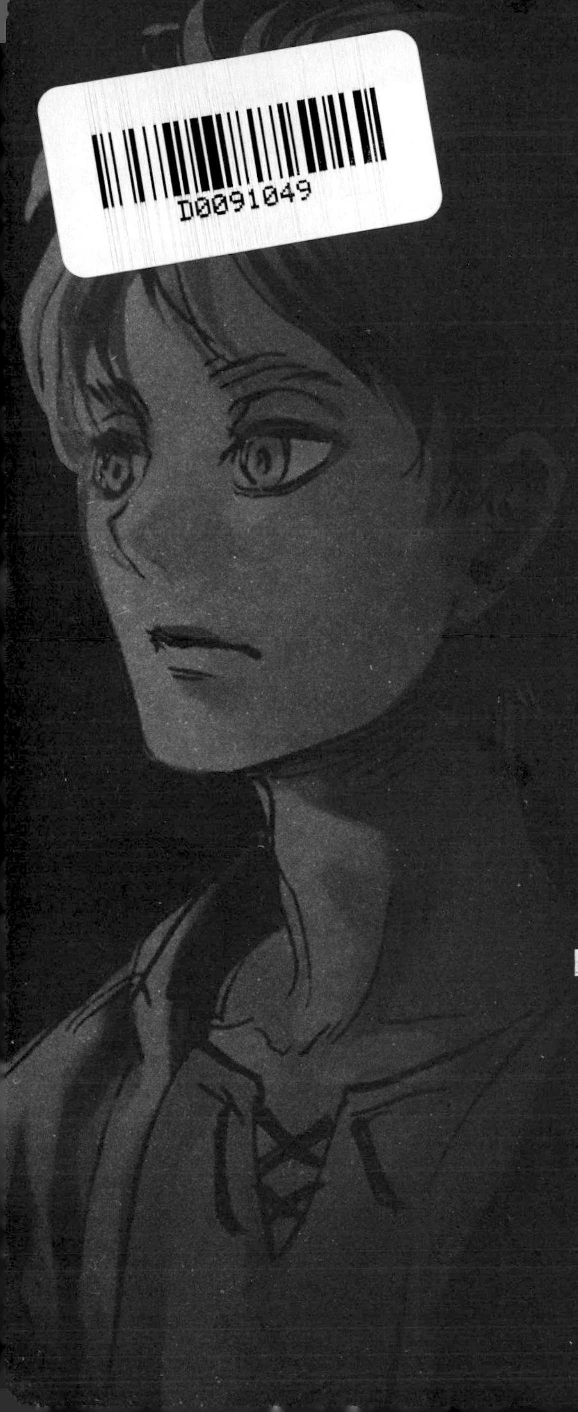

ATTACK ON TITAN 17

HAJIME ISAYAMA

"Attack on Titan" Character Introduction

104th Corps

Eren joined the Survey Corps out of his longing for the outside world and his hatred of the Titans. He has the power to turn himself into a Titan, but its origins are unknown.

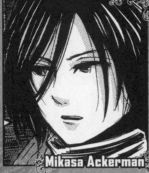

raduated at he top of her aining corps, ikasa is a ghly talented oldier. Her arents were urdered efore her yes when she as a child, ut Eren saved er life. Since en, she has ade it her ission to rotect him.

en and Mikasa's ildhood friend. ough Armin isn't hletic in the least, possesses both arp observational wers and keen sight, and he hibits an traordinary ability develop rategies.

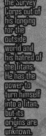

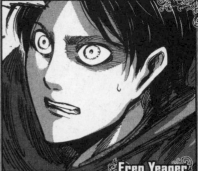

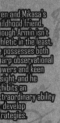

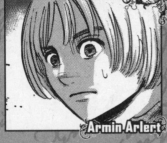

Eren Yeager
Mikasa Ackerman
Armin Arlert
Military Police Brigade
Annie Leonhart
Reiner Braun
Bertolt Hoover
The Female Titan
The Armored Titan
The Colossus Titan

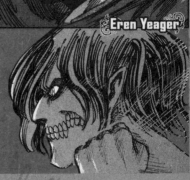

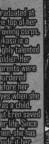

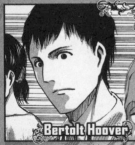

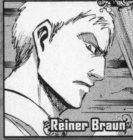

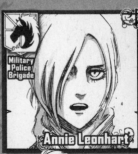

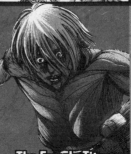

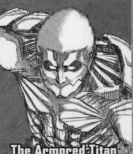

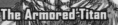

Head of the Reiss family

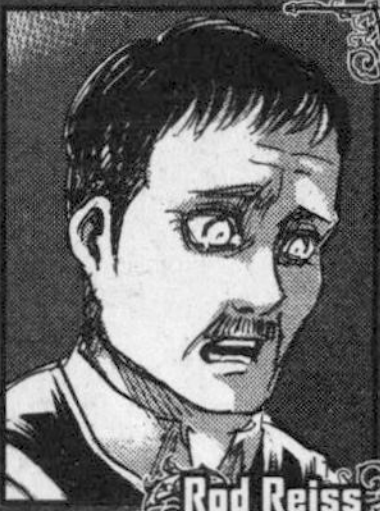

Rod Reiss

Military Police Anti-Personnel Control Squad Leader

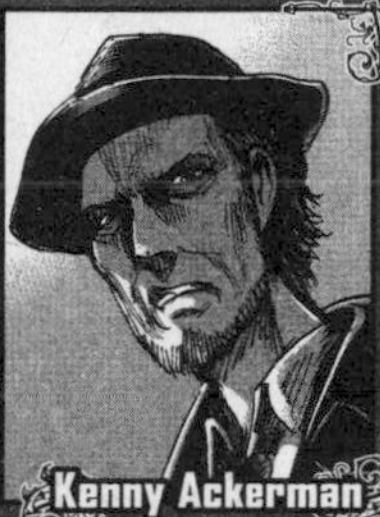

Kenny Ackerman

Survey Corps

Soldiers who are prepared to sacrifice themselves as they brave the Titan territory outside the walls.

Squad Captain

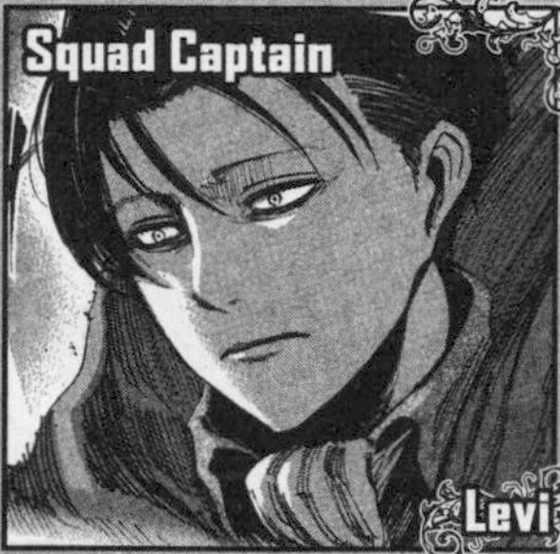

Levi

13th Commander of the Survey Corps

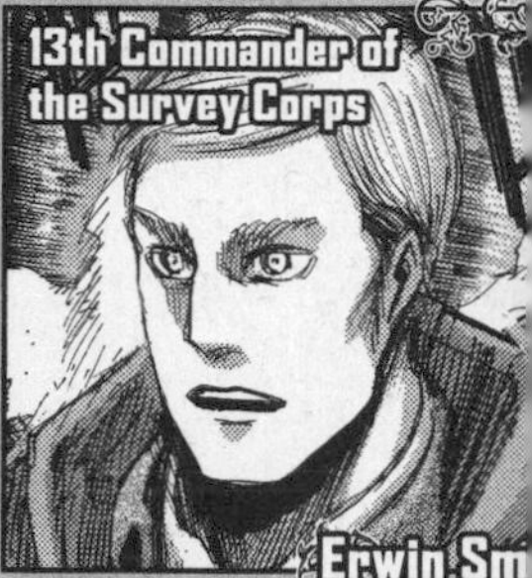

Erwin Sm

Squad Leader

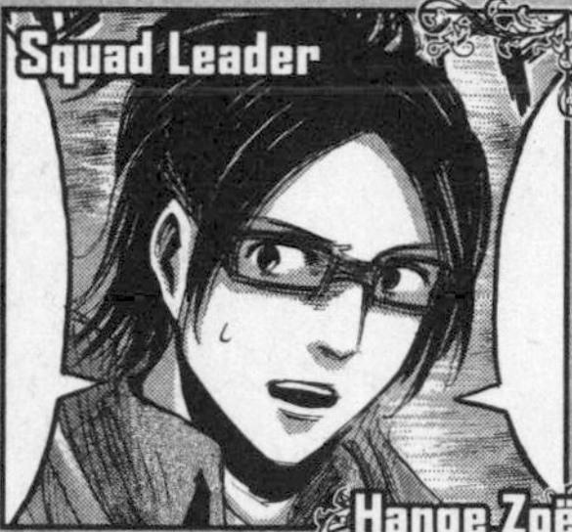

Hange Zoë

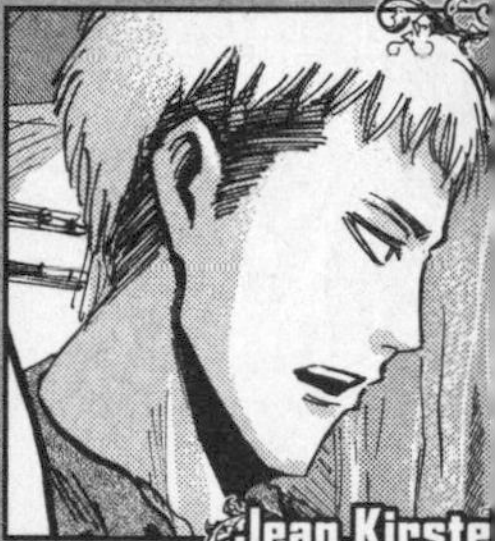

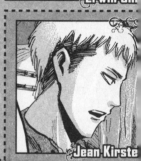

Jean Kirste

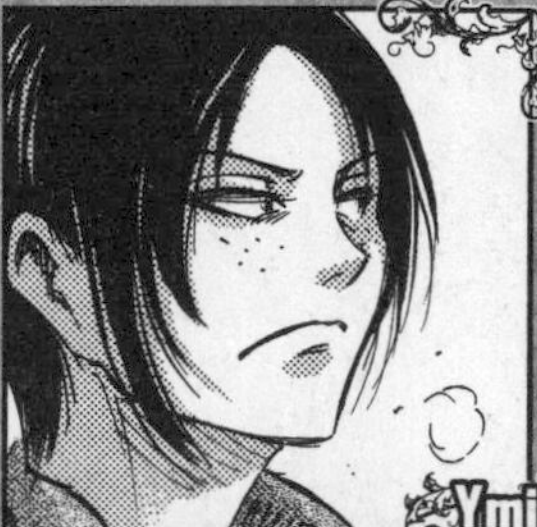

Ymir

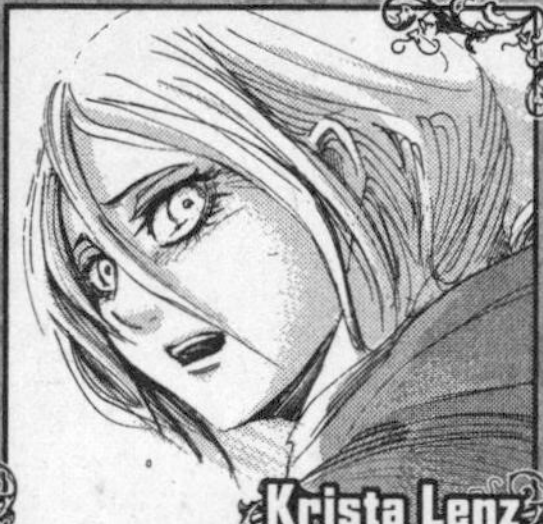

Krista Lenz
(Historia Reiss)

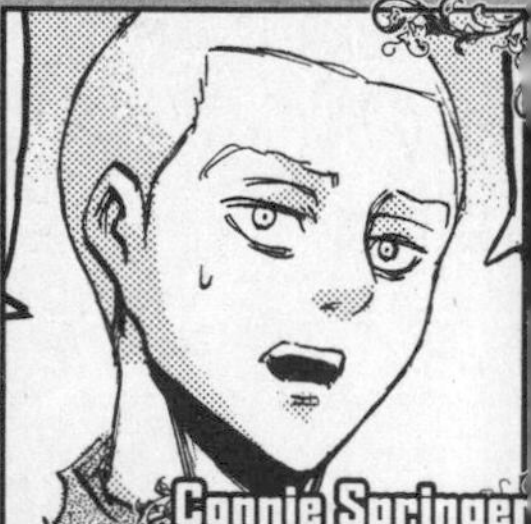

Connie Springer

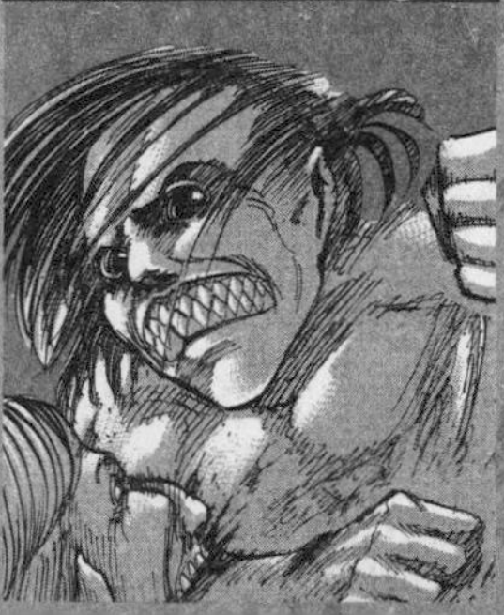

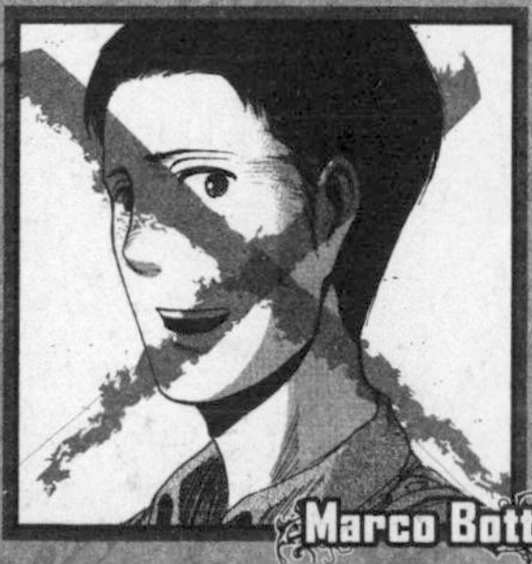

Marco Bott

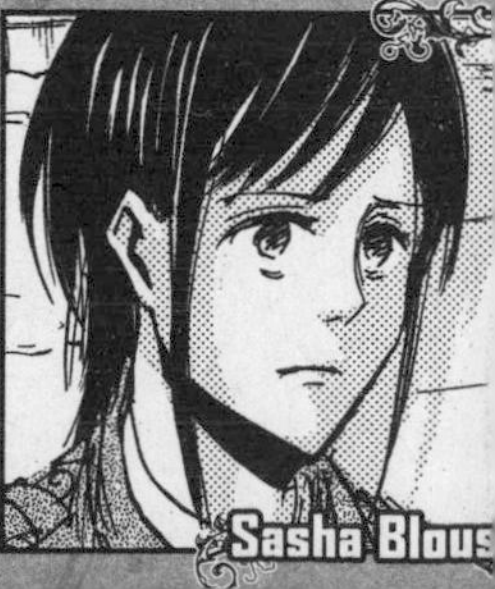

Sasha Blous

ATTACK on TITAN

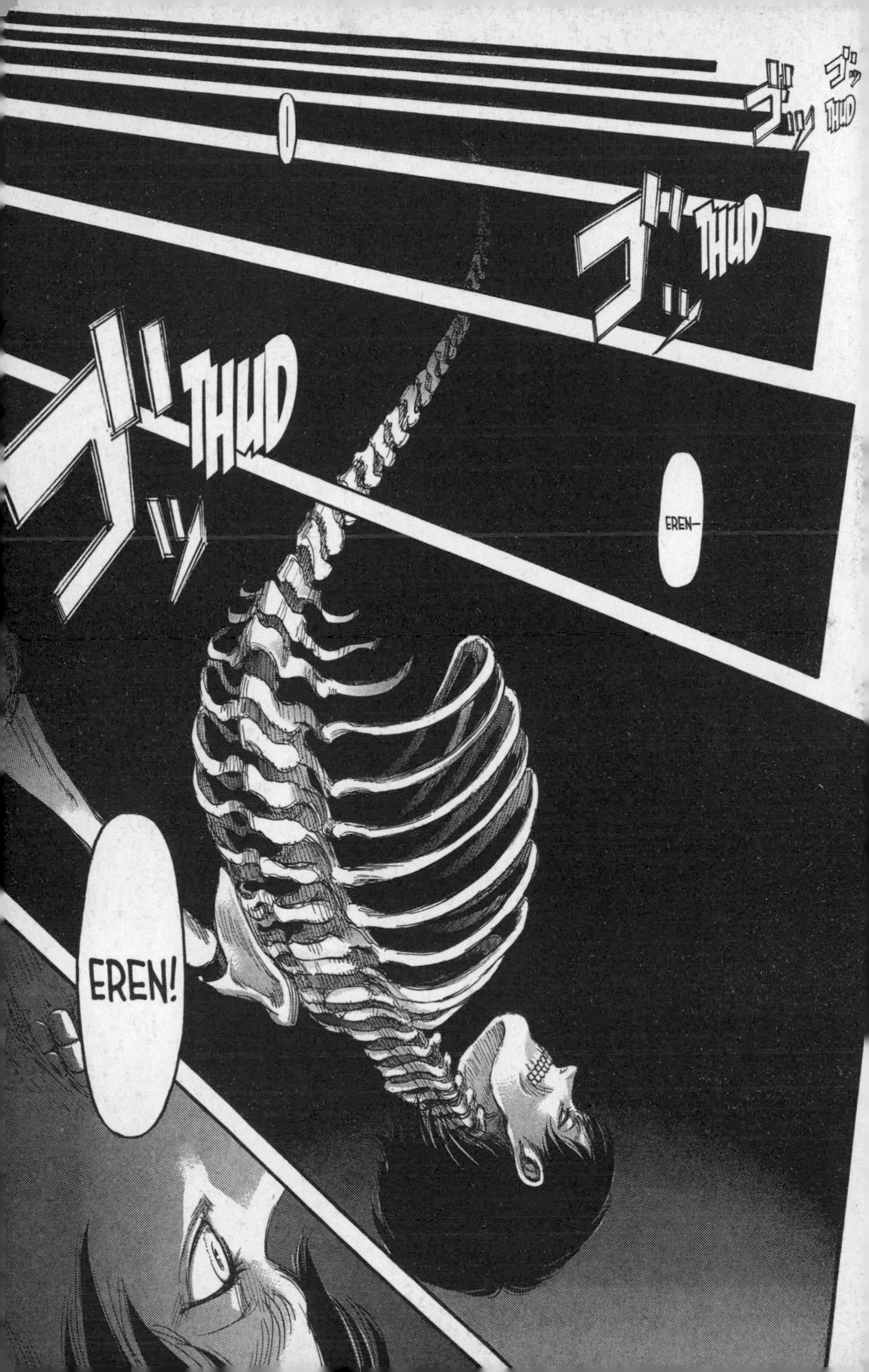
ゴッ
THUD
ゴッ
THUD
ゴッ
THUD
ゴッ
THUD
EREN—
EREN!

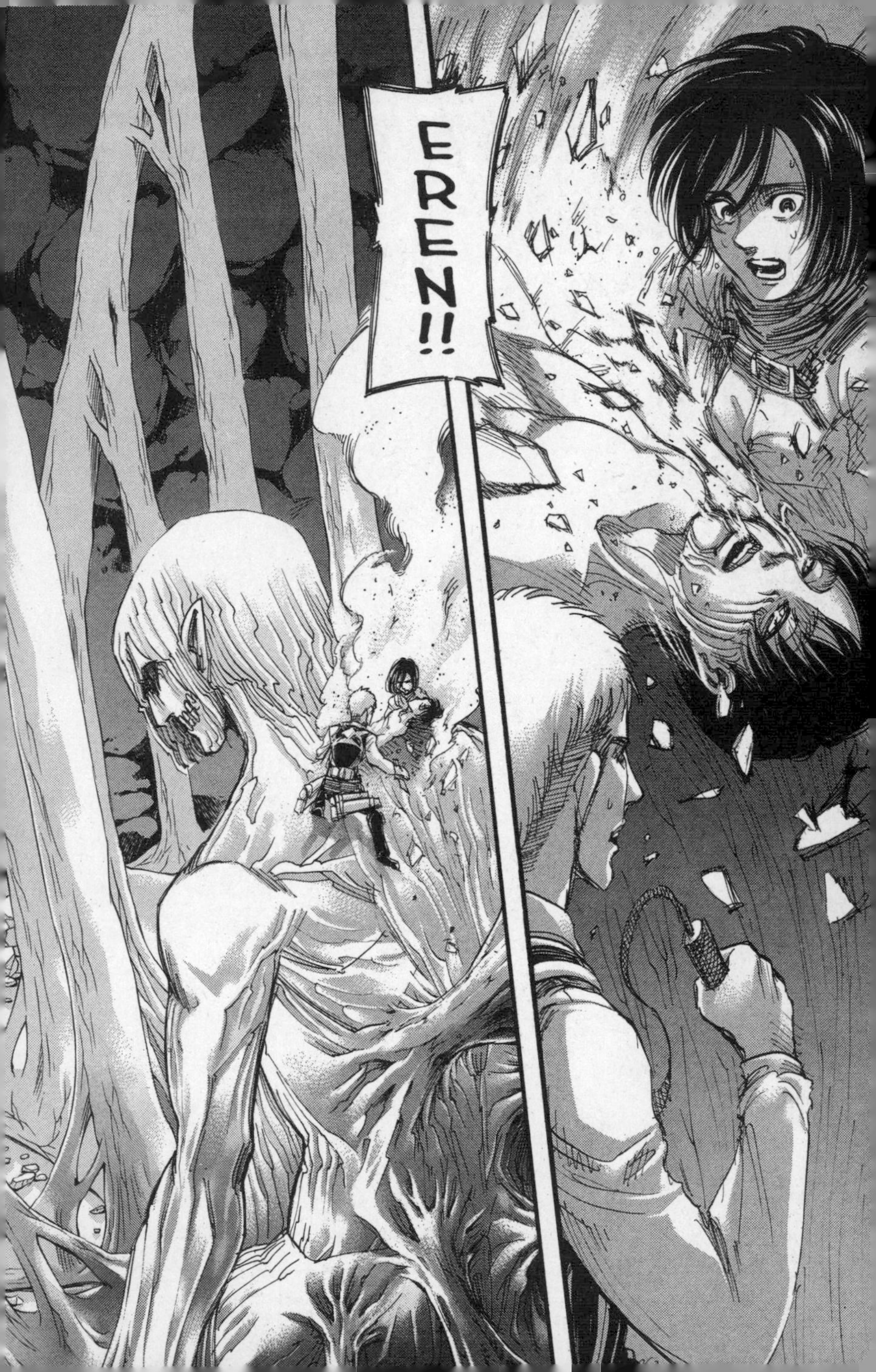
EREN!!

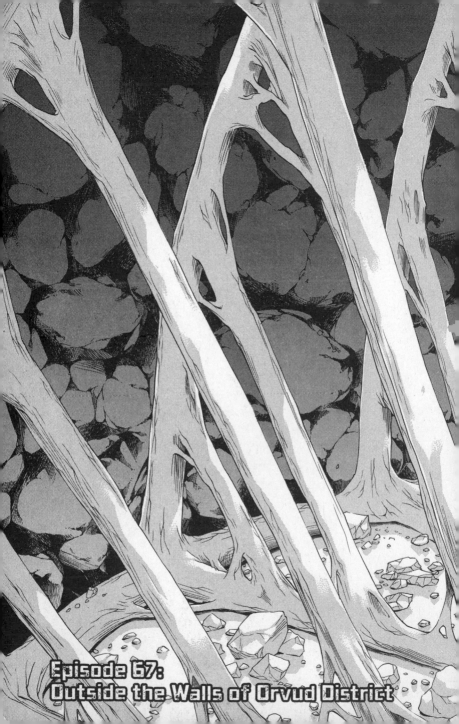

Episode 67:
Outside the Walls of Orvud District

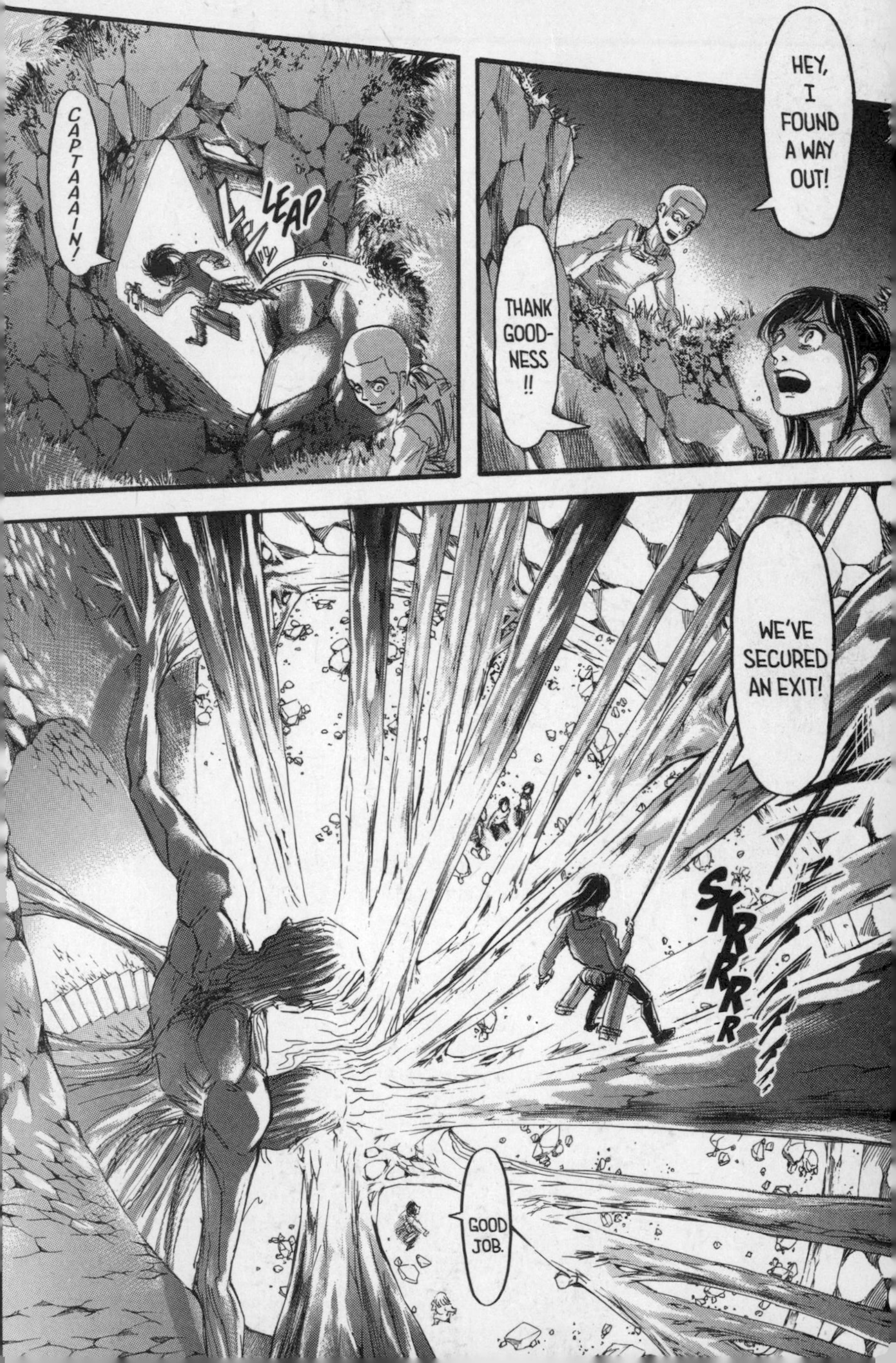
HEY, I FOUND A WAY OUT!
THANK GOODNESS!!
CAPTAAAAIN!
LEAP
WE'VE SECURED AN EXIT!
SKRRRR
GOOD JOB.

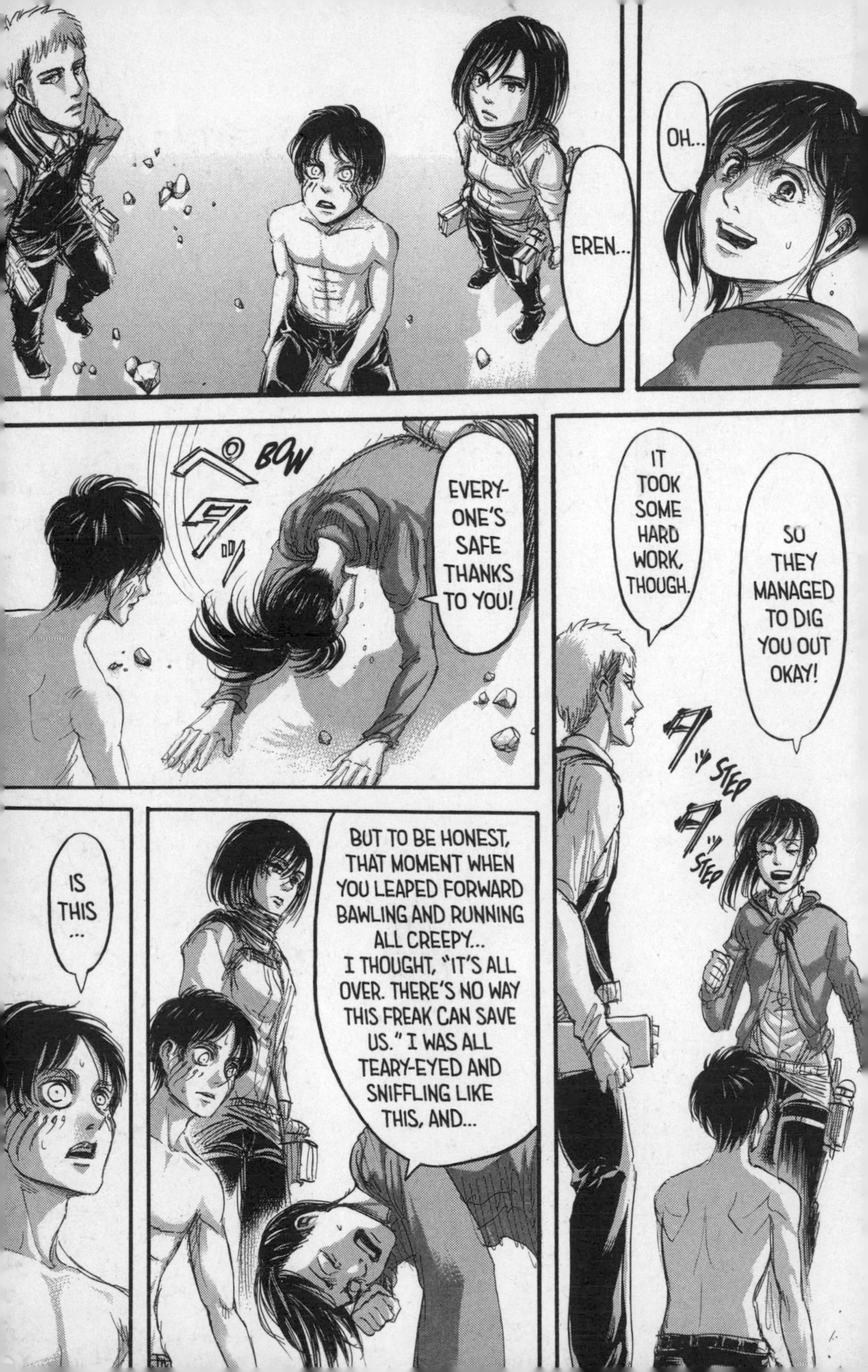
OH...
EREN...
SO THEY MANAGED TO DIG YOU OUT OKAY!
IT TOOK SOME HARD WORK, THOUGH.
STEP
STEP
BOW
EVERY-ONE'S SAFE THANKS TO YOU!
BUT TO BE HONEST, THAT MOMENT WHEN YOU LEAPED FORWARD BAWLING AND RUNNING ALL CREEPY... I THOUGHT, "IT'S ALL OVER. THERE'S NO WAY THIS FREAK CAN SAVE US." I WAS ALL TEARY-EYED AND SNIFFLING LIKE THIS, AND...
IS THIS ...

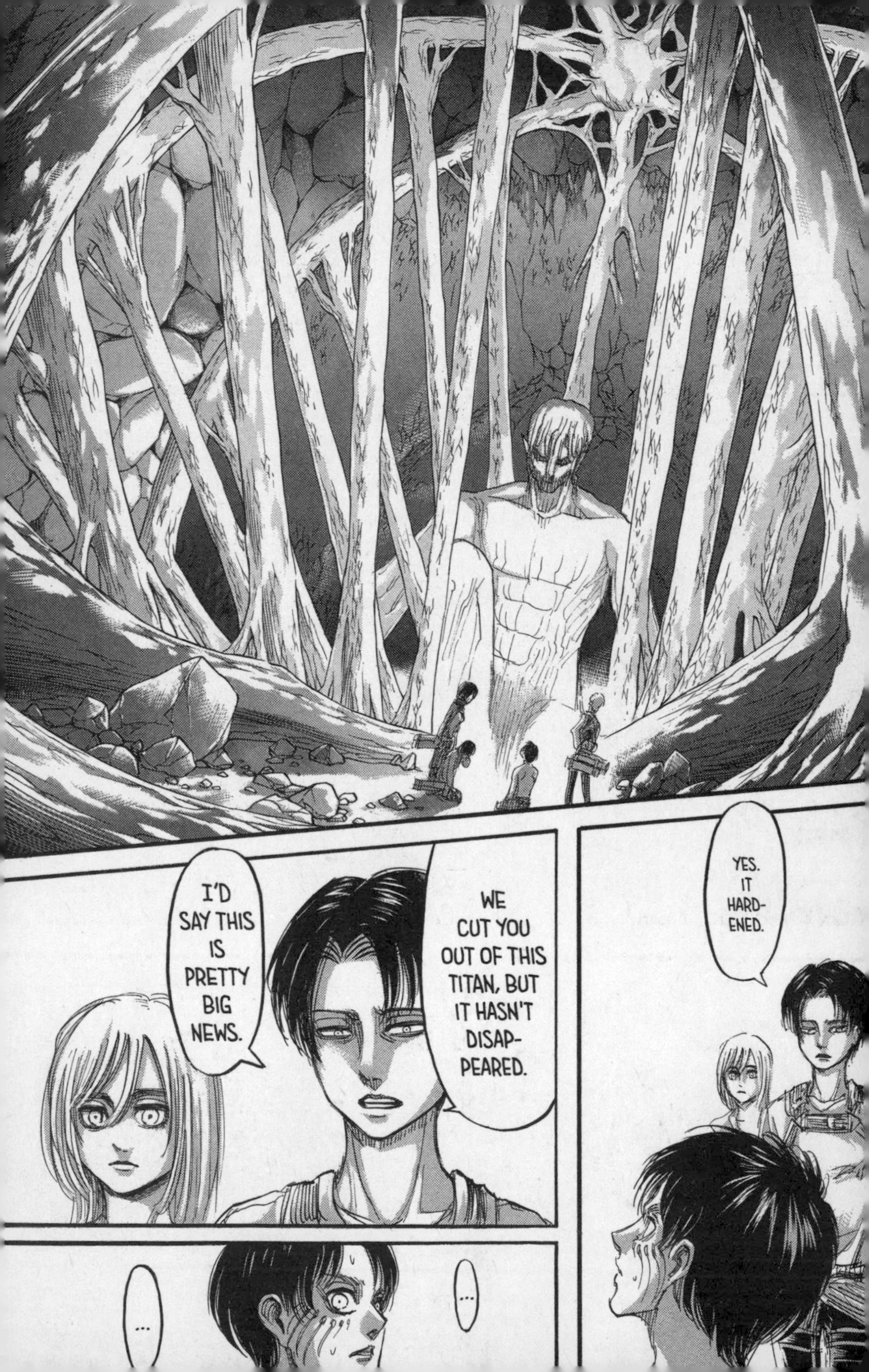
YES. IT HARD-ENED.
WE CUT YOU OUT OF THIS TITAN, BUT IT HASN'T DISAP-PEARED.
I'D SAY THIS IS PRETTY BIG NEWS.
...
...

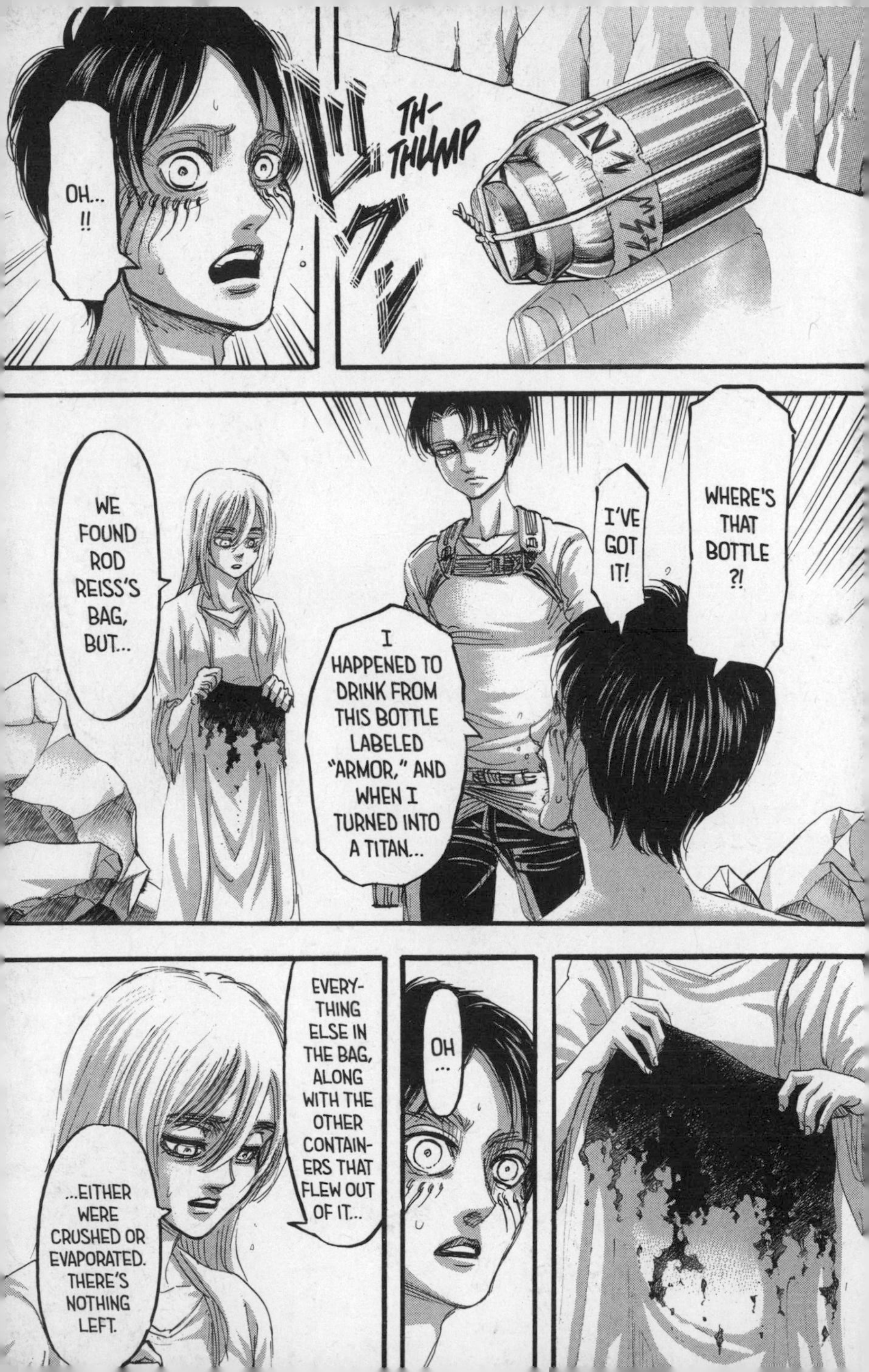
TH-THUMP
OH... !!
WHERE'S THAT BOTTLE ?!
I'VE GOT IT!
I HAPPENED TO DRINK FROM THIS BOTTLE LABELED "ARMOR," AND WHEN I TURNED INTO A TITAN...
WE FOUND ROD REISS'S BAG, BUT...
OH ...
EVERYTHING ELSE IN THE BAG, ALONG WITH THE OTHER CONTAINERS THAT FLEW OUT OF IT...
...EITHER WERE CRUSHED OR EVAPORATED. THERE'S NOTHING LEFT.

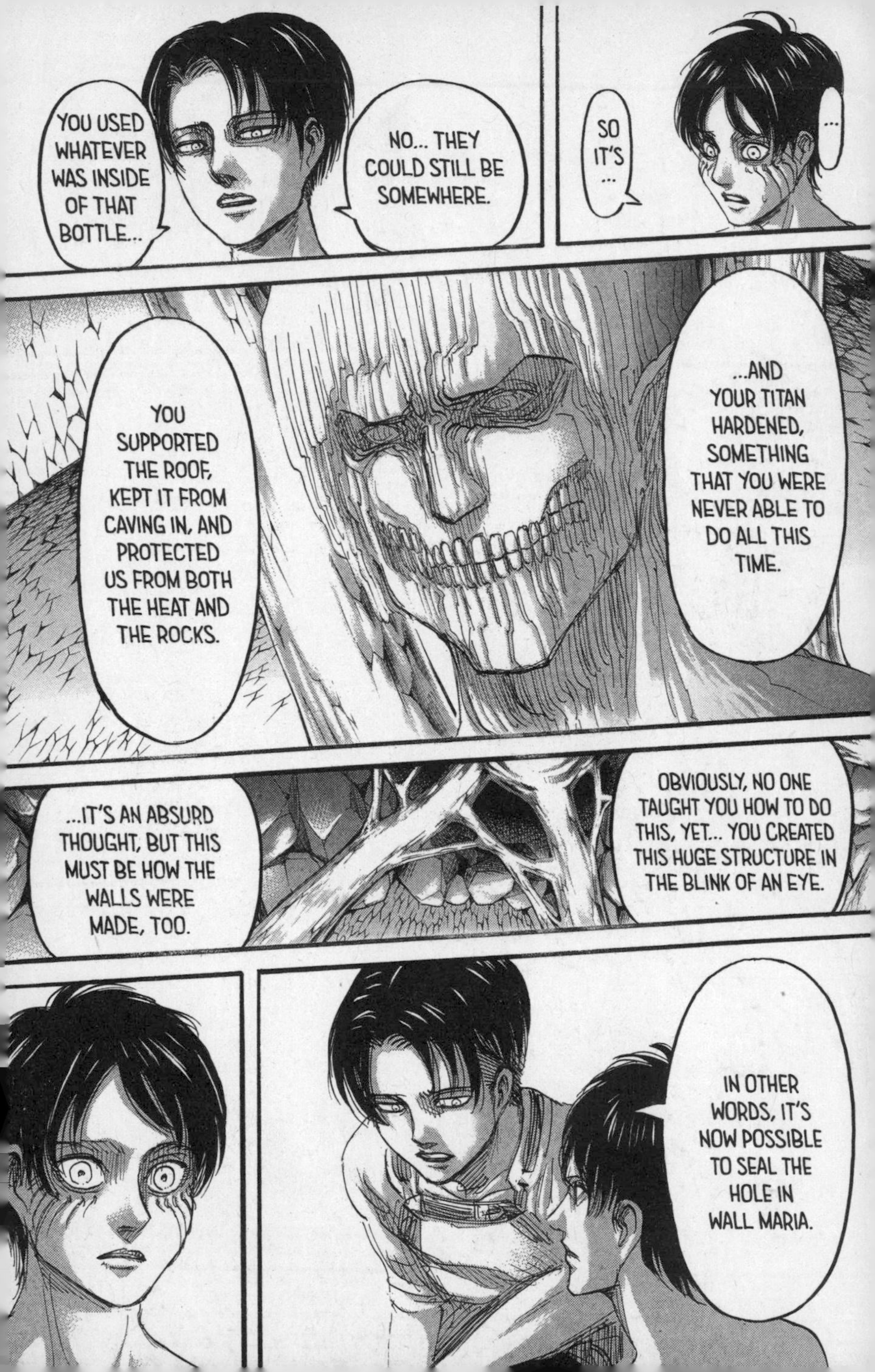
...
SO IT'S ...
NO... THEY COULD STILL BE SOMEWHERE.
YOU USED WHATEVER WAS INSIDE OF THAT BOTTLE...
...AND YOUR TITAN HARDENED, SOMETHING THAT YOU WERE NEVER ABLE TO DO ALL THIS TIME.
YOU SUPPORTED THE ROOF, KEPT IT FROM CAVING IN, AND PROTECTED US FROM BOTH THE HEAT AND THE ROCKS.
OBVIOUSLY, NO ONE TAUGHT YOU HOW TO DO THIS, YET... YOU CREATED THIS HUGE STRUCTURE IN THE BLINK OF AN EYE.
...IT'S AN ABSURD THOUGHT, BUT THIS MUST BE HOW THE WALLS WERE MADE, TOO.
IN OTHER WORDS, IT'S NOW POSSIBLE TO SEAL THE HOLE IN WALL MARIA.

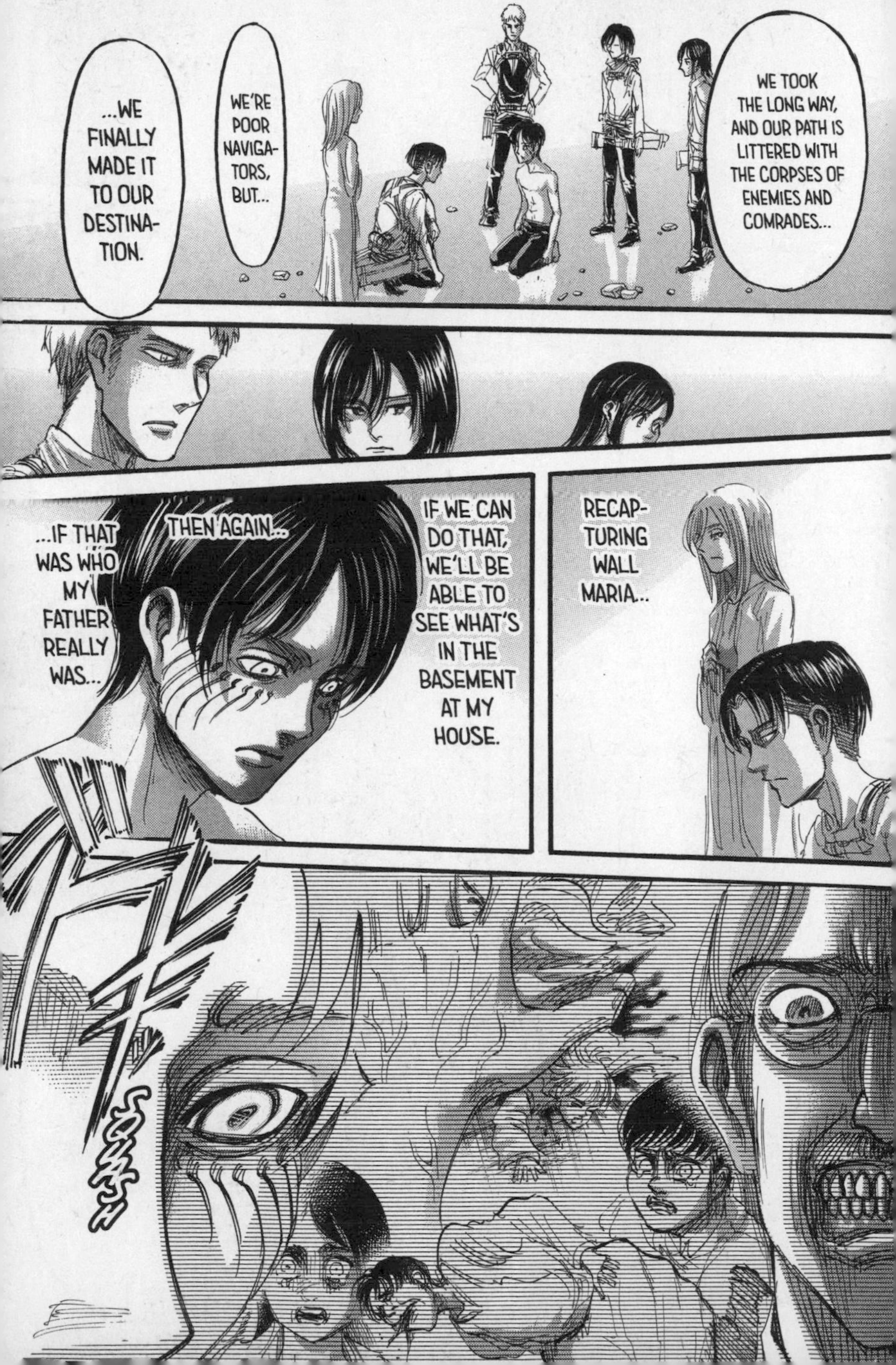
WE TOOK THE LONG WAY, AND OUR PATH IS LITTERED WITH THE CORPSES OF ENEMIES AND COMRADES...
WE'RE POOR NAVIGATORS, BUT...
...WE FINALLY MADE IT TO OUR DESTINATION.
RECAPTURING WALL MARIA...
IF WE CAN DO THAT, WE'LL BE ABLE TO SEE WHAT'S IN THE BASEMENT AT MY HOUSE.
THEN AGAIN...
...IF THAT WAS WHO MY FATHER REALLY WAS...

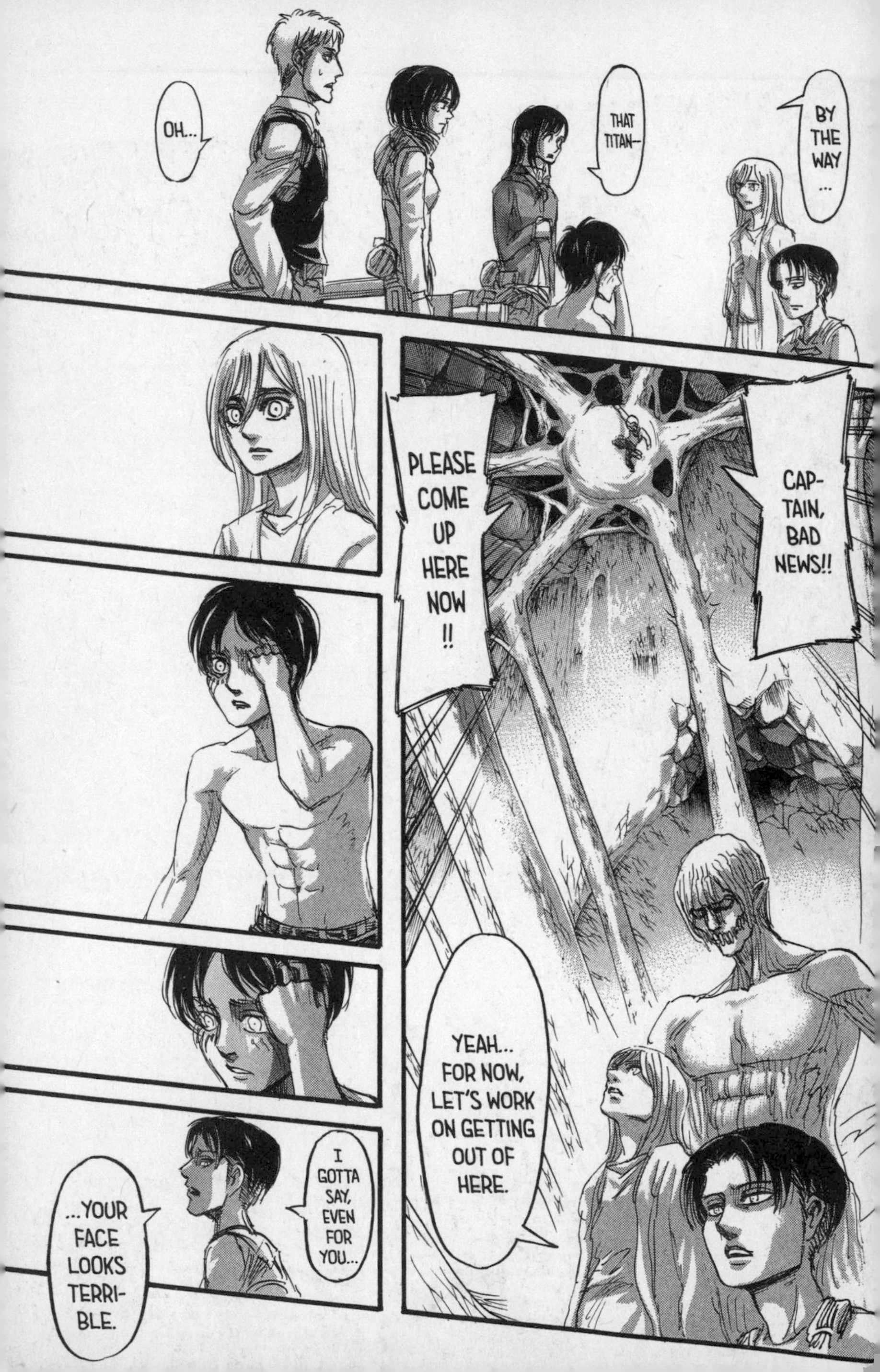
BY THE WAY ...
THAT TITAN—
OH...
CAP-TAIN, BAD NEWS!!
PLEASE COME UP HERE NOW !!
YEAH... FOR NOW, LET'S WORK ON GETTING OUT OF HERE.
I GOTTA SAY, EVEN FOR YOU...
...YOUR FACE LOOKS TERRI-BLE.

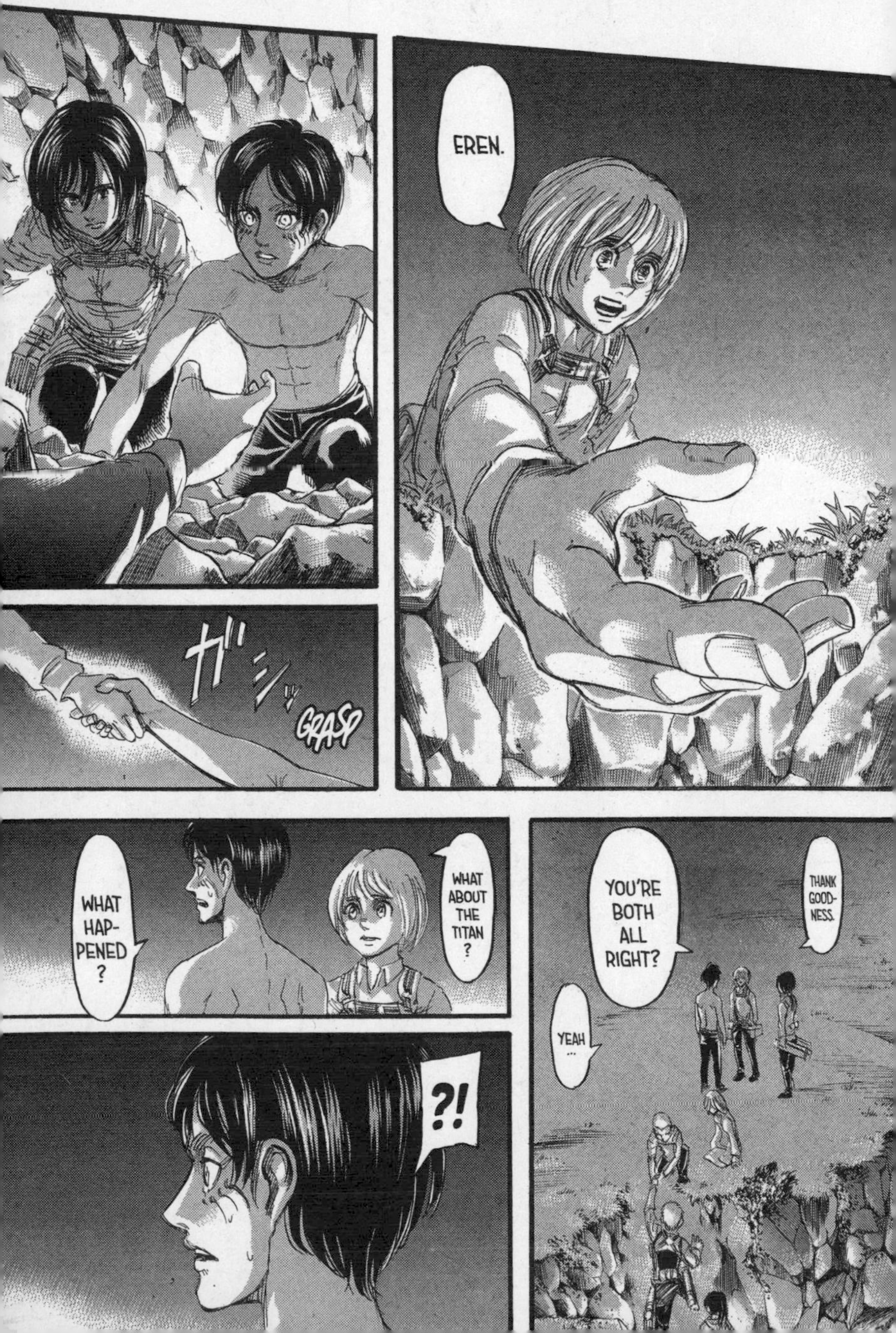
EREN.
ガシッ
GRASP
THANK GOODNESS.
YOU'RE BOTH ALL RIGHT?
YEAH...
WHAT ABOUT THE TITAN?
WHAT HAPPENED?
?!

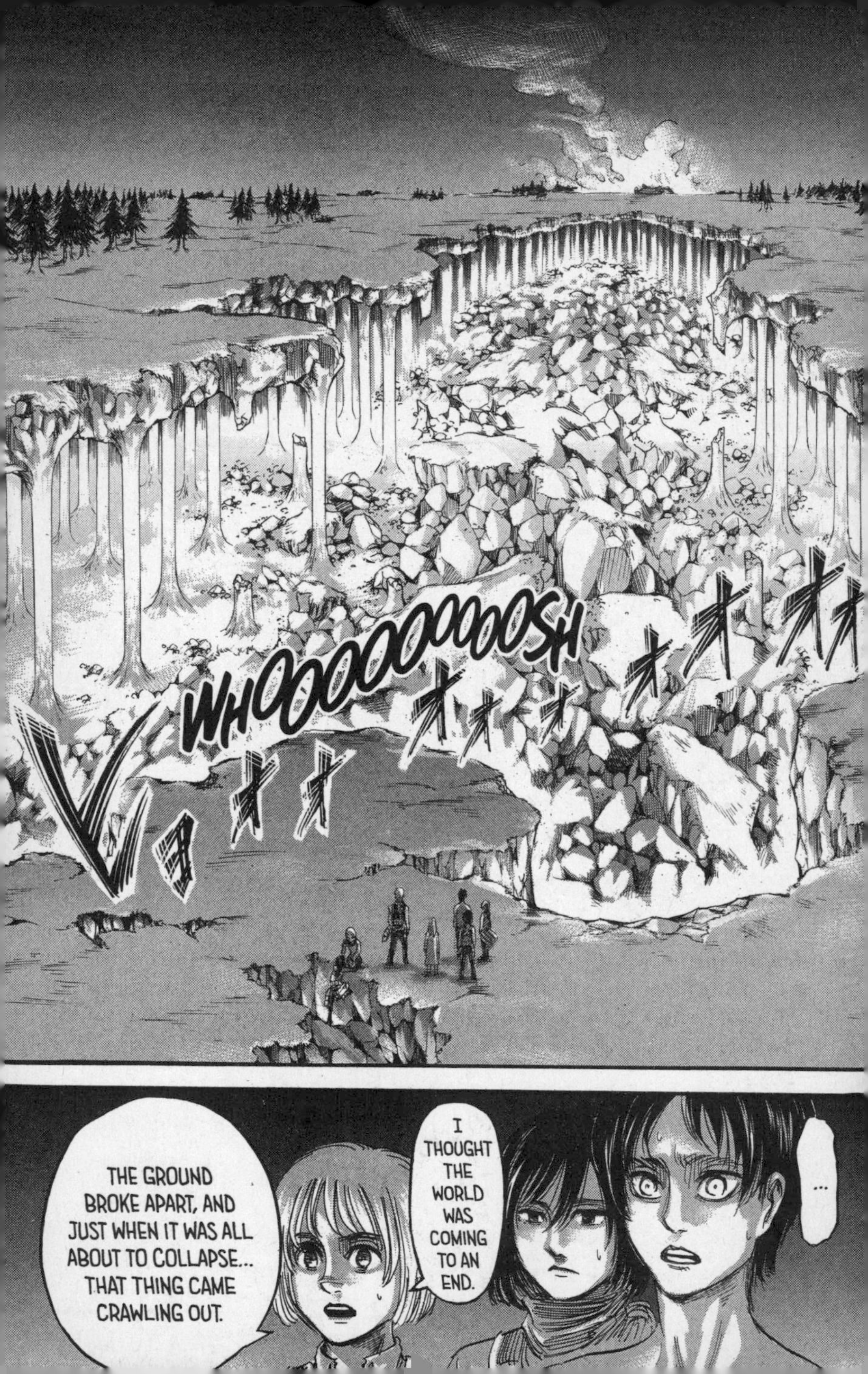
WHOOOOOOOOOOSH
...
I THOUGHT THE WORLD WAS COMING TO AN END.
THE GROUND BROKE APART, AND JUST WHEN IT WAS ALL ABOUT TO COLLAPSE... THAT THING CAME CRAWLING OUT.

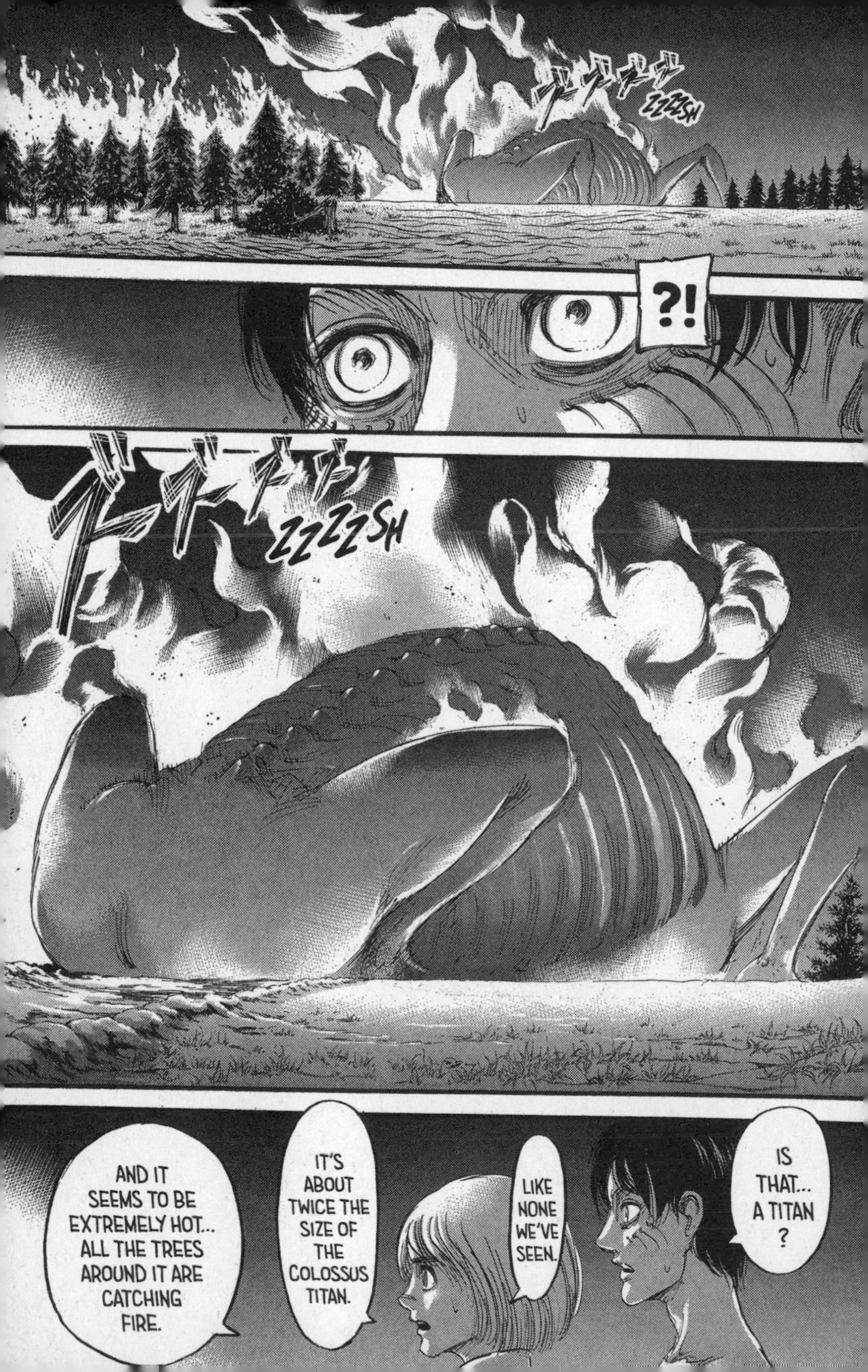
ZZZZSH
?!
ZZZZZSH
IS THAT... A TITAN?
LIKE NONE WE'VE SEEN.
IT'S ABOUT TWICE THE SIZE OF THE COLOSSUS TITAN.
AND IT SEEMS TO BE EXTREMELY HOT... ALL THE TREES AROUND IT ARE CATCHING FIRE.

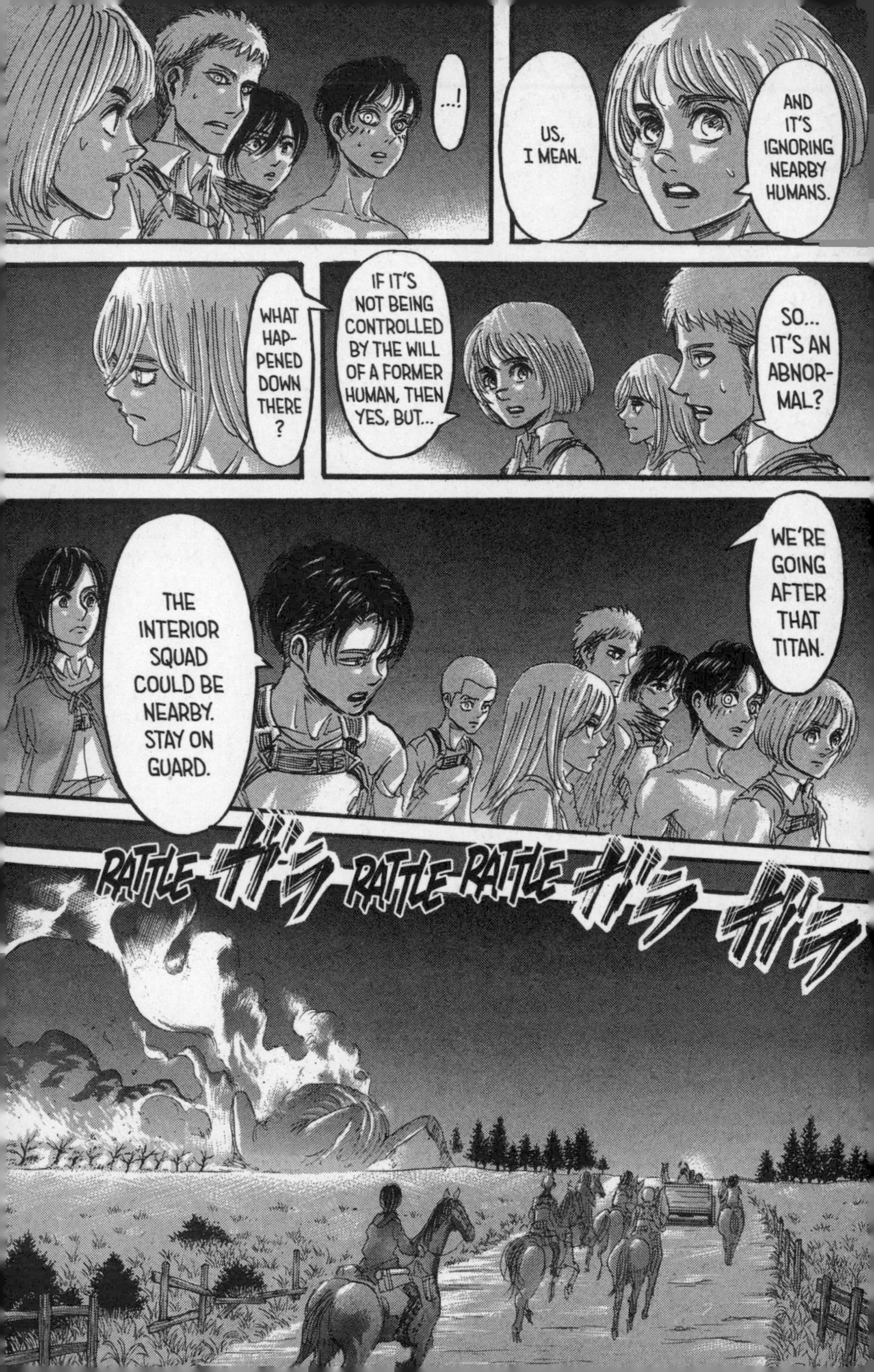
AND IT'S IGNORING NEARBY HUMANS.
US, I MEAN.
...!
SO... IT'S AN ABNORMAL?
IF IT'S NOT BEING CONTROLLED BY THE WILL OF A FORMER HUMAN, THEN YES, BUT...
WHAT HAPPENED DOWN THERE?
WE'RE GOING AFTER THAT TITAN.
THE INTERIOR SQUAD COULD BE NEARBY. STAY ON GUARD.
RATTLE ガラ RATTLE RATTLE ガラ ガラ

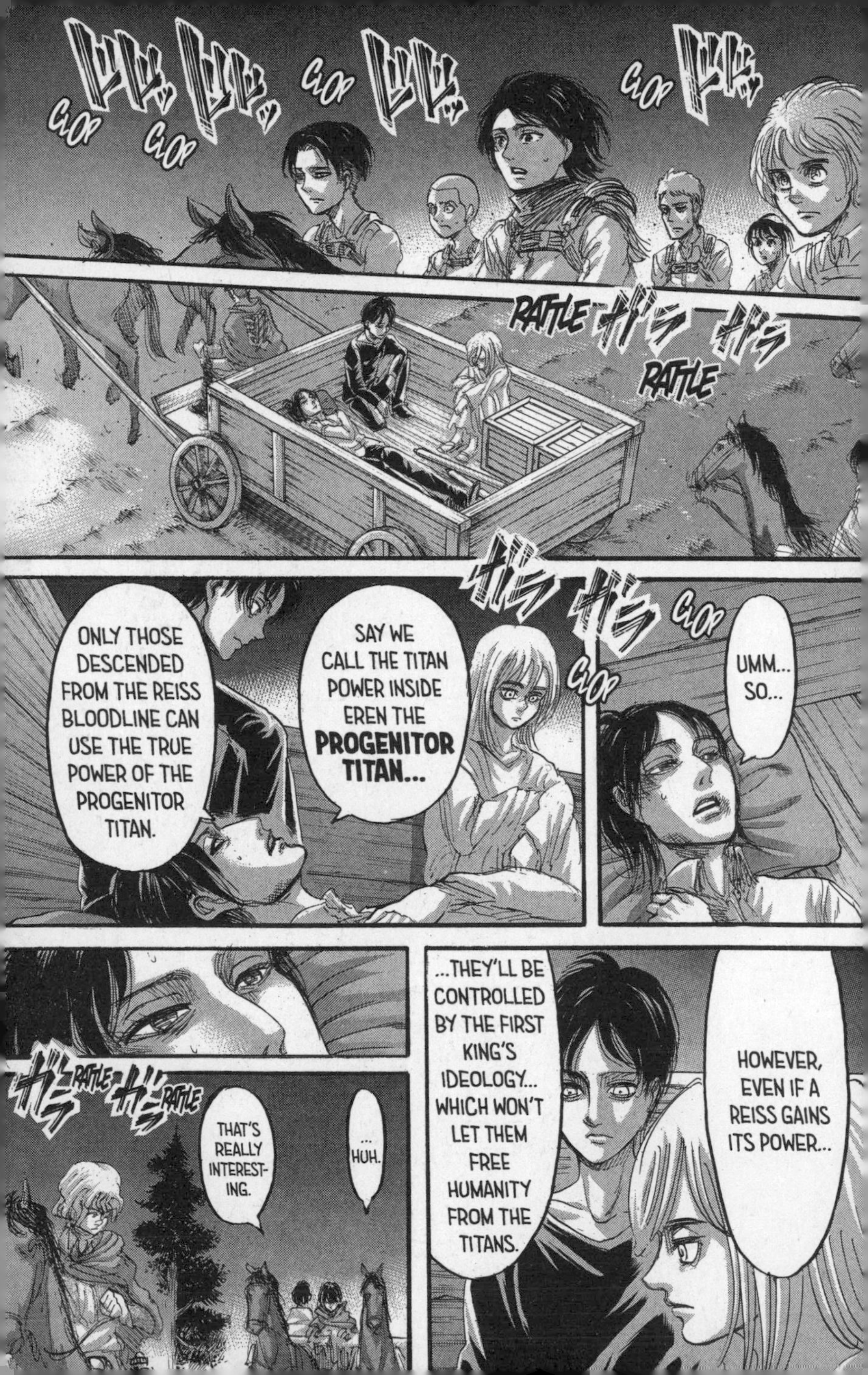
CLOP
CLOP
CLOP
CLOP
CLOP
RATTLE
RATTLE
CLOP
CLOP
UMM... SO...
SAY WE CALL THE TITAN POWER INSIDE EREN THE **PROGENITOR TITAN...**
ONLY THOSE DESCENDED FROM THE REISS BLOODLINE CAN USE THE TRUE POWER OF THE PROGENITOR TITAN.
HOWEVER, EVEN IF A REISS GAINS ITS POWER...
...THEY'LL BE CONTROLLED BY THE FIRST KING'S IDEOLOGY... WHICH WON'T LET THEM FREE HUMANITY FROM THE TITANS.
RATTLE
RATTLE
... HUH.
THAT'S REALLY INTEREST-ING.

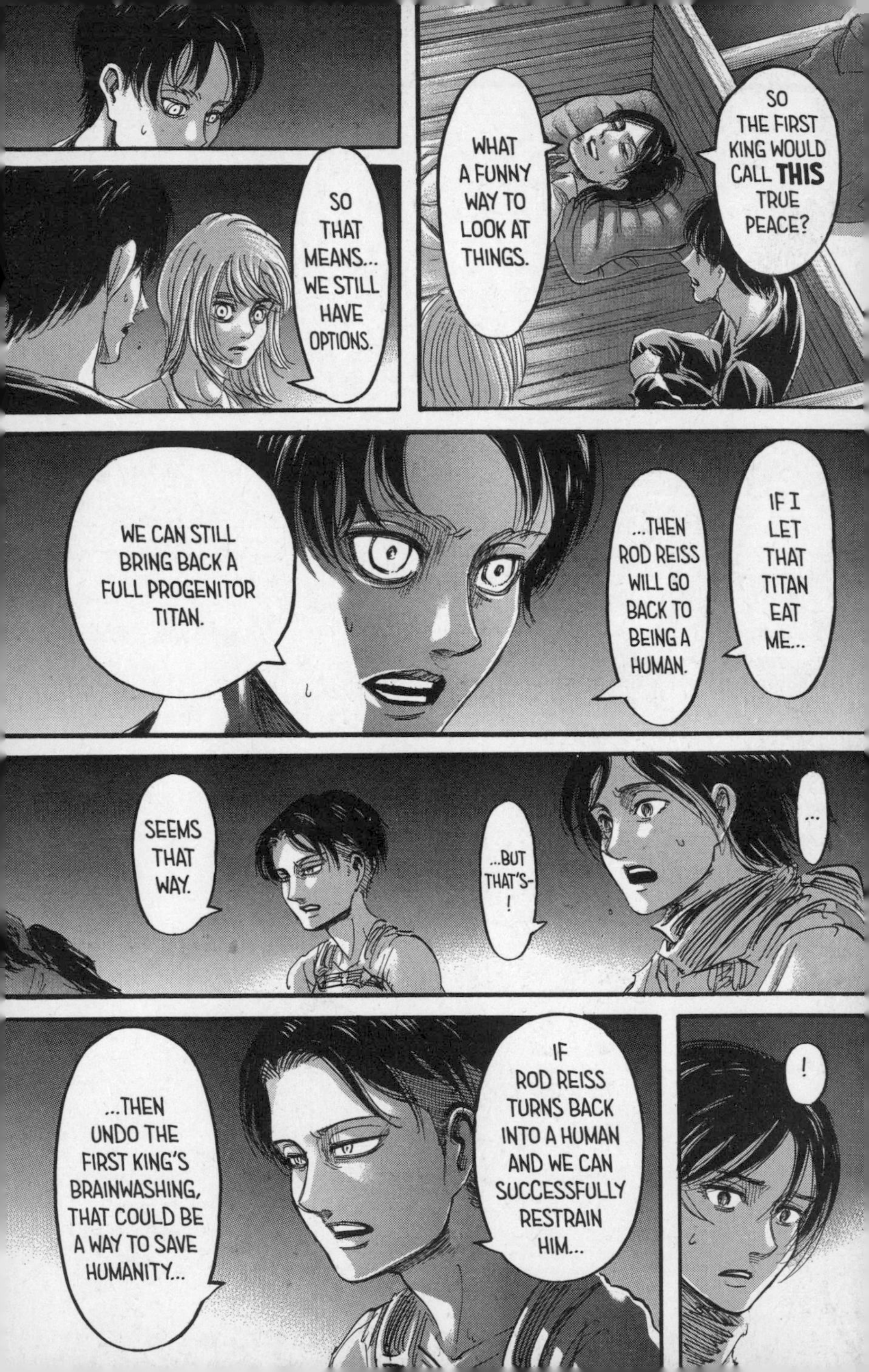
SO THE FIRST KING WOULD CALL **THIS** TRUE PEACE?
WHAT A FUNNY WAY TO LOOK AT THINGS.
SO THAT MEANS... WE STILL HAVE OPTIONS.
IF I LET THAT TITAN EAT ME...
...THEN ROD REISS WILL GO BACK TO BEING A HUMAN.
WE CAN STILL BRING BACK A FULL PROGENITOR TITAN.
...
...BUT THAT'S- !
SEEMS THAT WAY.
!
IF ROD REISS TURNS BACK INTO A HUMAN AND WE CAN SUCCESSFULLY RESTRAIN HIM...
...THEN UNDO THE FIRST KING'S BRAINWASHING, THAT COULD BE A WAY TO SAVE HUMANITY...

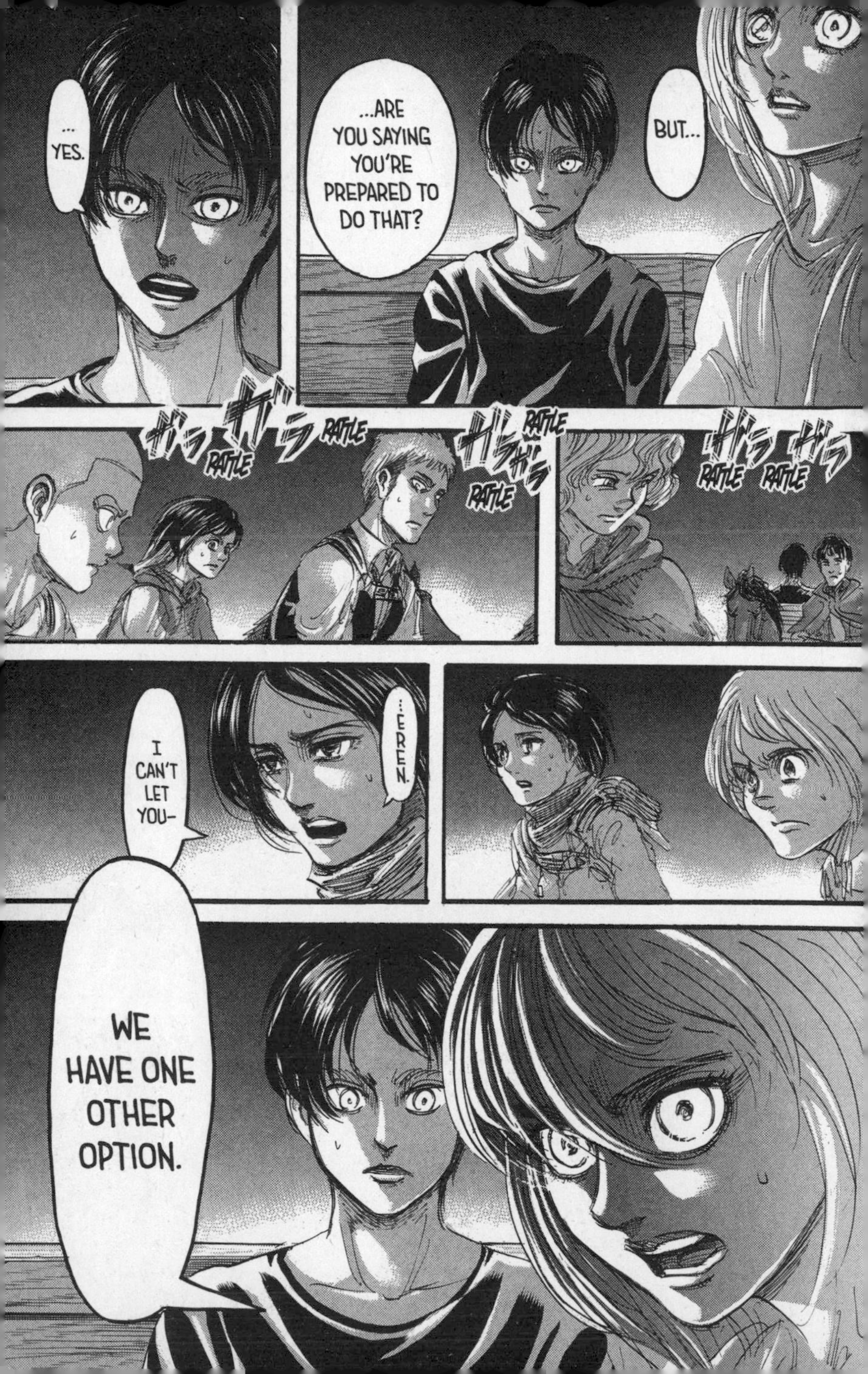
BUT...
...ARE YOU SAYING YOU'RE PREPARED TO DO THAT?
... YES.
RATTLE
RATTLE
RATTLE
RATTLE
RATTLE
RATTLE
...EREN.
I CAN'T LET YOU–
WE HAVE ONE OTHER OPTION.

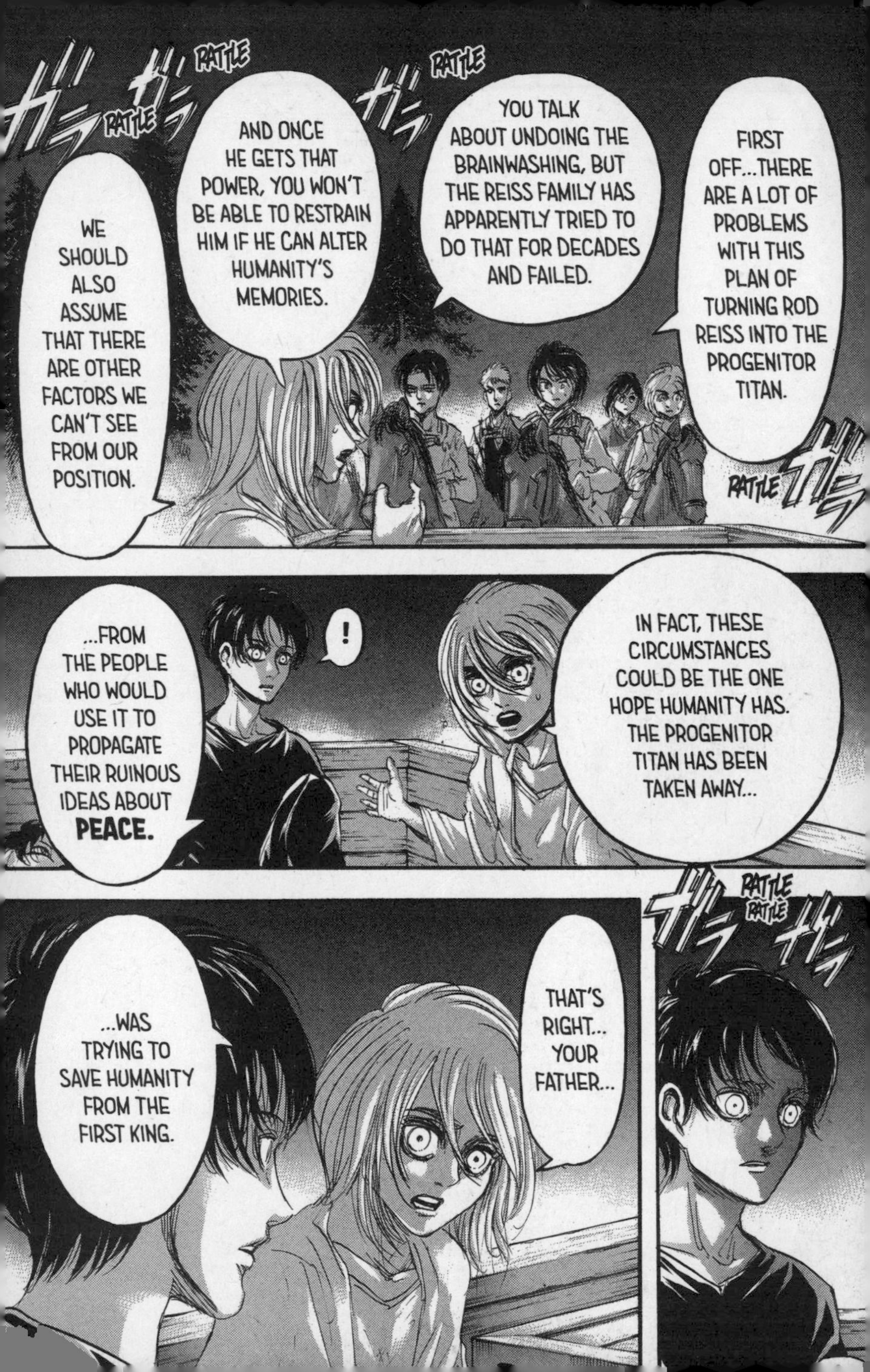
RATTLE
FIRST OFF...THERE ARE A LOT OF PROBLEMS WITH THIS PLAN OF TURNING ROD REISS INTO THE PROGENITOR TITAN.
RATTLE
YOU TALK ABOUT UNDOING THE BRAINWASHING, BUT THE REISS FAMILY HAS APPARENTLY TRIED TO DO THAT FOR DECADES AND FAILED.
RATTLE
RATTLE
AND ONCE HE GETS THAT POWER, YOU WON'T BE ABLE TO RESTRAIN HIM IF HE CAN ALTER HUMANITY'S MEMORIES.
WE SHOULD ALSO ASSUME THAT THERE ARE OTHER FACTORS WE CAN'T SEE FROM OUR POSITION.
IN FACT, THESE CIRCUMSTANCES COULD BE THE ONE HOPE HUMANITY HAS. THE PROGENITOR TITAN HAS BEEN TAKEN AWAY...
!
...FROM THE PEOPLE WHO WOULD USE IT TO PROPAGATE THEIR RUINOUS IDEAS ABOUT PEACE.
RATTLE
RATTLE
THAT'S RIGHT... YOUR FATHER...
...WAS TRYING TO SAVE HUMANITY FROM THE FIRST KING.

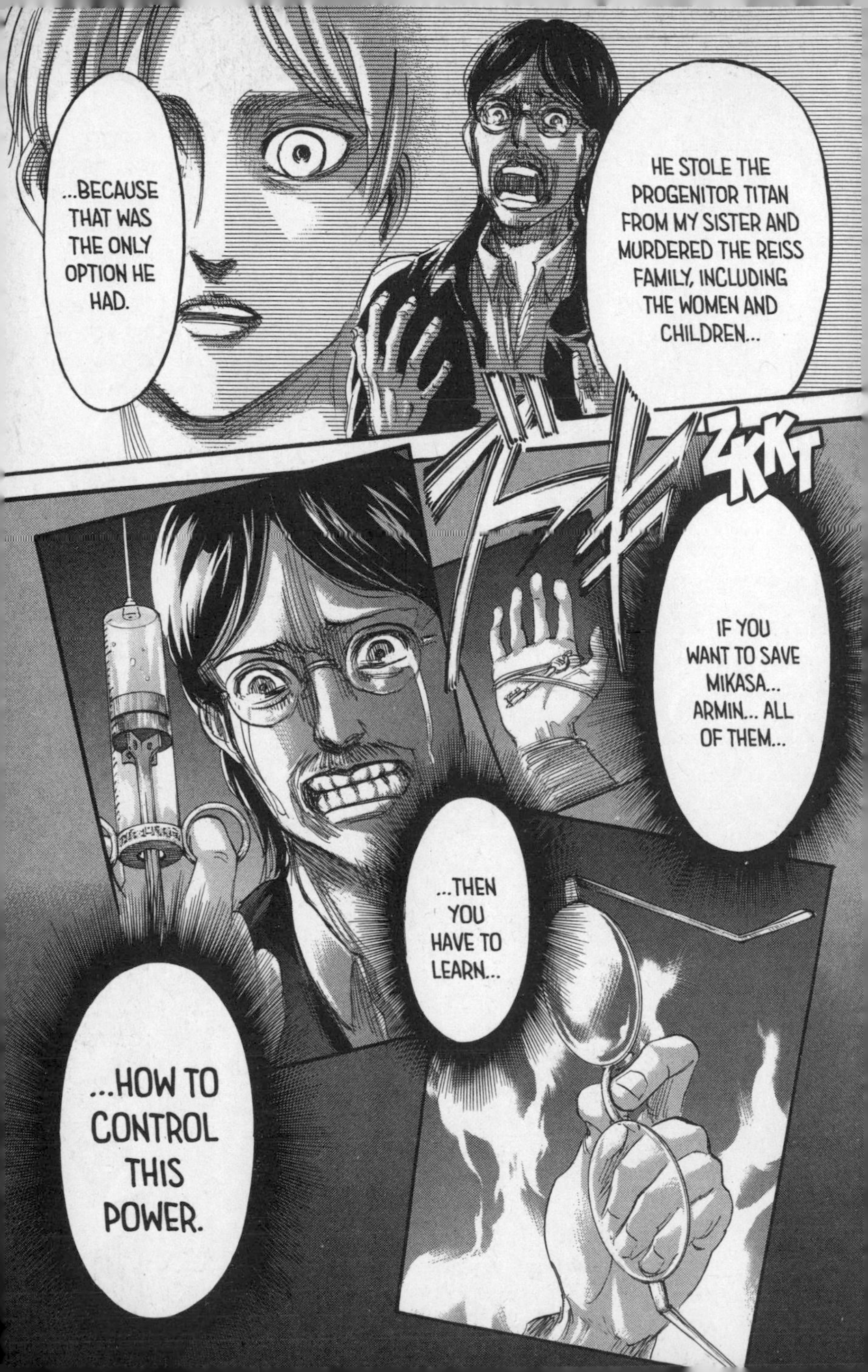
HE STOLE THE PROGENITOR TITAN FROM MY SISTER AND MURDERED THE REISS FAMILY, INCLUDING THE WOMEN AND CHILDREN...
...BECAUSE THAT WAS THE ONLY OPTION HE HAD.
ZKKT
IF YOU WANT TO SAVE MIKASA... ARMIN... ALL OF THEM...
...THEN YOU HAVE TO LEARN...
...HOW TO CONTROL THIS POWER.

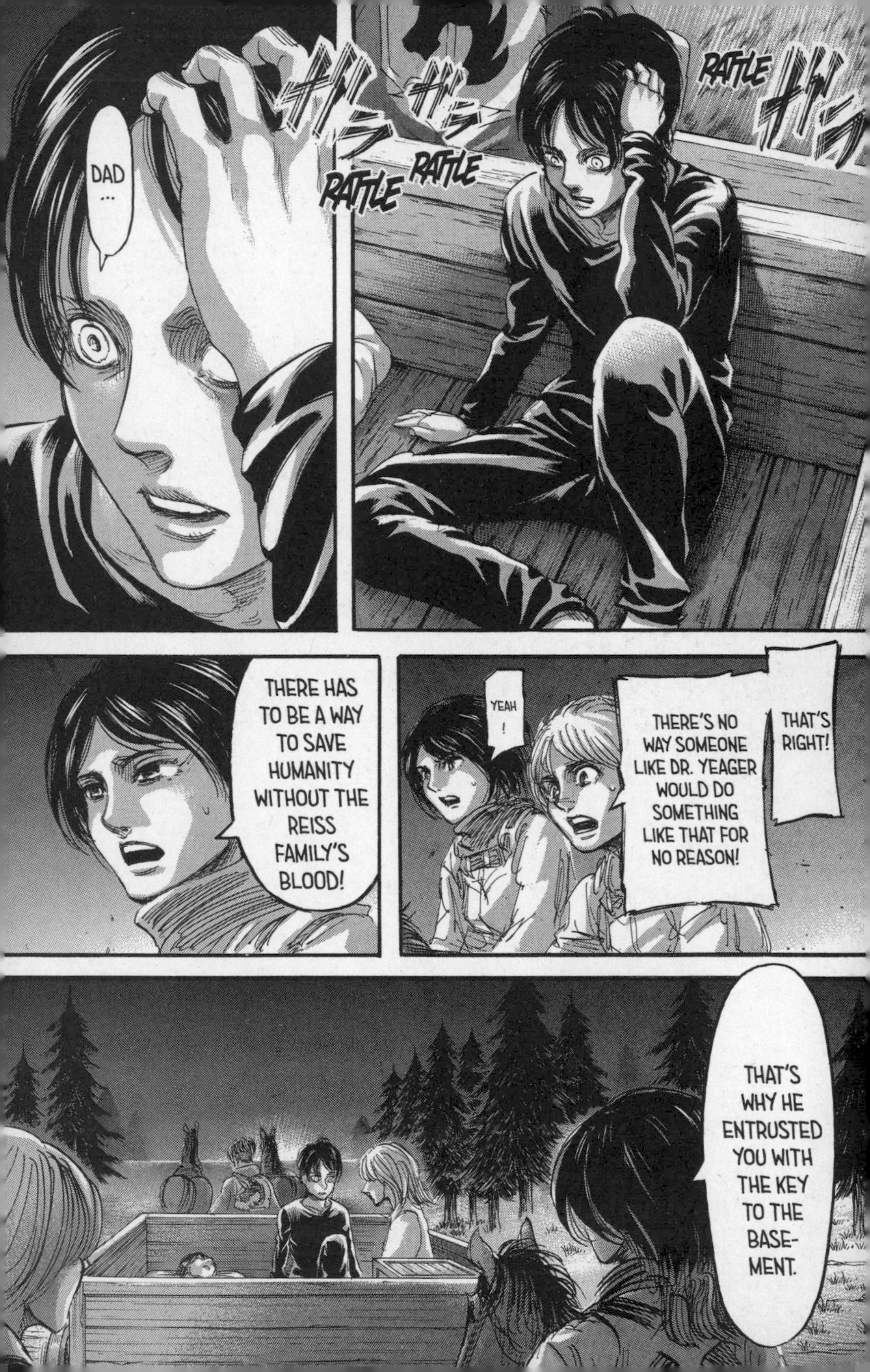
RATTLE
RATTLE
RATTLE
DAD ...
THAT'S RIGHT!
THERE'S NO WAY SOMEONE LIKE DR. YEAGER WOULD DO SOMETHING LIKE THAT FOR NO REASON!
YEAH!
THERE HAS TO BE A WAY TO SAVE HUMANITY WITHOUT THE REISS FAMILY'S BLOOD!
THAT'S WHY HE ENTRUSTED YOU WITH THE KEY TO THE BASE- MENT.

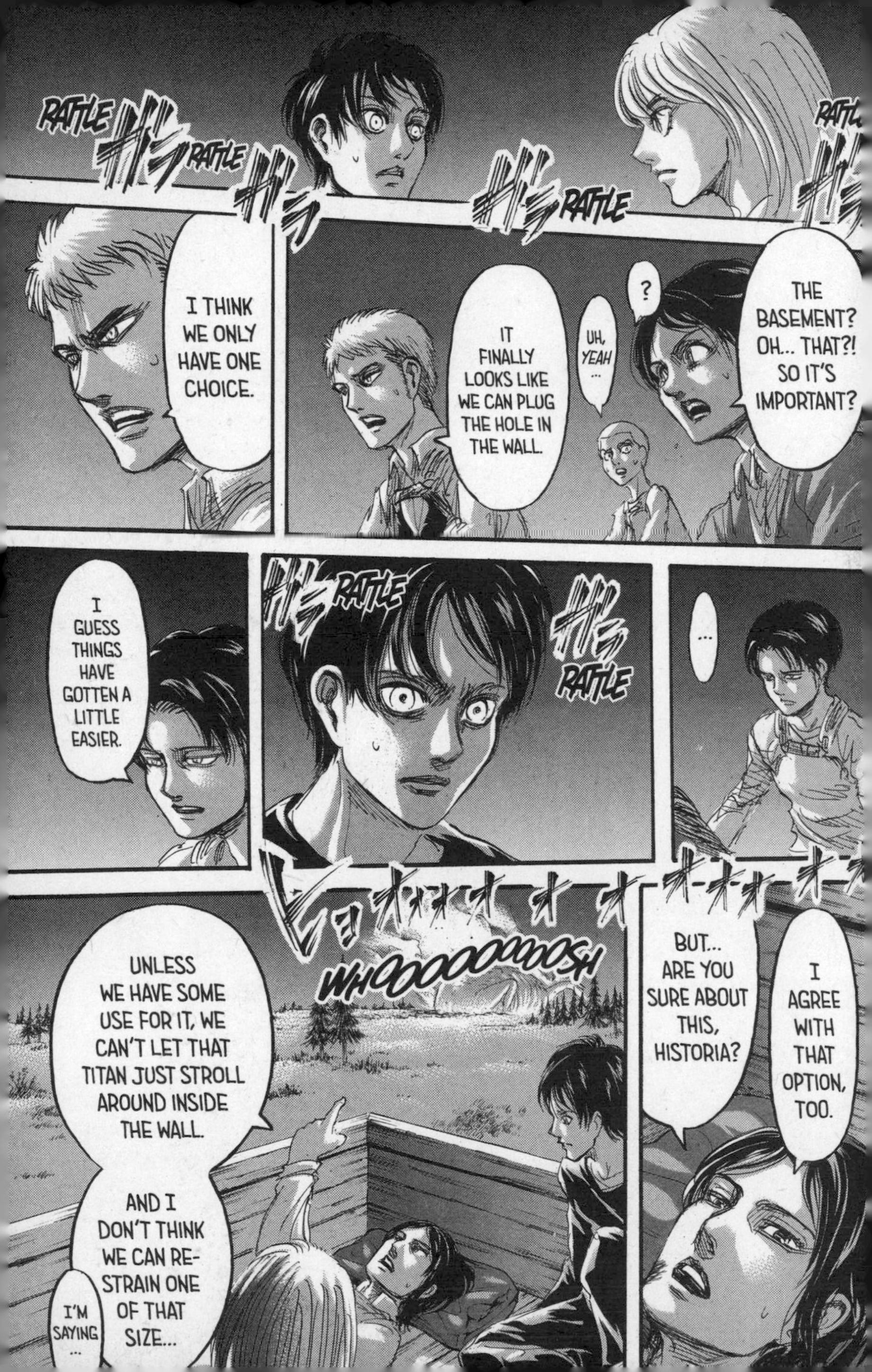
RATTLE
RATTLE
RATTLE
RATTLE
?
THE BASEMENT? OH... THAT?! SO IT'S IMPORTANT?
UH, YEAH ...
IT FINALLY LOOKS LIKE WE CAN PLUG THE HOLE IN THE WALL.
I THINK WE ONLY HAVE ONE CHOICE.
...
RATTLE
RATTLE
I GUESS THINGS HAVE GOTTEN A LITTLE EASIER.
I AGREE WITH THAT OPTION, TOO.
BUT... ARE YOU SURE ABOUT THIS, HISTORIA?
WHOOOOOOOOOOSH
UNLESS WE HAVE SOME USE FOR IT, WE CAN'T LET THAT TITAN JUST STROLL AROUND INSIDE THE WALL.
AND I DON'T THINK WE CAN RE-STRAIN ONE OF THAT SIZE...
I'M SAYING ...

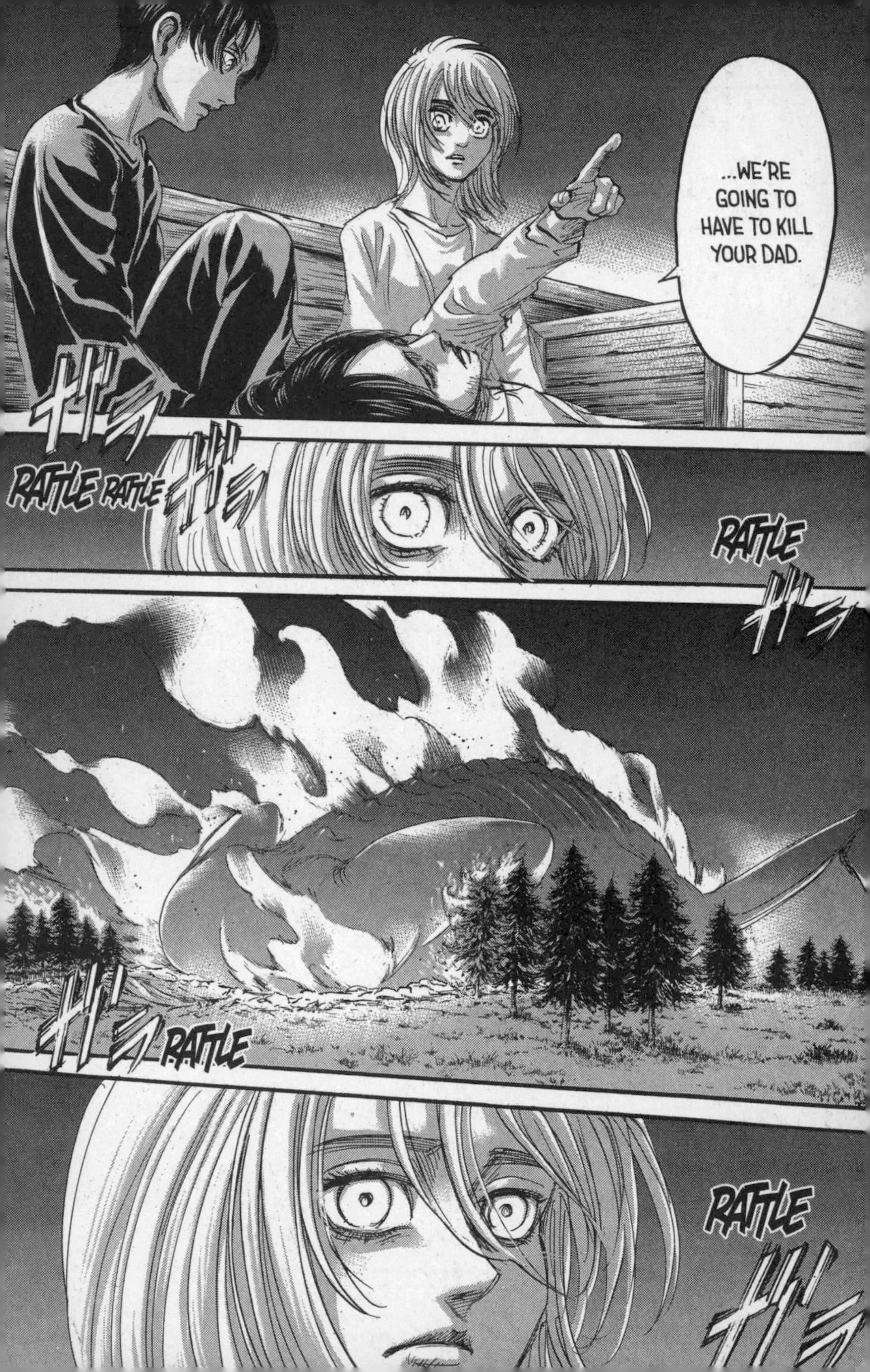
...WE'RE GOING TO HAVE TO KILL YOUR DAD.
RATTLE RATTLE
RATTLE
RATTLE
RATTLE
RATTLE

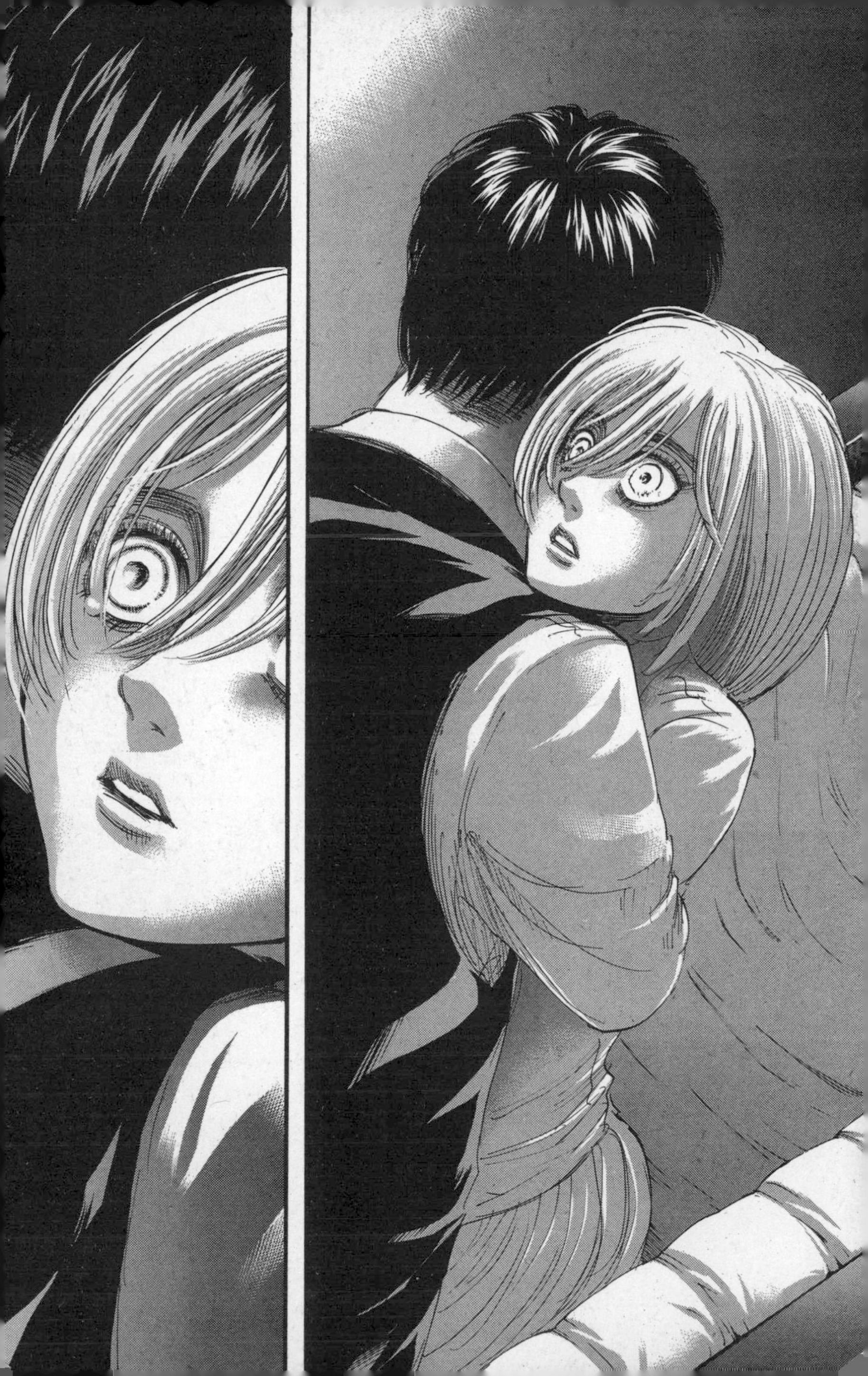

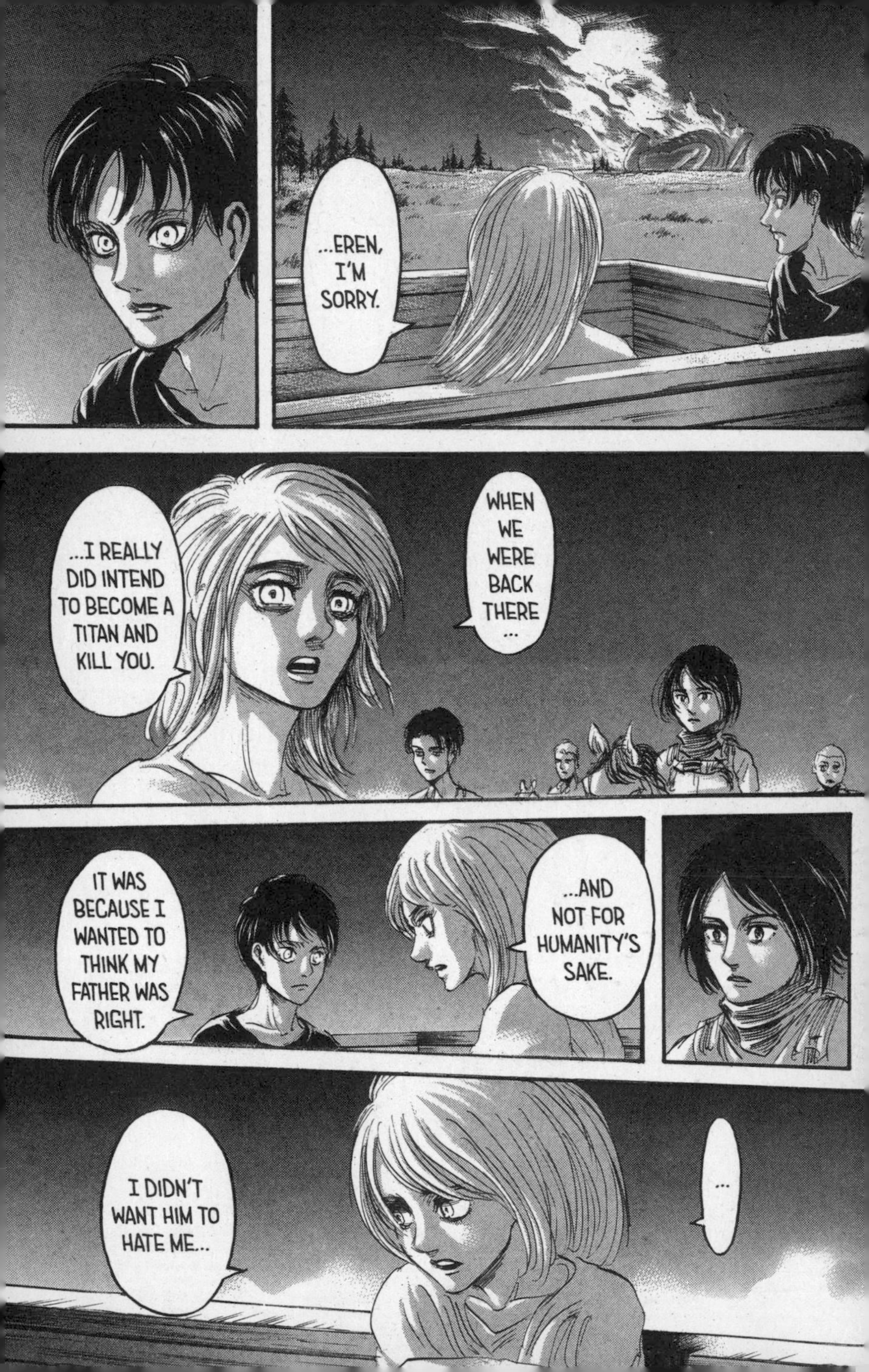
...EREN, I'M SORRY.
WHEN WE WERE BACK THERE ...
...I REALLY DID INTEND TO BECOME A TITAN AND KILL YOU.
...AND NOT FOR HUMANITY'S SAKE.
IT WAS BECAUSE I WANTED TO THINK MY FATHER WAS RIGHT.
...
I DIDN'T WANT HIM TO HATE ME...

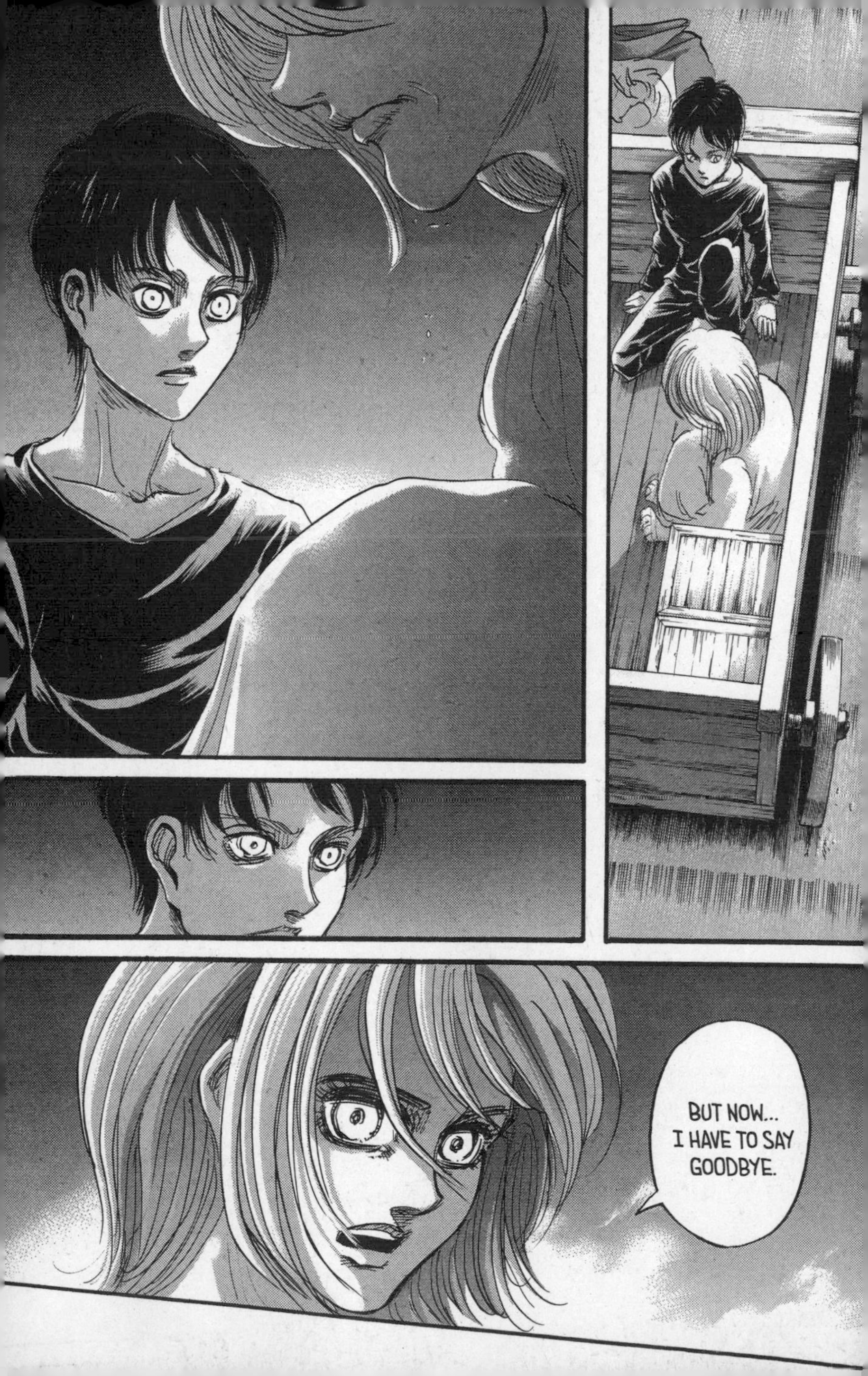
BUT NOW... I HAVE TO SAY GOODBYE.

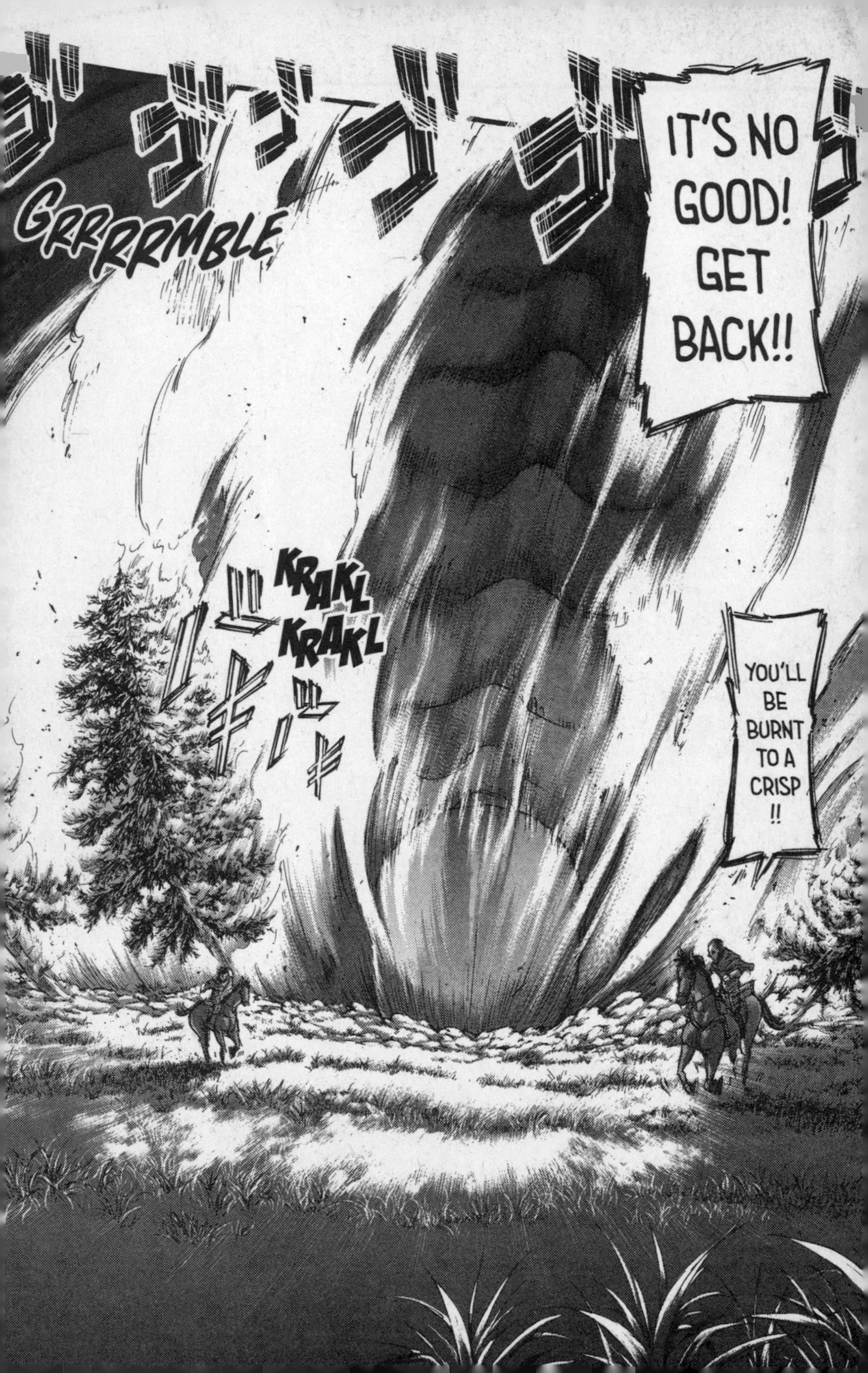
IT'S NO GOOD! GET BACK!!
GRRRRRMBLE
KRAKL KRAKL
YOU'LL BE BURNT TO A CRISP !!

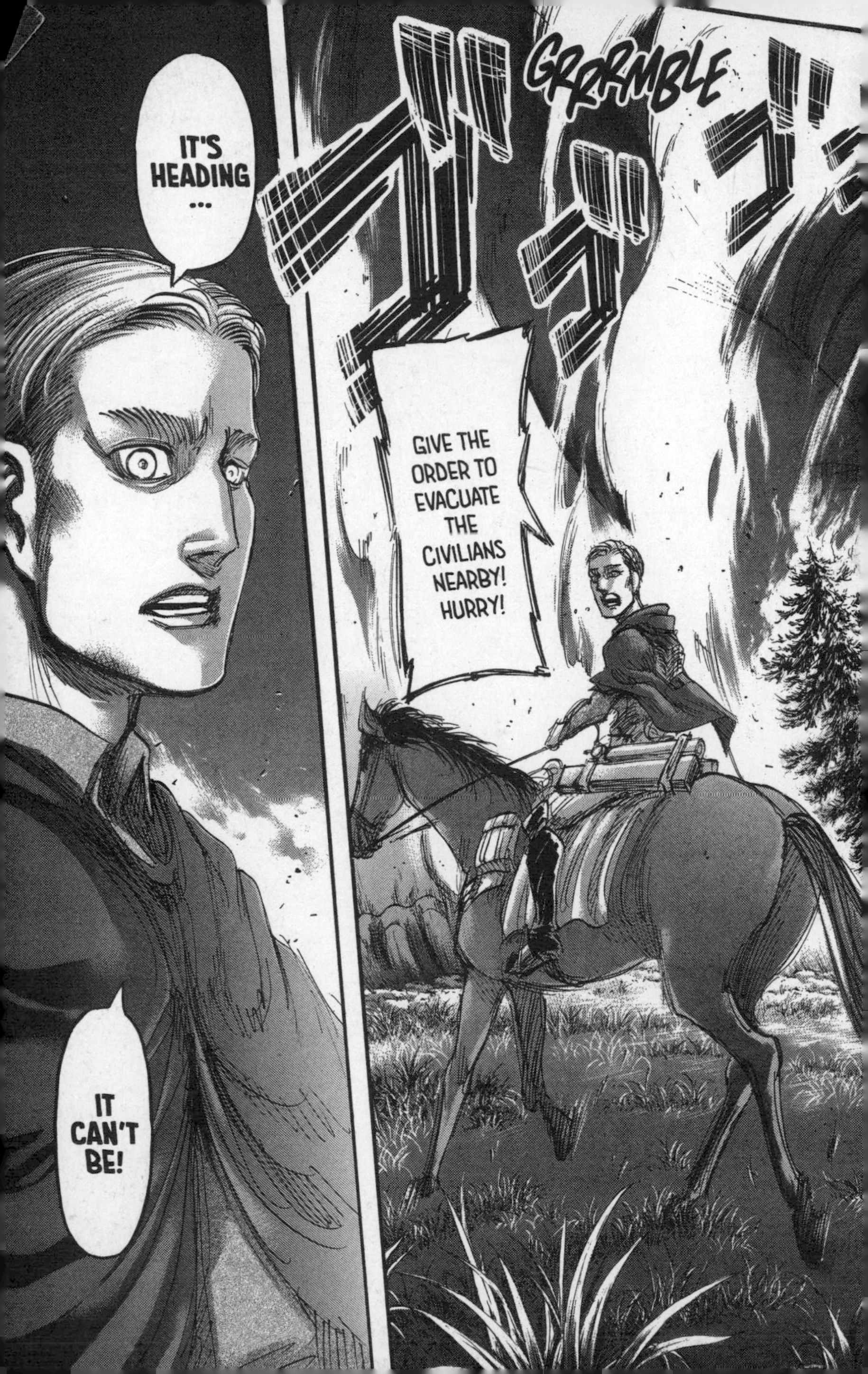
GRRRMBLE
GIVE THE ORDER TO EVACUATE THE CIVILIANS NEARBY! HURRY!
IT'S HEADING ...
IT CAN'T BE!

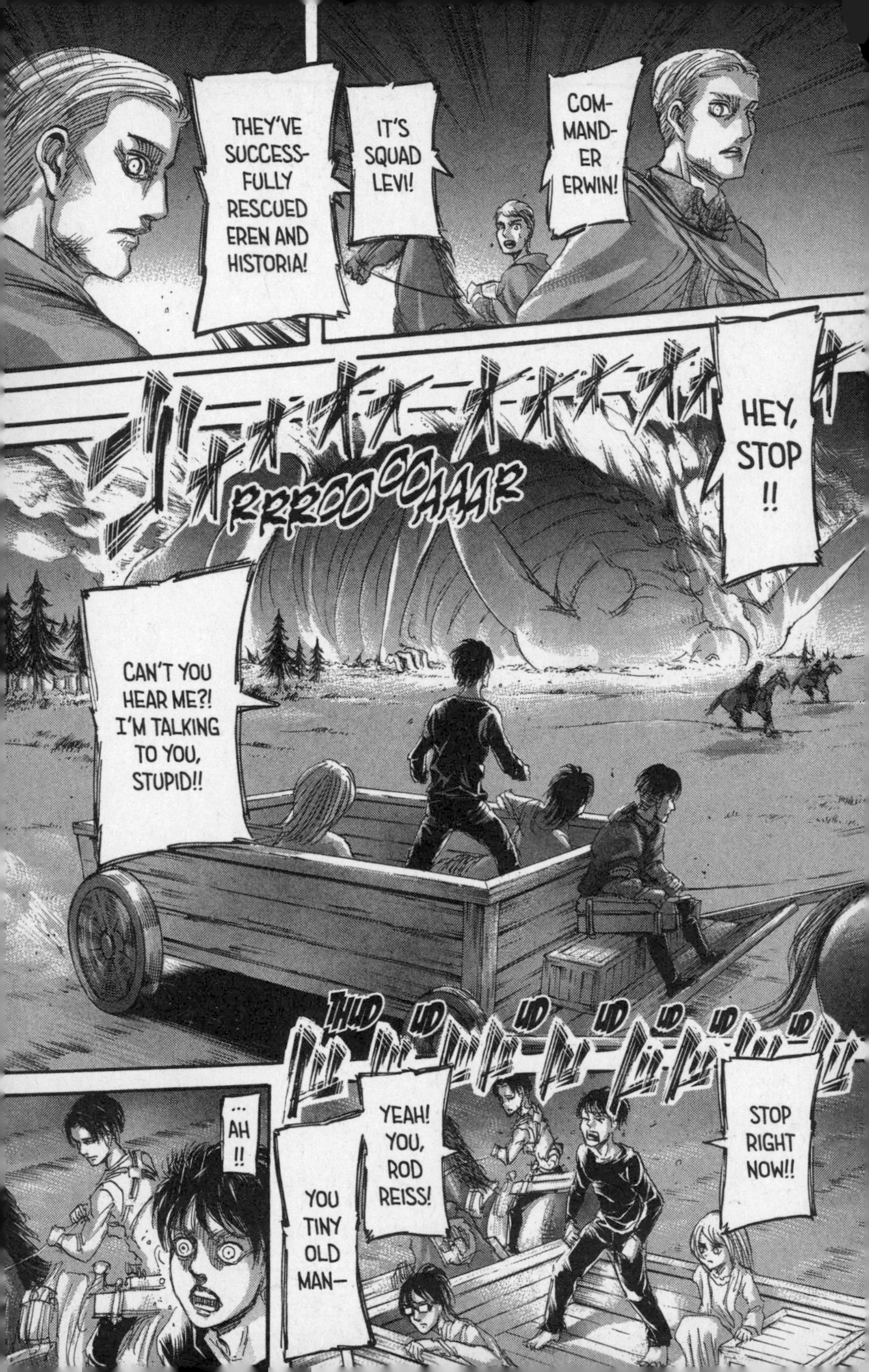
COMMANDER ERWIN!
IT'S SQUAD LEVI!
THEY'VE SUCCESSFULLY RESCUED EREN AND HISTORIA!
RRROOOOAAAR
HEY, STOP!!
CAN'T YOU HEAR ME?! I'M TALKING TO YOU, STUPID!!
THUD UD UD UD UD UD UD
STOP RIGHT NOW!!
YEAH! YOU, ROD REISS!
YOU TINY OLD MAN–
...AH!!

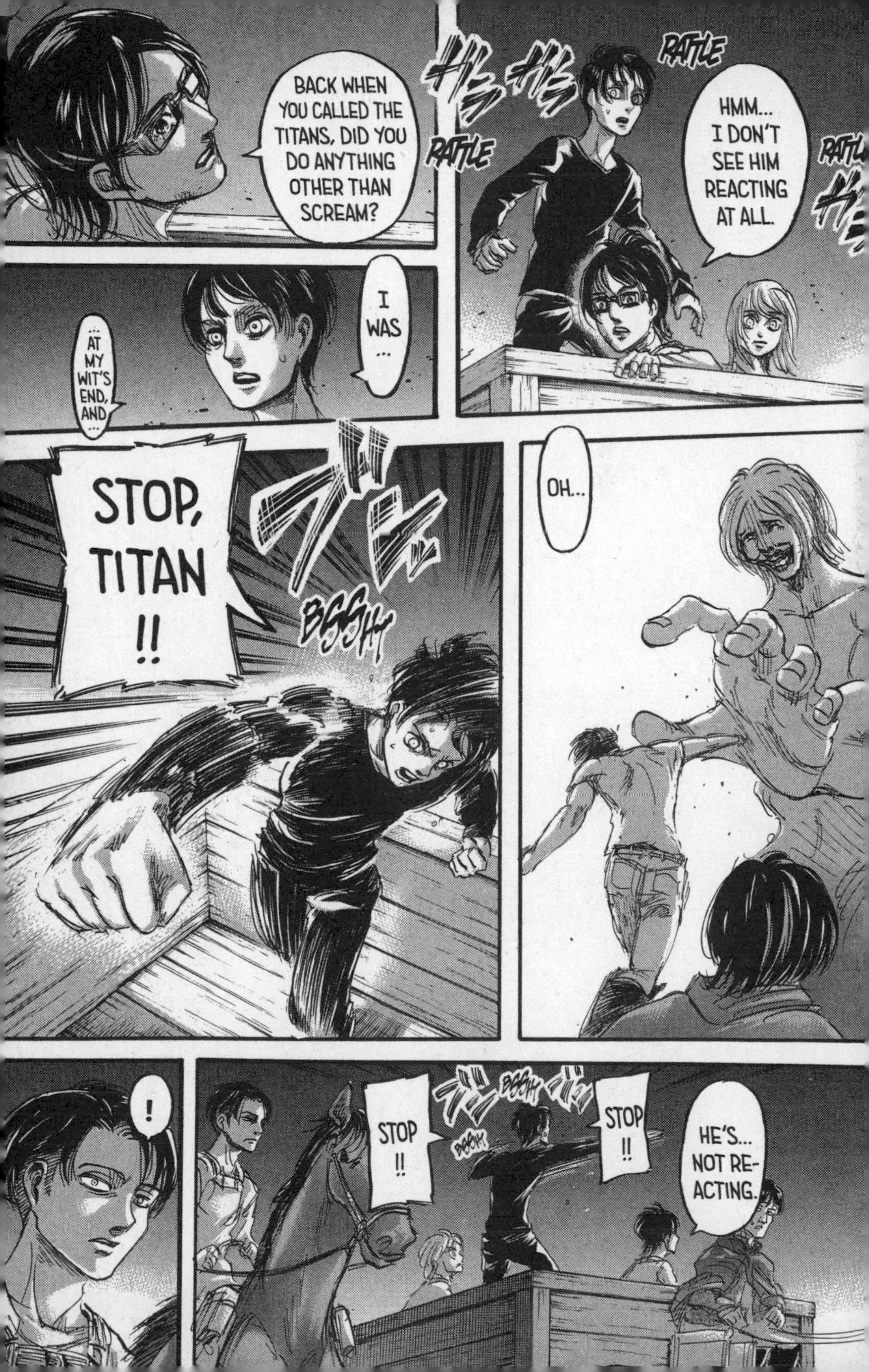
RATTLE
HMM... I DON'T SEE HIM REACTING AT ALL.
RATTLE
RATTLE
BACK WHEN YOU CALLED THE TITANS, DID YOU DO ANYTHING OTHER THAN SCREAM?
I WAS ...
... AT MY WIT'S END, AND ...
OH...
BGSSH
STOP, TITAN !!
HE'S... NOT RE-ACTING.
STOP !!
BGSSH
STOP !!
!

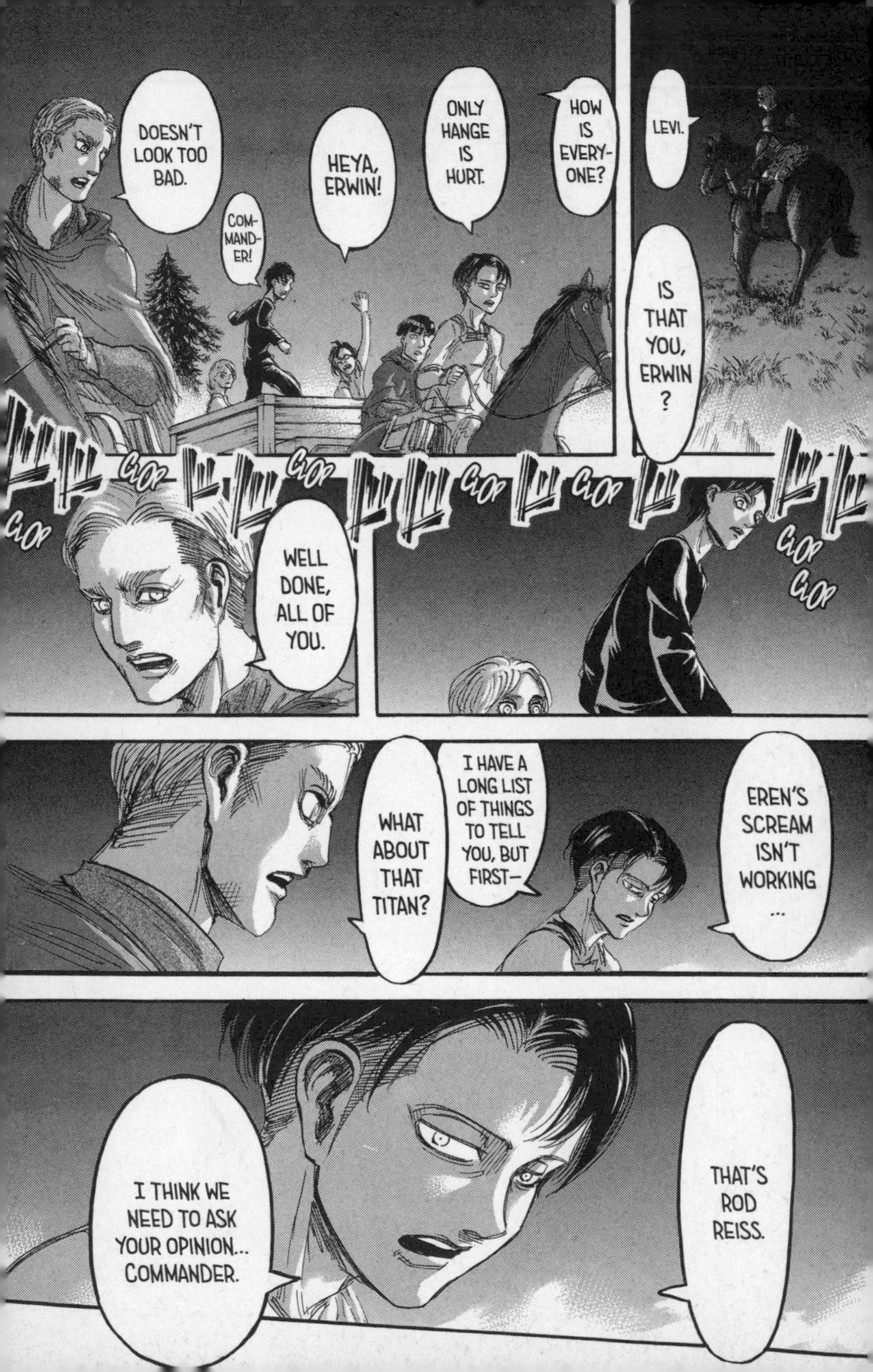
LEVI.
IS THAT YOU, ERWIN?
HOW IS EVERYONE?
ONLY HANGE IS HURT.
HEYA, ERWIN!
DOESN'T LOOK TOO BAD.
COMMANDER!
CLOP CLOP CLOP CLOP CLOP CLOP
CLOP CLOP
WELL DONE, ALL OF YOU.
EREN'S SCREAM ISN'T WORKING ...
I HAVE A LONG LIST OF THINGS TO TELL YOU, BUT FIRST—
WHAT ABOUT THAT TITAN?
THAT'S ROD REISS.
I THINK WE NEED TO ASK YOUR OPINION... COMMANDER.

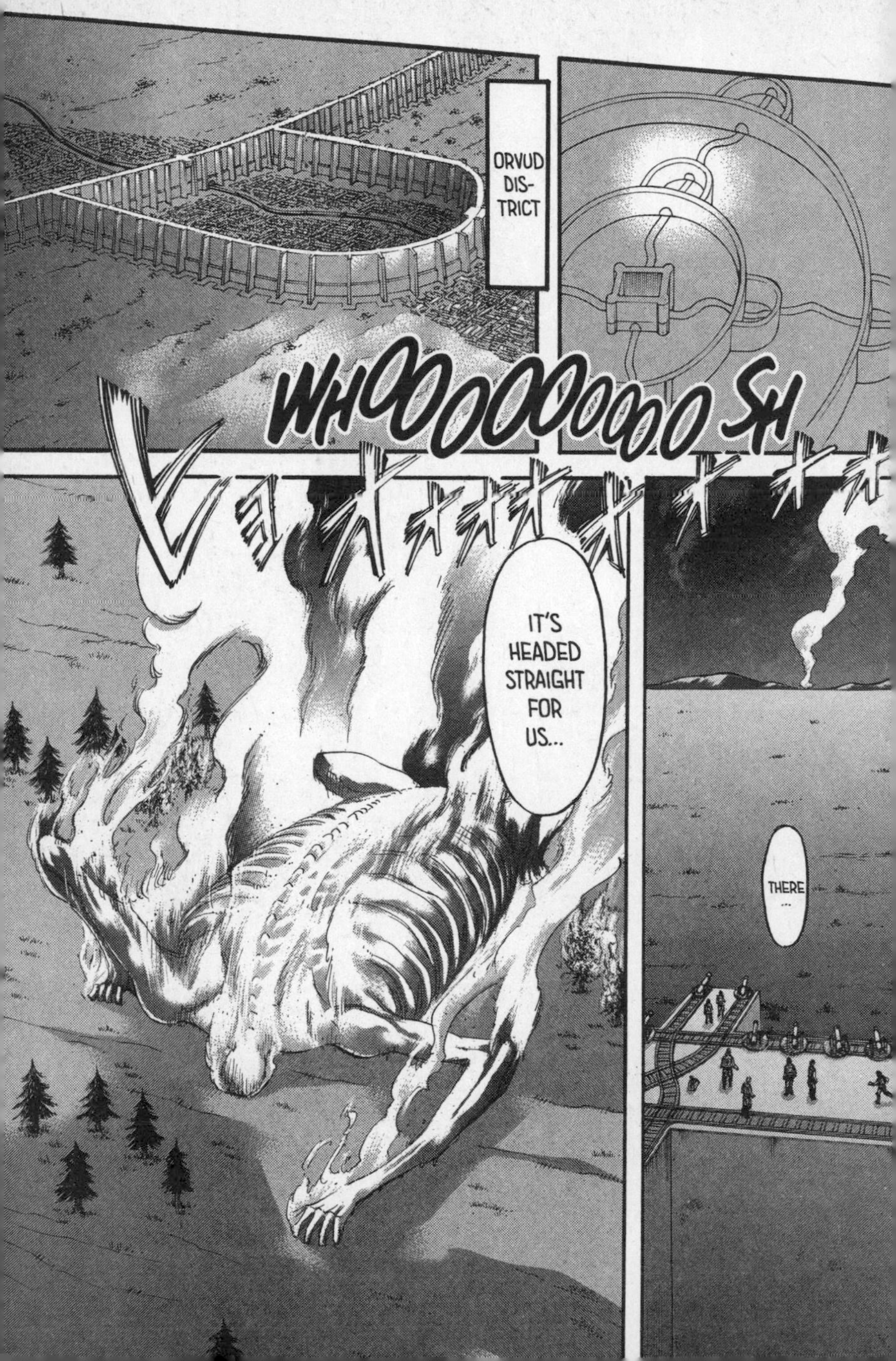
ORVUD DIS- TRICT
WHOOOOOOOOO SH
THERE ...
IT'S HEADED STRAIGHT FOR US...

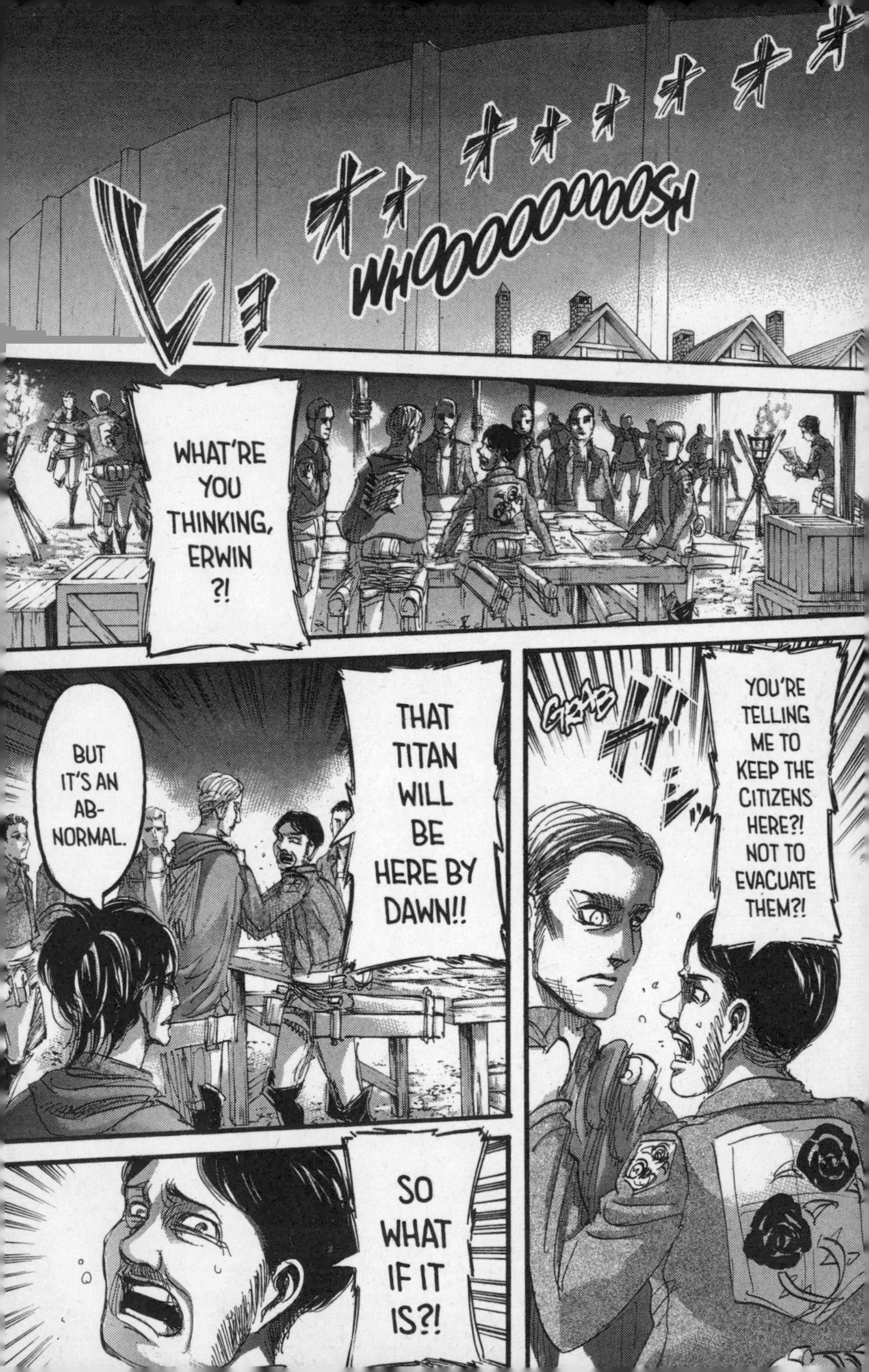
WHOOOOOOOOOSH
WHAT'RE YOU THINKING, ERWIN?!
GRAB
YOU'RE TELLING ME TO KEEP THE CITIZENS HERE?! NOT TO EVACUATE THEM?!
THAT TITAN WILL BE HERE BY DAWN!!
BUT IT'S AN AB-NORMAL.
SO WHAT IF IT IS?!

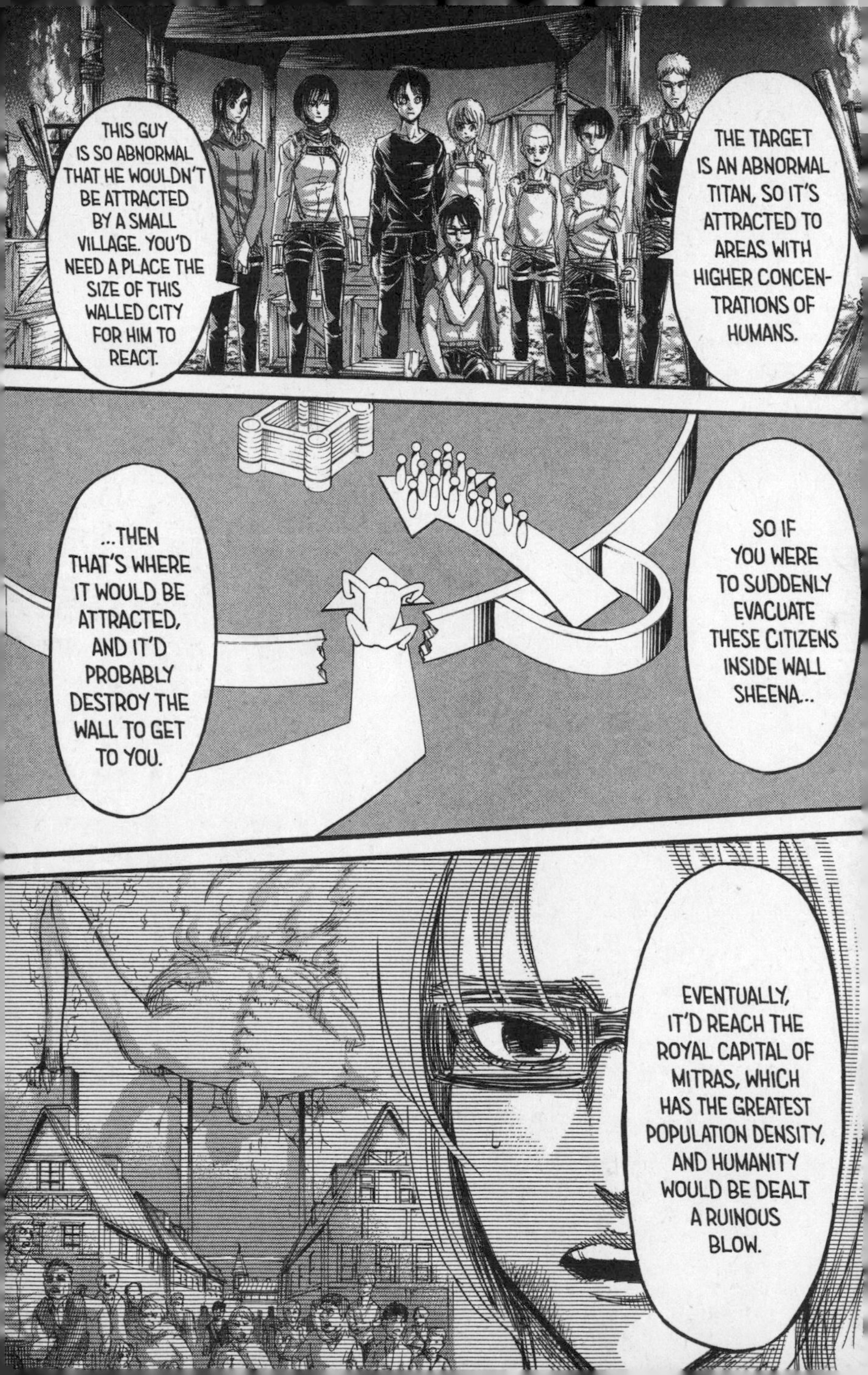
THE TARGET IS AN ABNORMAL TITAN, SO IT'S ATTRACTED TO AREAS WITH HIGHER CONCEN-TRATIONS OF HUMANS.
THIS GUY IS SO ABNORMAL THAT HE WOULDN'T BE ATTRACTED BY A SMALL VILLAGE. YOU'D NEED A PLACE THE SIZE OF THIS WALLED CITY FOR HIM TO REACT.
SO IF YOU WERE TO SUDDENLY EVACUATE THESE CITIZENS INSIDE WALL SHEENA...
...THEN THAT'S WHERE IT WOULD BE ATTRACTED, AND IT'D PROBABLY DESTROY THE WALL TO GET TO YOU.
EVENTUALLY, IT'D REACH THE ROYAL CAPITAL OF MITRAS, WHICH HAS THE GREATEST POPULATION DENSITY, AND HUMANITY WOULD BE DEALT A RUINOUS BLOW.

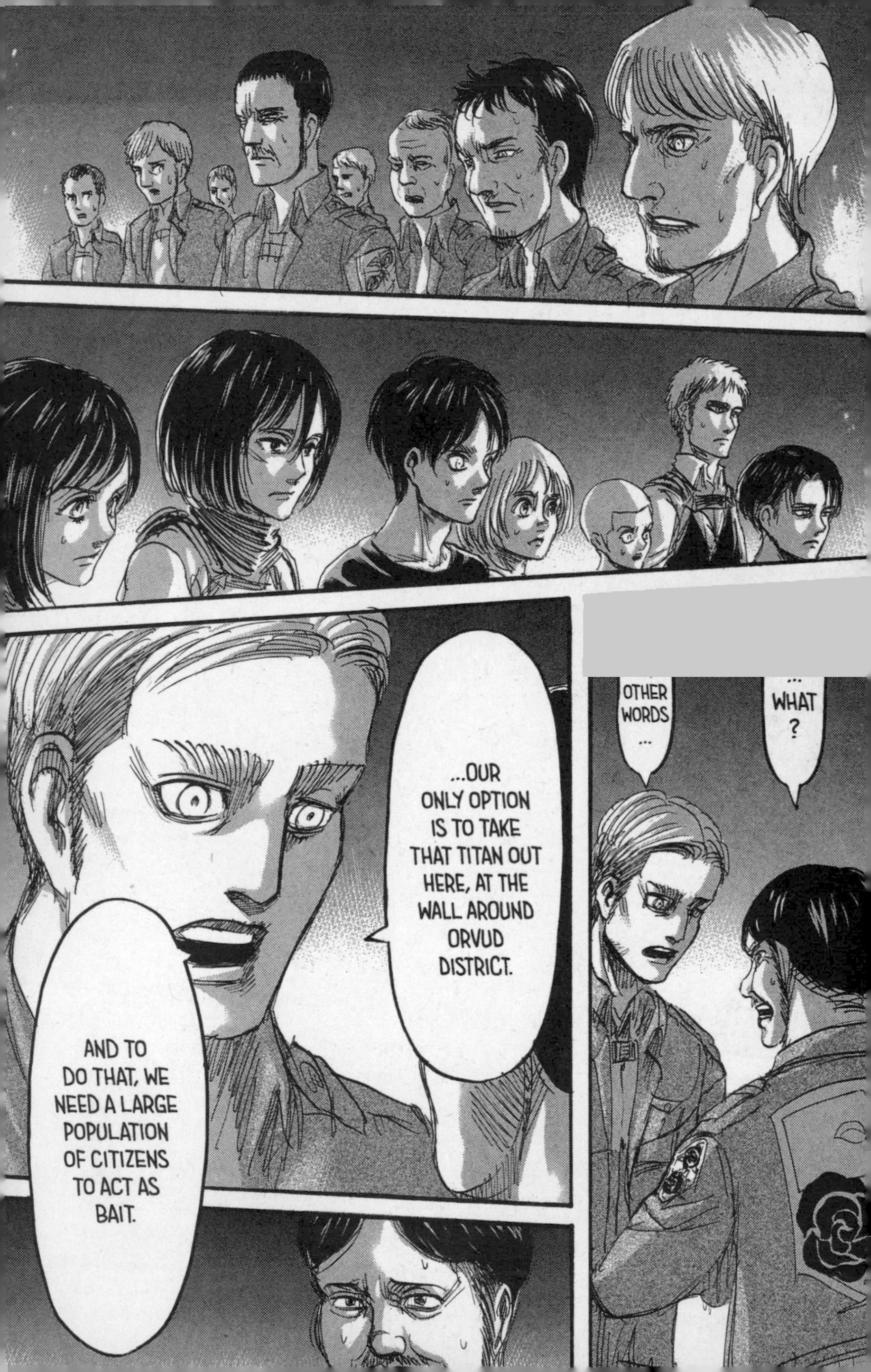
... WHAT?
OTHER WORDS ...
...OUR ONLY OPTION IS TO TAKE THAT TITAN OUT HERE, AT THE WALL AROUND ORVUD DISTRICT.
AND TO DO THAT, WE NEED A LARGE POPULATION OF CITIZENS TO ACT AS BAIT.

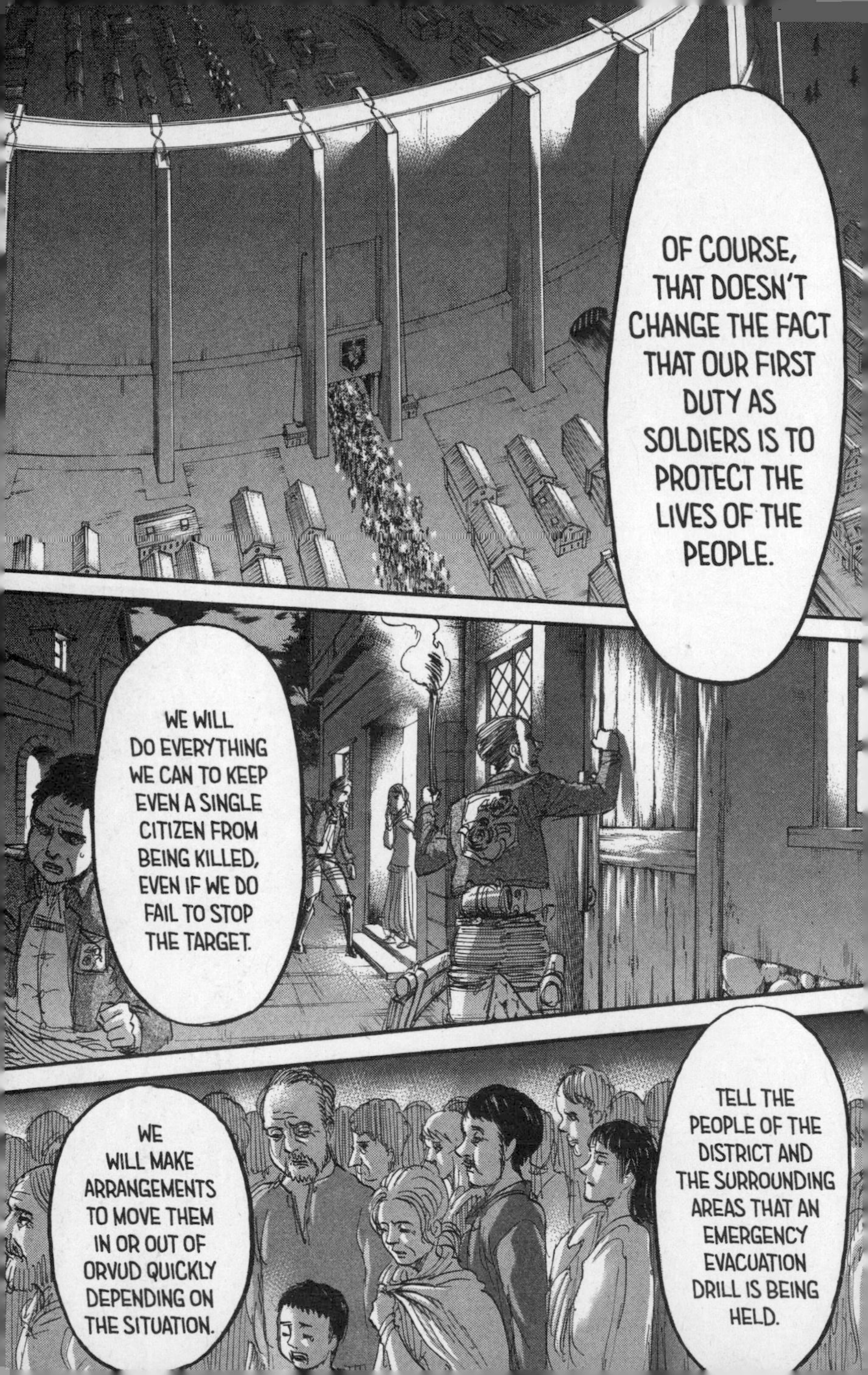
OF COURSE, THAT DOESN'T CHANGE THE FACT THAT OUR FIRST DUTY AS SOLDIERS IS TO PROTECT THE LIVES OF THE PEOPLE.
WE WILL DO EVERYTHING WE CAN TO KEEP EVEN A SINGLE CITIZEN FROM BEING KILLED, EVEN IF WE DO FAIL TO STOP THE TARGET.
TELL THE PEOPLE OF THE DISTRICT AND THE SURROUNDING AREAS THAT AN EMERGENCY EVACUATION DRILL IS BEING HELD.
WE WILL MAKE ARRANGEMENTS TO MOVE THEM IN OR OUT OF ORVUD QUICKLY DEPENDING ON THE SITUATION.

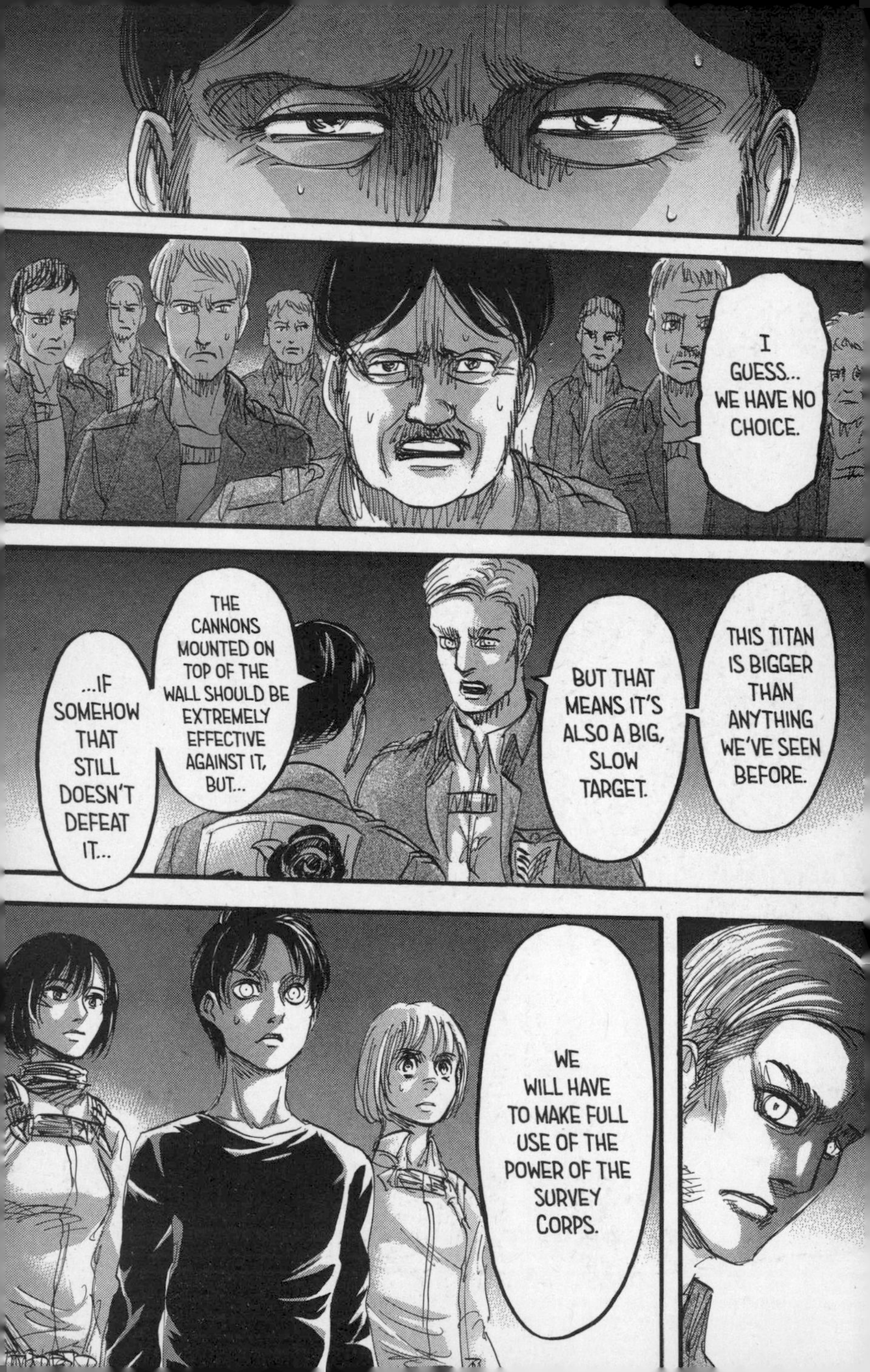
I GUESS... WE HAVE NO CHOICE.
THIS TITAN IS BIGGER THAN ANYTHING WE'VE SEEN BEFORE.
BUT THAT MEANS IT'S ALSO A BIG, SLOW TARGET.
THE CANNONS MOUNTED ON TOP OF THE WALL SHOULD BE EXTREMELY EFFECTIVE AGAINST IT, BUT...
...IF SOMEHOW THAT STILL DOESN'T DEFEAT IT...
WE WILL HAVE TO MAKE FULL USE OF THE POWER OF THE SURVEY CORPS.

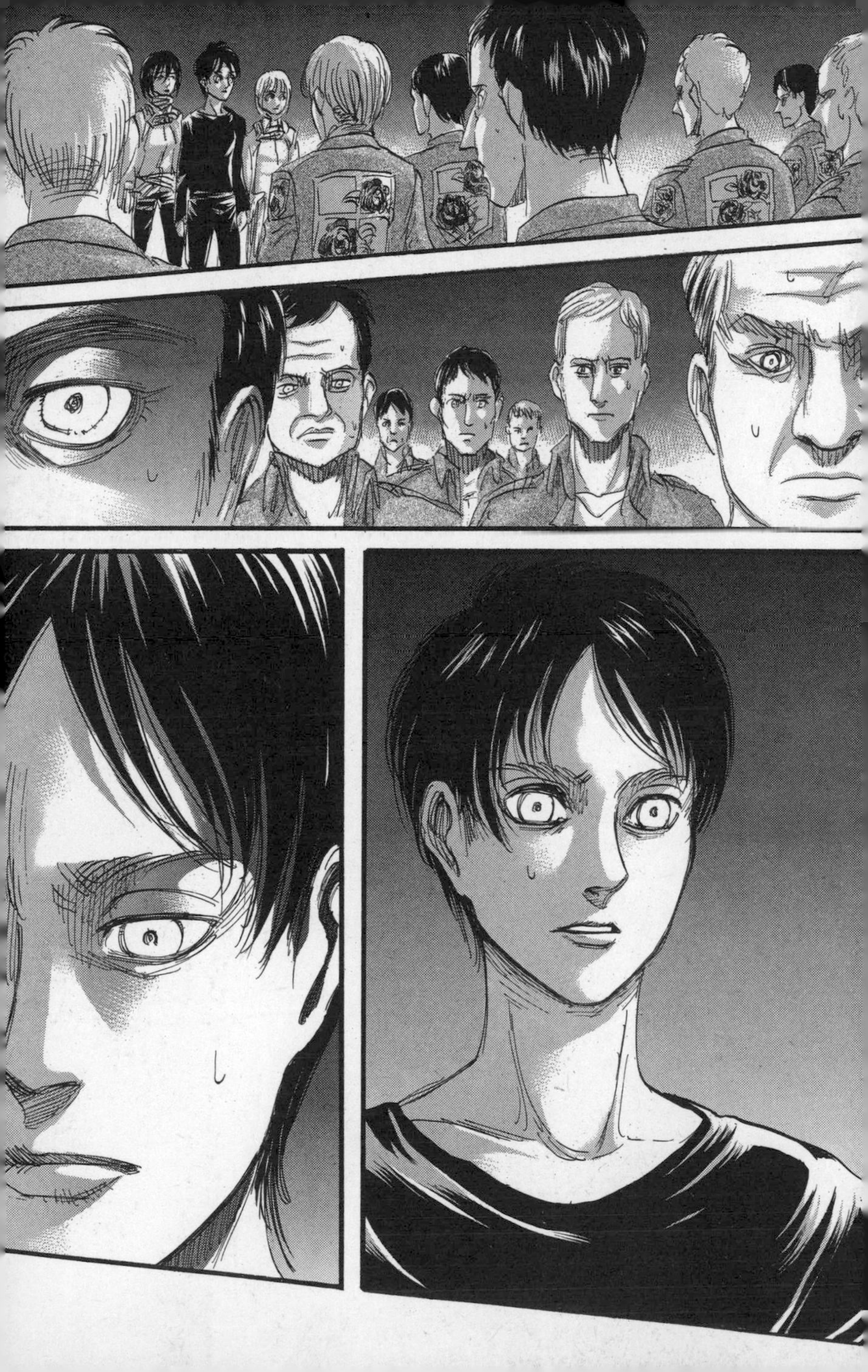

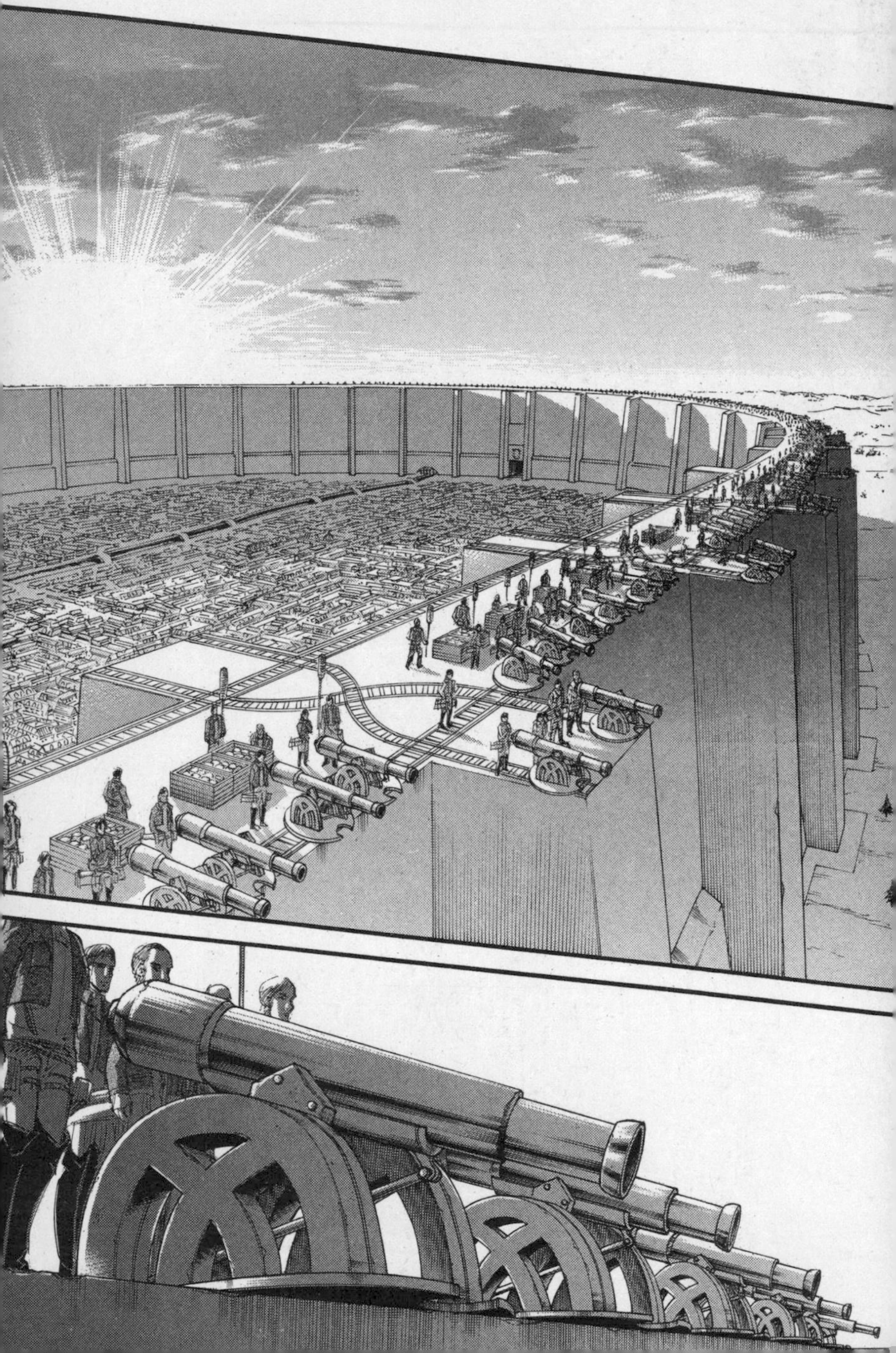

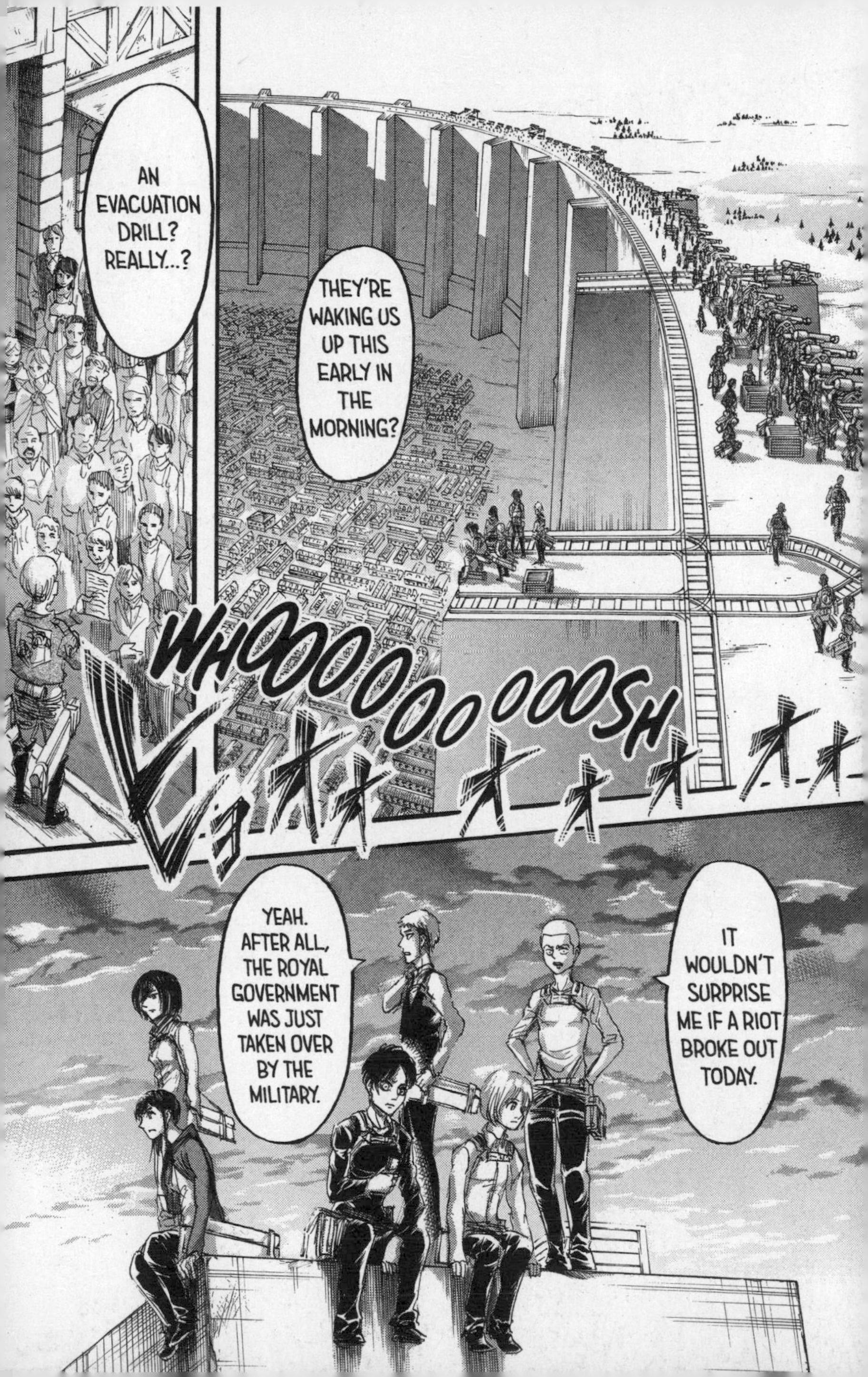
THEY'RE WAKING US UP THIS EARLY IN THE MORNING?
WHOOOOOOOOOOSH
AN EVACUATION DRILL? REALLY...?
IT WOULDN'T SURPRISE ME IF A RIOT BROKE OUT TODAY.
YEAH. AFTER ALL, THE ROYAL GOVERNMENT WAS JUST TAKEN OVER BY THE MILITARY.

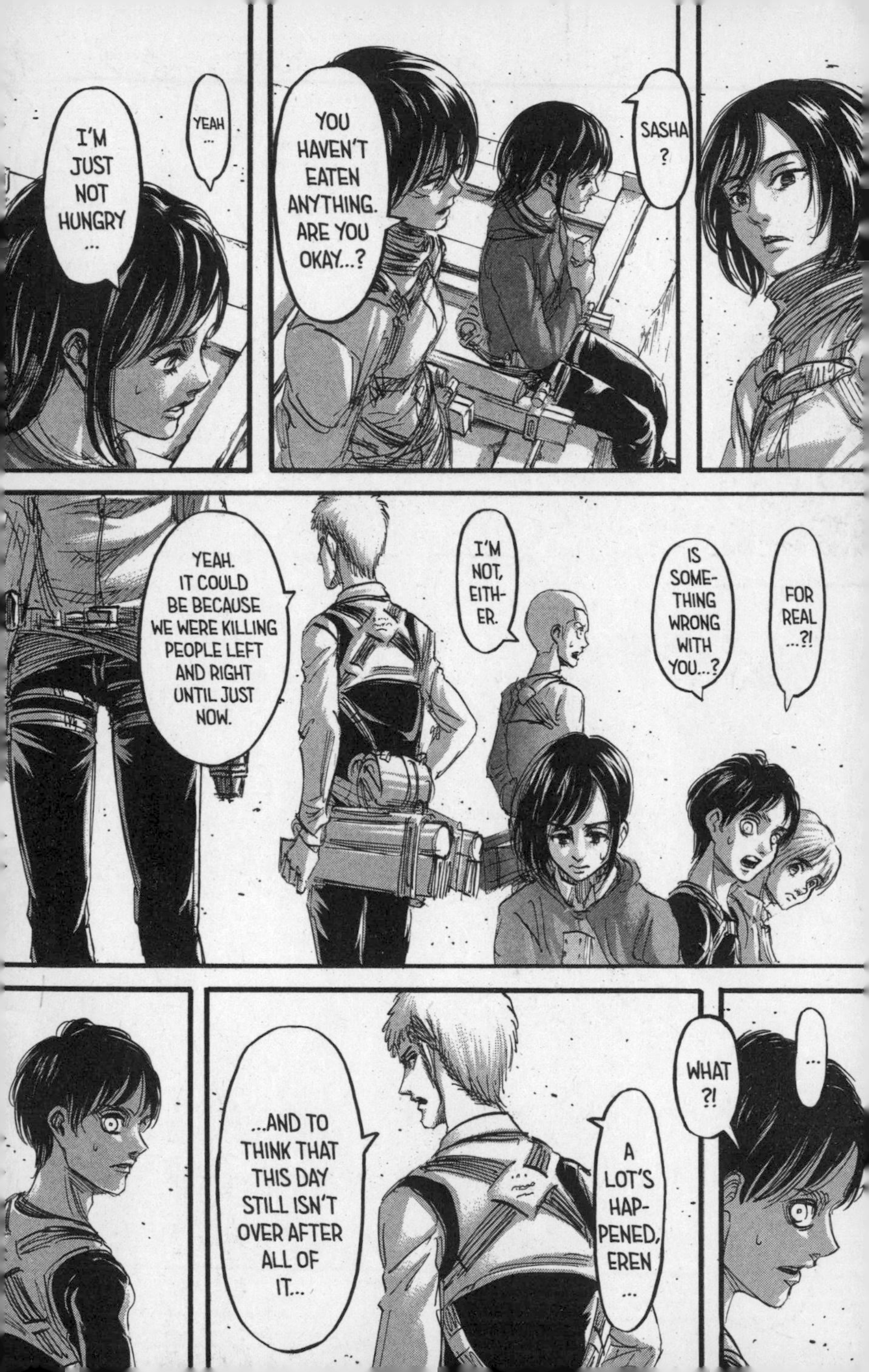
SASHA ?
YOU HAVEN'T EATEN ANYTHING. ARE YOU OKAY...?
YEAH ...
I'M JUST NOT HUNGRY ...
FOR REAL ...?!
IS SOME-THING WRONG WITH YOU...?
I'M NOT, EITH-ER.
YEAH. IT COULD BE BECAUSE WE WERE KILLING PEOPLE LEFT AND RIGHT UNTIL JUST NOW.
...
WHAT ?!
A LOT'S HAP-PENED, EREN ...
...AND TO THINK THAT THIS DAY STILL ISN'T OVER AFTER ALL OF IT...

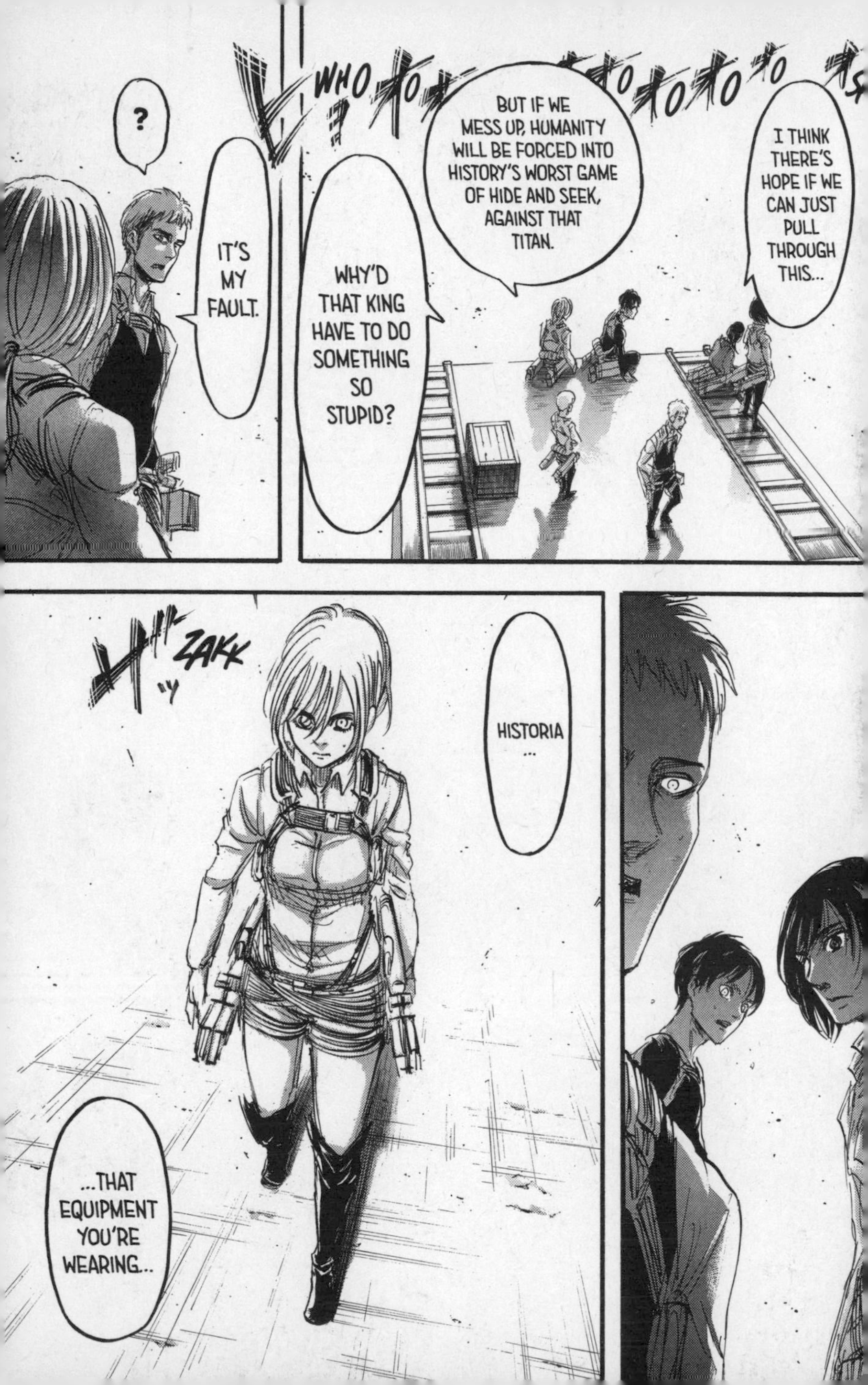
I THINK THERE'S HOPE IF WE CAN JUST PULL THROUGH THIS...
BUT IF WE MESS UP, HUMANITY WILL BE FORCED INTO HISTORY'S WORST GAME OF HIDE AND SEEK, AGAINST THAT TITAN.
WHO
WHY'D THAT KING HAVE TO DO SOMETHING SO STUPID?
IT'S MY FAULT.
?
HISTORIA ...
ZAKK
...THAT EQUIPMENT YOU'RE WEARING...

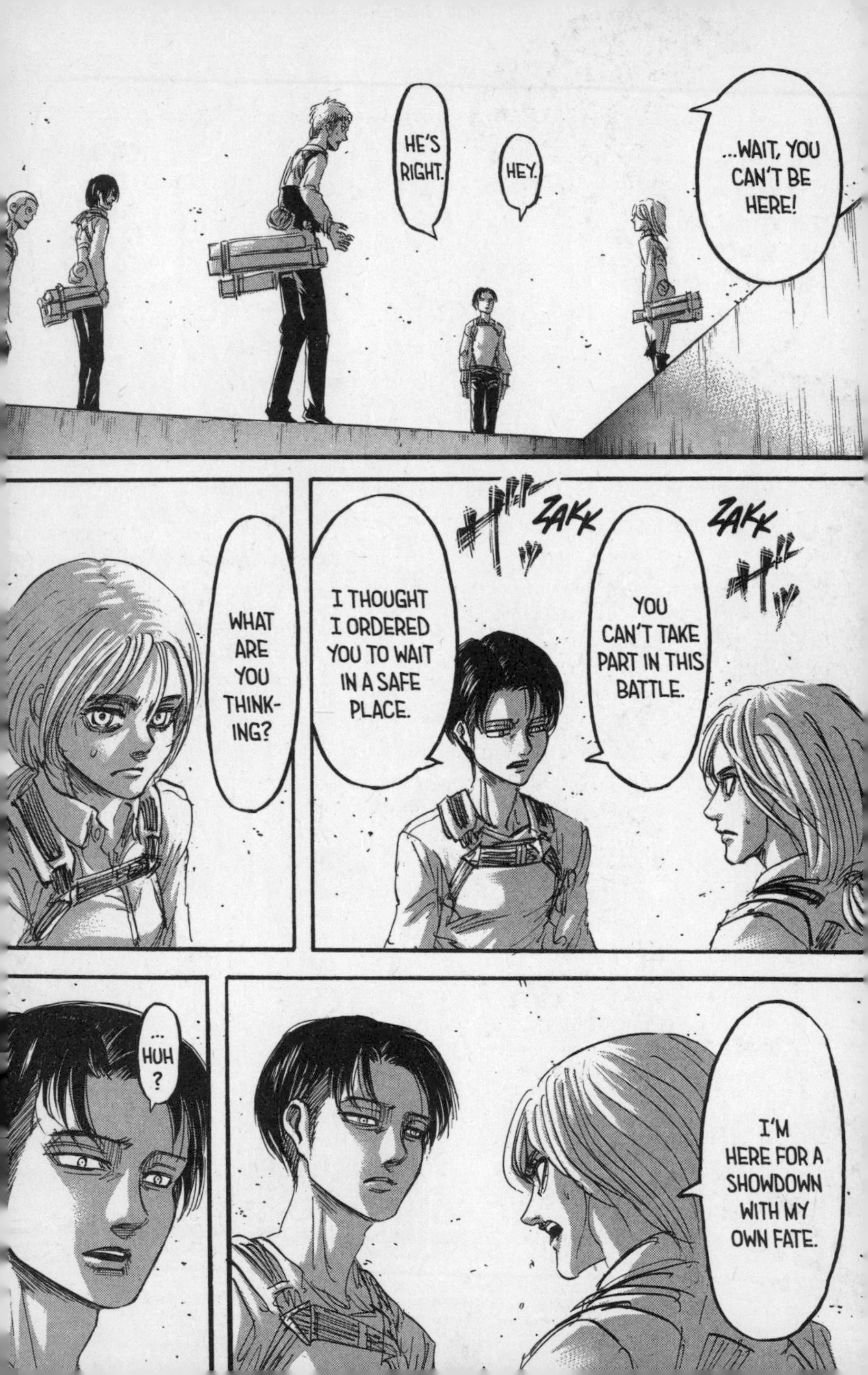
...WAIT, YOU CAN'T BE HERE!
HEY.
HE'S RIGHT.
ZAKK
ZAKK
YOU CAN'T TAKE PART IN THIS BATTLE.
I THOUGHT I ORDERED YOU TO WAIT IN A SAFE PLACE.
WHAT ARE YOU THINKING?
I'M HERE FOR A SHOWDOWN WITH MY OWN FATE.
...HUH?

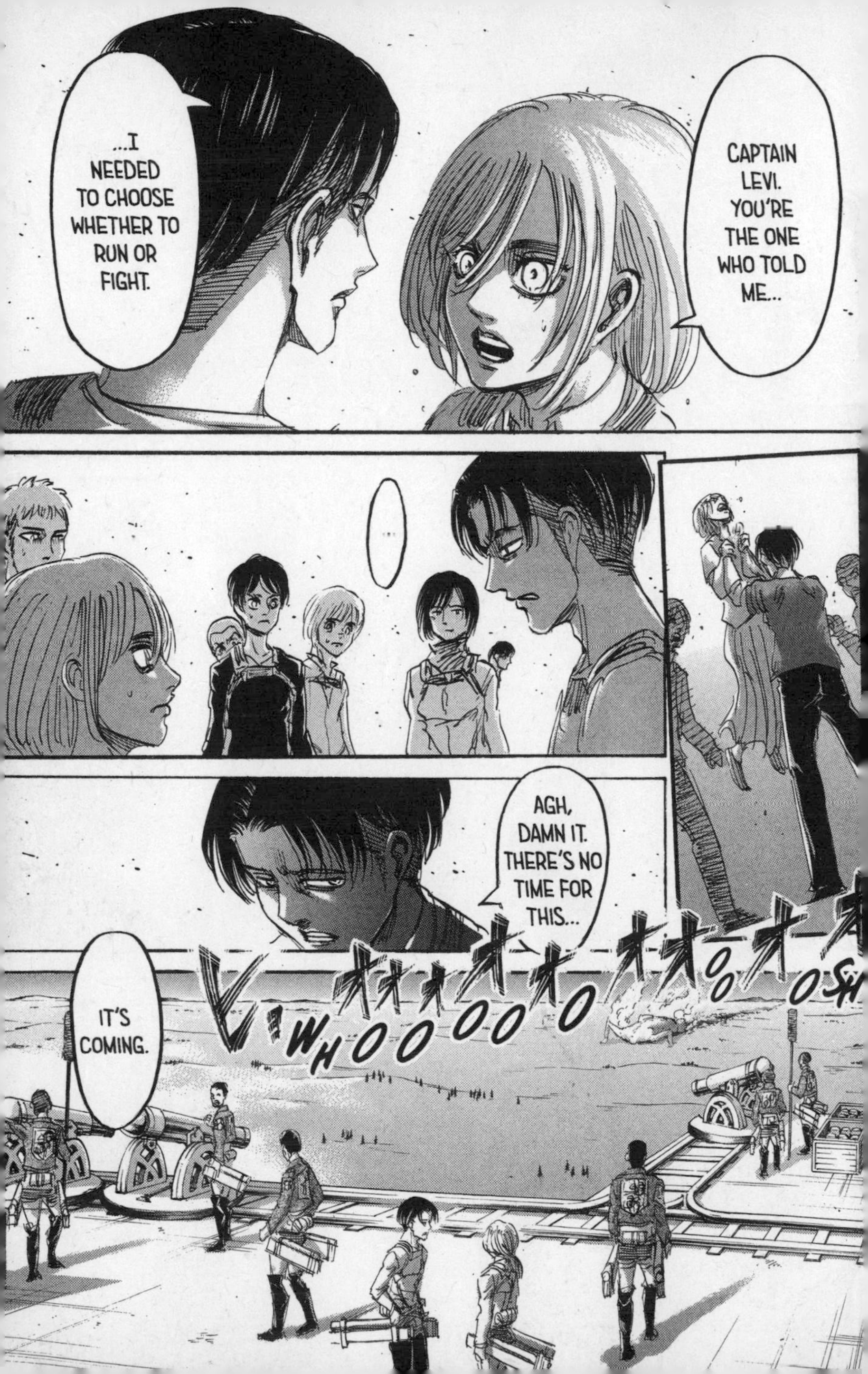
CAPTAIN LEVI. YOU'RE THE ONE WHO TOLD ME...
...I NEEDED TO CHOOSE WHETHER TO RUN OR FIGHT.
...
AGH, DAMN IT. THERE'S NO TIME FOR THIS...
VWHOOOOOOOSH
IT'S COMING.

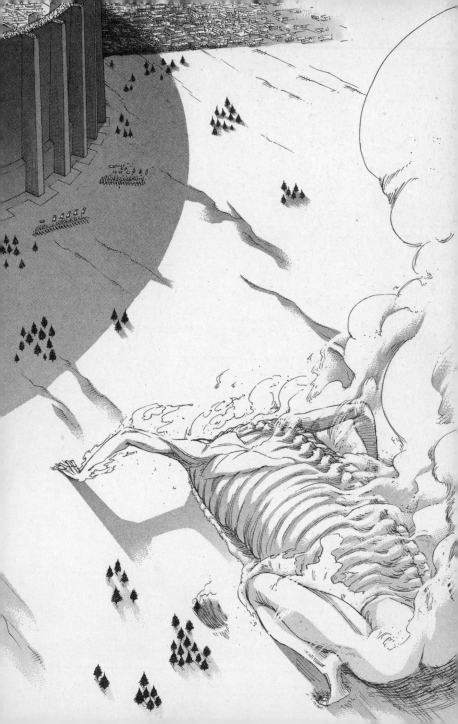

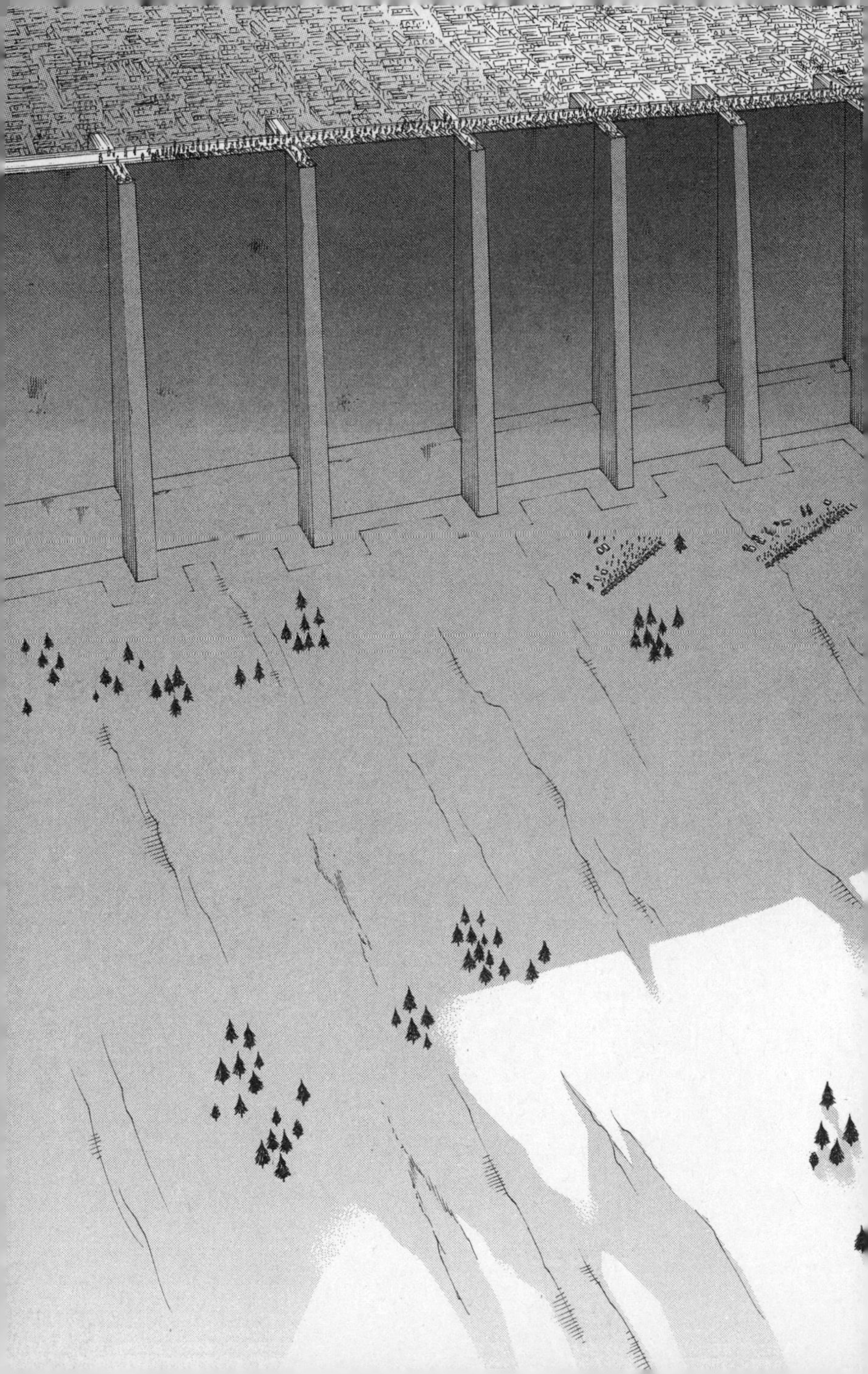

ATTACK on TITAN

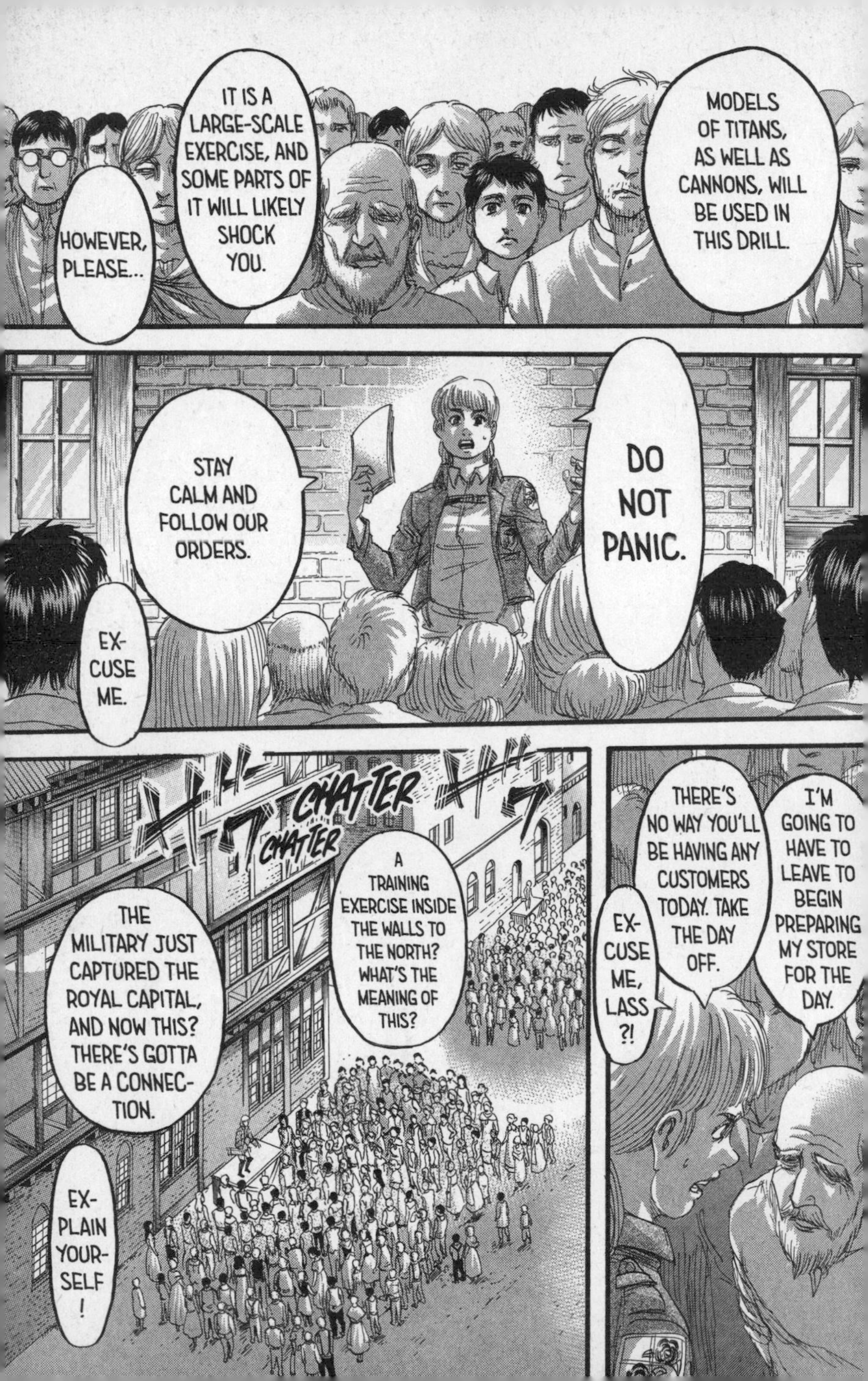
MODELS OF TITANS, AS WELL AS CANNONS, WILL BE USED IN THIS DRILL.
IT IS A LARGE-SCALE EXERCISE, AND SOME PARTS OF IT WILL LIKELY SHOCK YOU.
HOWEVER, PLEASE...
DO NOT PANIC.
STAY CALM AND FOLLOW OUR ORDERS.
EX-CUSE ME.
I'M GOING TO HAVE TO LEAVE TO BEGIN PREPARING MY STORE FOR THE DAY.
THERE'S NO WAY YOU'LL BE HAVING ANY CUSTOMERS TODAY. TAKE THE DAY OFF.
EX-CUSE ME, LASS ?!
CHATTER
CHATTER
A TRAINING EXERCISE INSIDE THE WALLS TO THE NORTH? WHAT'S THE MEANING OF THIS?
THE MILITARY JUST CAPTURED THE ROYAL CAPITAL, AND NOW THIS? THERE'S GOTTA BE A CONNEC-TION.
EX-PLAIN YOUR-SELF !

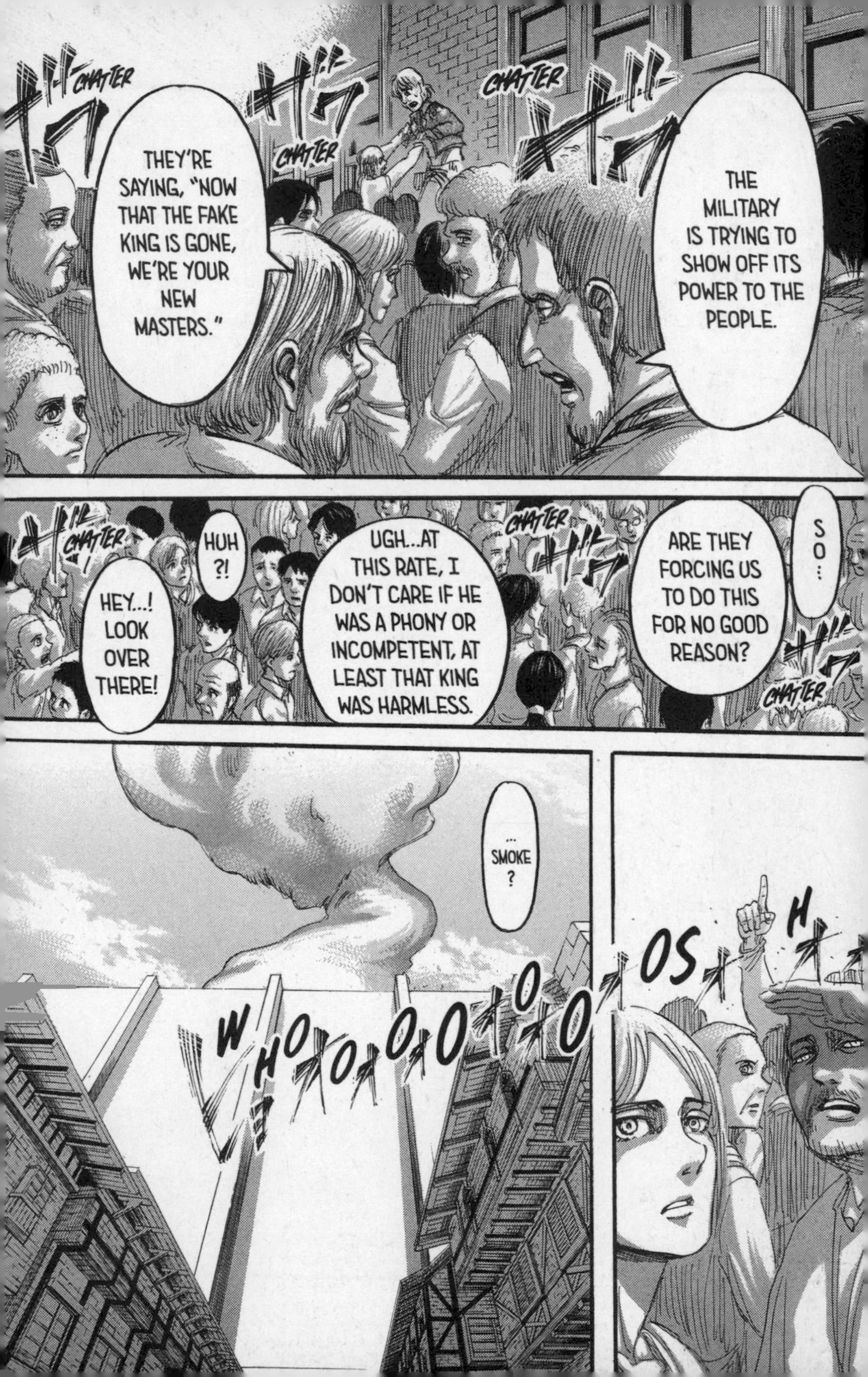
CHATTER
CHATTER
THE MILITARY IS TRYING TO SHOW OFF ITS POWER TO THE PEOPLE.
CHATTER
THEY'RE SAYING, "NOW THAT THE FAKE KING IS GONE, WE'RE YOUR NEW MASTERS."
CHATTER
SO...
CHATTER
ARE THEY FORCING US TO DO THIS FOR NO GOOD REASON?
CHATTER
UGH...AT THIS RATE, I DON'T CARE IF HE WAS A PHONY OR INCOMPETENT, AT LEAST THAT KING WAS HARMLESS.
HUH ?!
CHATTER
HEY...! LOOK OVER THERE!
WHOOOOOOOSH
... SMOKE ?

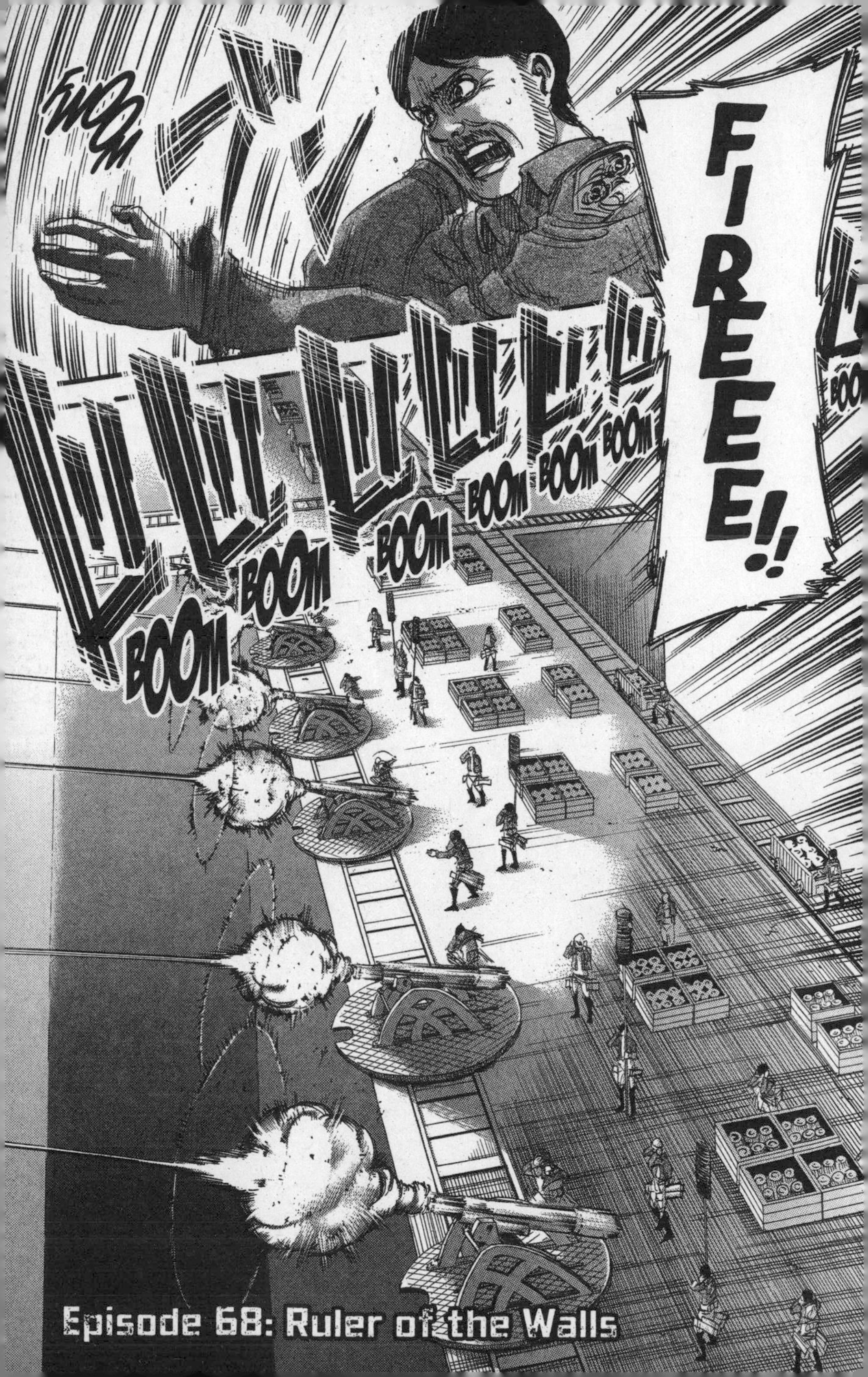
FIREEE!!
BOOM
FWOOM
BOOM BOOM BOOM BOOM BOOM BOOM
Episode 68: Ruler of the Walls

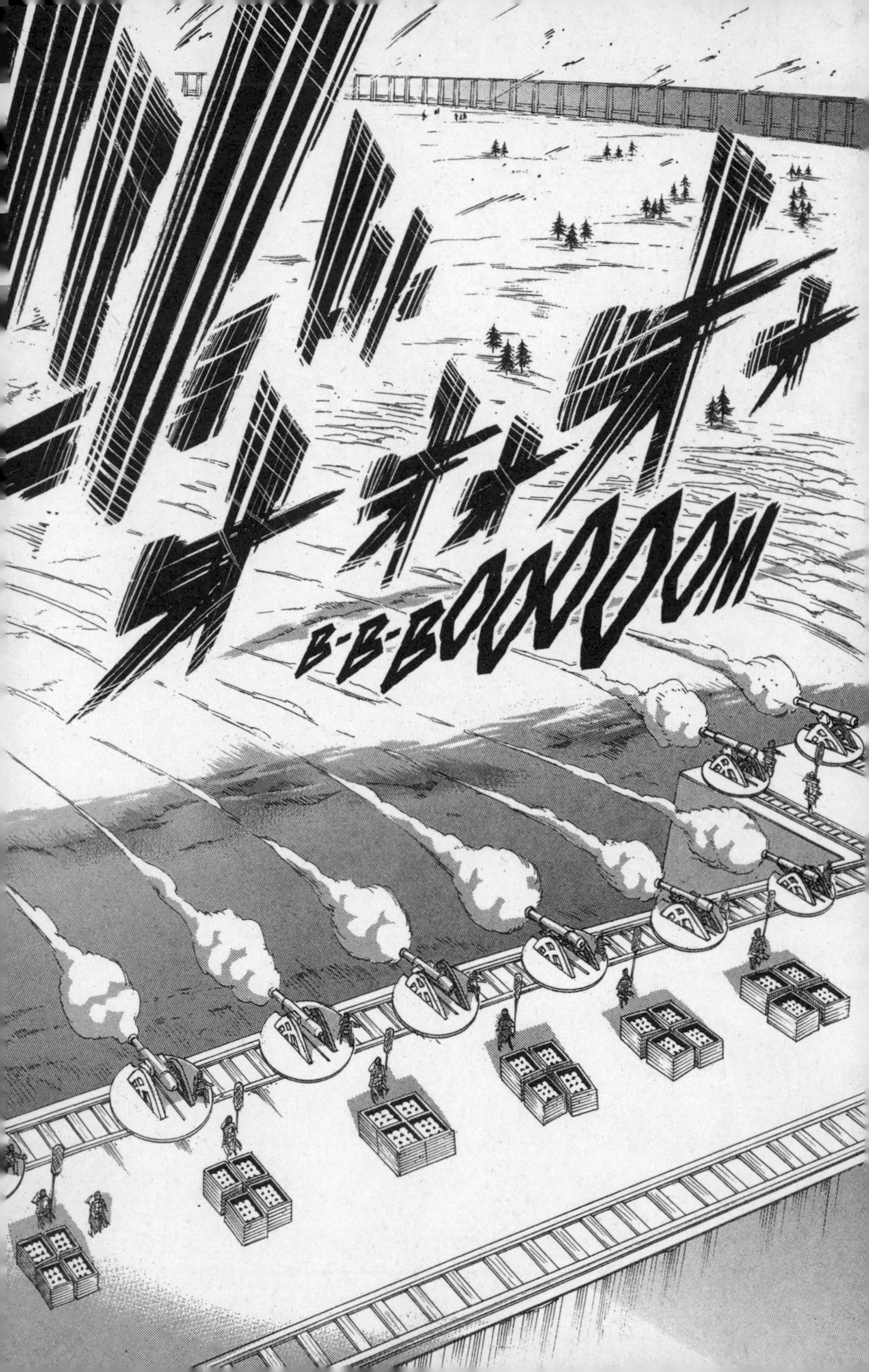
B-B-BOOOOOM

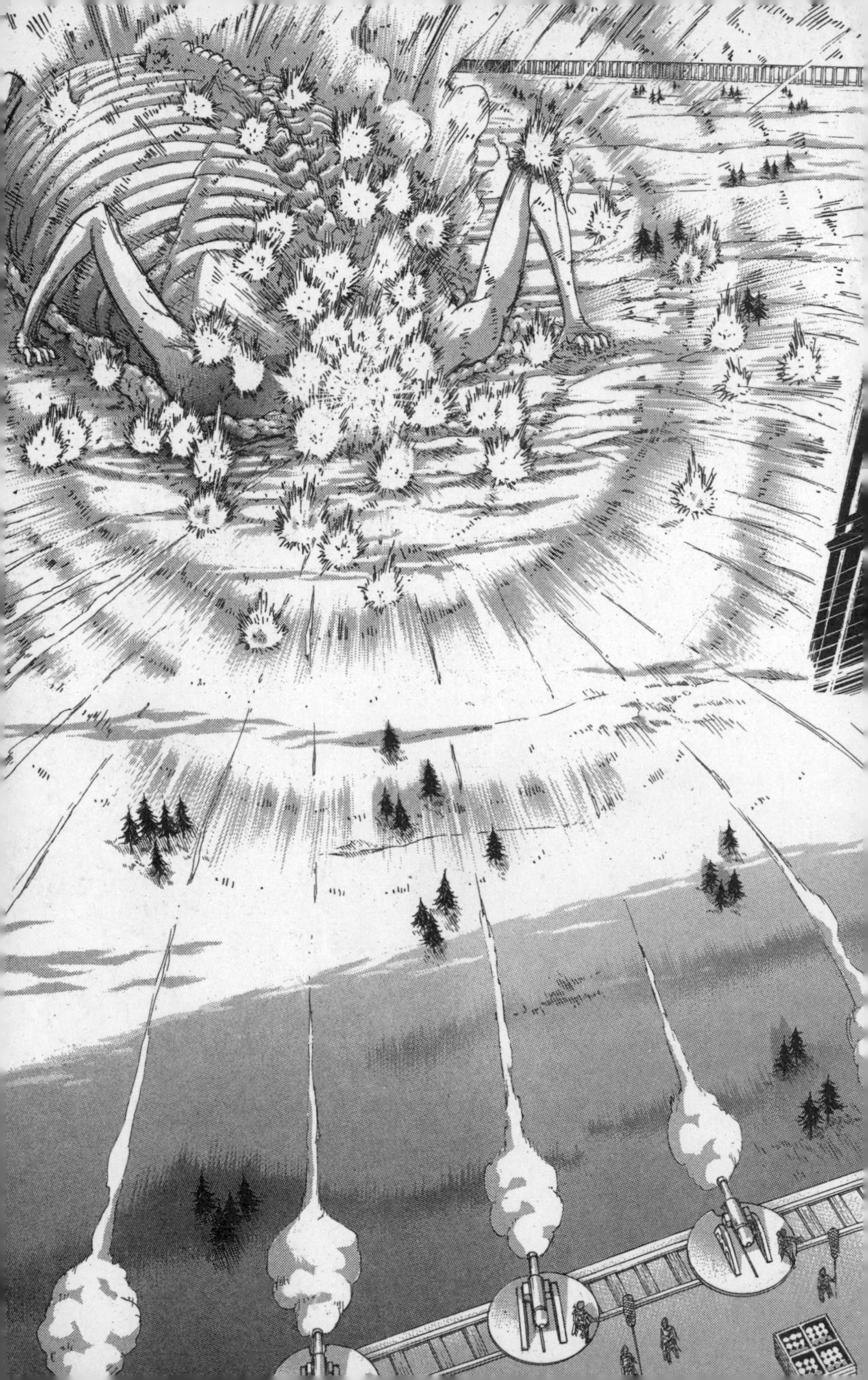

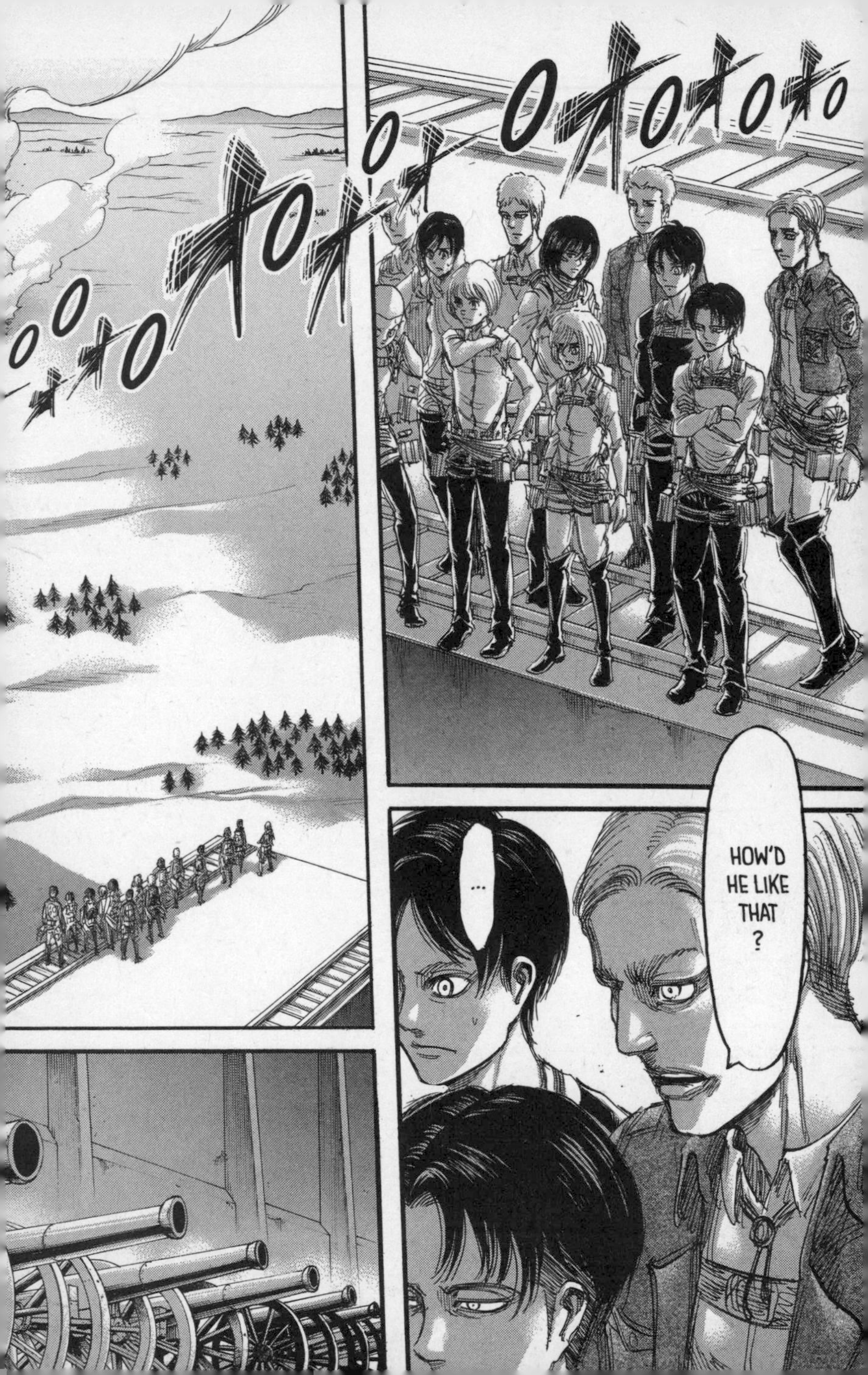
HOW'D HE LIKE THAT ?
...

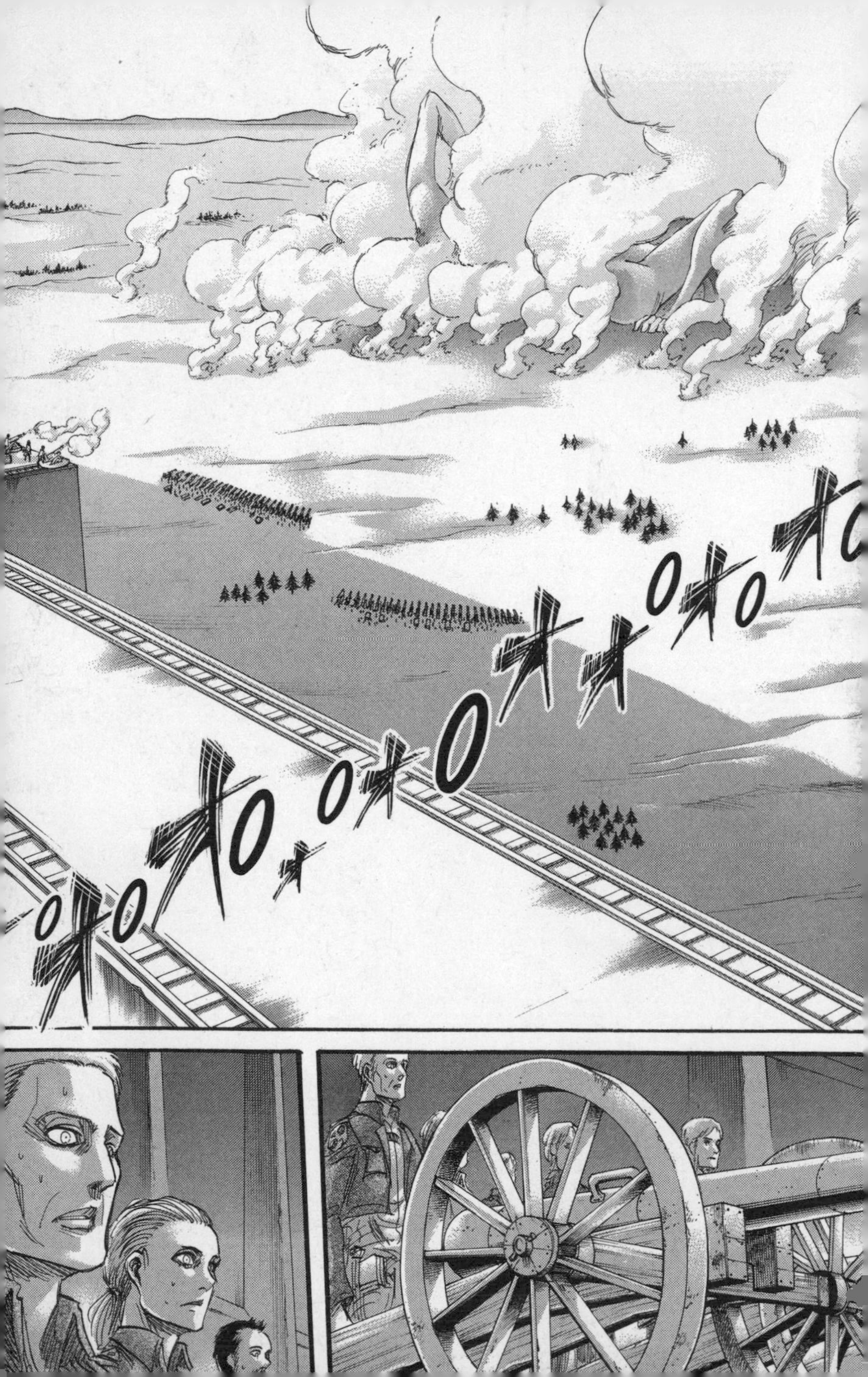

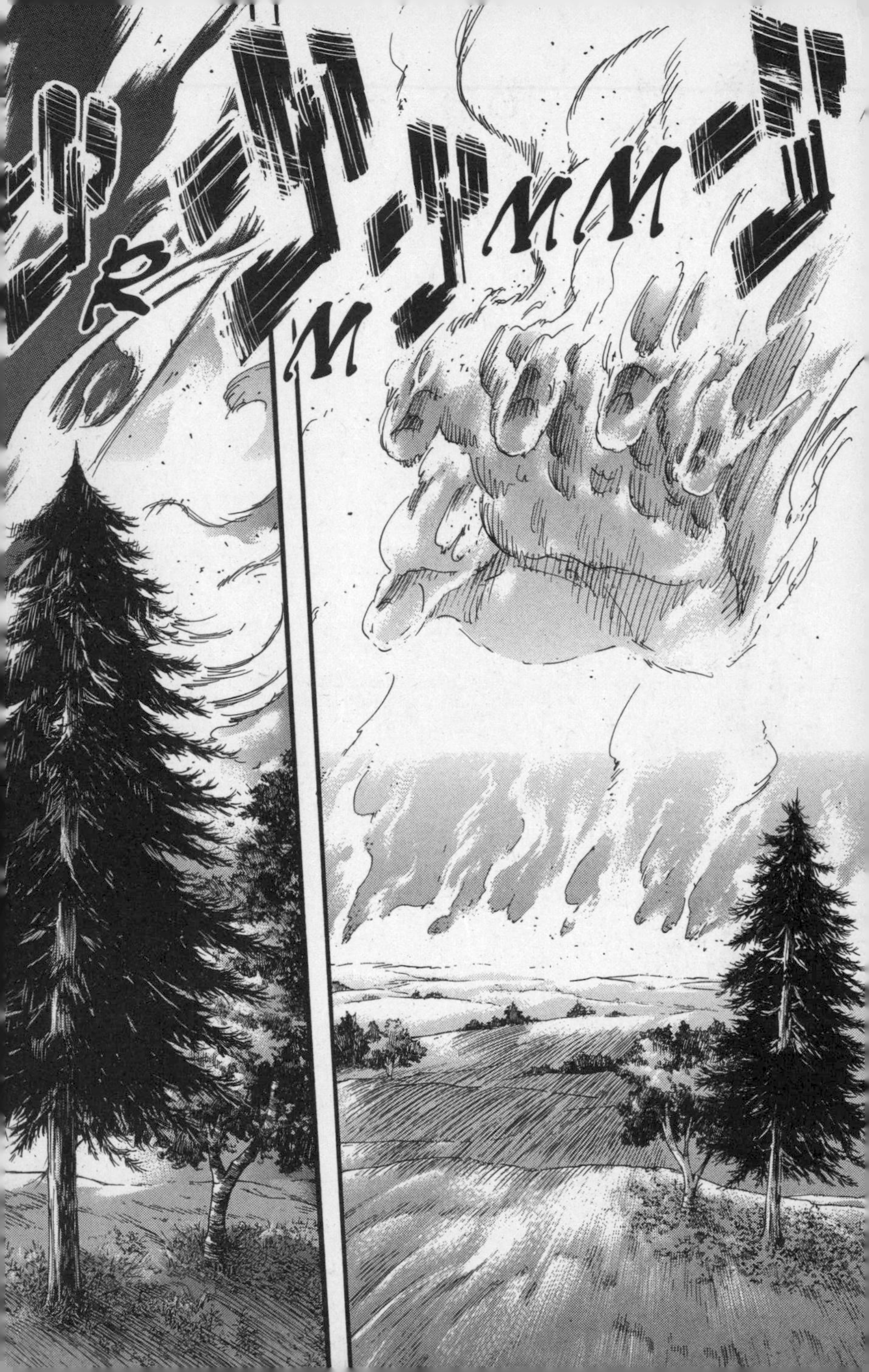

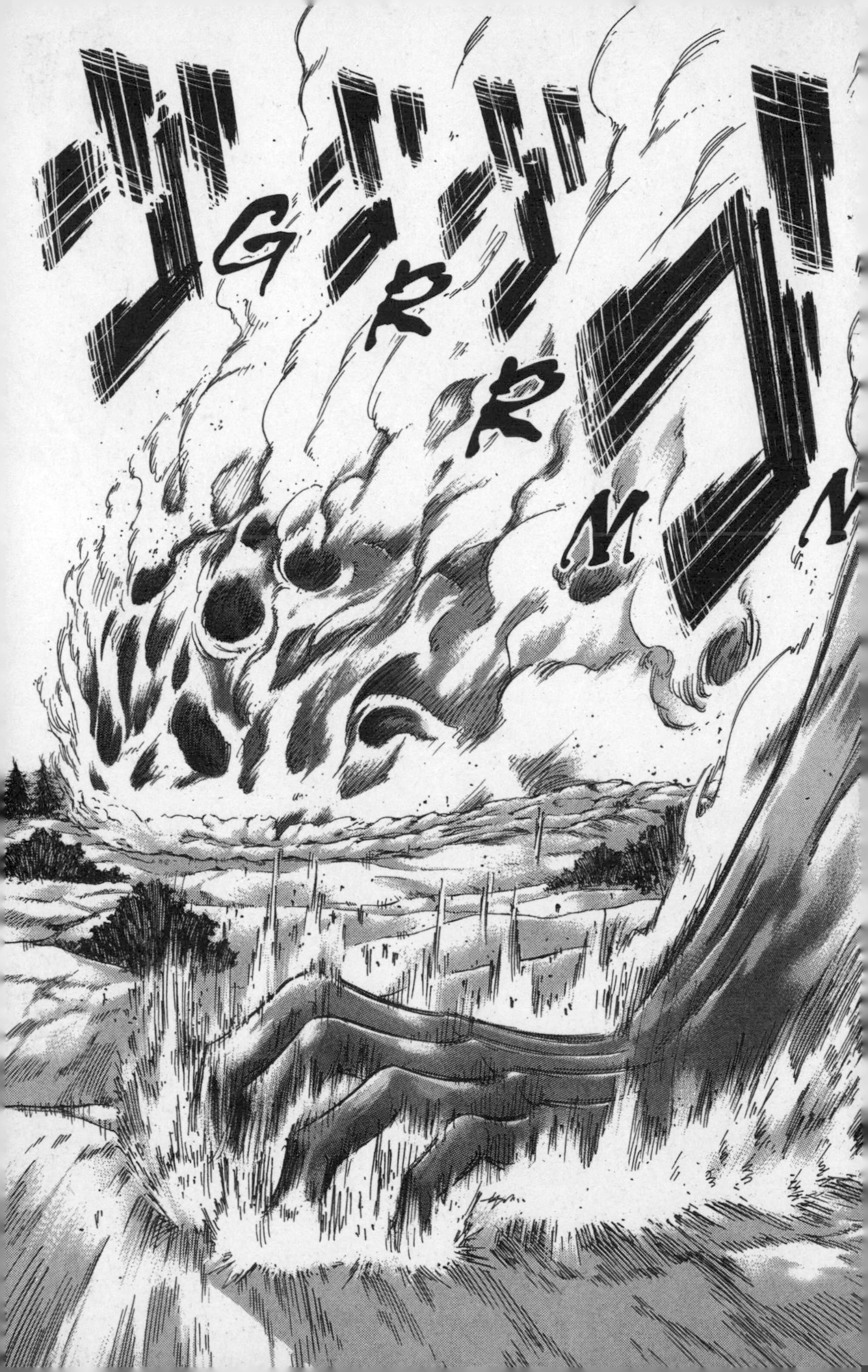
GRRMM

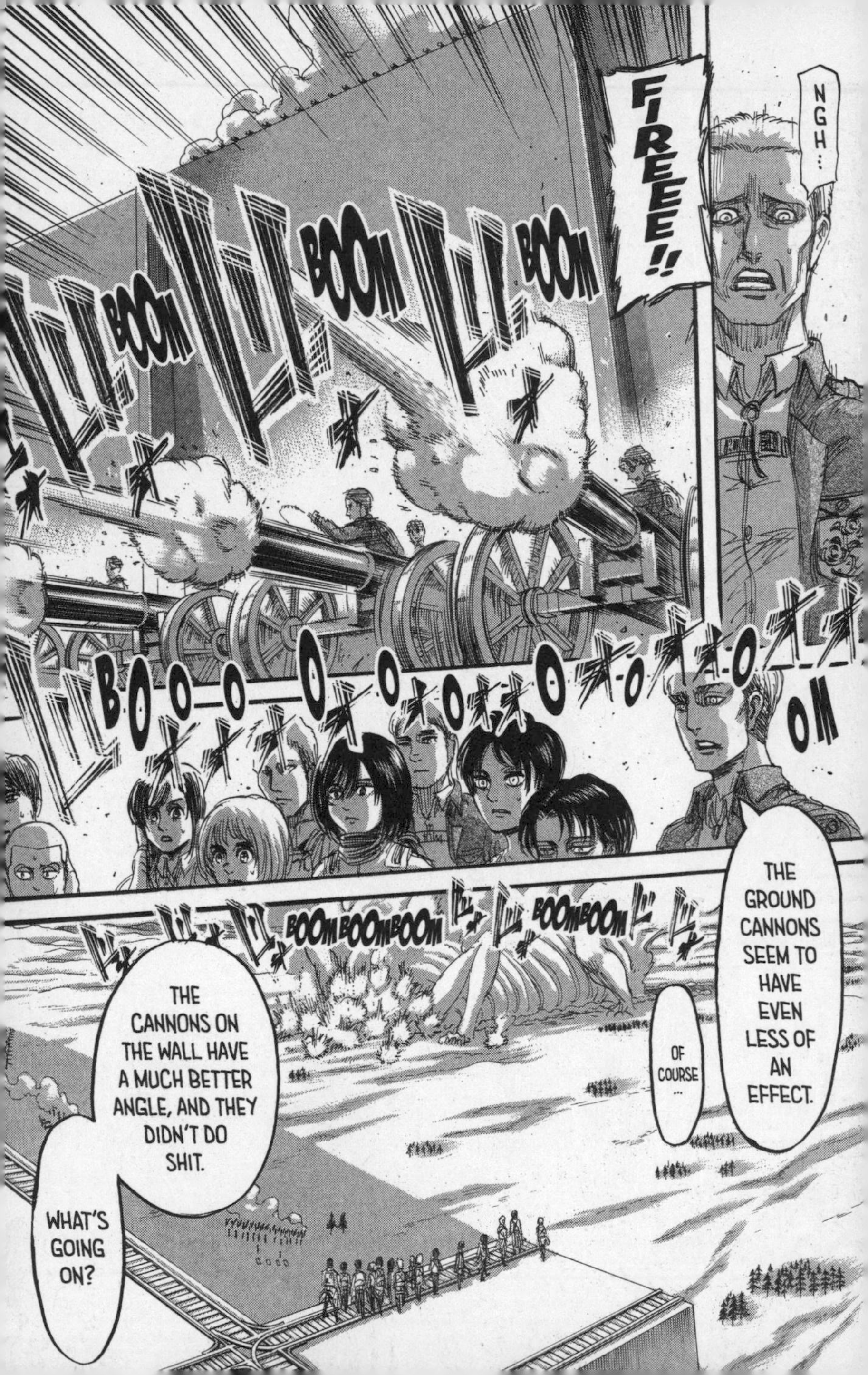
NGH...
FIREEEE!!
BOOM
BOOM
BOOM
BOOOOOOOOOOOM
THE GROUND CANNONS SEEM TO HAVE EVEN LESS OF AN EFFECT.
OF COURSE...
BOOMBOOM
BOOMBOOMBOOM
THE CANNONS ON THE WALL HAVE A MUCH BETTER ANGLE, AND THEY DIDN'T DO SHIT.
WHAT'S GOING ON?

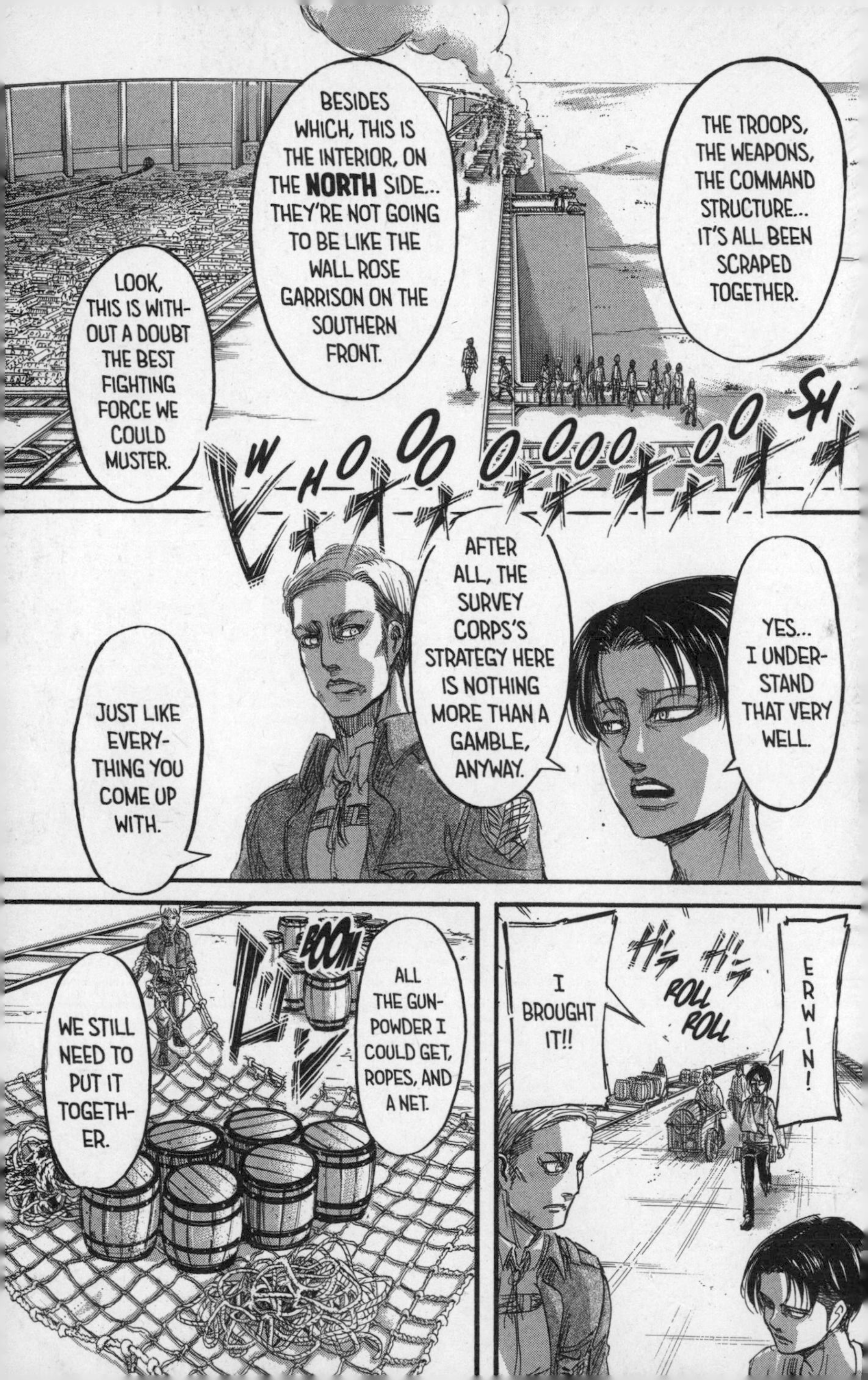
THE TROOPS, THE WEAPONS, THE COMMAND STRUCTURE... IT'S ALL BEEN SCRAPED TOGETHER.
BESIDES WHICH, THIS IS THE INTERIOR, ON THE **NORTH** SIDE... THEY'RE NOT GOING TO BE LIKE THE WALL ROSE GARRISON ON THE SOUTHERN FRONT.
LOOK, THIS IS WITHOUT A DOUBT THE BEST FIGHTING FORCE WE COULD MUSTER.
WHOOOOOOOOOSH
YES... I UNDERSTAND THAT VERY WELL.
AFTER ALL, THE SURVEY CORPS'S STRATEGY HERE IS NOTHING MORE THAN A GAMBLE, ANYWAY.
JUST LIKE EVERYTHING YOU COME UP WITH.
ERWIN!
ROLL ROLL
I BROUGHT IT!!
ALL THE GUNPOWDER I COULD GET, ROPES, AND A NET.
BOOM
WE STILL NEED TO PUT IT TOGETHER.

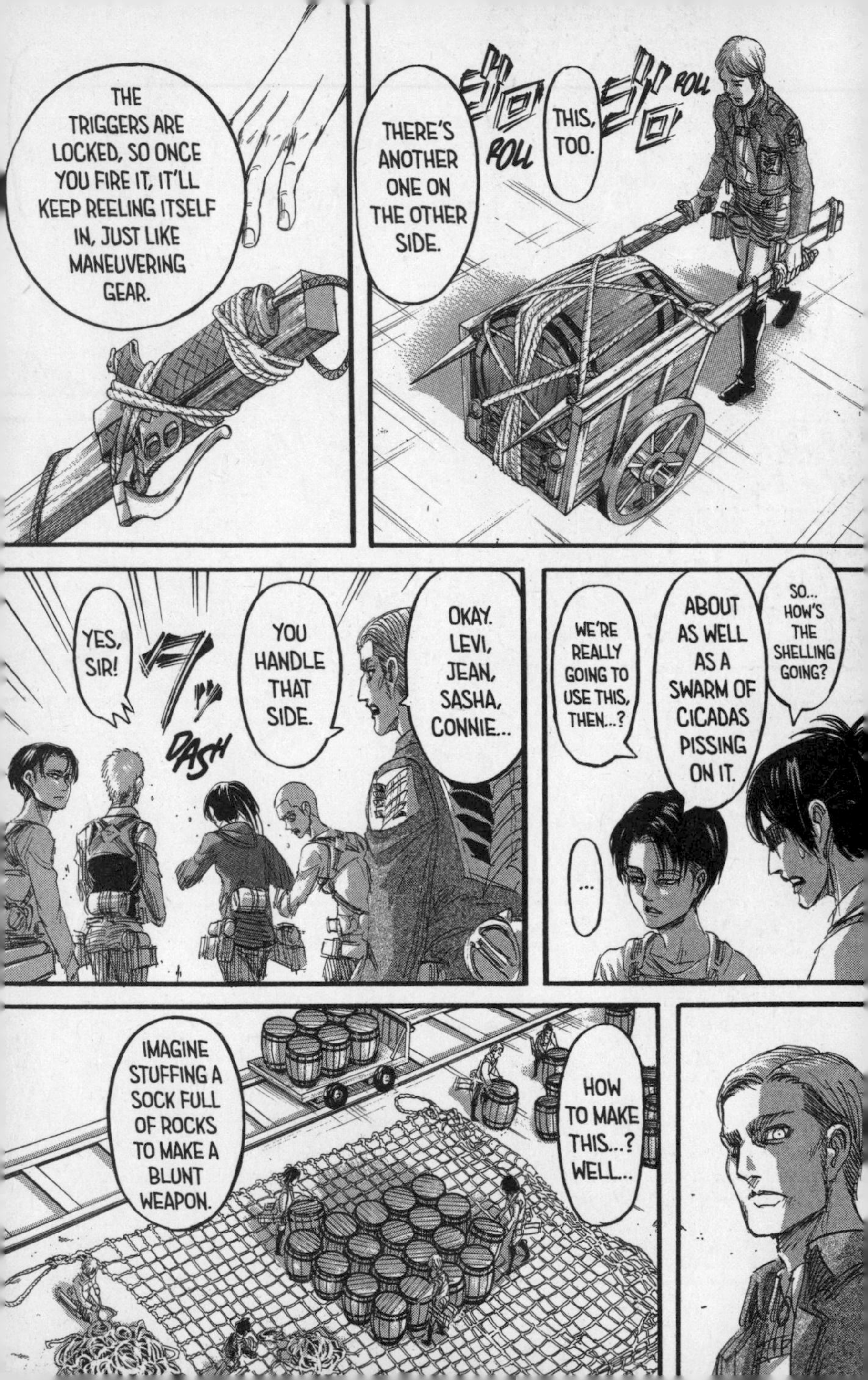
ROLL
THIS, TOO.
ROLL
THERE'S ANOTHER ONE ON THE OTHER SIDE.
THE TRIGGERS ARE LOCKED, SO ONCE YOU FIRE IT, IT'LL KEEP REELING ITSELF IN, JUST LIKE MANEUVERING GEAR.
SO... HOW'S THE SHELLING GOING?
ABOUT AS WELL AS A SWARM OF CICADAS PISSING ON IT.
WE'RE REALLY GOING TO USE THIS, THEN...?
...
OKAY. LEVI, JEAN, SASHA, CONNIE...
YOU HANDLE THAT SIDE.
YES, SIR!
DASH
HOW TO MAKE THIS...? WELL...
IMAGINE STUFFING A SOCK FULL OF ROCKS TO MAKE A BLUNT WEAPON.

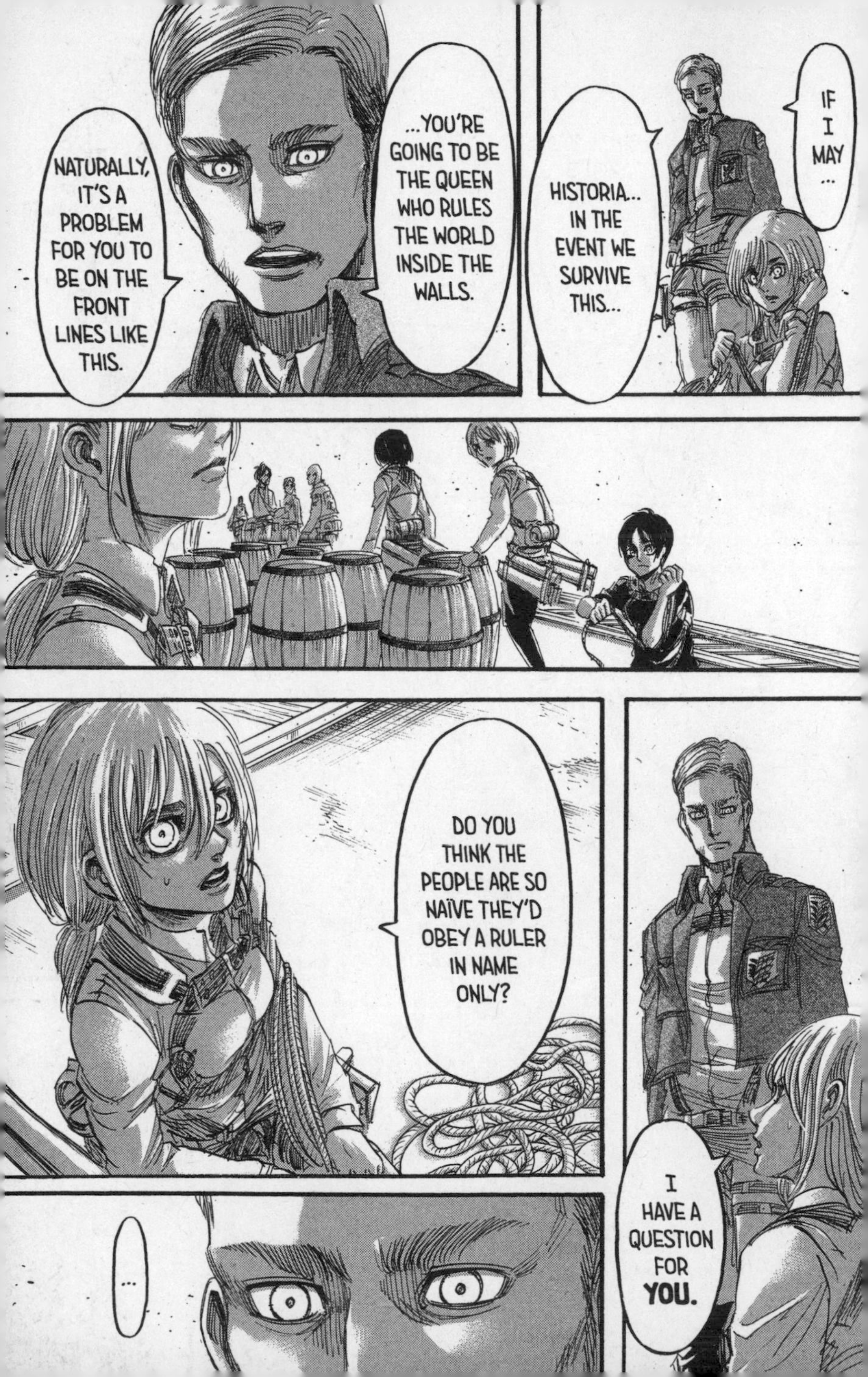
IF I MAY...
HISTORIA... IN THE EVENT WE SURVIVE THIS...
...YOU'RE GOING TO BE THE QUEEN WHO RULES THE WORLD INSIDE THE WALLS.
NATURALLY, IT'S A PROBLEM FOR YOU TO BE ON THE FRONT LINES LIKE THIS.
I HAVE A QUESTION FOR **YOU.**
DO YOU THINK THE PEOPLE ARE SO NAÏVE THEY'D OBEY A RULER IN NAME ONLY?
...

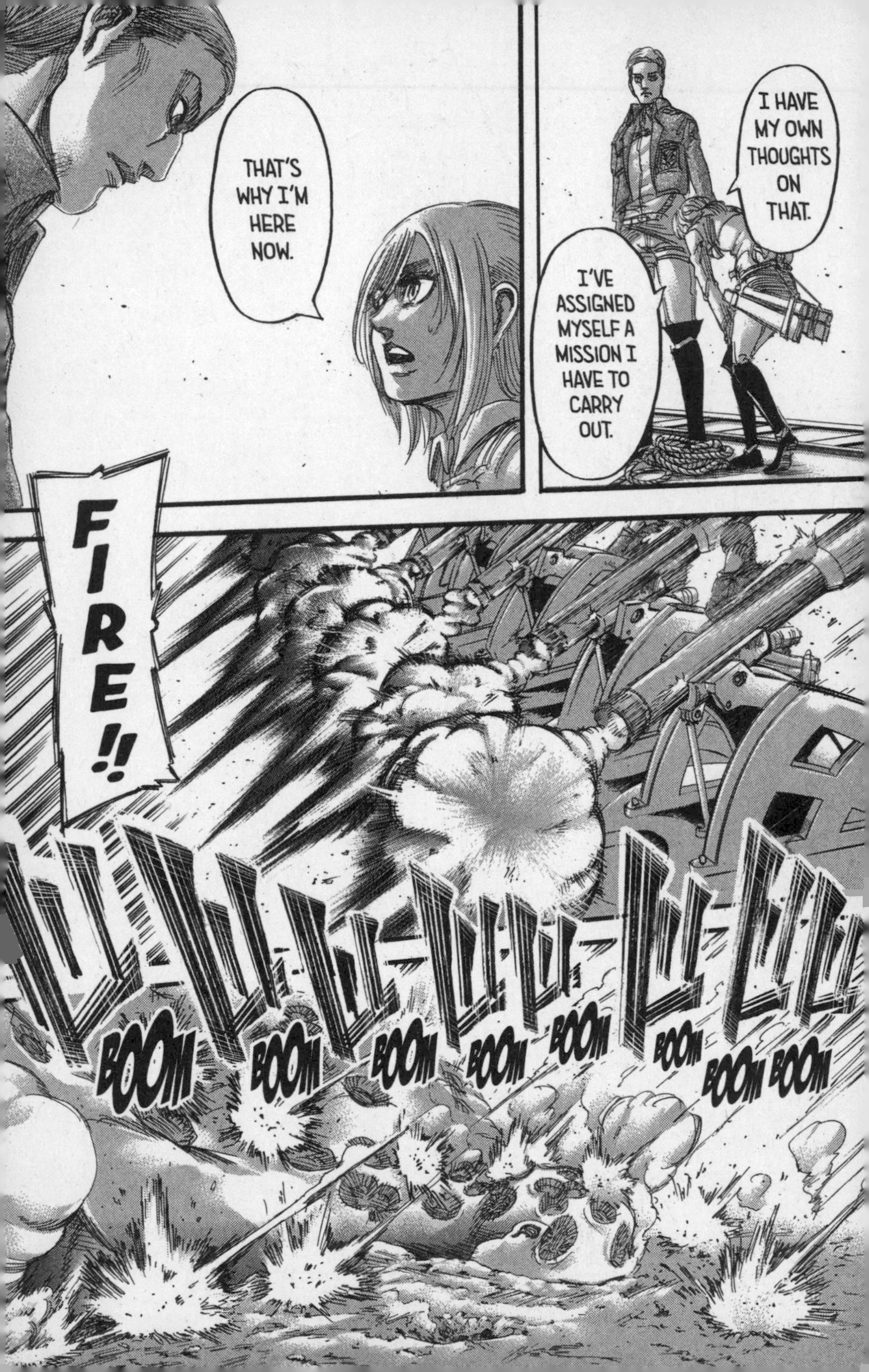

I HAVE MY OWN THOUGHTS ON THAT.
I'VE ASSIGNED MYSELF A MISSION I HAVE TO CARRY OUT.
THAT'S WHY I'M HERE NOW.
FIRE!!
BOOM BOOM BOOM BOOM BOOM BOOM BOOM BOOM

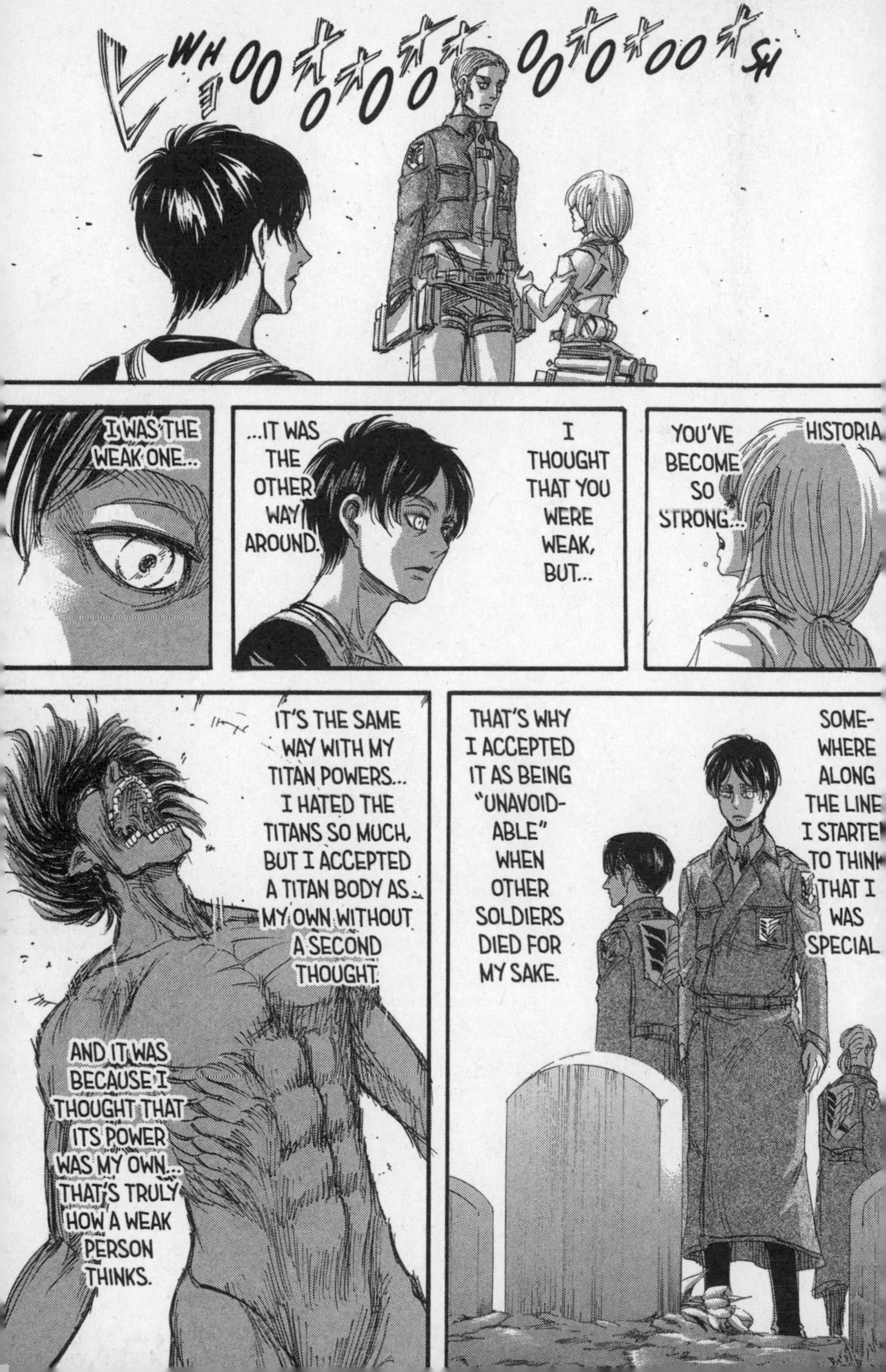
WHOOOOOOOOOOSH
HISTORIA
YOU'VE BECOME SO STRONG...
I THOUGHT THAT YOU WERE WEAK, BUT...
...IT WAS THE OTHER WAY AROUND.
I WAS THE WEAK ONE...
SOME-WHERE ALONG THE LINE I STARTE TO THINK THAT I WAS SPECIAL.
THAT'S WHY I ACCEPTED IT AS BEING "UNAVOID-ABLE" WHEN OTHER SOLDIERS DIED FOR MY SAKE.
IT'S THE SAME WAY WITH MY TITAN POWERS... I HATED THE TITANS SO MUCH, BUT I ACCEPTED A TITAN BODY AS MY OWN WITHOUT A SECOND THOUGHT.
AND IT WAS BECAUSE I THOUGHT THAT ITS POWER WAS MY OWN... THAT'S TRULY HOW A WEAK PERSON THINKS.

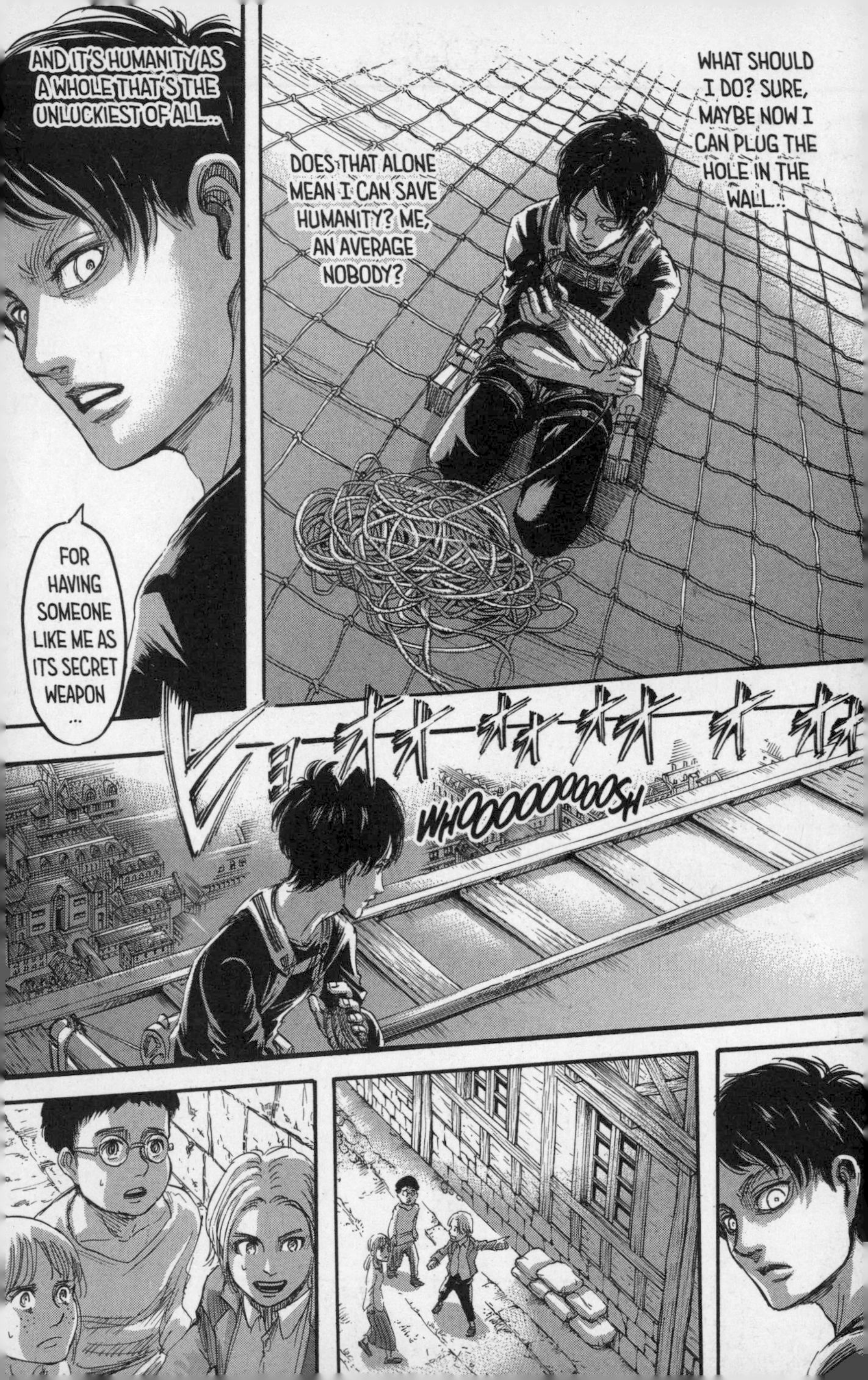
WHAT SHOULD I DO? SURE, MAYBE NOW I CAN PLUG THE HOLE IN THE WALL...
DOES THAT ALONE MEAN I CAN SAVE HUMANITY? ME, AN AVERAGE NOBODY?
AND IT'S HUMANITY AS A WHOLE THAT'S THE UNLUCKIEST OF ALL...
FOR HAVING SOMEONE LIKE ME AS ITS SECRET WEAPON ...
WHOOOOOOOOOSH

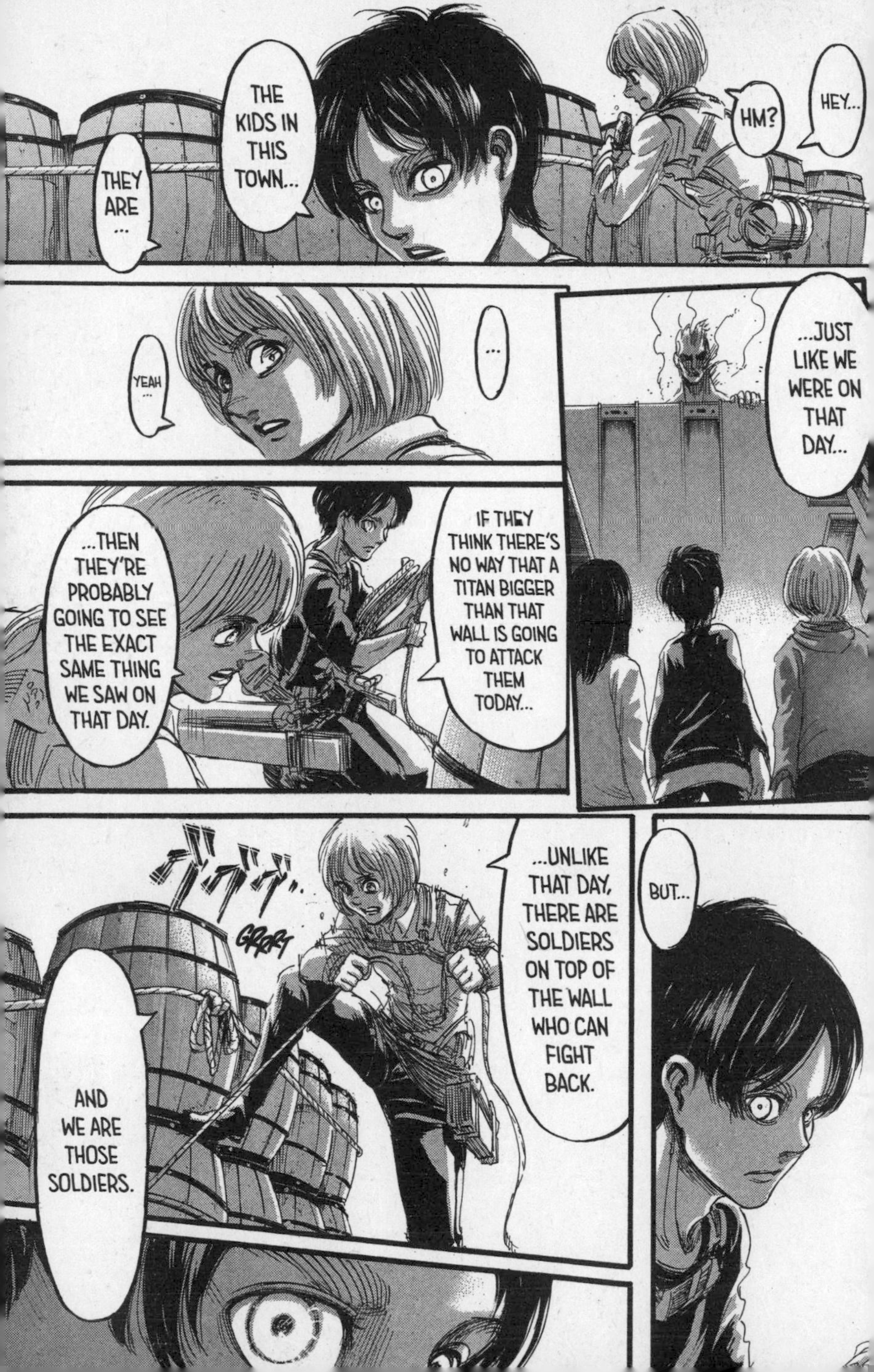
HEY...
HM?
THE KIDS IN THIS TOWN...
THEY ARE ...
...JUST LIKE WE WERE ON THAT DAY...
...
YEAH ...
IF THEY THINK THERE'S NO WAY THAT A TITAN BIGGER THAN THAT WALL IS GOING TO ATTACK THEM TODAY...
...THEN THEY'RE PROBABLY GOING TO SEE THE EXACT SAME THING WE SAW ON THAT DAY.
BUT...
...UNLIKE THAT DAY, THERE ARE SOLDIERS ON TOP OF THE WALL WHO CAN FIGHT BACK.
AND WE ARE THOSE SOLDIERS.

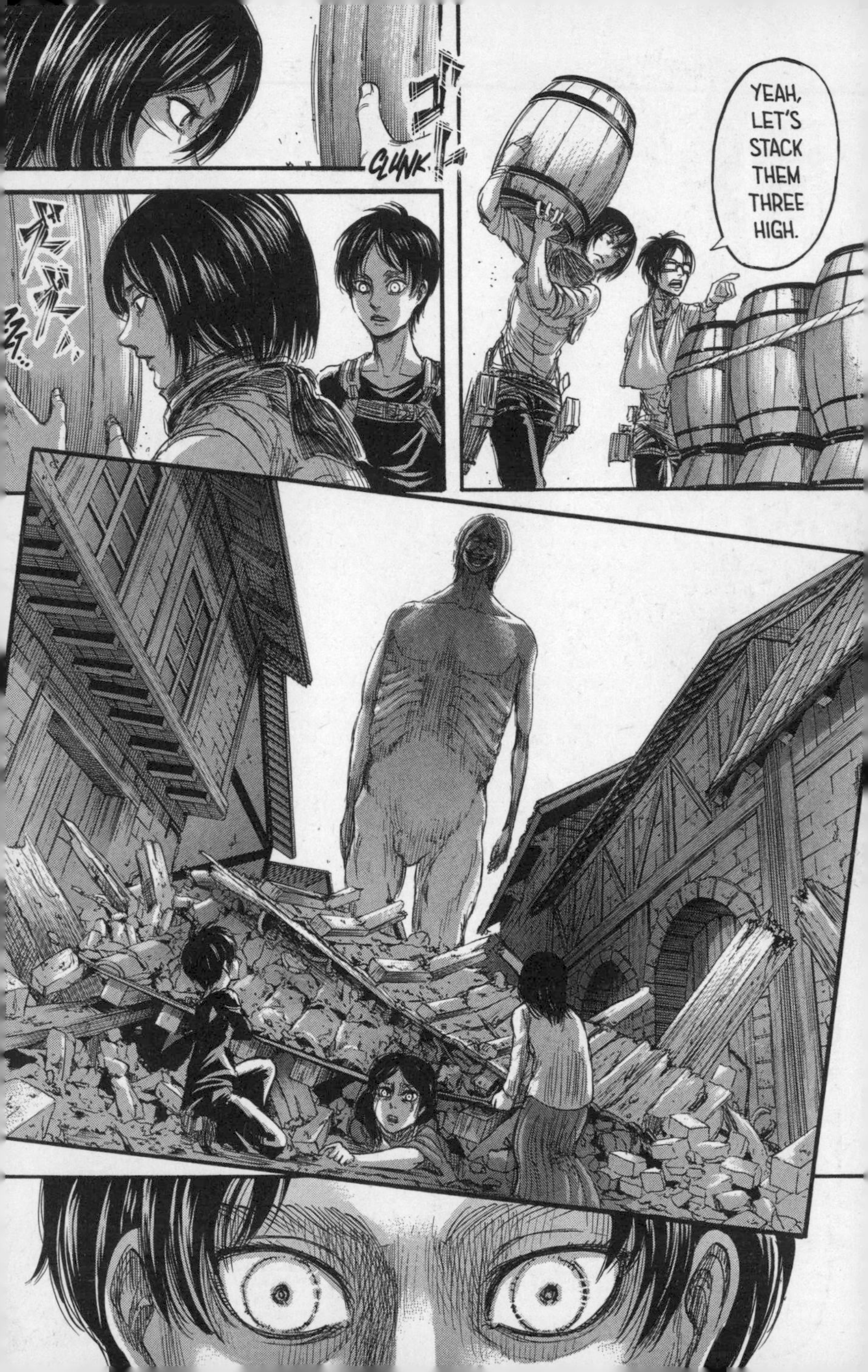
YEAH, LET'S STACK THEM THREE HIGH.
CLUNK

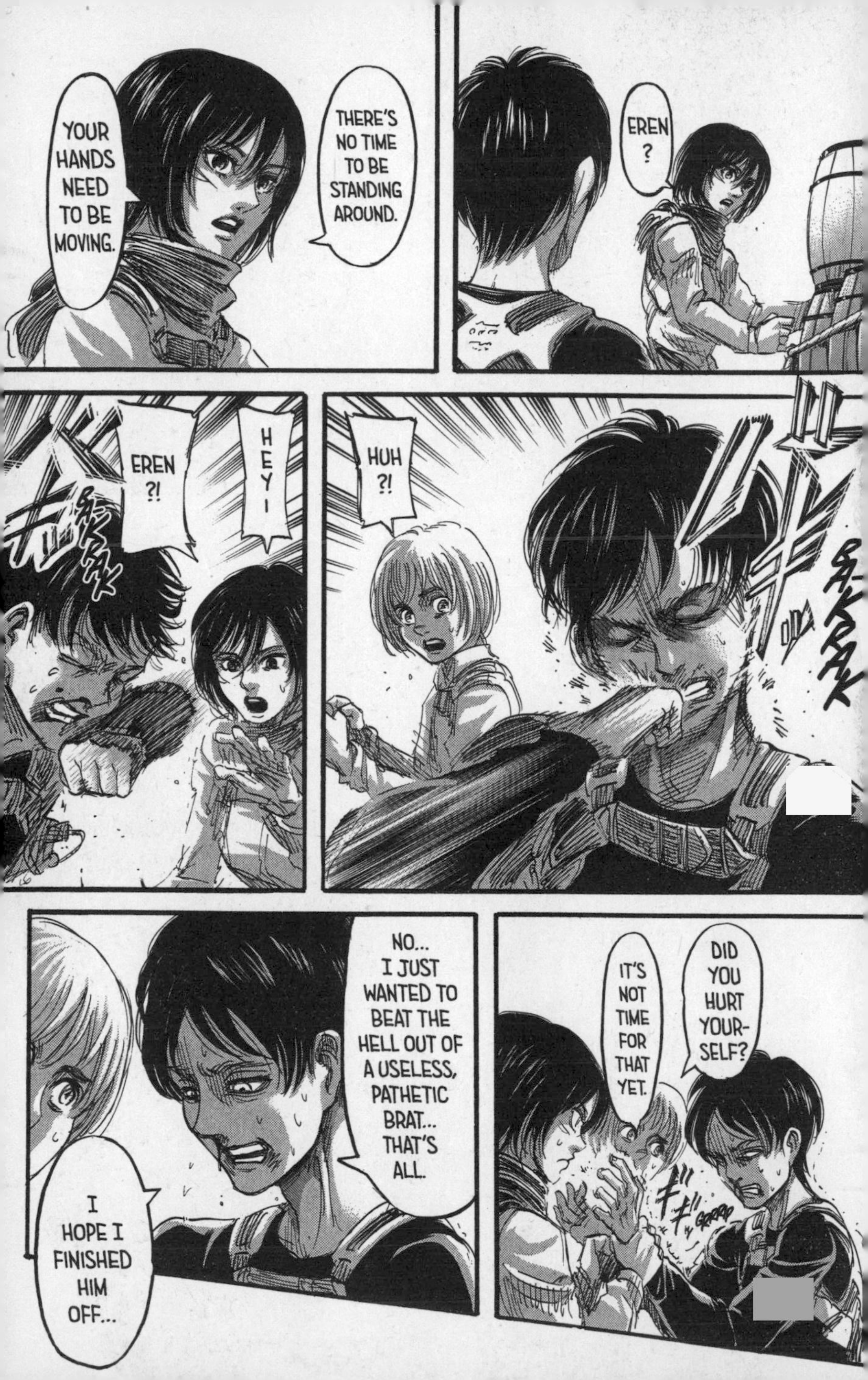
EREN ?
THERE'S NO TIME TO BE STANDING AROUND.
YOUR HANDS NEED TO BE MOVING.
SAKRAK
HUH ?!
HEY!
EREN ?!
SAKRAK
DID YOU HURT YOURSELF?
IT'S NOT TIME FOR THAT YET.
NO... I JUST WANTED TO BEAT THE HELL OUT OF A USELESS, PATHETIC BRAT... THAT'S ALL.
I HOPE I FINISHED HIM OFF...

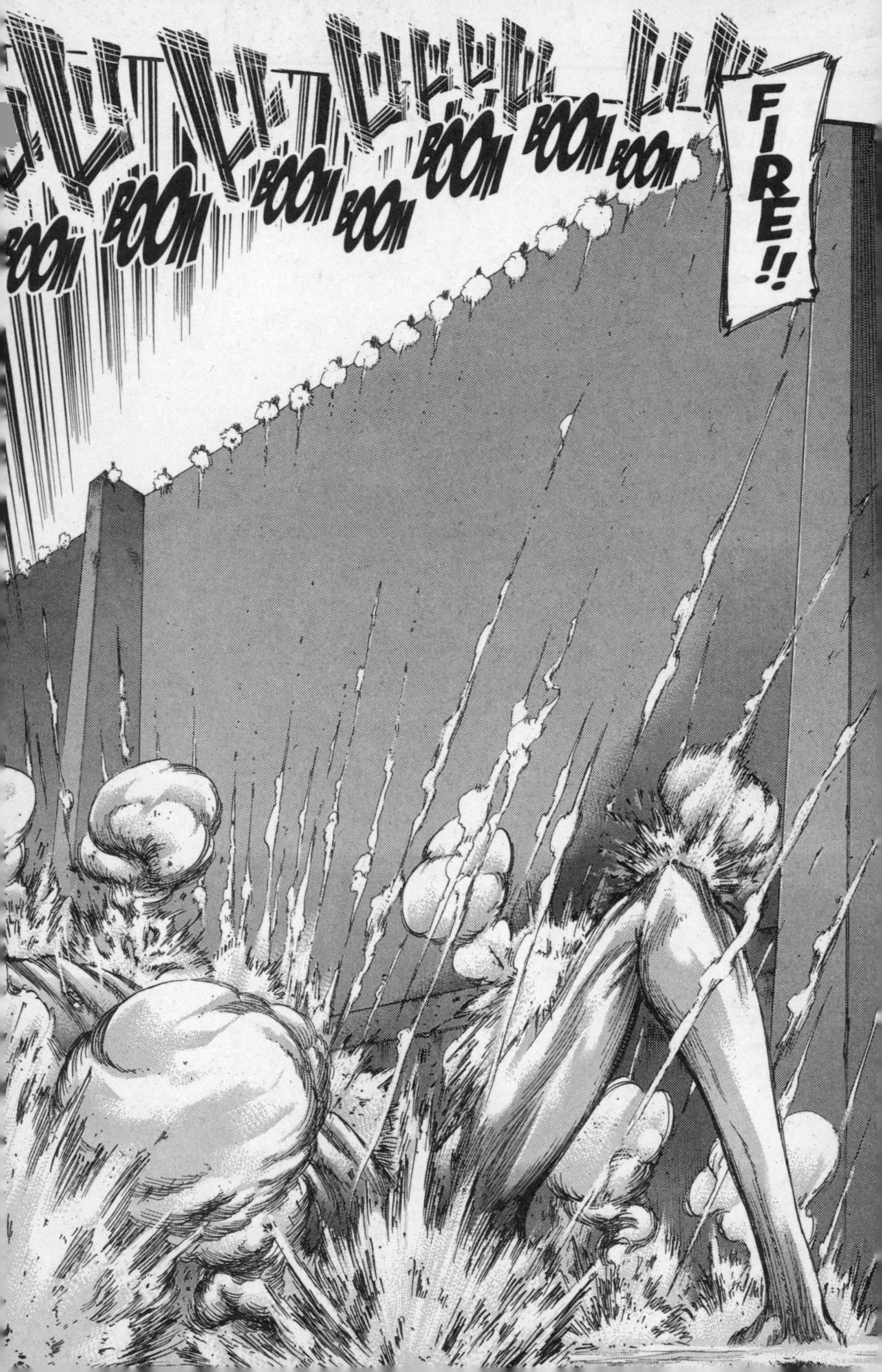
FIRE!!
BOOM
BOOM
BOOM
BOOM
BOOM
BOOM

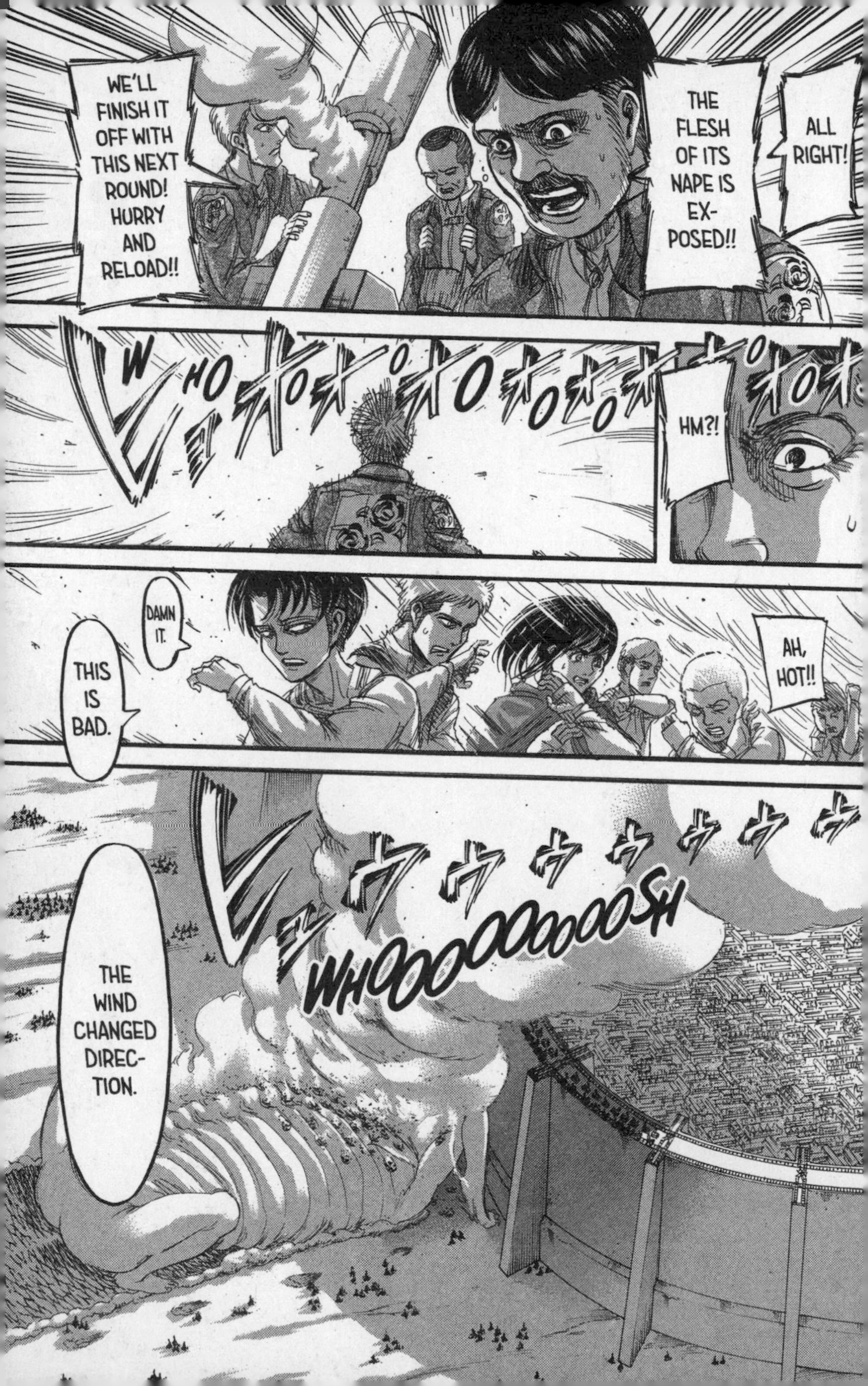
ALL RIGHT!
THE FLESH OF ITS NAPE IS EX-POSED!!
WE'LL FINISH IT OFF WITH THIS NEXT ROUND! HURRY AND RELOAD!!
HM?!
AH, HOT!!
DAMN IT.
THIS IS BAD.
WHOOOOOOOOOOSH
THE WIND CHANGED DIREC-TION.

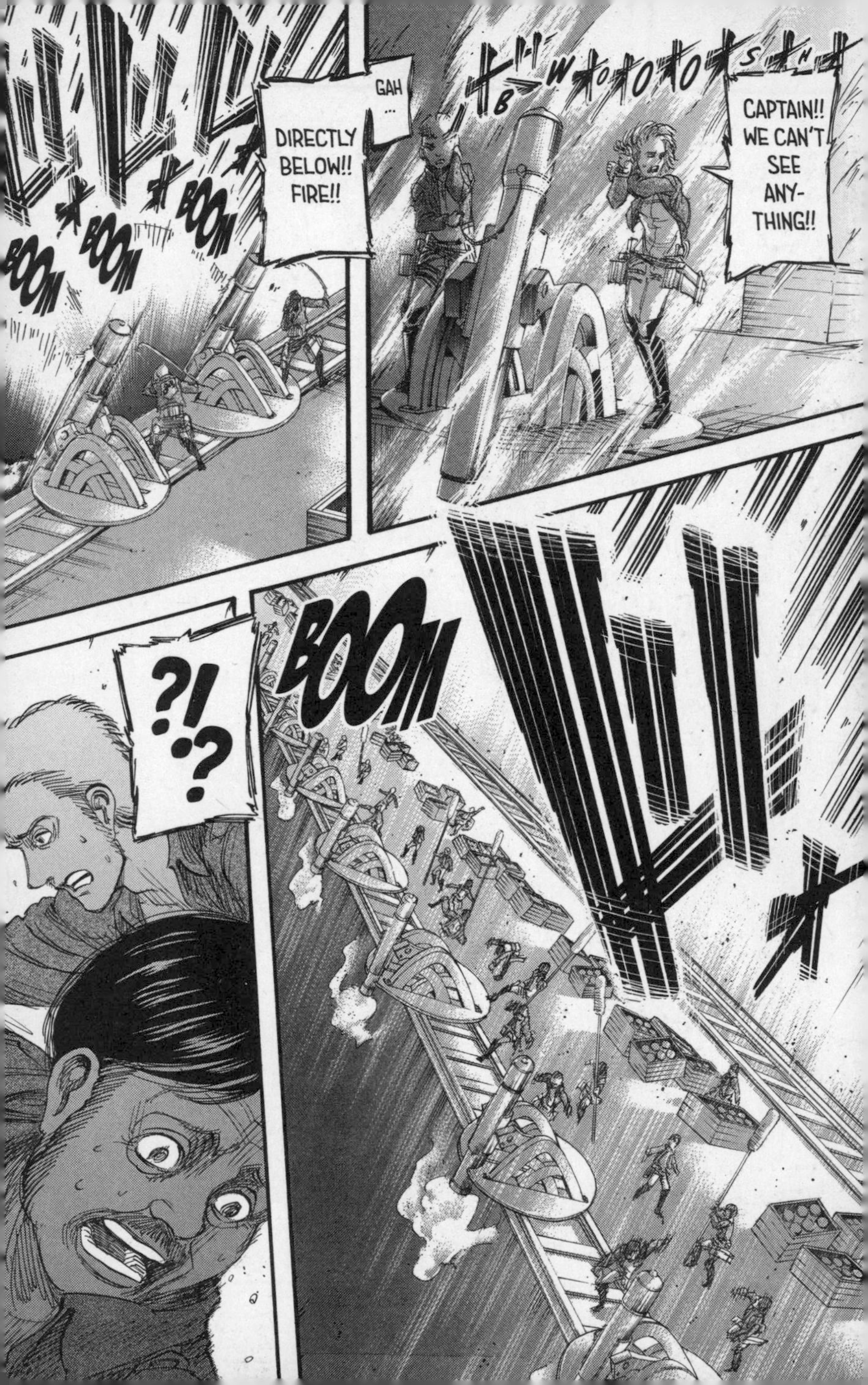
BWOOOOSH
CAPTAIN!! WE CAN'T SEE ANYTHING!!
GAH ...
DIRECTLY BELOW!! FIRE!!
BOOM
BOOM
BOOM
BOOM
?!?

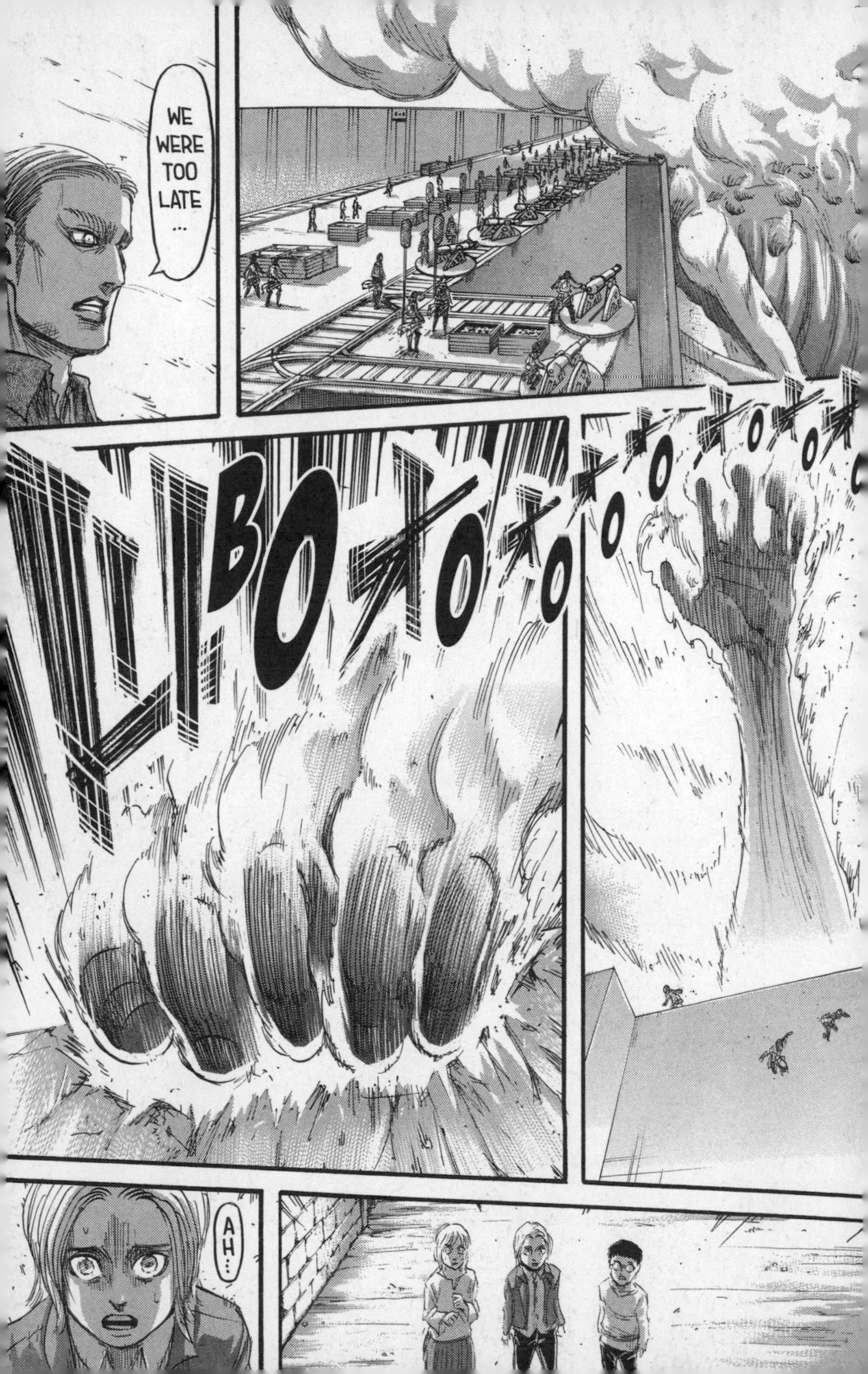
WE WERE TOO LATE ...
BOOOOOOOOOOO
AH...

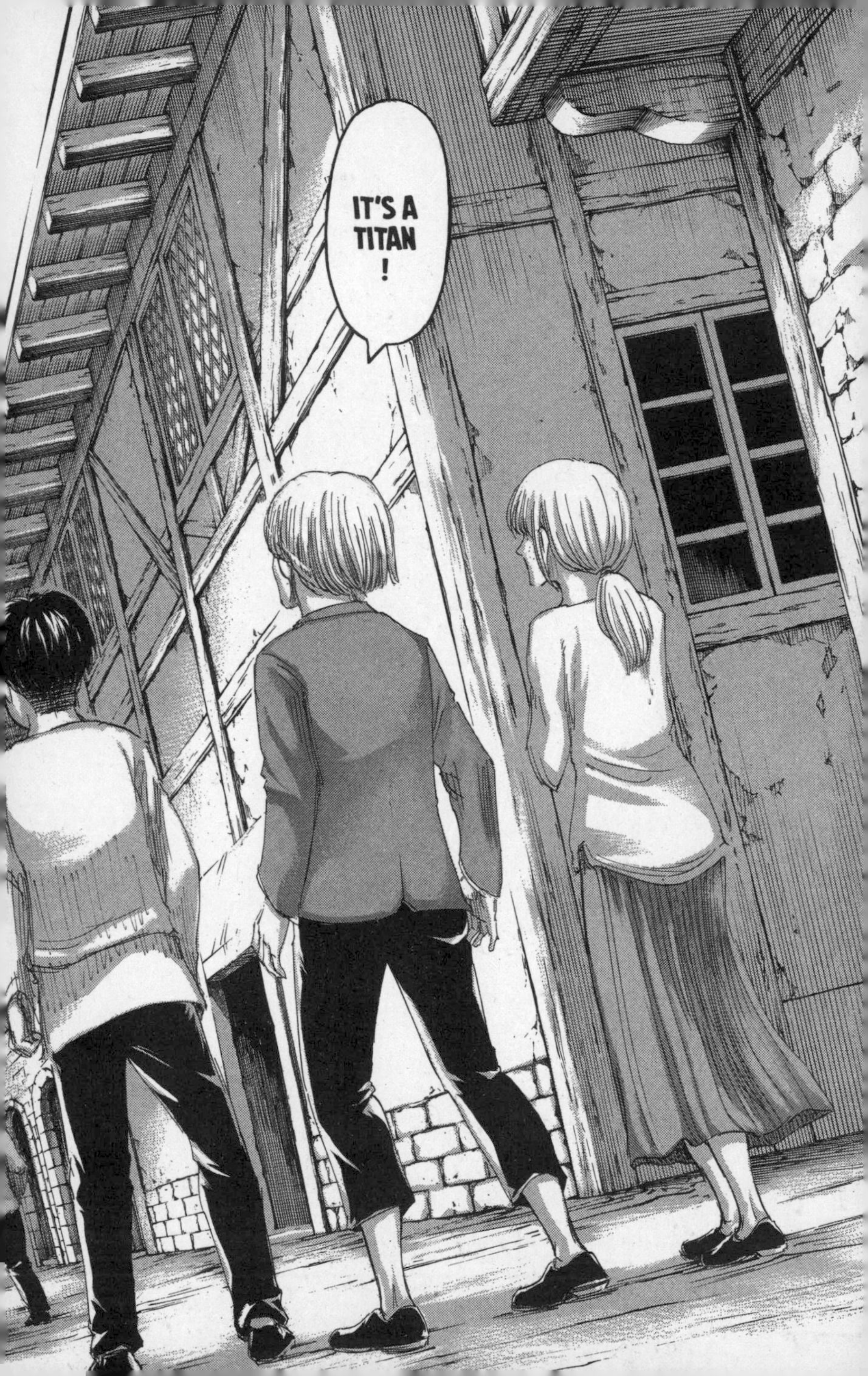
IT'S A TITAN!

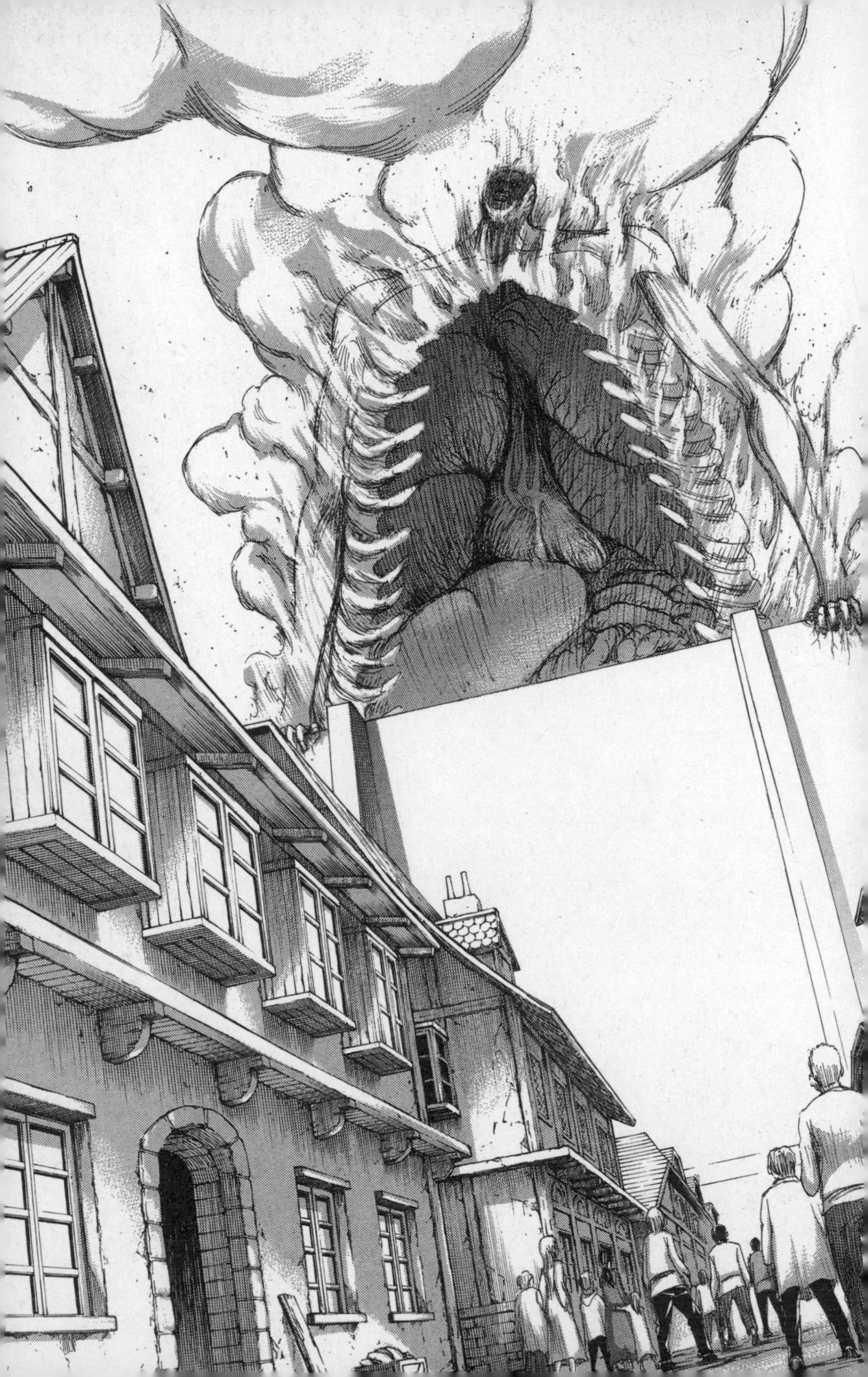

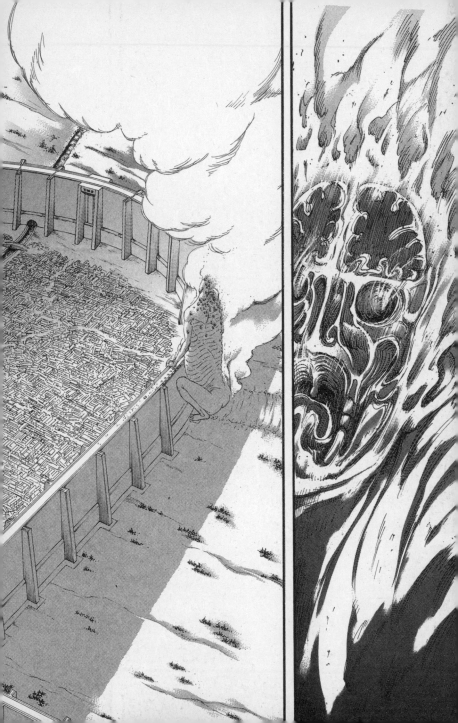

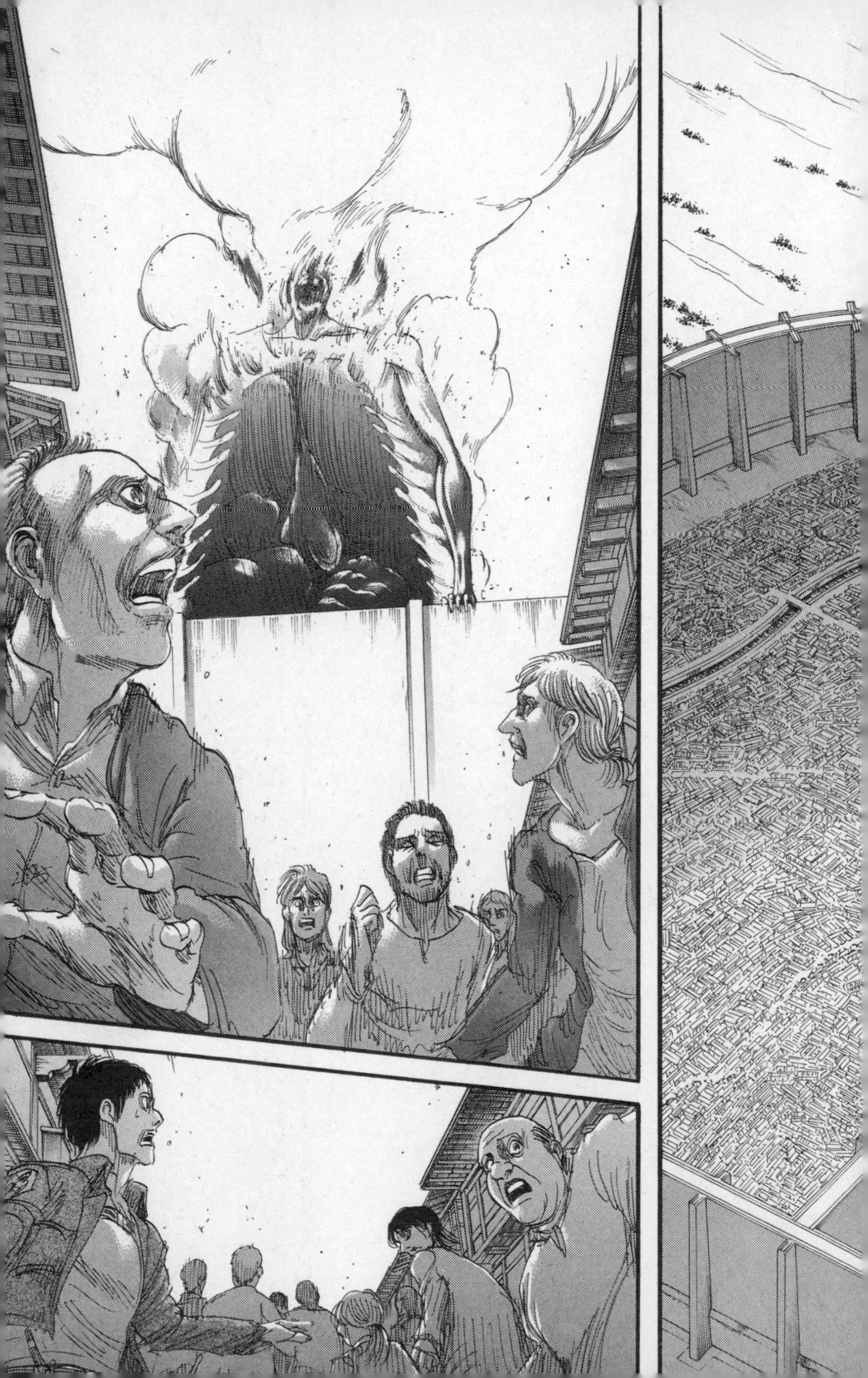

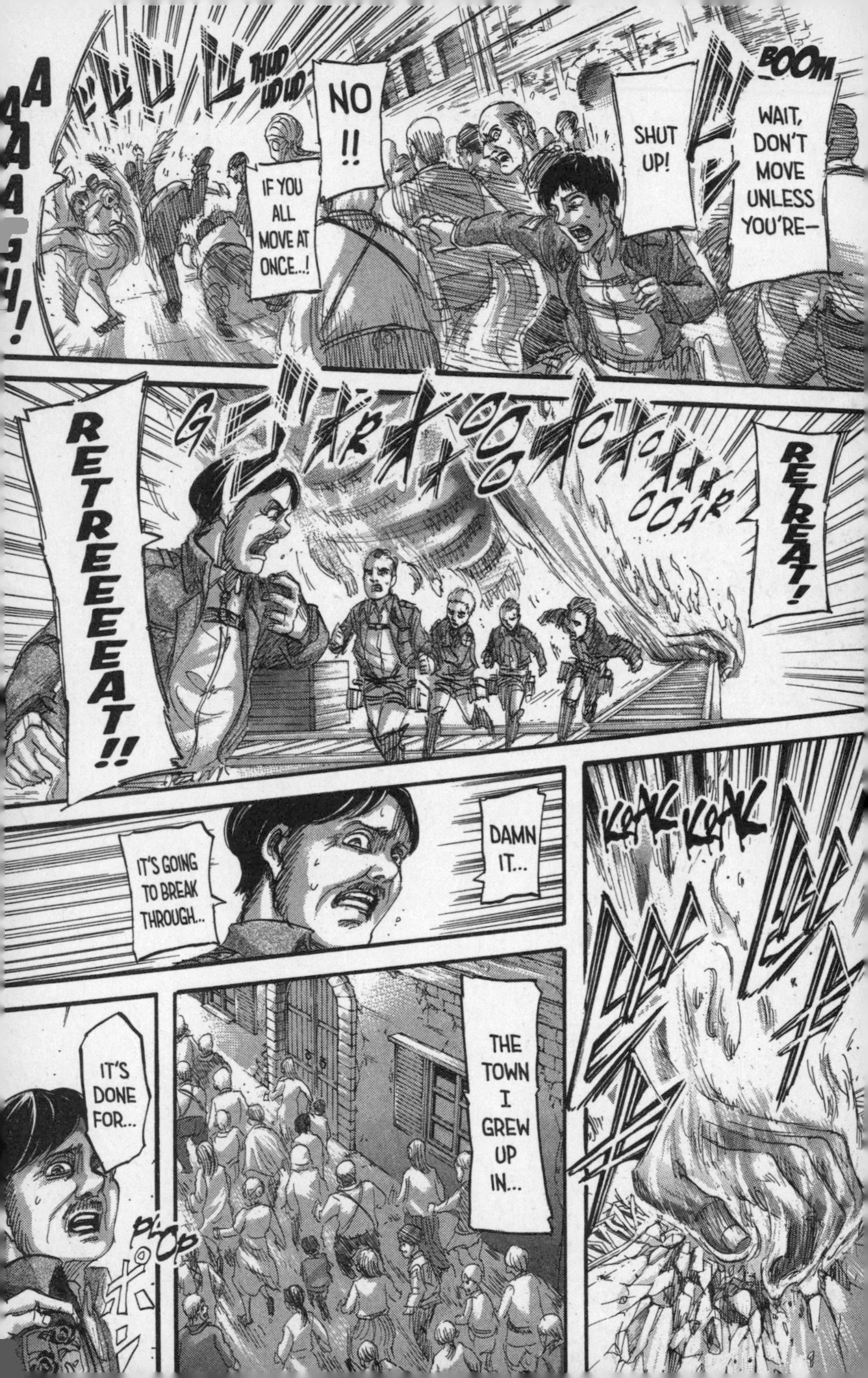
BOOM
WAIT, DON'T MOVE UNLESS YOU'RE—
SHUT UP!
NO!!
IF YOU ALL MOVE AT ONCE...!
THUD UD UD
AAAAGGH!
RETREAT!
RETREEEEEAT!!
KRAK KRAK
DAMN IT...
IT'S GOING TO BREAK THROUGH...
THE TOWN I GREW UP IN...
IT'S DONE FOR...
PLOP

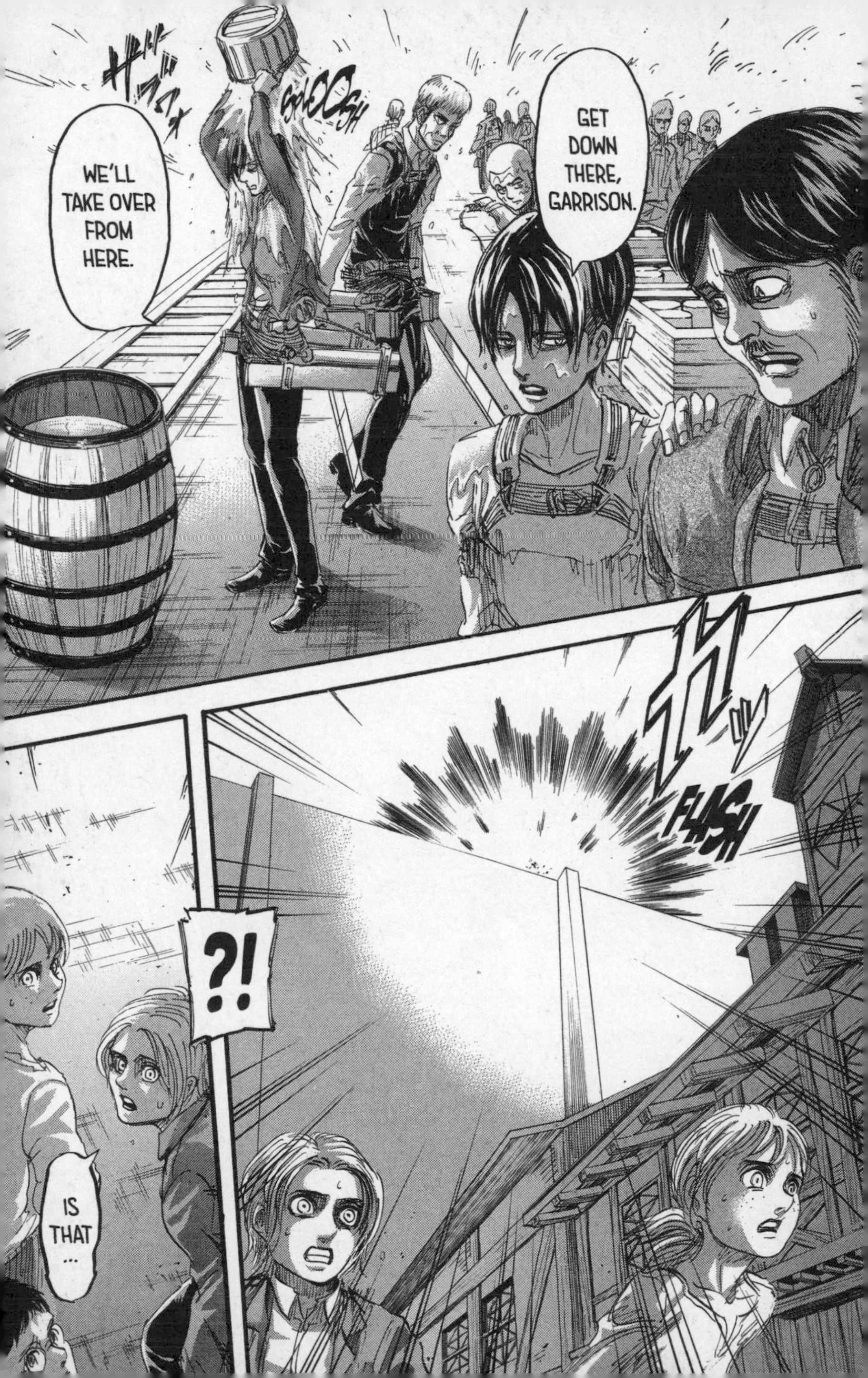
GET DOWN THERE, GARRISON.
SPLOOSH
WE'LL TAKE OVER FROM HERE.
FLASH
?!
IS THAT ...

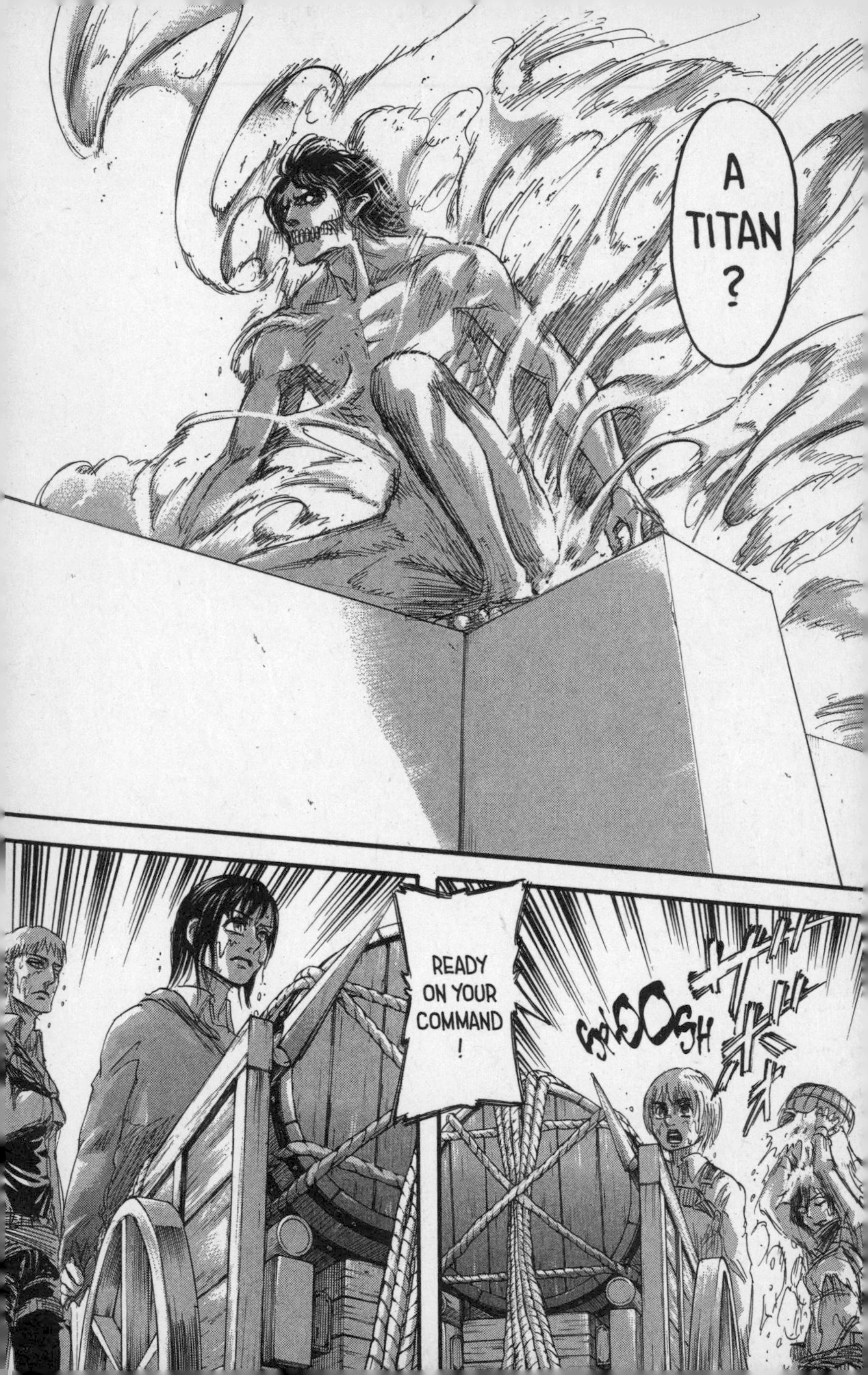
A TITAN ?
READY ON YOUR COMMAND !
GOOOSH

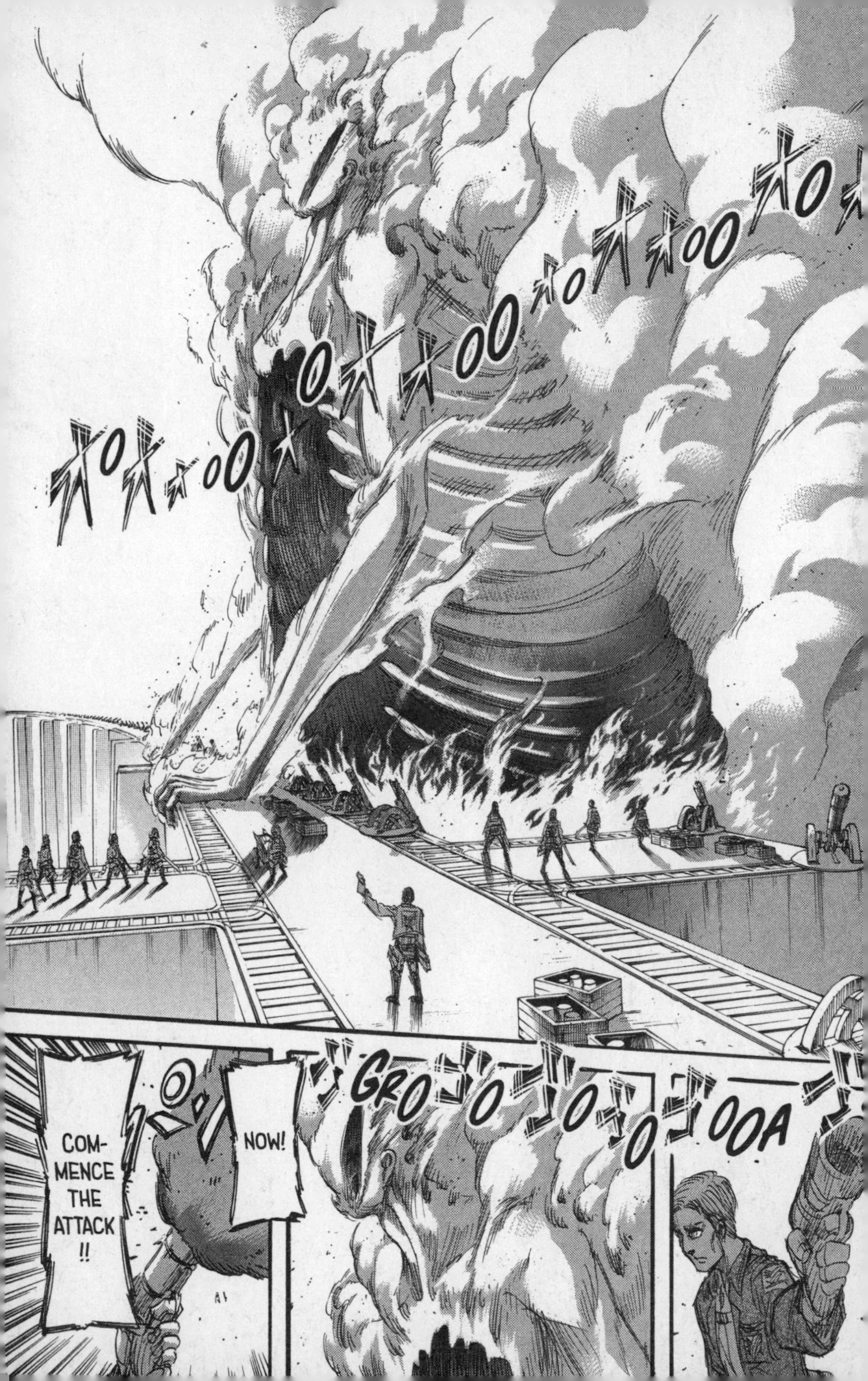

GROOOOOOA
NOW!
COM-
MENCE
THE
ATTACK
!!

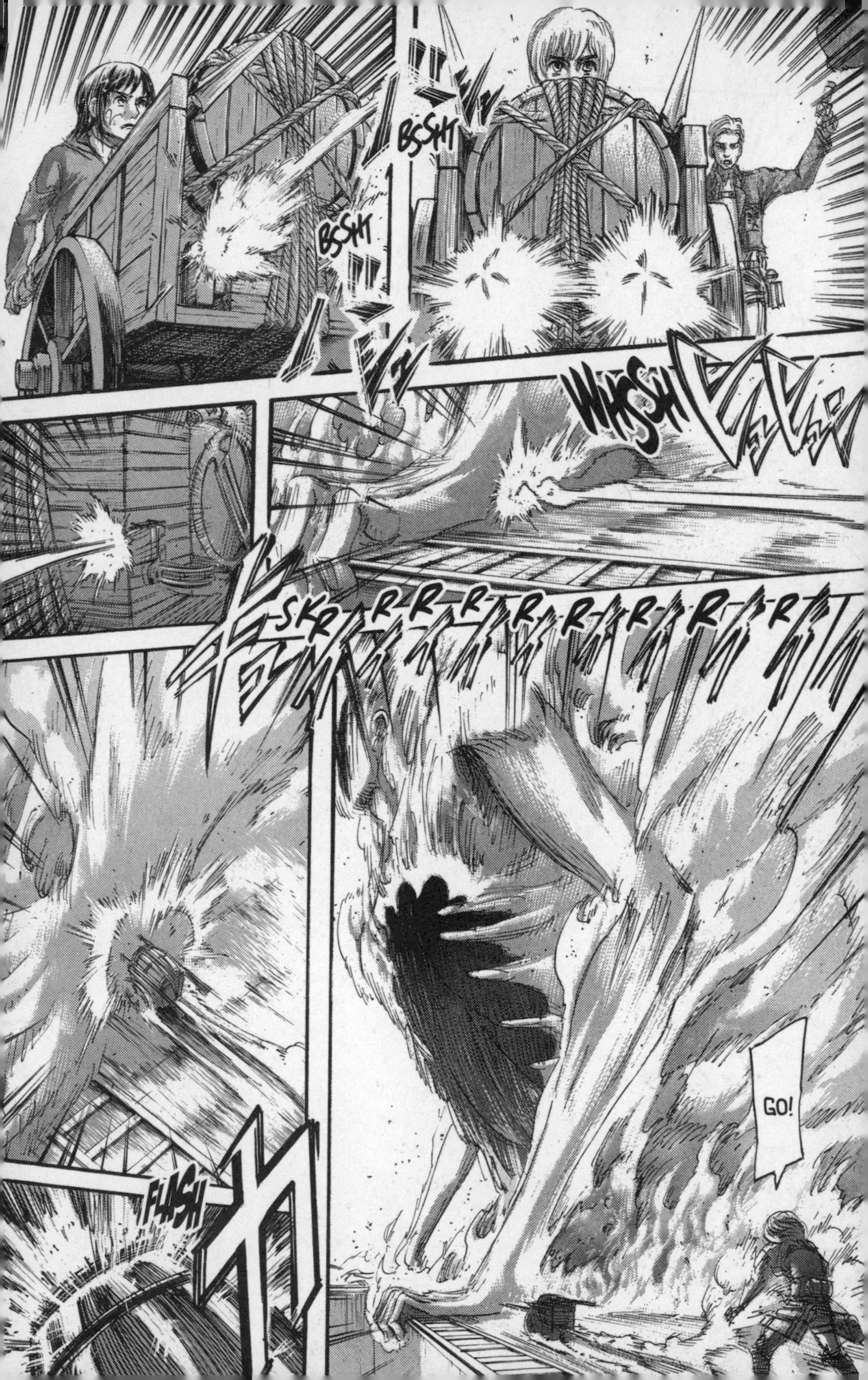
BSSHT
BSSHT
WHSSH
SKRRRRRRRRRRR
FLASH
GO!

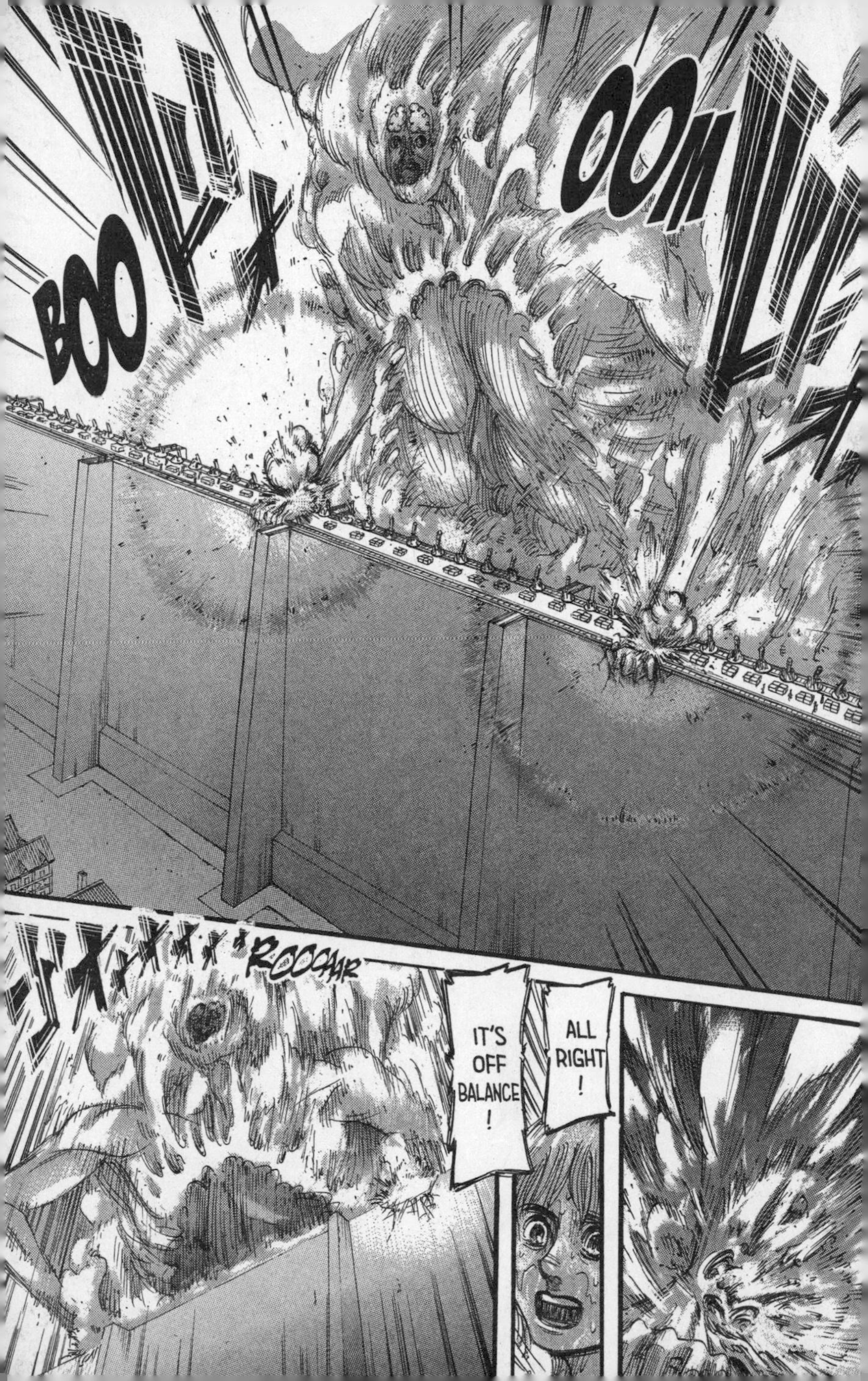
BOO
OOM
ALL RIGHT!
IT'S OFF BALANCE!
ROOOAR

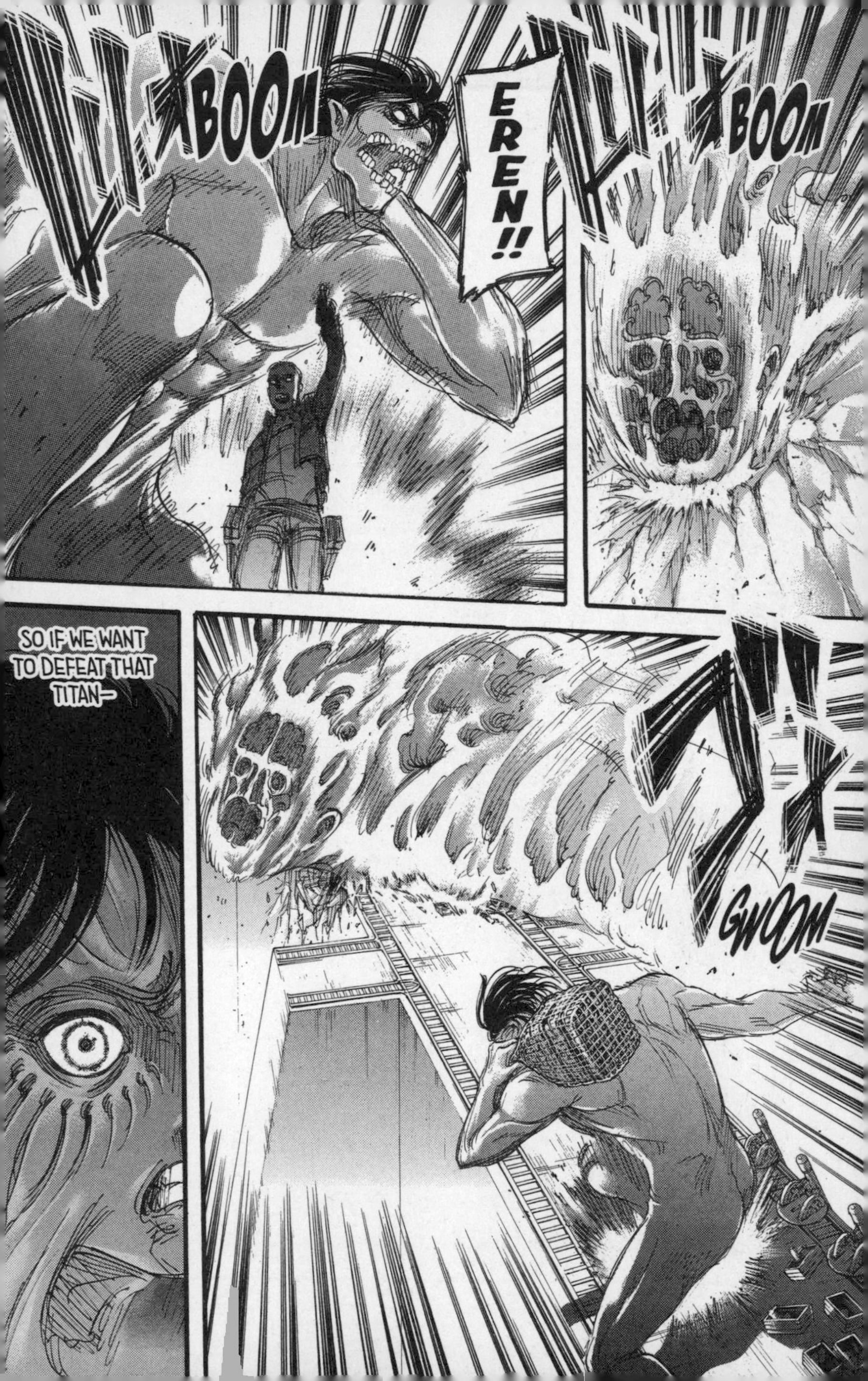
BOOM
BOOM
EREN!!
GWOOM
SO IF WE WANT TO DEFEAT THAT TITAN—

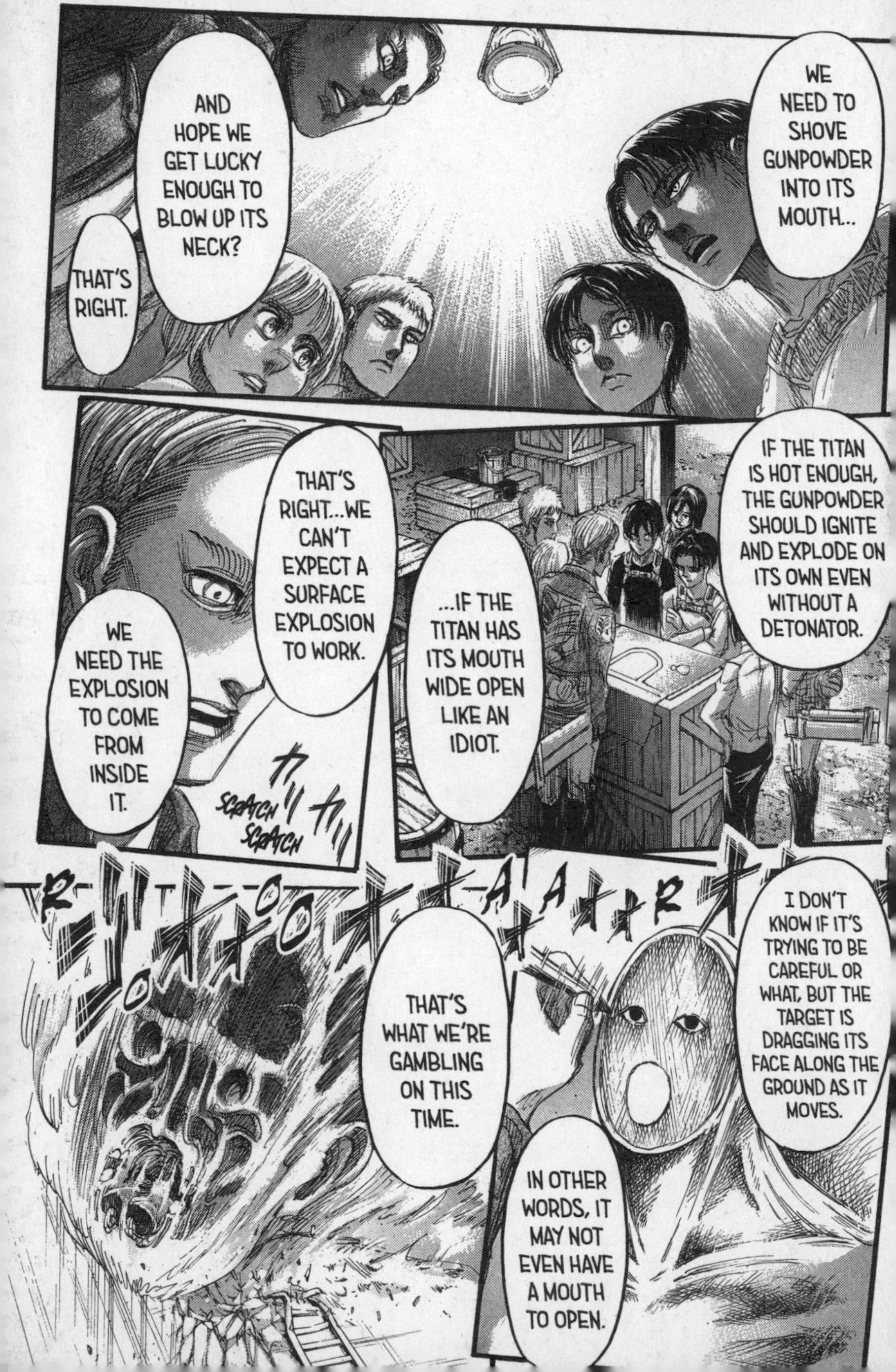
WE NEED TO SHOVE GUNPOWDER INTO ITS MOUTH...
AND HOPE WE GET LUCKY ENOUGH TO BLOW UP ITS NECK?
THAT'S RIGHT.
IF THE TITAN IS HOT ENOUGH, THE GUNPOWDER SHOULD IGNITE AND EXPLODE ON ITS OWN EVEN WITHOUT A DETONATOR.
...IF THE TITAN HAS ITS MOUTH WIDE OPEN LIKE AN IDIOT.
THAT'S RIGHT...WE CAN'T EXPECT A SURFACE EXPLOSION TO WORK.
WE NEED THE EXPLOSION TO COME FROM INSIDE IT.
SCRATCH SCRATCH
I DON'T KNOW IF IT'S TRYING TO BE CAREFUL OR WHAT, BUT THE TARGET IS DRAGGING ITS FACE ALONG THE GROUND AS IT MOVES.
IN OTHER WORDS, IT MAY NOT EVEN HAVE A MOUTH TO OPEN.
THAT'S WHAT WE'RE GAMBLING ON THIS TIME.

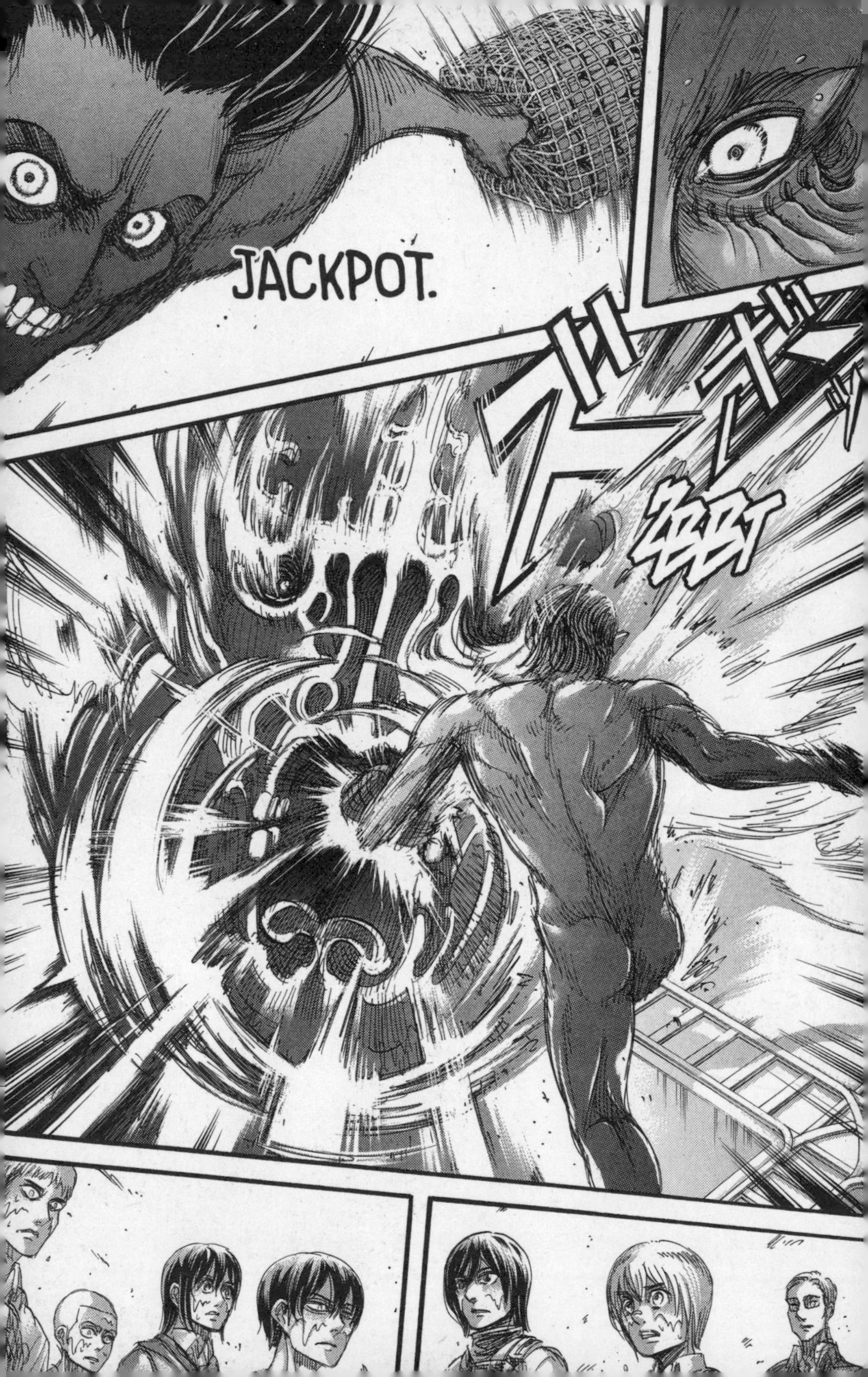
JACKPOT.

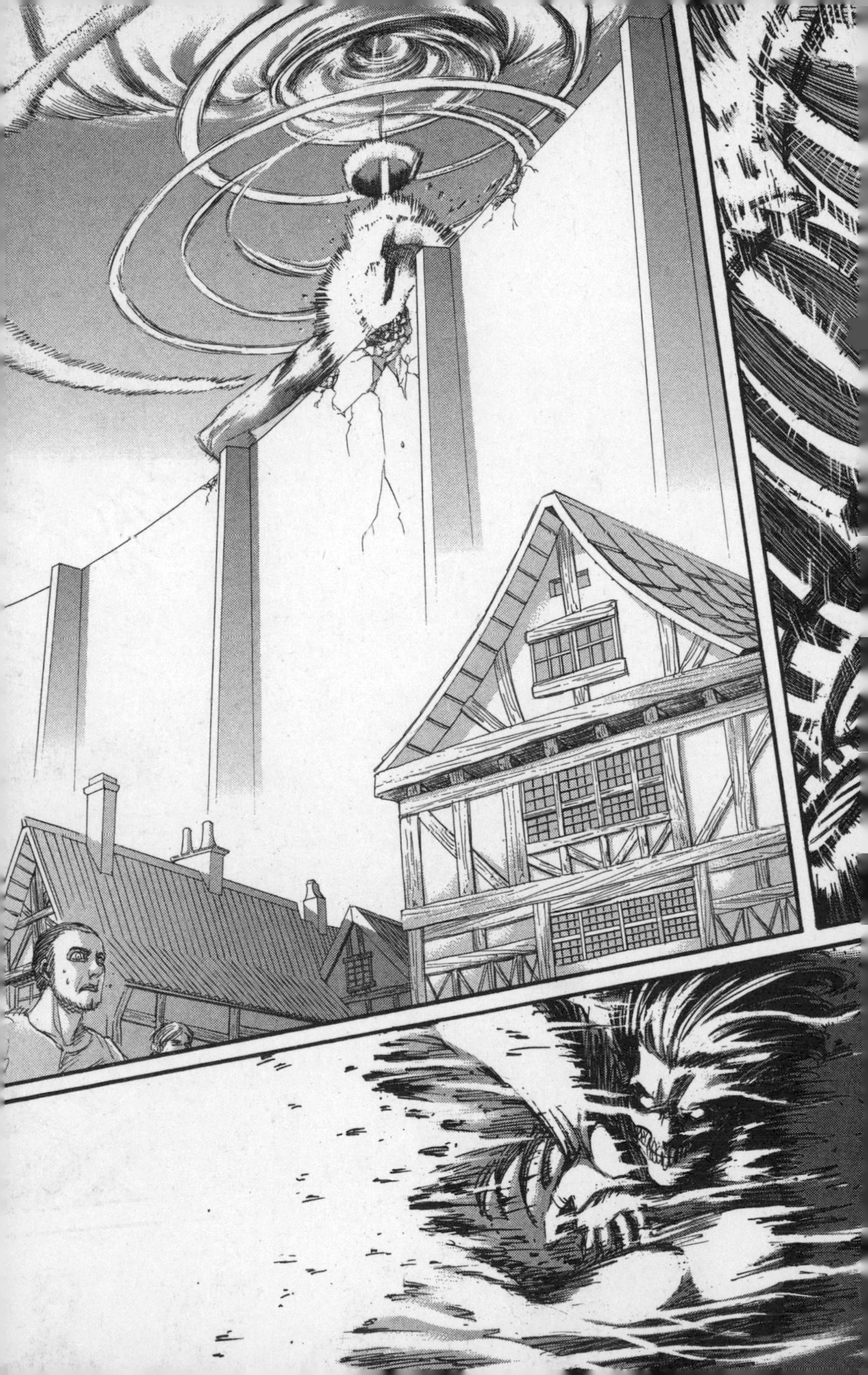

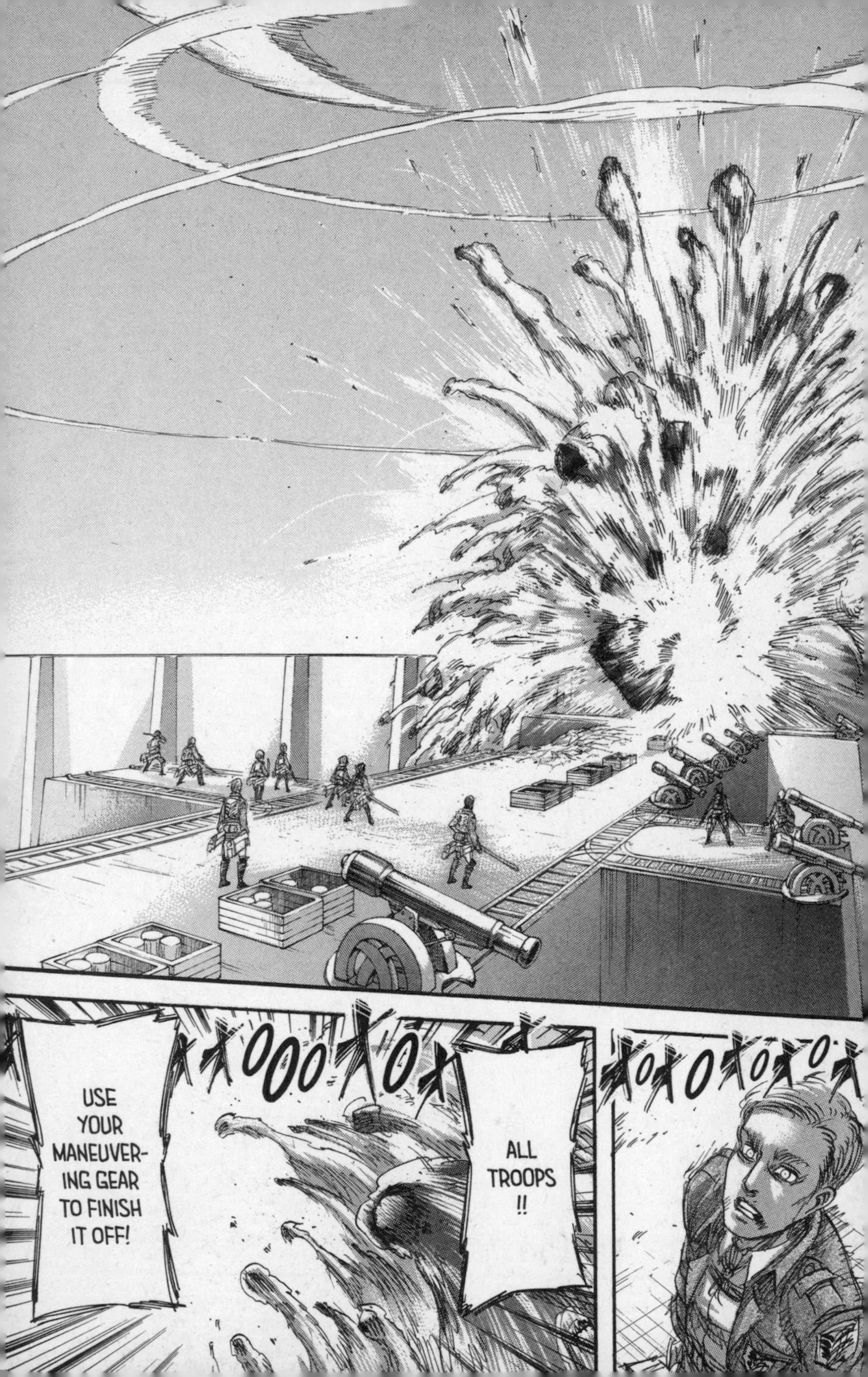
OOOOO
OOOOO
ALL TROOPS !!
USE YOUR MANEUVER-ING GEAR TO FINISH IT OFF!

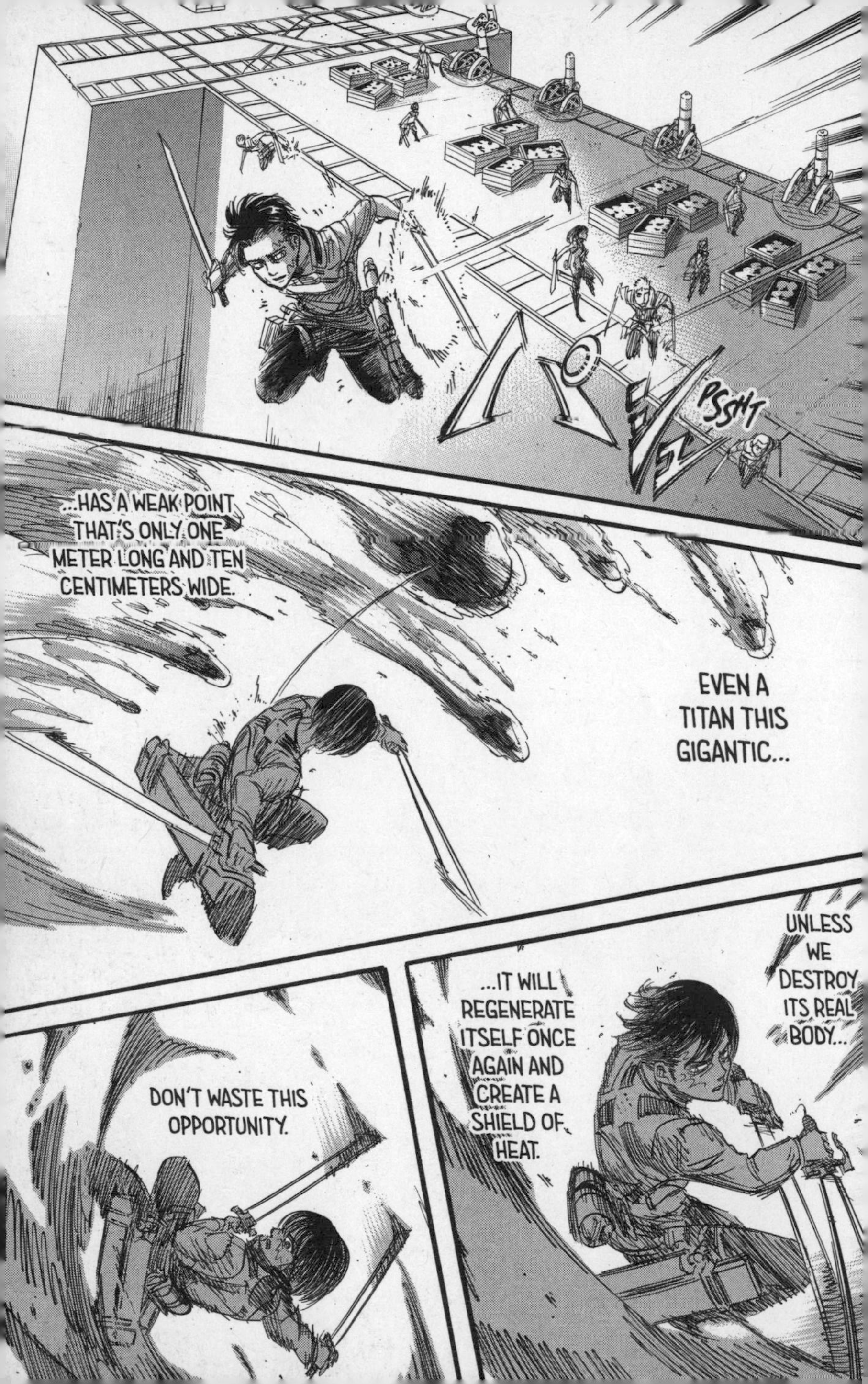
PSSHT
EVEN A TITAN THIS GIGANTIC...
...HAS A WEAK POINT THAT'S ONLY ONE METER LONG AND TEN CENTIMETERS WIDE.
UNLESS WE DESTROY ITS REAL BODY...
...IT WILL REGENERATE ITSELF ONCE AGAIN AND CREATE A SHIELD OF HEAT.
DON'T WASTE THIS OPPORTUNITY.

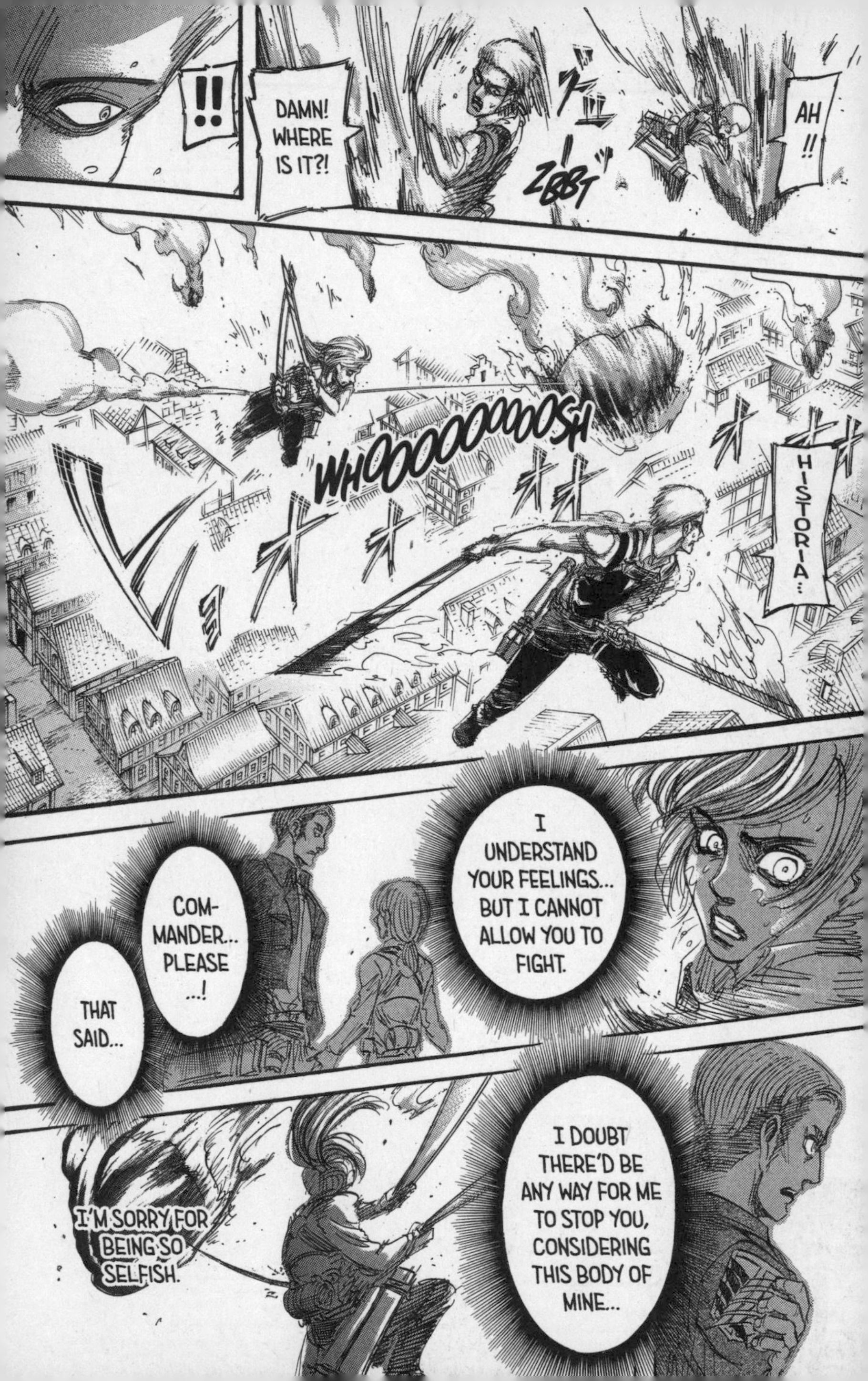
AH !!
ZBBT
DAMN! WHERE IS IT?!
!!
HISTORIA...
WHOOOOOOOOOSH
I UNDERSTAND YOUR FEELINGS... BUT I CANNOT ALLOW YOU TO FIGHT.
COM-MANDER... PLEASE ...!
THAT SAID...
I DOUBT THERE'D BE ANY WAY FOR ME TO STOP YOU, CONSIDERING THIS BODY OF MINE...
I'M SORRY FOR BEING SO SELFISH.

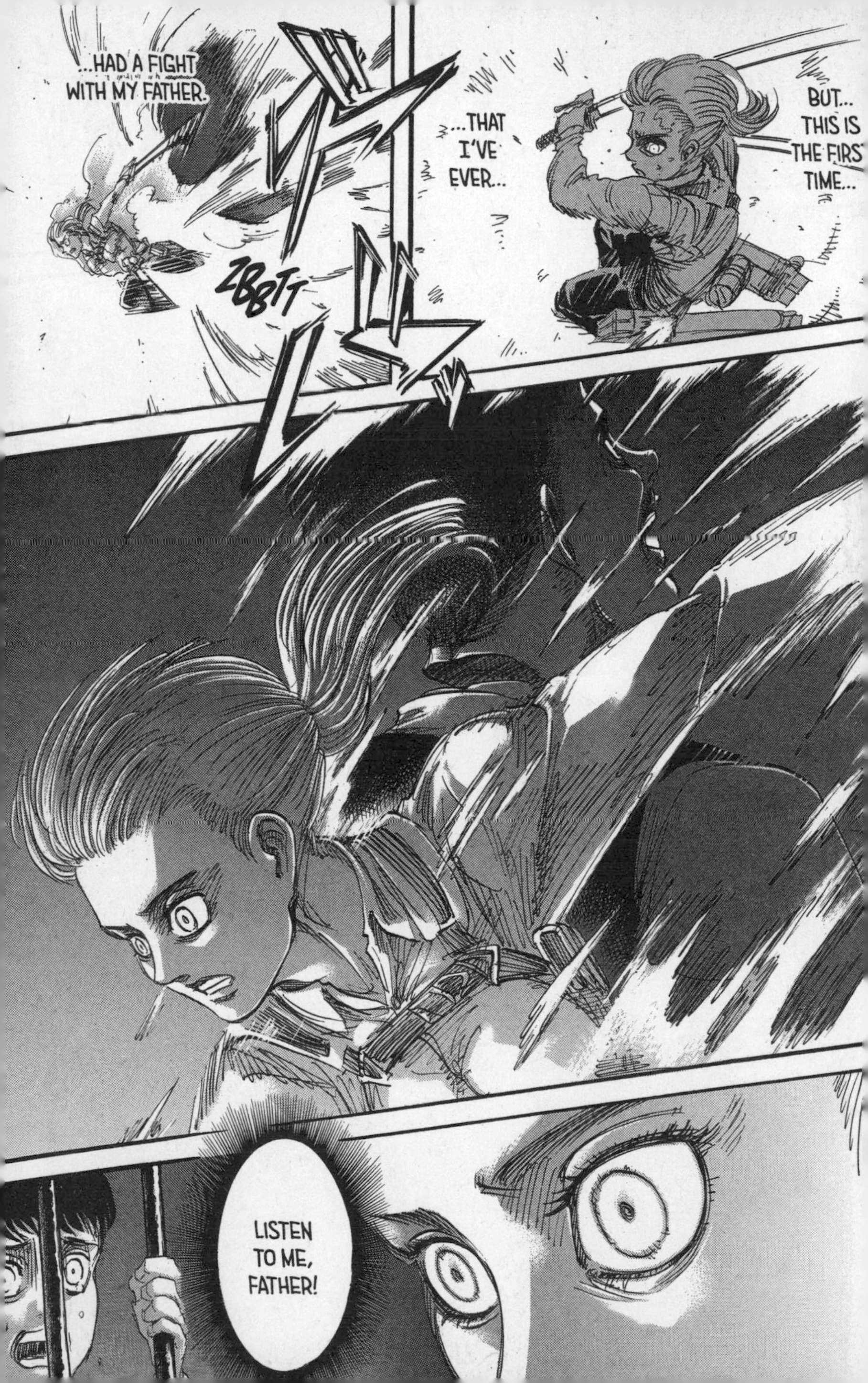
BUT... THIS IS THE FIRS TIME...
...THAT I'VE EVER...
...HAD A FIGHT WITH MY FATHER.
ZBBTT
LISTEN TO ME, FATHER!

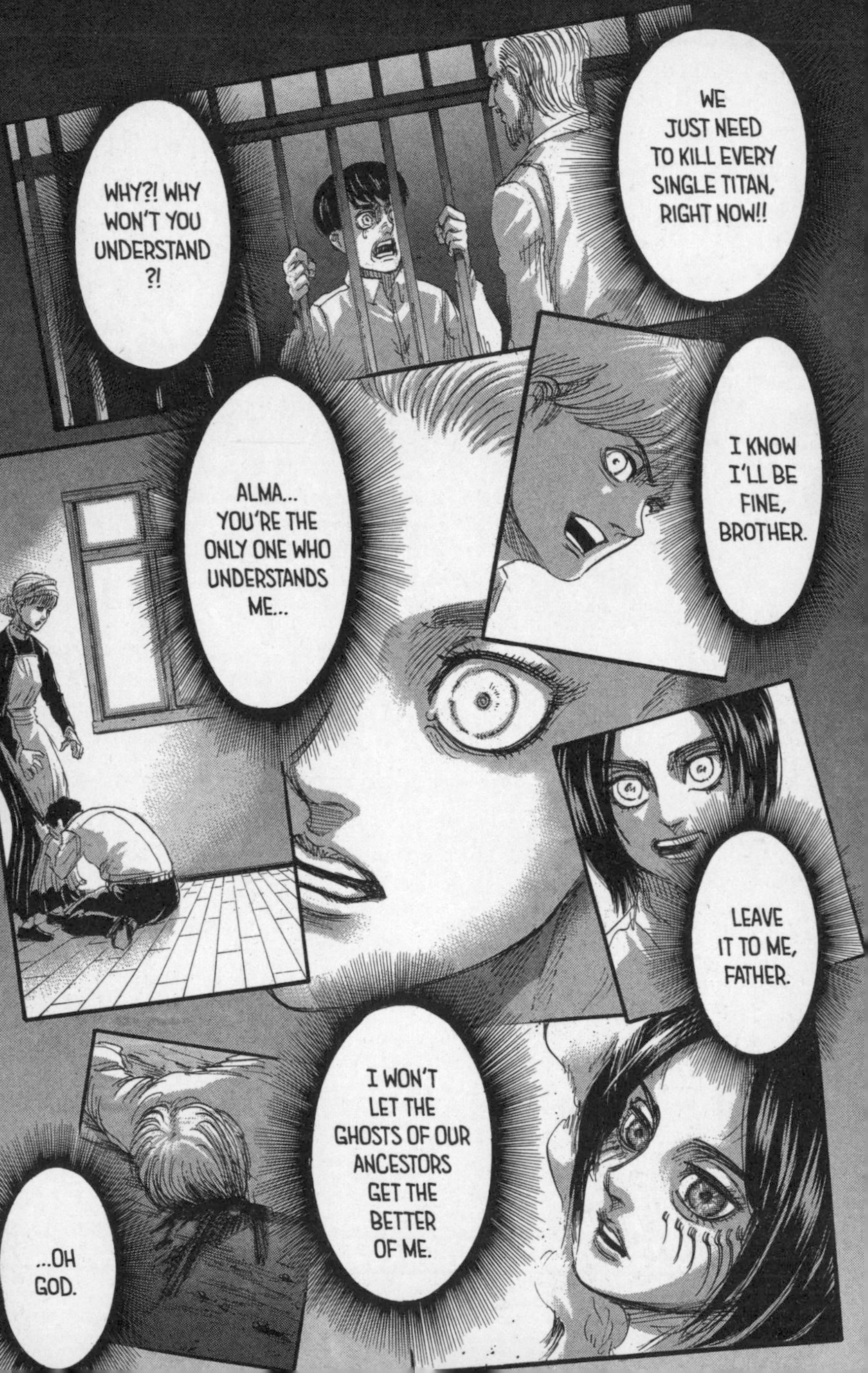
WE JUST NEED TO KILL EVERY SINGLE TITAN, RIGHT NOW!!
WHY?! WHY WON'T YOU UNDERSTAND ?!
I KNOW I'LL BE FINE, BROTHER.
LEAVE IT TO ME, FATHER.
ALMA... YOU'RE THE ONLY ONE WHO UNDERSTANDS ME...
I WON'T LET THE GHOSTS OF OUR ANCESTORS GET THE BETTER OF ME.
...OH GOD.

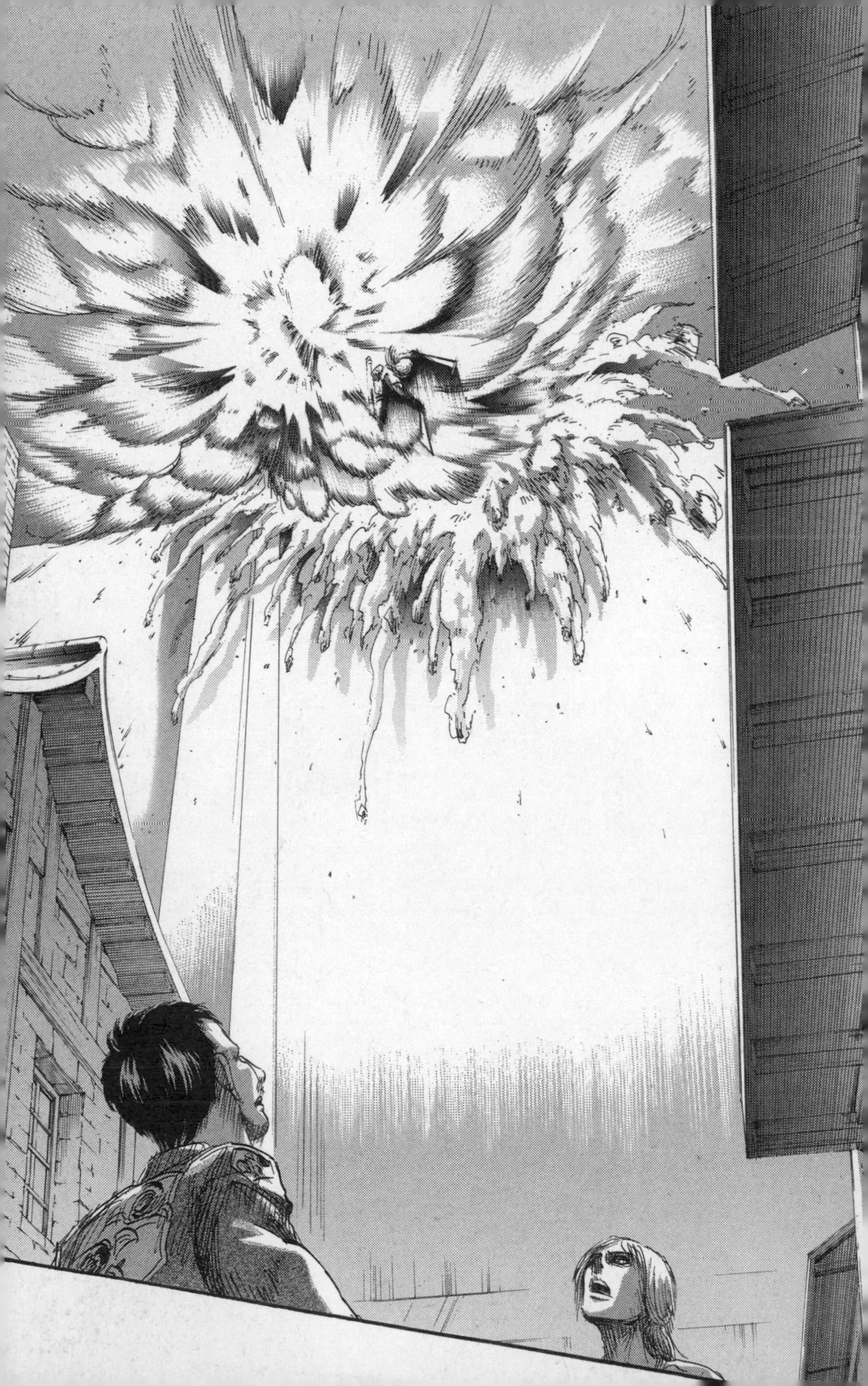

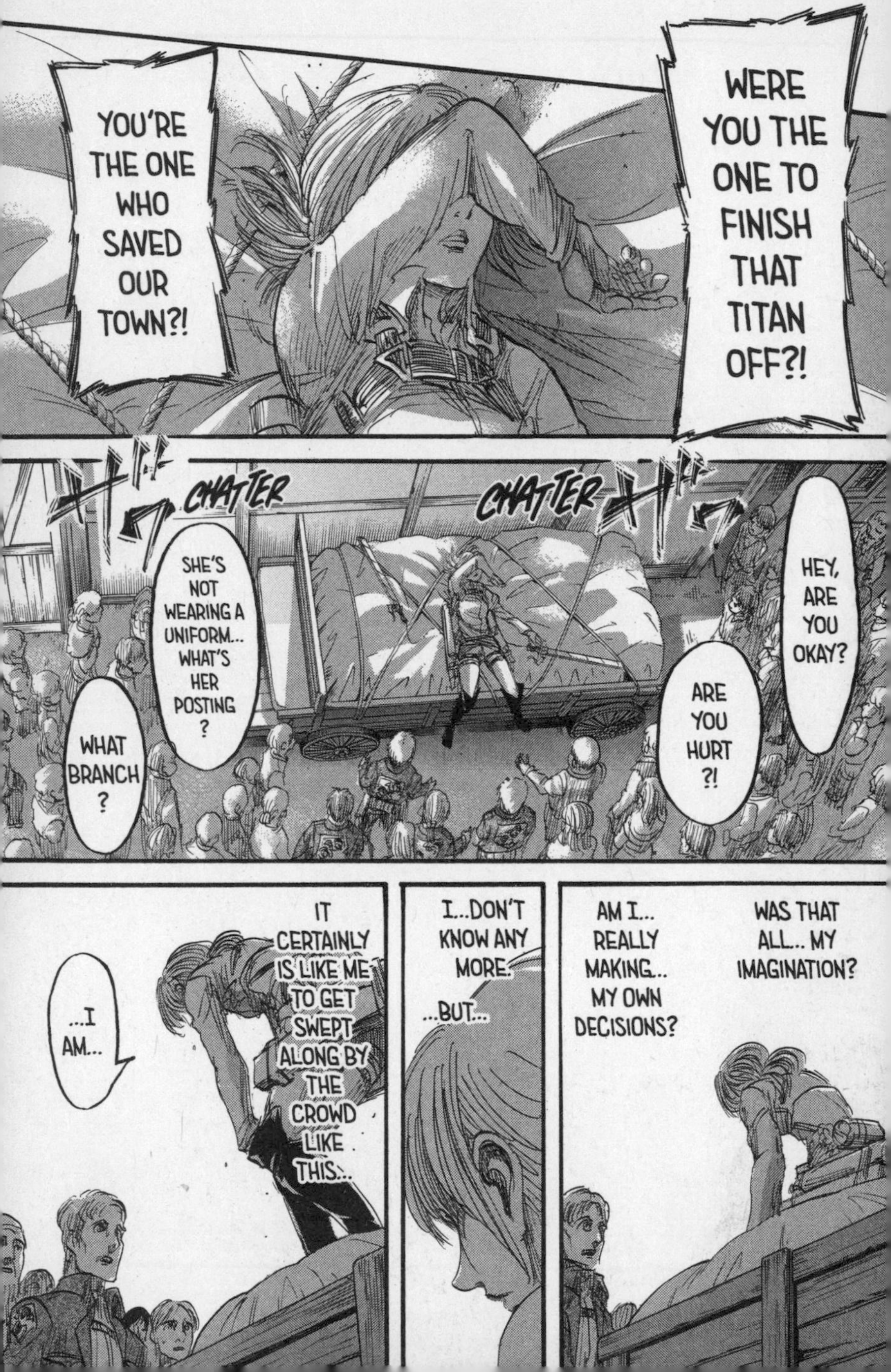
WERE YOU THE ONE TO FINISH THAT TITAN OFF?!
YOU'RE THE ONE WHO SAVED OUR TOWN?!
HEY, ARE YOU OKAY?
ARE YOU HURT?!
CHATTER
CHATTER
SHE'S NOT WEARING A UNIFORM... WHAT'S HER POSTING?
WHAT BRANCH?
WAS THAT ALL... MY IMAGINATION?
AM I... REALLY MAKING... MY OWN DECISIONS?
I...DON'T KNOW ANY MORE.
...BUT...
IT CERTAINLY IS LIKE ME TO GET SWEPT ALONG BY THE CROWD LIKE THIS...
...I AM...

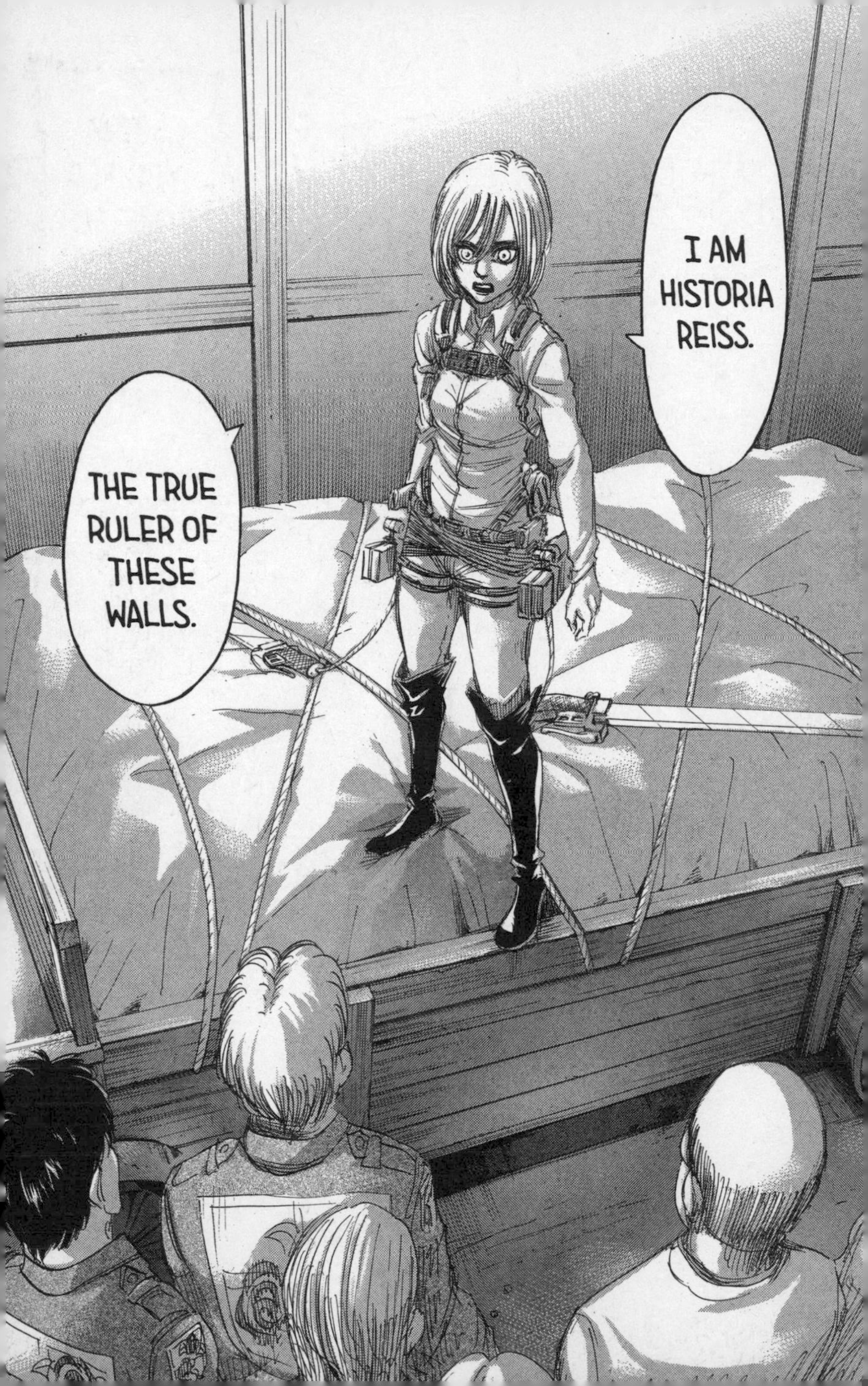
I AM HISTORIA REISS.
THE TRUE RULER OF THESE WALLS.

ATTACK on TITAN

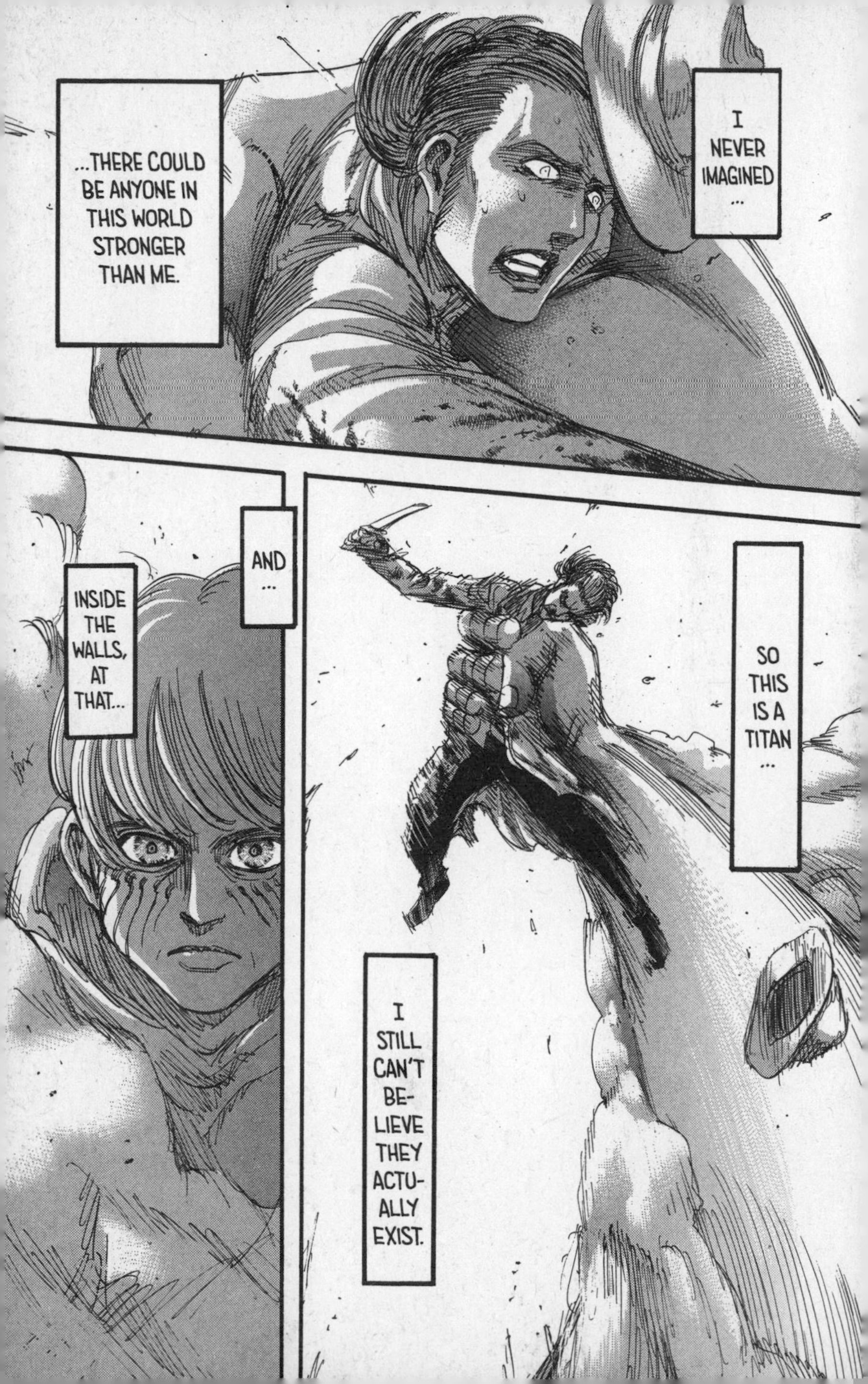
I NEVER IMAGINED...
...THERE COULD BE ANYONE IN THIS WORLD STRONGER THAN ME.
SO THIS IS A TITAN...
I STILL CAN'T BE-LIEVE THEY ACTU-ALLY EXIST.
AND...
INSIDE THE WALLS, AT THAT...

Episode 69: Friends

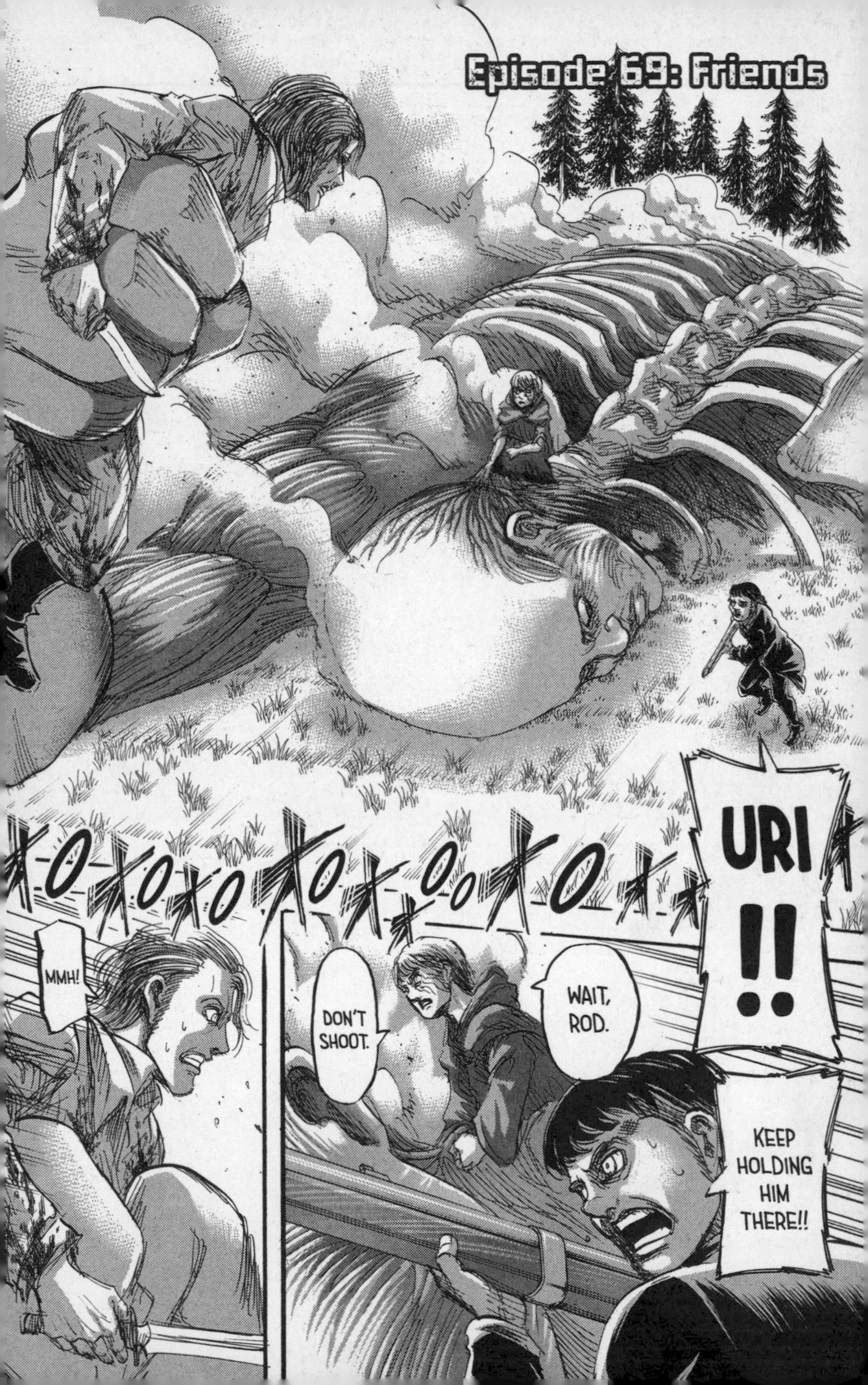
URI!!
KEEP HOLDING HIM THERE!!
WAIT, ROD.
DON'T SHOOT.
MMH!

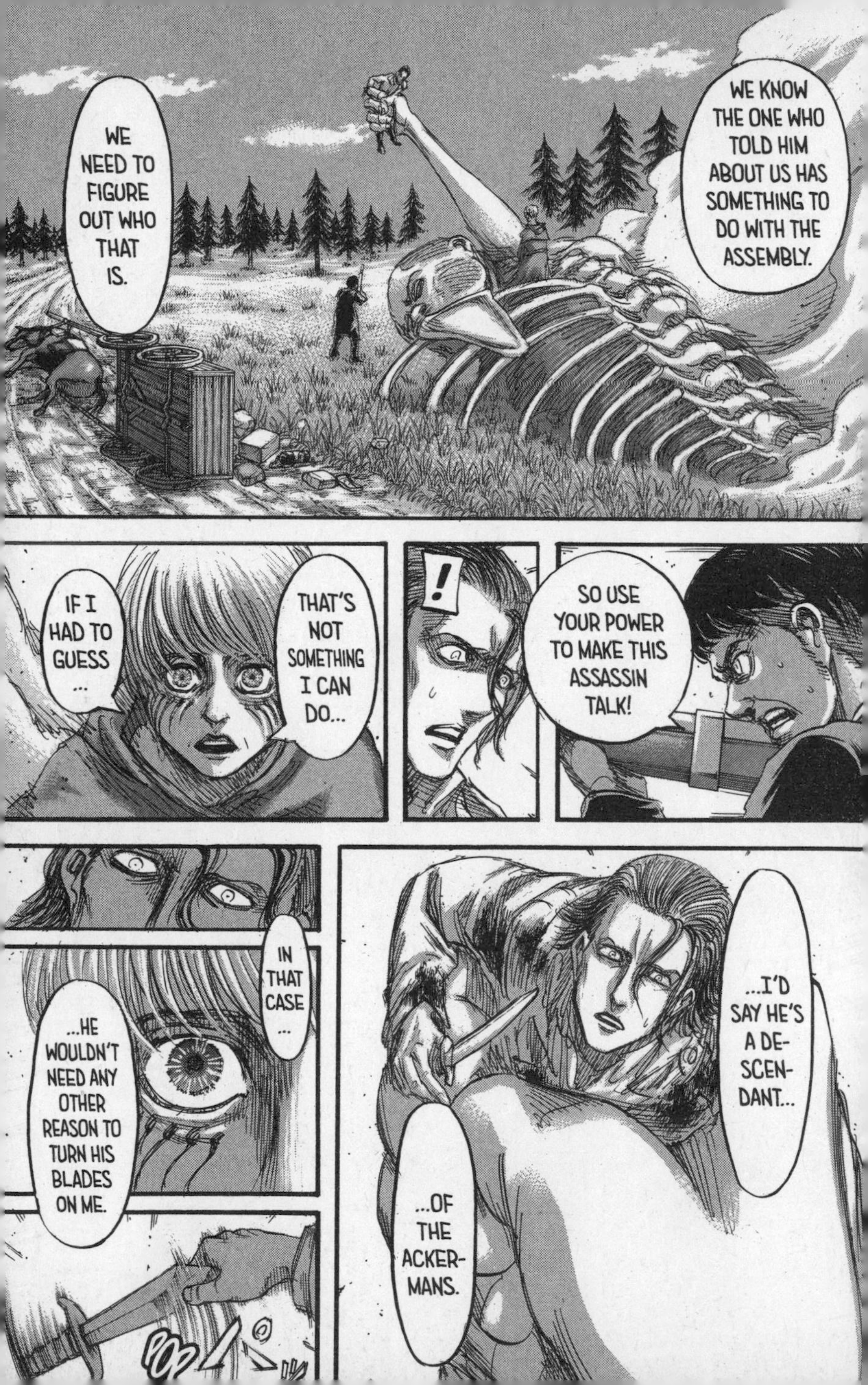
WE KNOW THE ONE WHO TOLD HIM ABOUT US HAS SOMETHING TO DO WITH THE ASSEMBLY.
WE NEED TO FIGURE OUT WHO THAT IS.
SO USE YOUR POWER TO MAKE THIS ASSASSIN TALK!
!
THAT'S NOT SOMETHING I CAN DO...
IF I HAD TO GUESS...
...I'D SAY HE'S A DE-SCEN-DANT...
...OF THE ACKER-MANS.
IN THAT CASE...
...HE WOULDN'T NEED ANY OTHER REASON TO TURN HIS BLADES ON ME.
POP

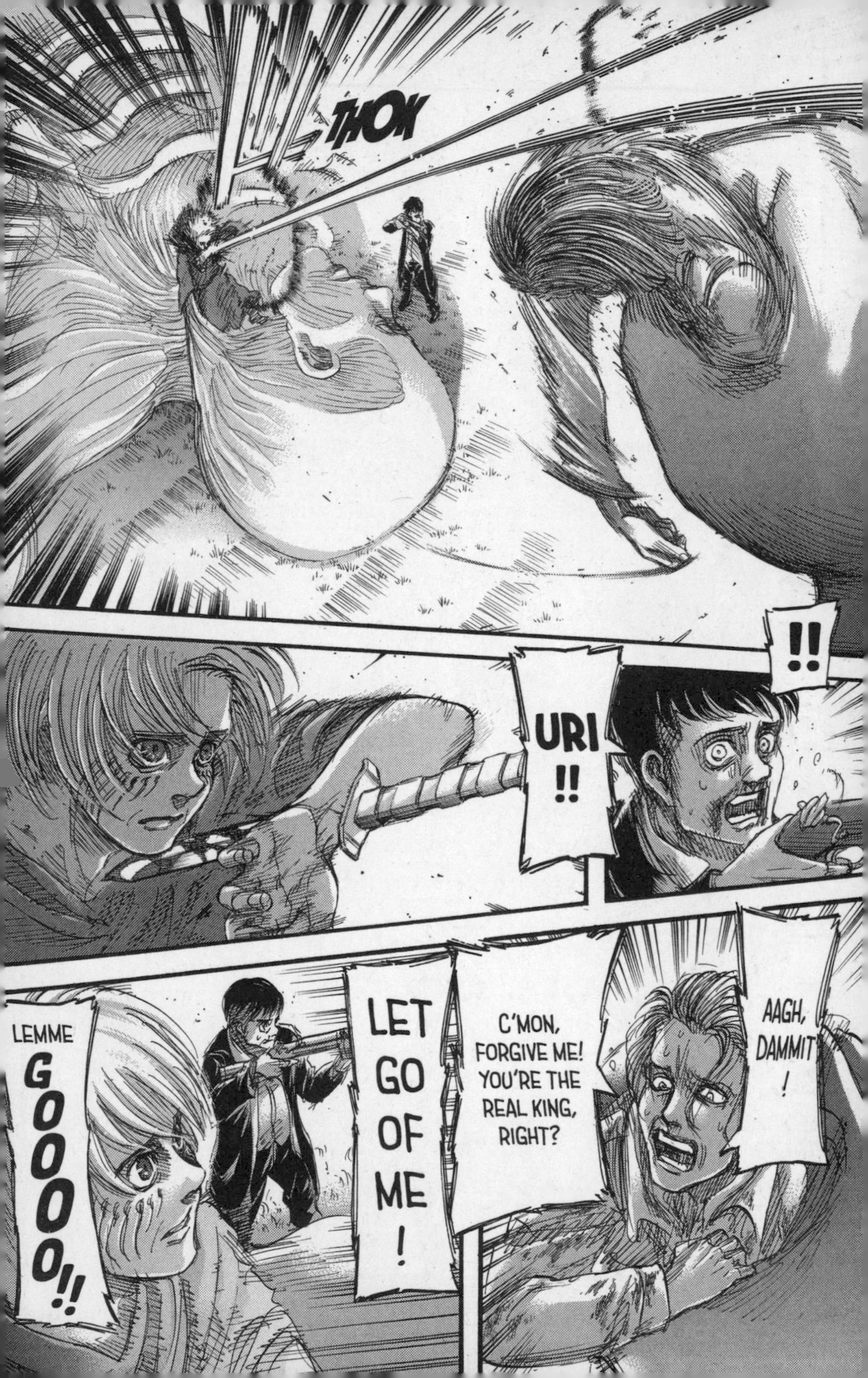
THOK
!!
URI !!
AAGH, DAMMIT !
C'MON, FORGIVE ME! YOU'RE THE REAL KING, RIGHT?
LET GO OF ME !
LEMME GOOOOO!!

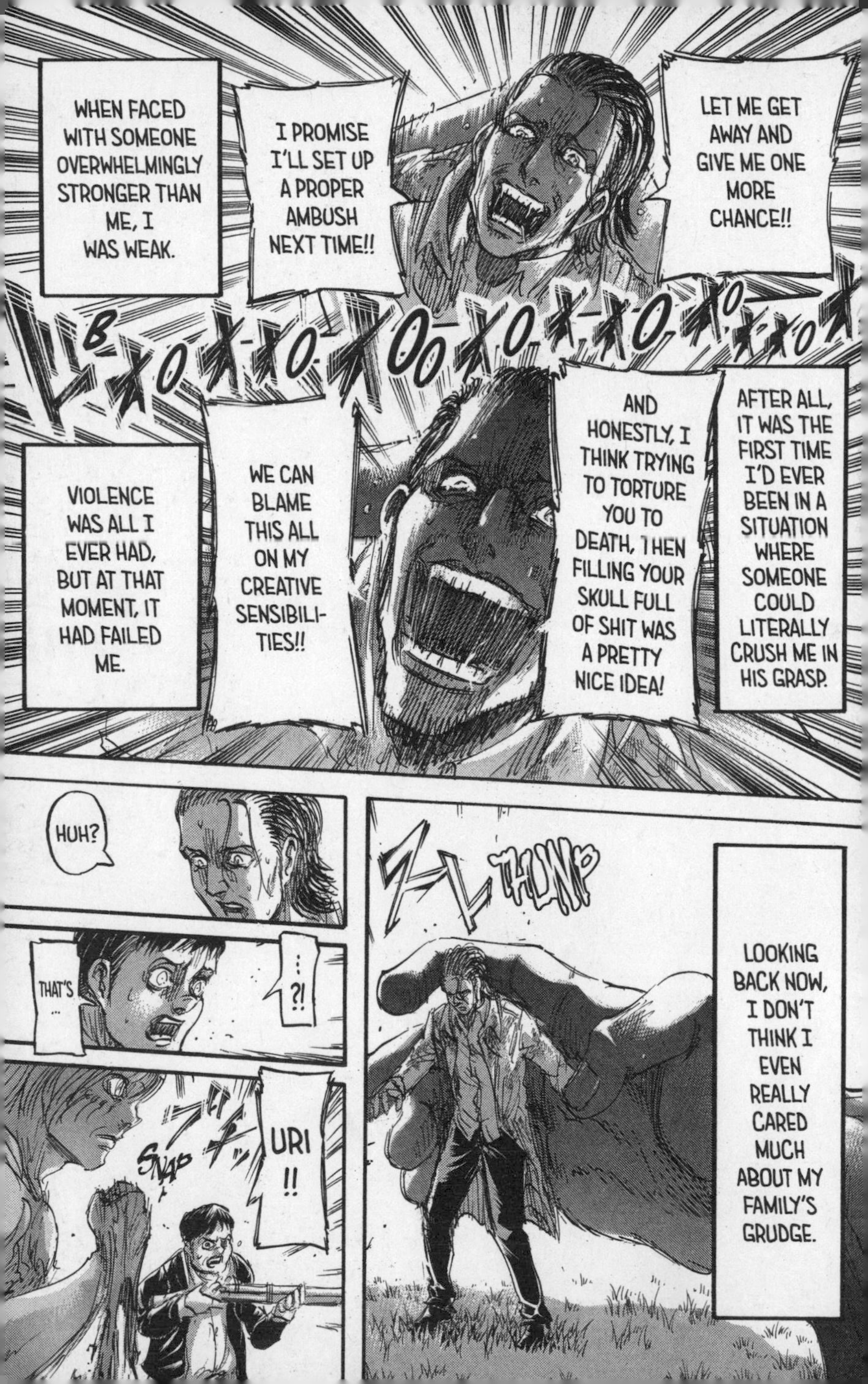
LET ME GET AWAY AND GIVE ME ONE MORE CHANCE!!
I PROMISE I'LL SET UP A PROPER AMBUSH NEXT TIME!!
WHEN FACED WITH SOMEONE OVERWHELMINGLY STRONGER THAN ME, I WAS WEAK.
AFTER ALL, IT WAS THE FIRST TIME I'D EVER BEEN IN A SITUATION WHERE SOMEONE COULD LITERALLY CRUSH ME IN HIS GRASP.
AND HONESTLY, I THINK TRYING TO TORTURE YOU TO DEATH, THEN FILLING YOUR SKULL FULL OF SHIT WAS A PRETTY NICE IDEA!
WE CAN BLAME THIS ALL ON MY CREATIVE SENSIBILI-TIES!!
VIOLENCE WAS ALL I EVER HAD, BUT AT THAT MOMENT, IT HAD FAILED ME.
THUMP
LOOKING BACK NOW, I DON'T THINK I EVEN REALLY CARED MUCH ABOUT MY FAMILY'S GRUDGE.
HUH?
…?!
THAT'S …
URI!!
SNAP

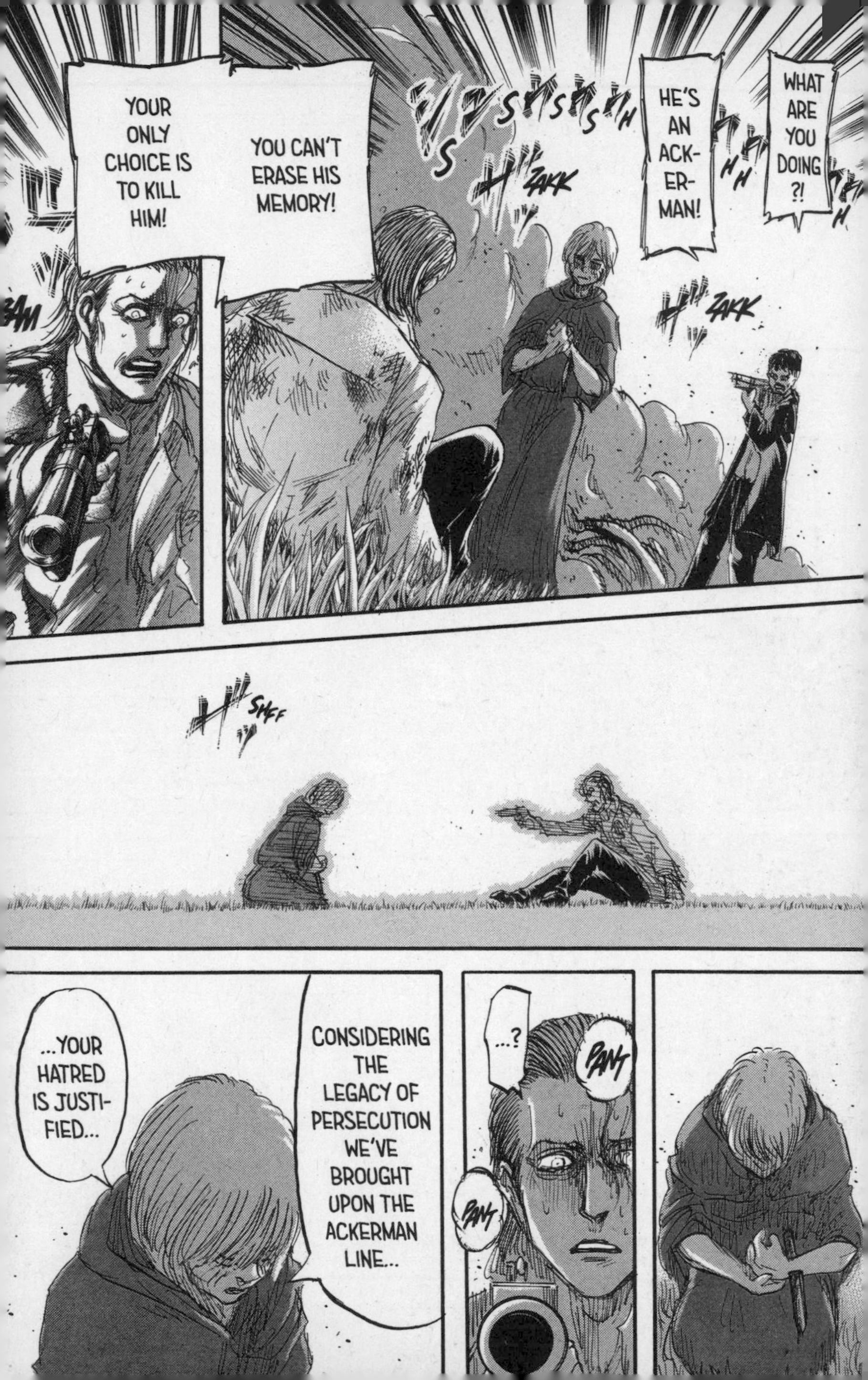
WHAT ARE YOU DOING?!
HE'S AN ACK-ER-MAN!
ZAKK
ZAKK
YOU CAN'T ERASE HIS MEMORY!
YOUR ONLY CHOICE IS TO KILL HIM!
SHFF
...?
PANT
PANT
...YOUR HATRED IS JUSTI-FIED...
CONSIDERING THE LEGACY OF PERSECUTION WE'VE BROUGHT UPON THE ACKERMAN LINE...

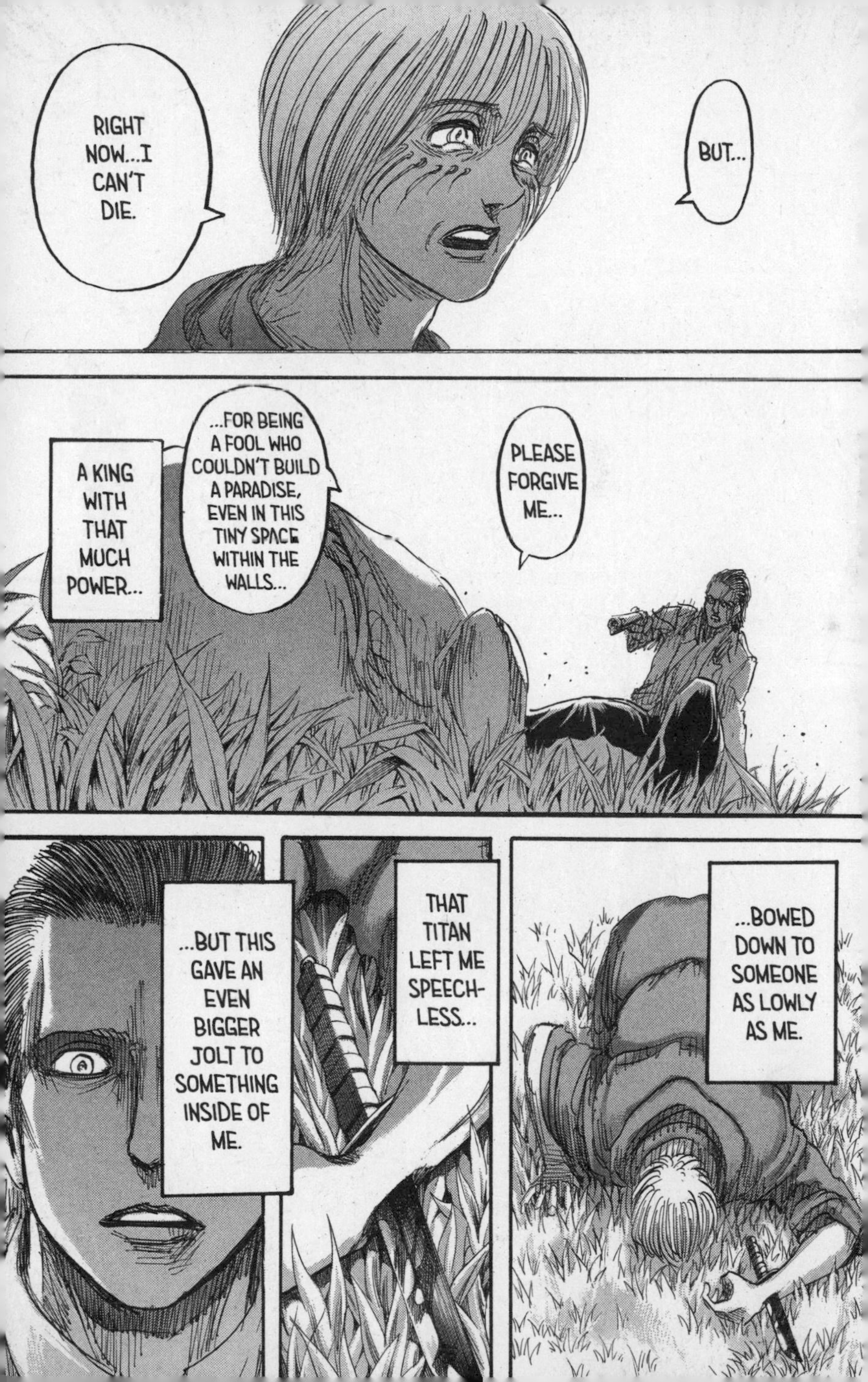
BUT...
RIGHT NOW...I CAN'T DIE.
PLEASE FORGIVE ME...
...FOR BEING A FOOL WHO COULDN'T BUILD A PARADISE, EVEN IN THIS TINY SPACE WITHIN THE WALLS...
A KING WITH THAT MUCH POWER...
...BOWED DOWN TO SOMEONE AS LOWLY AS ME.
THAT TITAN LEFT ME SPEECHLESS...
...BUT THIS GAVE AN EVEN BIGGER JOLT TO SOMETHING INSIDE OF ME.

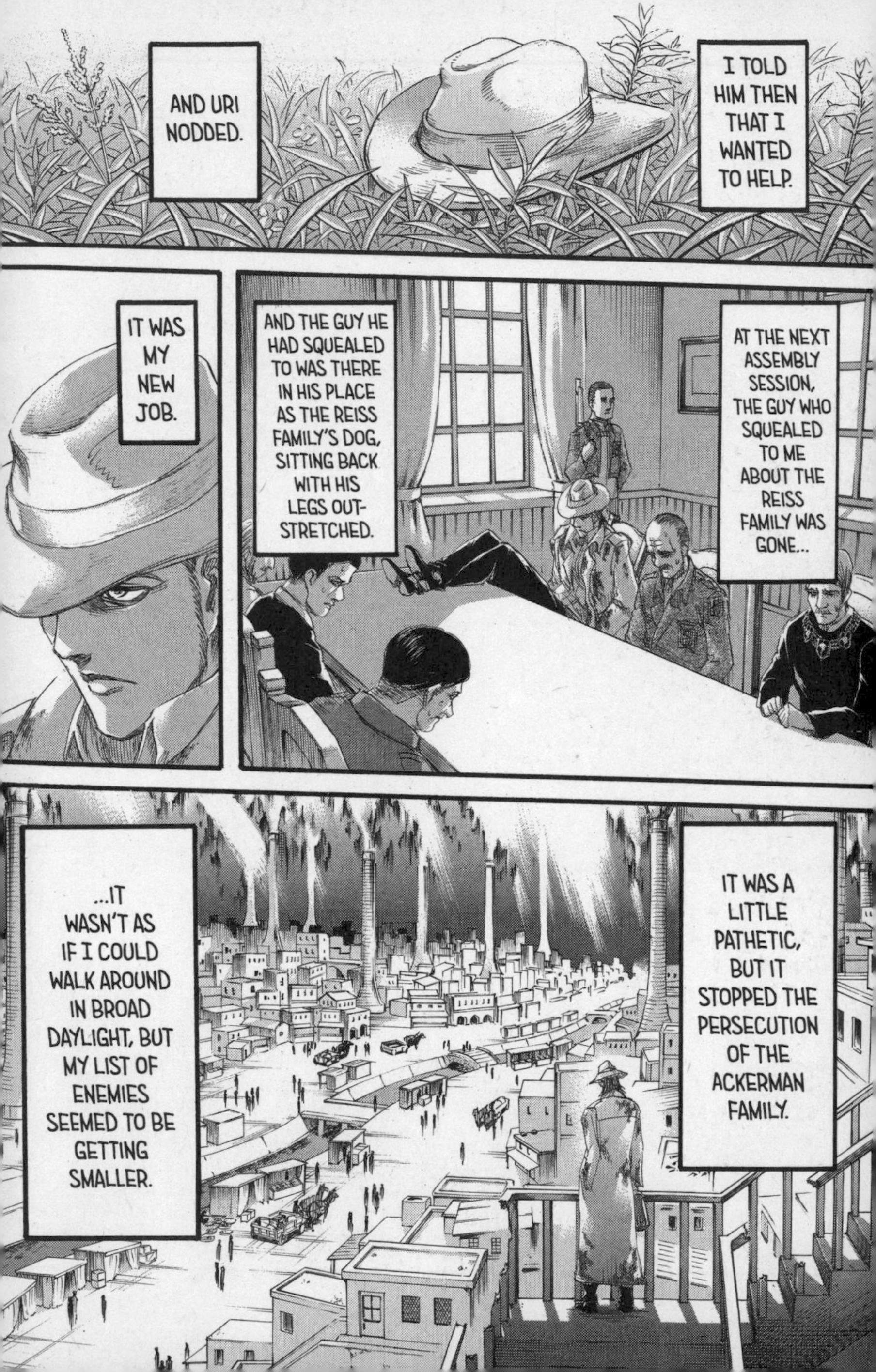
I TOLD HIM THEN THAT I WANTED TO HELP.
AND URI NODDED.
AT THE NEXT ASSEMBLY SESSION, THE GUY WHO SQUEALED TO ME ABOUT THE REISS FAMILY WAS GONE...
AND THE GUY HE HAD SQUEALED TO WAS THERE IN HIS PLACE AS THE REISS FAMILY'S DOG, SITTING BACK WITH HIS LEGS OUT-STRETCHED.
IT WAS MY NEW JOB.
IT WAS A LITTLE PATHETIC, BUT IT STOPPED THE PERSECUTION OF THE ACKERMAN FAMILY.
...IT WASN'T AS IF I COULD WALK AROUND IN BROAD DAYLIGHT, BUT MY LIST OF ENEMIES SEEMED TO BE GETTING SMALLER.

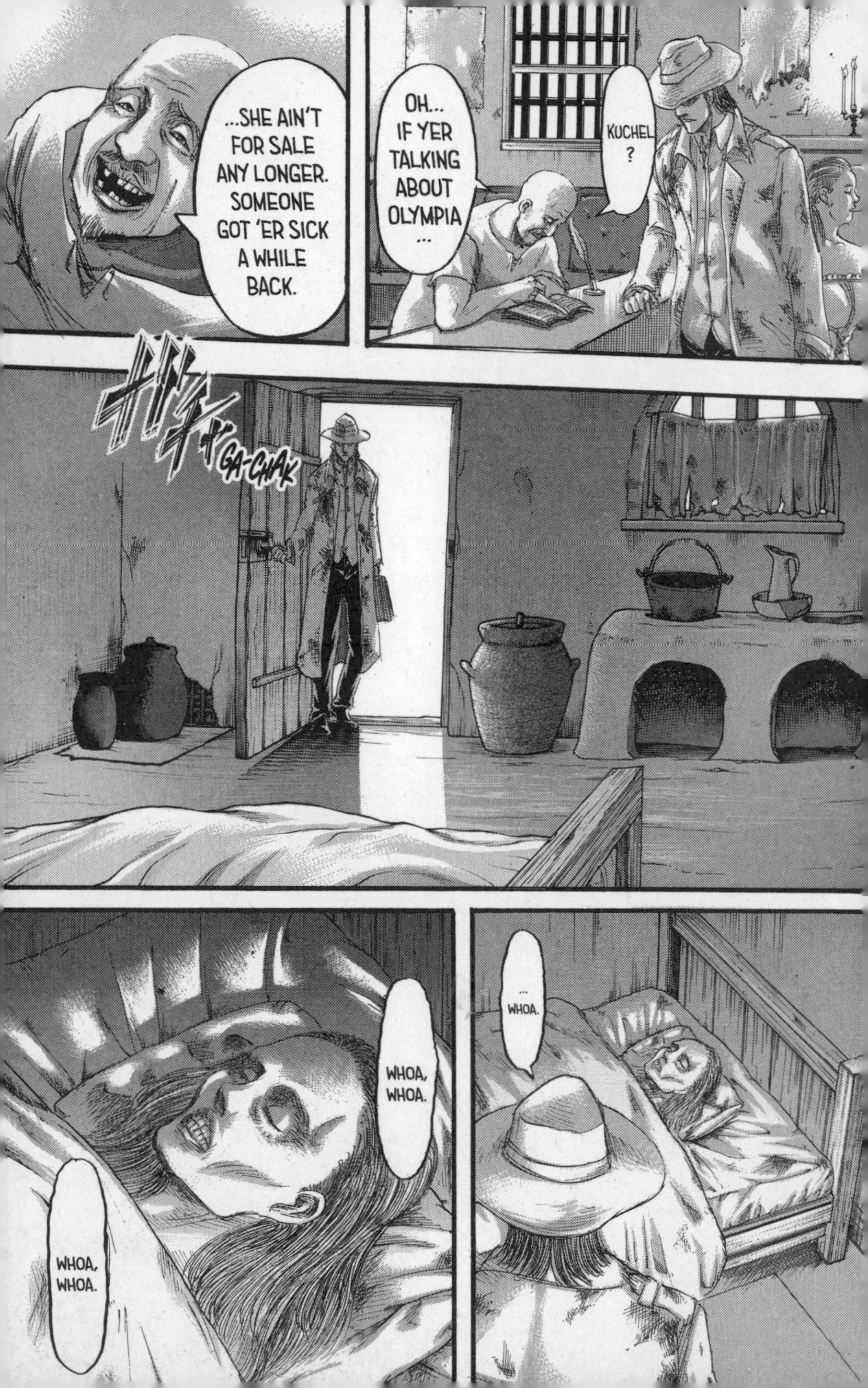
KUCHEL?
OH... IF YER TALKING ABOUT OLYMPIA...
...SHE AIN'T FOR SALE ANY LONGER. SOMEONE GOT 'ER SICK A WHILE BACK.
GA-CHAK
... WHOA.
WHOA, WHOA.
WHOA, WHOA.

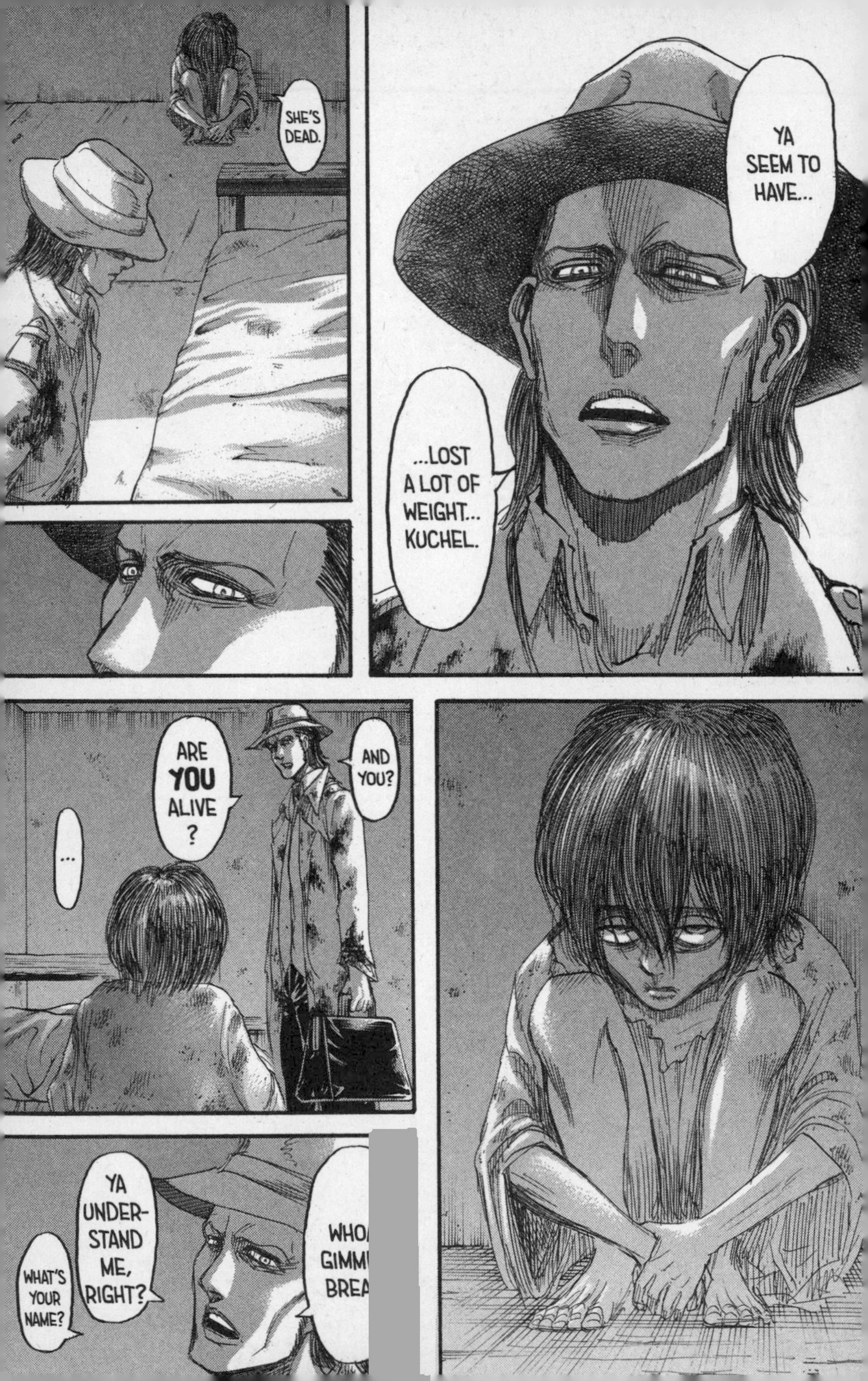
YA SEEM TO HAVE...
...LOST A LOT OF WEIGHT... KUCHEL.
SHE'S DEAD.
AND YOU?
ARE **YOU** ALIVE ?
...
WHO
GIMM
BREA
YA UNDER-STAND ME, RIGHT?
WHAT'S YOUR NAME?

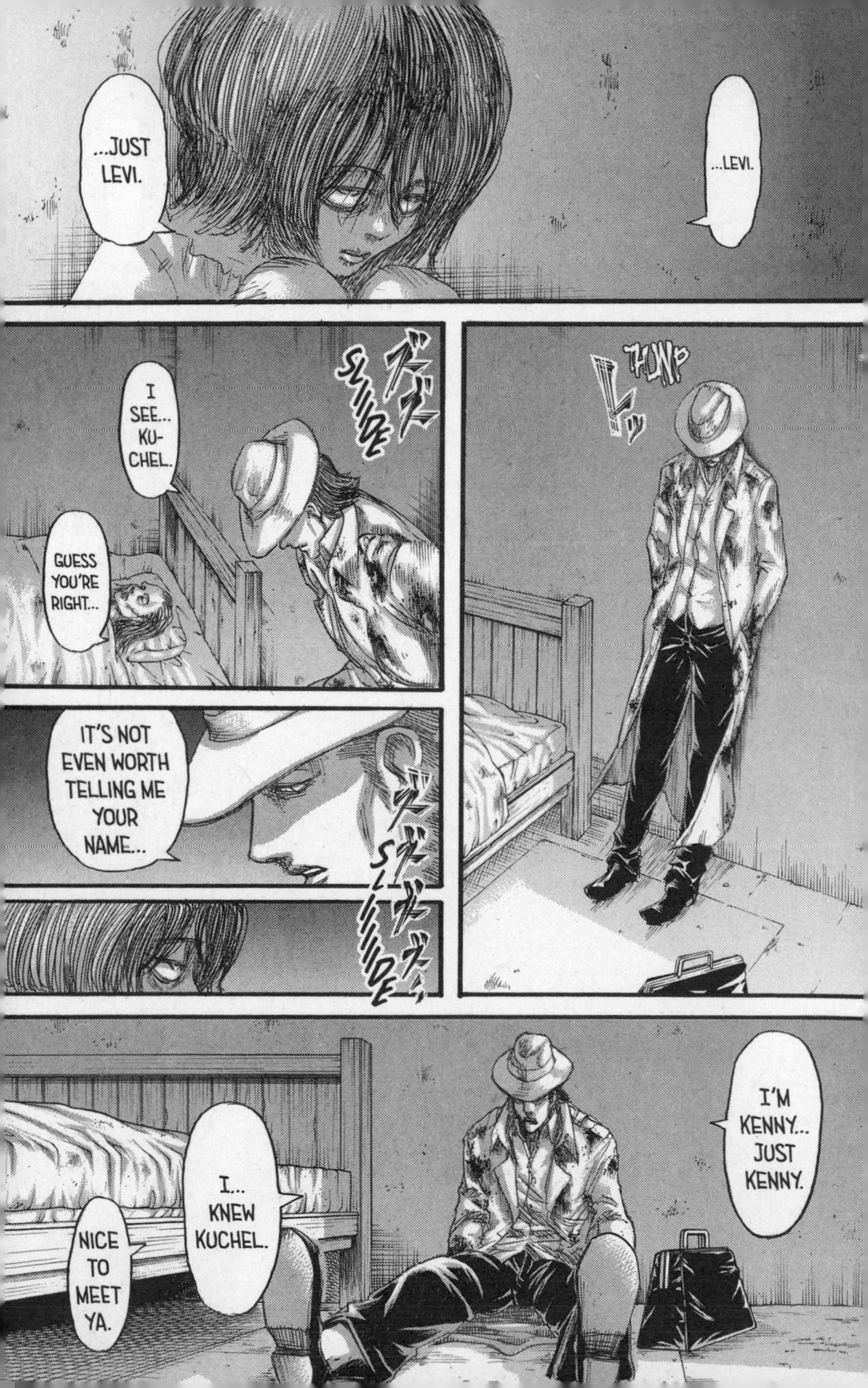
...LEVI.
...JUST LEVI.
THUMP
I SEE... KU-CHEL.
SLIIIDE
GUESS YOU'RE RIGHT...
IT'S NOT EVEN WORTH TELLING ME YOUR NAME...
SLIIIIIIDE
I'M KENNY... JUST KENNY.
I... KNEW KUCHEL.
NICE TO MEET YA.

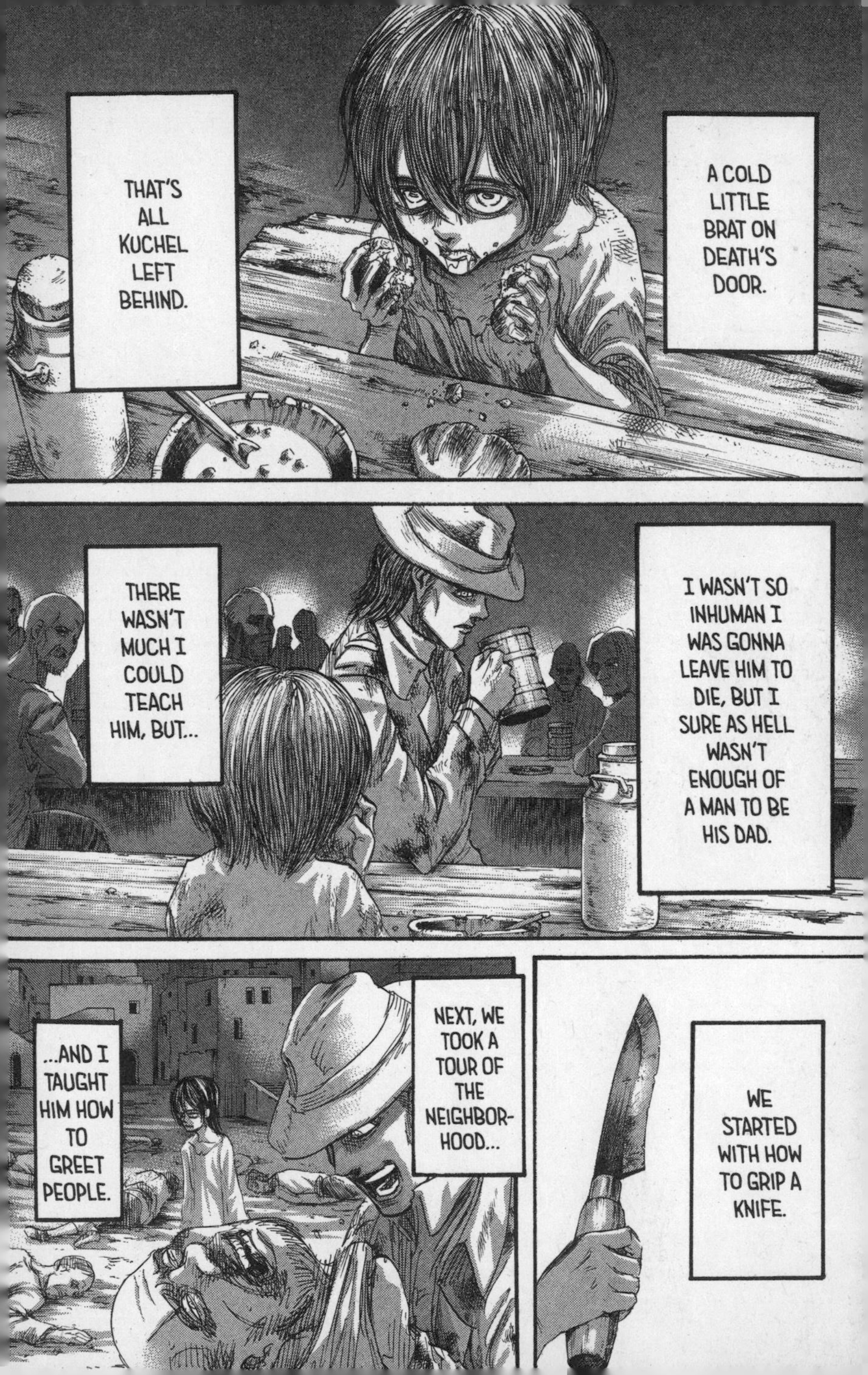
A COLD LITTLE BRAT ON DEATH'S DOOR.
THAT'S ALL KUCHEL LEFT BEHIND.
I WASN'T SO INHUMAN I WAS GONNA LEAVE HIM TO DIE, BUT I SURE AS HELL WASN'T ENOUGH OF A MAN TO BE HIS DAD.
THERE WASN'T MUCH I COULD TEACH HIM, BUT...
WE STARTED WITH HOW TO GRIP A KNIFE.
NEXT, WE TOOK A TOUR OF THE NEIGHBOR-HOOD...
...AND I TAUGHT HIM HOW TO GREET PEOPLE.

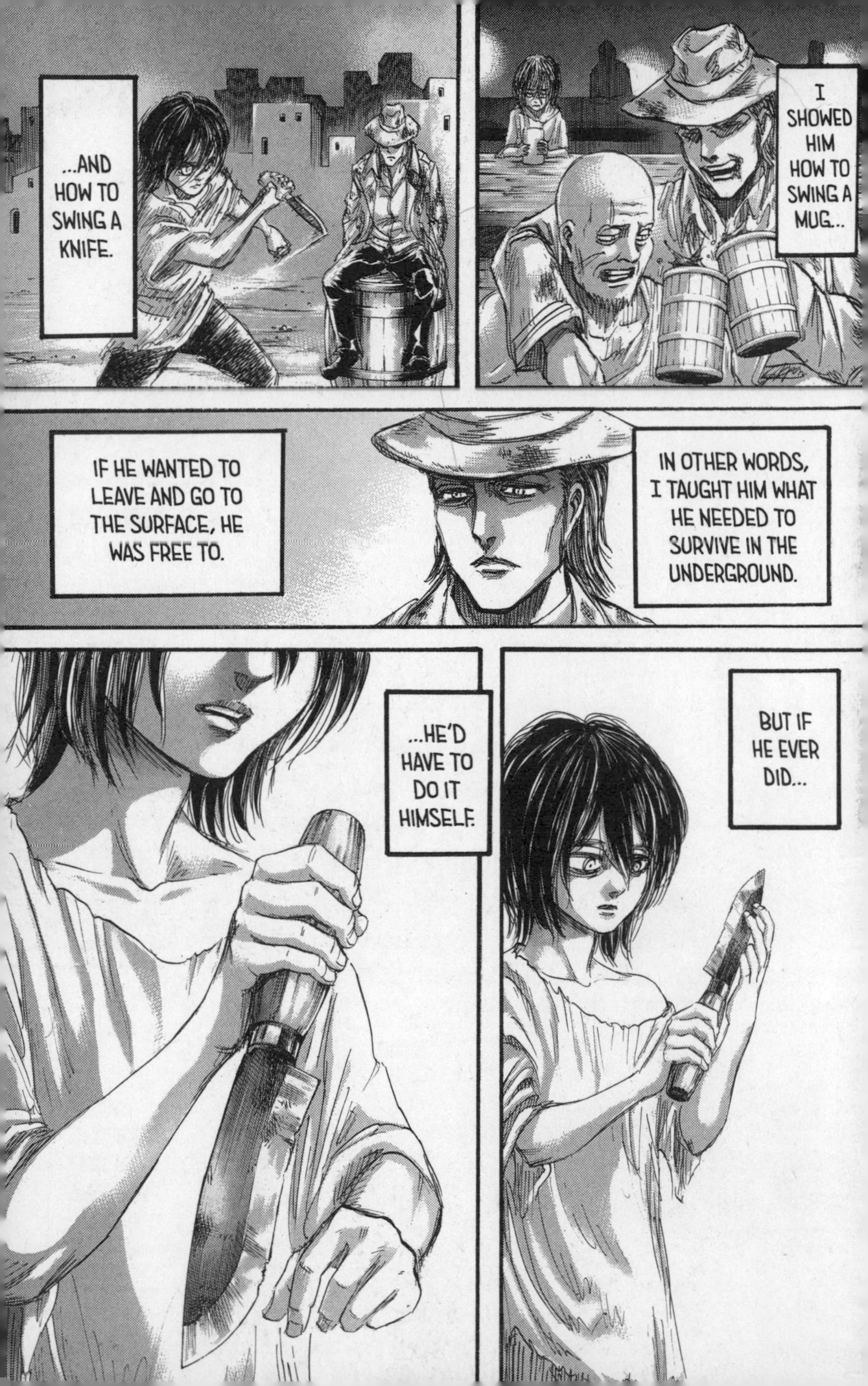
I SHOWED HIM HOW TO SWING A MUG...
...AND HOW TO SWING A KNIFE.
IN OTHER WORDS, I TAUGHT HIM WHAT HE NEEDED TO SURVIVE IN THE UNDERGROUND.
IF HE WANTED TO LEAVE AND GO TO THE SURFACE, HE WAS FREE TO.
BUT IF HE EVER DID...
...HE'D HAVE TO DO IT HIMSELF.

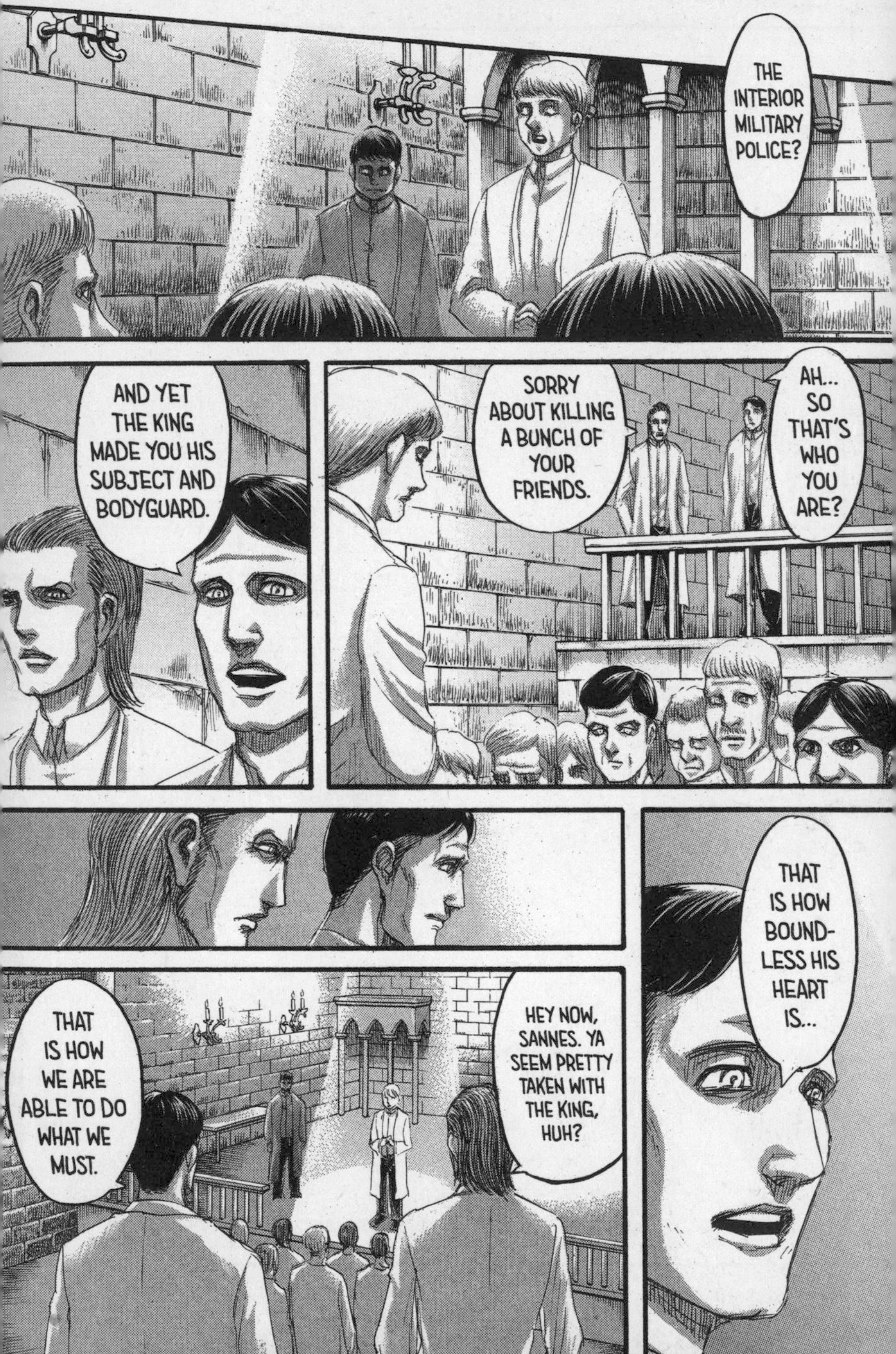
THE INTERIOR MILITARY POLICE?
AH... SO THAT'S WHO YOU ARE?
SORRY ABOUT KILLING A BUNCH OF YOUR FRIENDS.
AND YET THE KING MADE YOU HIS SUBJECT AND BODYGUARD.
THAT IS HOW BOUND-LESS HIS HEART IS...
HEY NOW, SANNES. YA SEEM PRETTY TAKEN WITH THE KING, HUH?
THAT IS HOW WE ARE ABLE TO DO WHAT WE MUST.

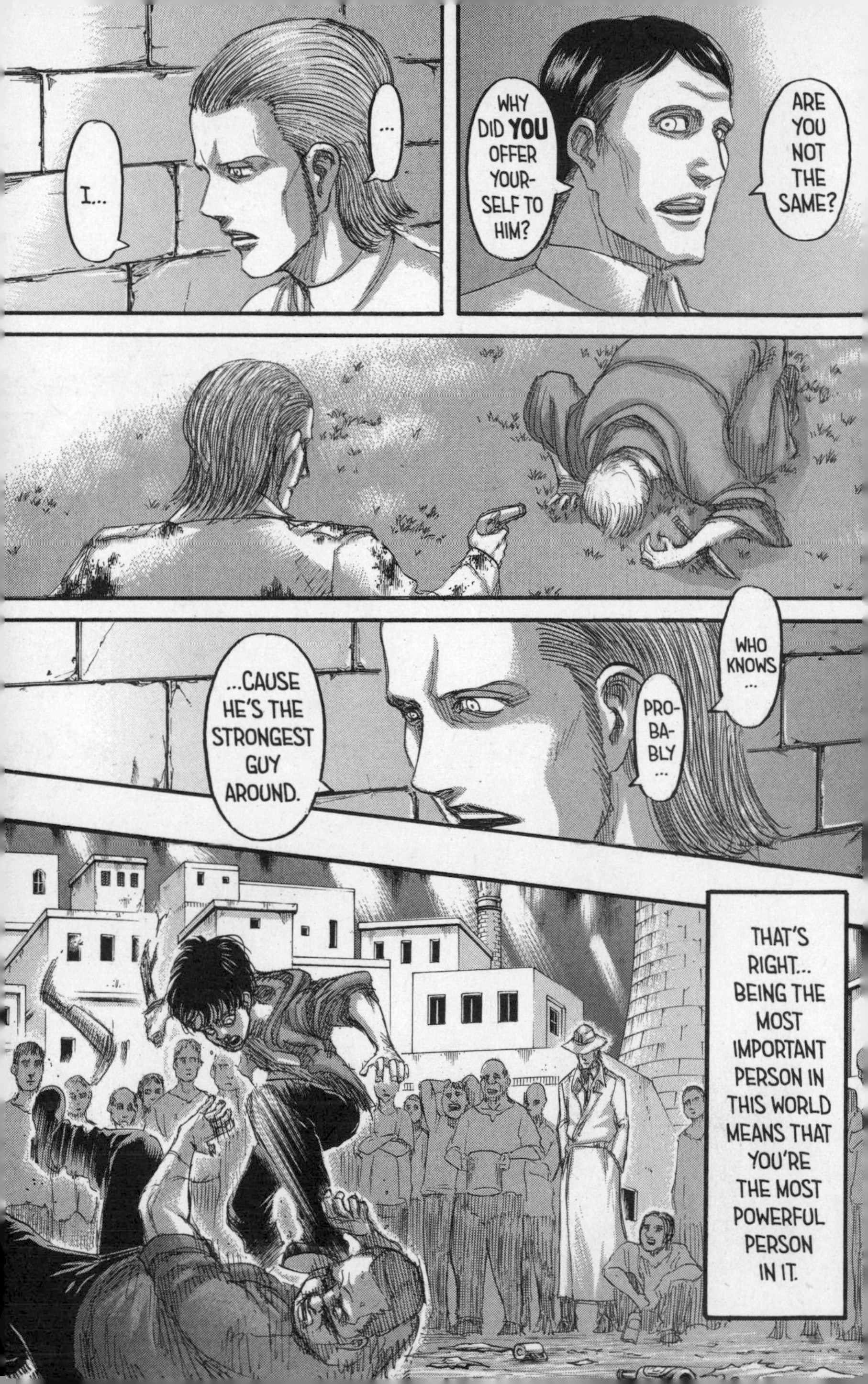
ARE YOU NOT THE SAME?
WHY DID **YOU** OFFER YOURSELF TO HIM?
...
I...
WHO KNOWS...
PROBABLY...
...CAUSE HE'S THE STRONGEST GUY AROUND.
THAT'S RIGHT... BEING THE MOST IMPORTANT PERSON IN THIS WORLD MEANS THAT YOU'RE THE MOST POWERFUL PERSON IN IT.

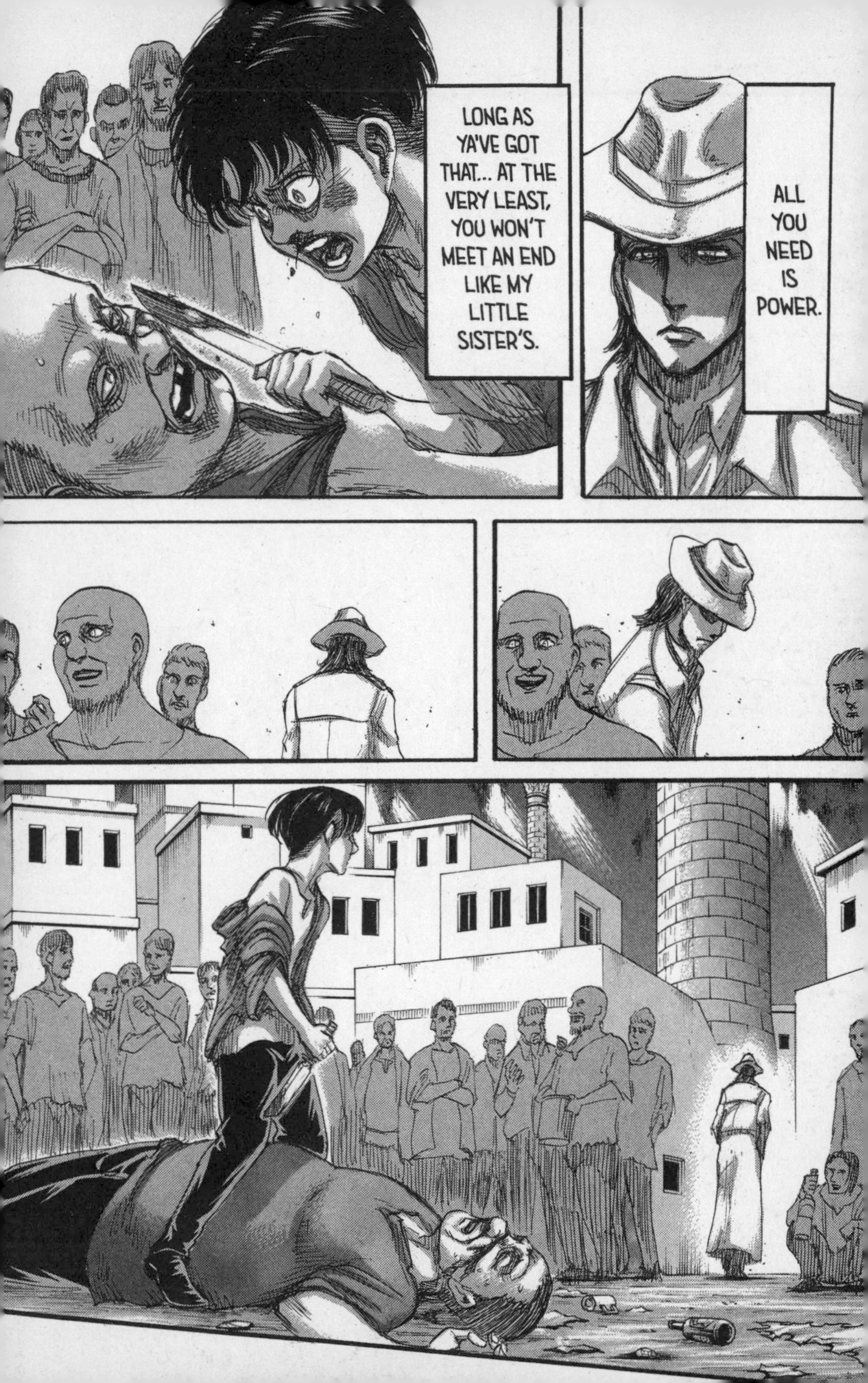
ALL YOU NEED IS POWER.
LONG AS YA'VE GOT THAT... AT THE VERY LEAST, YOU WON'T MEET AN END LIKE MY LITTLE SISTER'S.

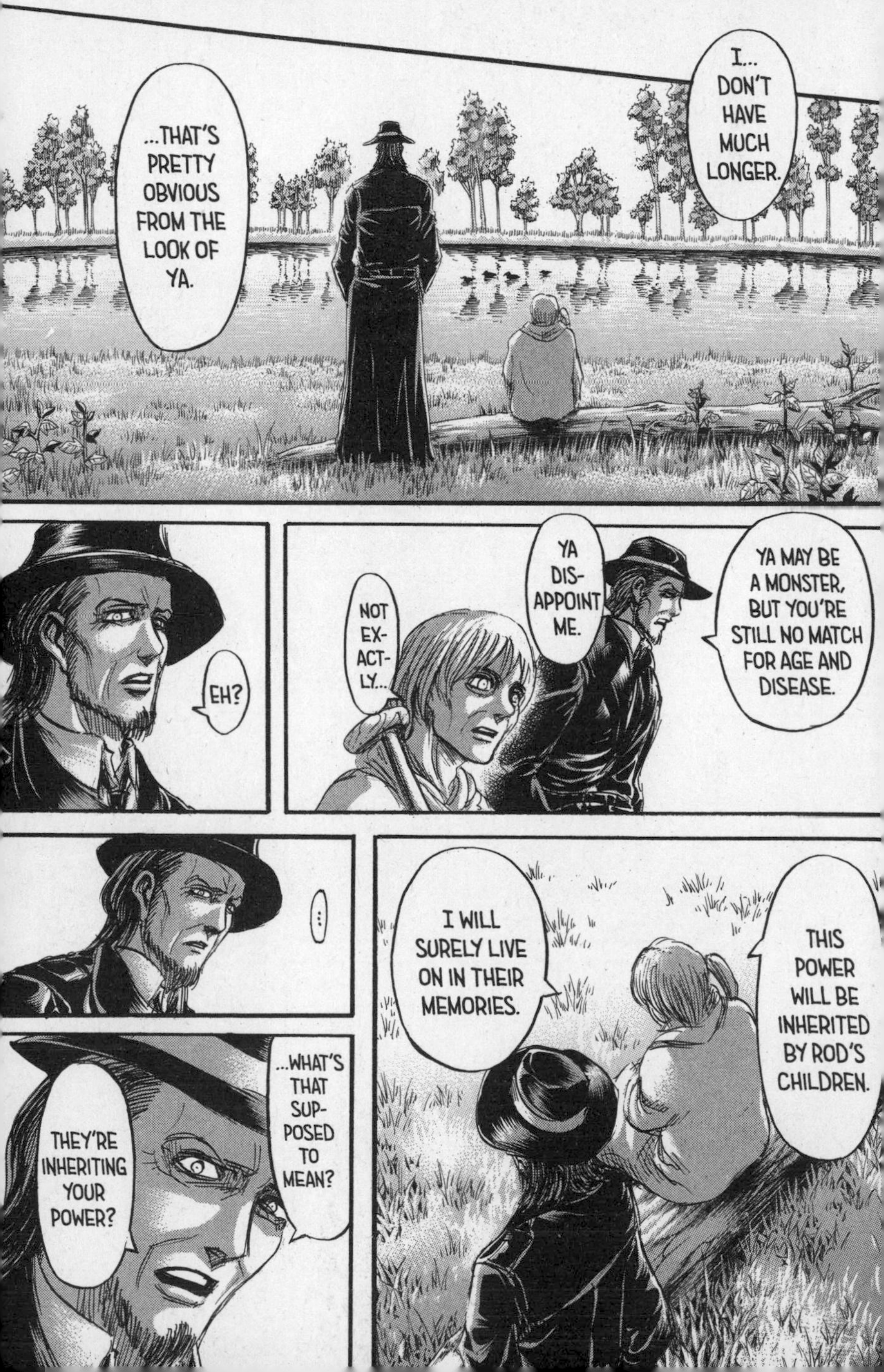
I... DON'T HAVE MUCH LONGER.
...THAT'S PRETTY OBVIOUS FROM THE LOOK OF YA.
YA MAY BE A MONSTER, BUT YOU'RE STILL NO MATCH FOR AGE AND DISEASE.
YA DIS-APPOINT ME.
NOT EX-ACT-LY...
EH?
THIS POWER WILL BE INHERITED BY ROD'S CHILDREN.
I WILL SURELY LIVE ON IN THEIR MEMORIES.
...
...WHAT'S THAT SUP-POSED TO MEAN?
THEY'RE INHERITING YOUR POWER?

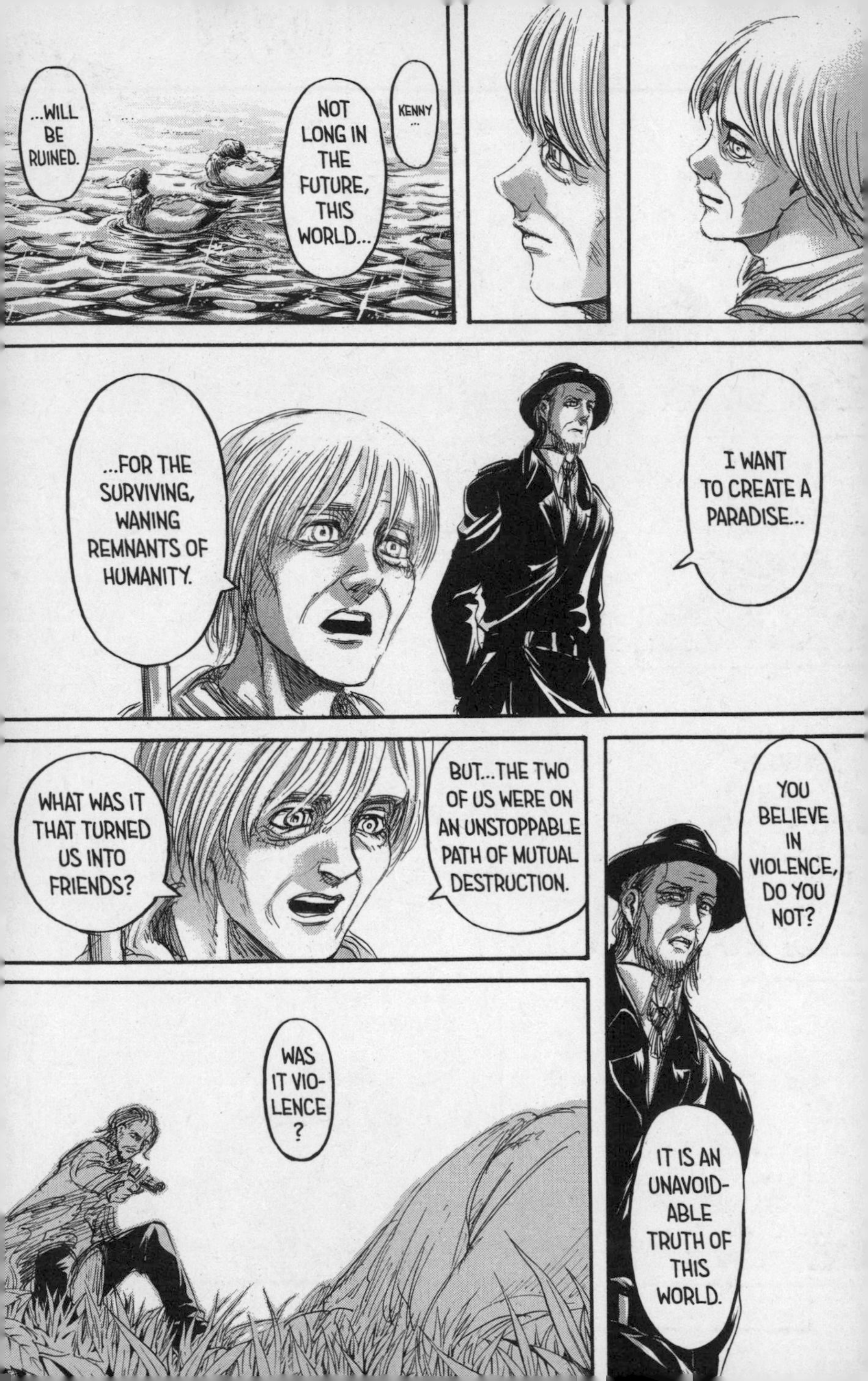
KENNY...
NOT LONG IN THE FUTURE, THIS WORLD...
...WILL BE RUINED.
I WANT TO CREATE A PARADISE...
...FOR THE SURVIVING, WANING REMNANTS OF HUMANITY.
YOU BELIEVE IN VIOLENCE, DO YOU NOT?
IT IS AN UNAVOIDABLE TRUTH OF THIS WORLD.
BUT...THE TWO OF US WERE ON AN UNSTOPPABLE PATH OF MUTUAL DESTRUCTION.
WHAT WAS IT THAT TURNED US INTO FRIENDS?
WAS IT VIOLENCE?

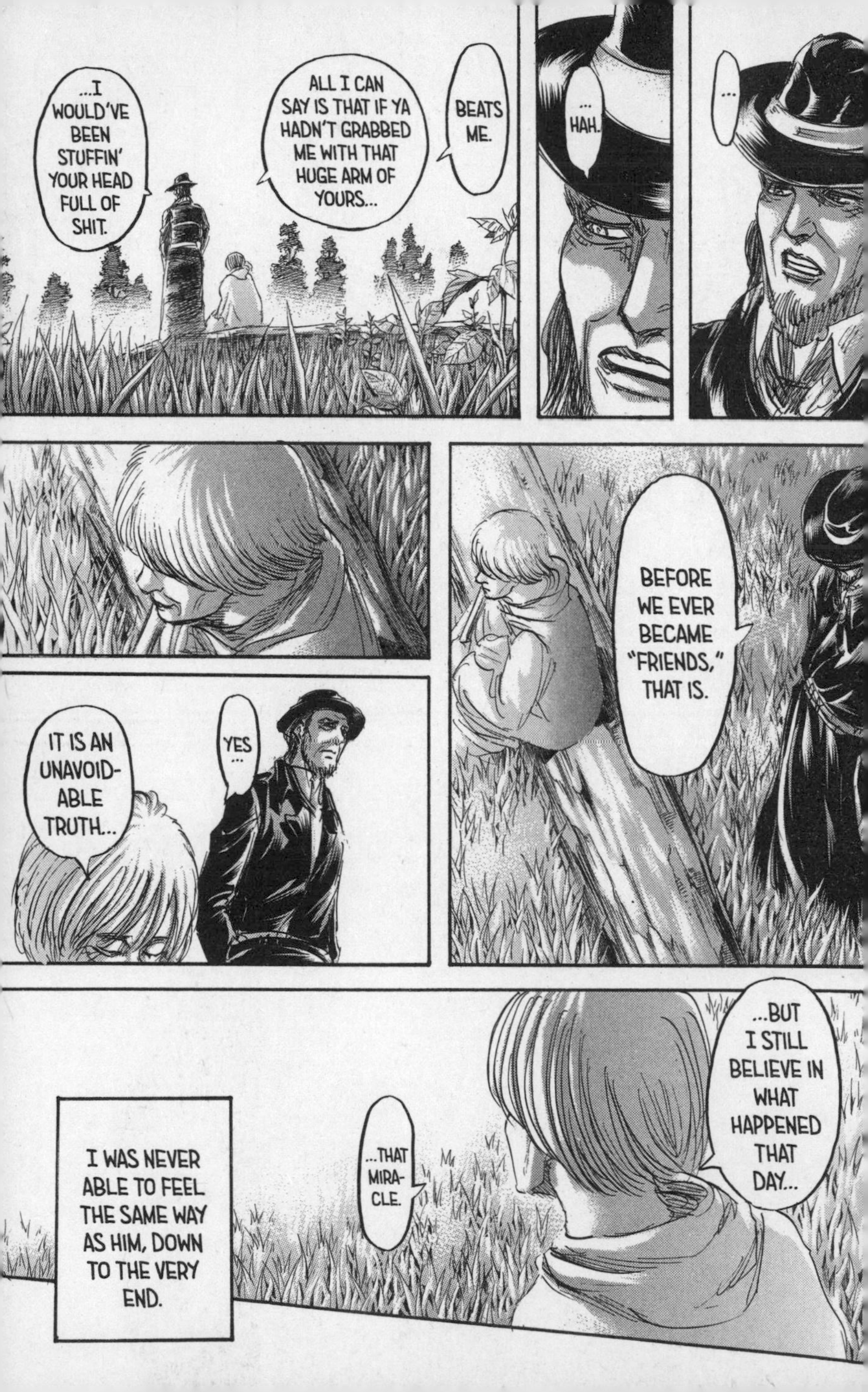
...
... HAH.
BEATS ME.
ALL I CAN SAY IS THAT IF YA HADN'T GRABBED ME WITH THAT HUGE ARM OF YOURS...
...I WOULD'VE BEEN STUFFIN' YOUR HEAD FULL OF SHIT.
BEFORE WE EVER BECAME "FRIENDS," THAT IS.
YES ...
IT IS AN UNAVOID-ABLE TRUTH...
...BUT I STILL BELIEVE IN WHAT HAPPENED THAT DAY...
...THAT MIRA-CLE.
I WAS NEVER ABLE TO FEEL THE SAME WAY AS HIM, DOWN TO THE VERY END.

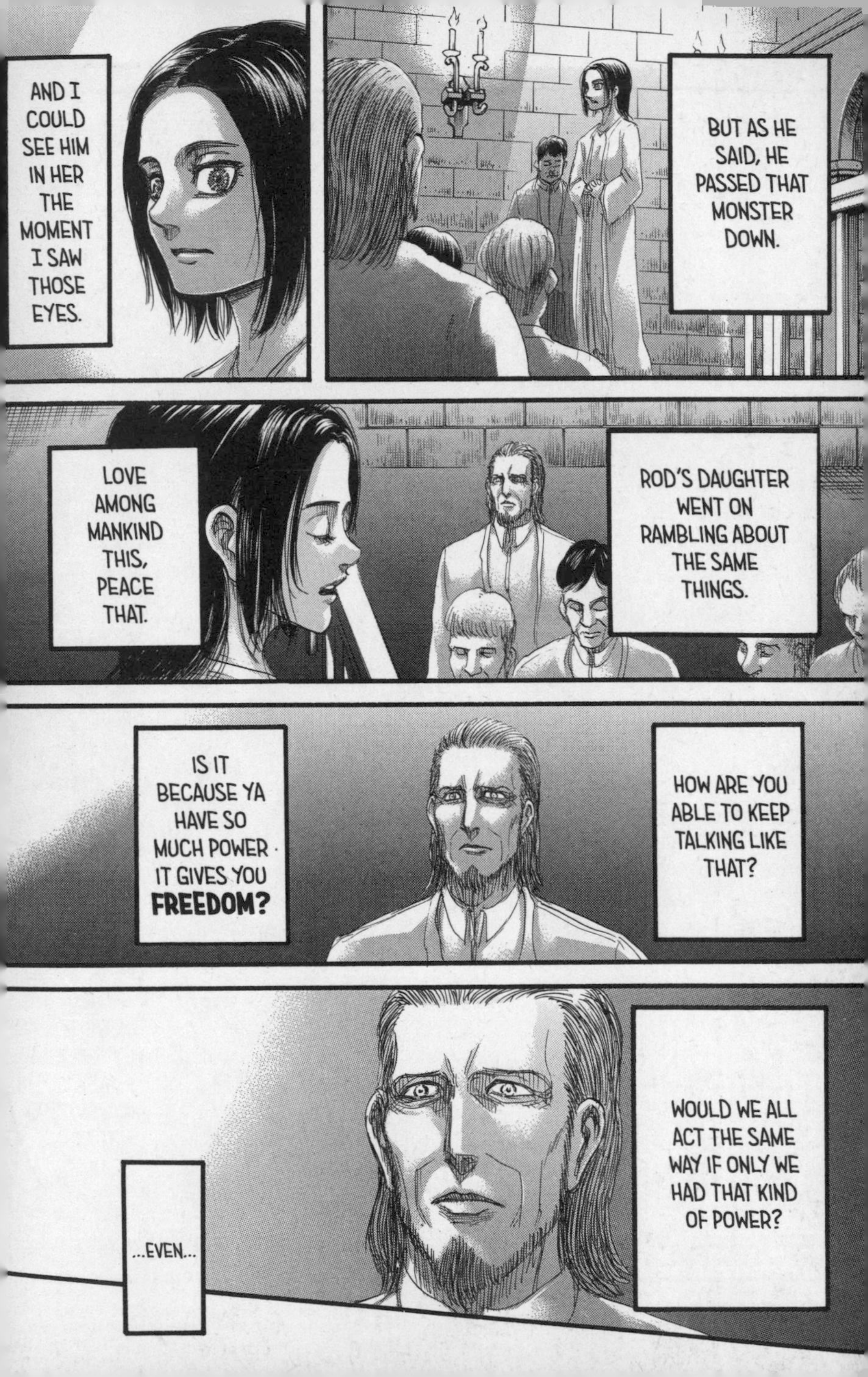
BUT AS HE SAID, HE PASSED THAT MONSTER DOWN.
AND I COULD SEE HIM IN HER THE MOMENT I SAW THOSE EYES.
ROD'S DAUGHTER WENT ON RAMBLING ABOUT THE SAME THINGS.
LOVE AMONG MANKIND THIS, PEACE THAT.
HOW ARE YOU ABLE TO KEEP TALKING LIKE THAT?
IS IT BECAUSE YA HAVE SO MUCH POWER IT GIVES YOU FREEDOM?
WOULD WE ALL ACT THE SAME WAY IF ONLY WE HAD THAT KIND OF POWER?
...EVEN...

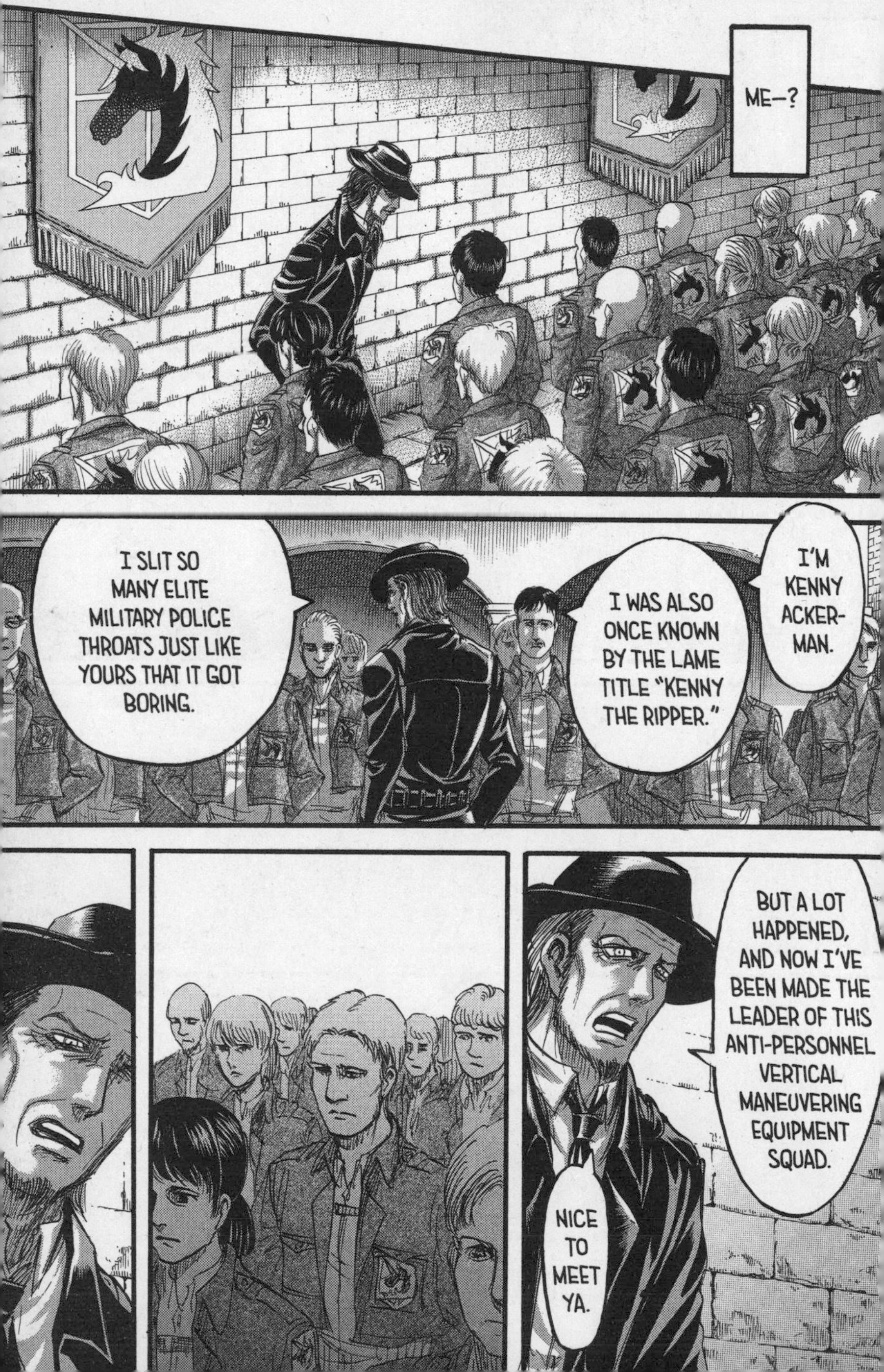
ME—?
I'M KENNY ACKER-MAN.
I WAS ALSO ONCE KNOWN BY THE LAME TITLE "KENNY THE RIPPER."
I SLIT SO MANY ELITE MILITARY POLICE THROATS JUST LIKE YOURS THAT IT GOT BORING.
BUT A LOT HAPPENED, AND NOW I'VE BEEN MADE THE LEADER OF THIS ANTI-PERSONNEL VERTICAL MANEUVERING EQUIPMENT SQUAD.
NICE TO MEET YA.

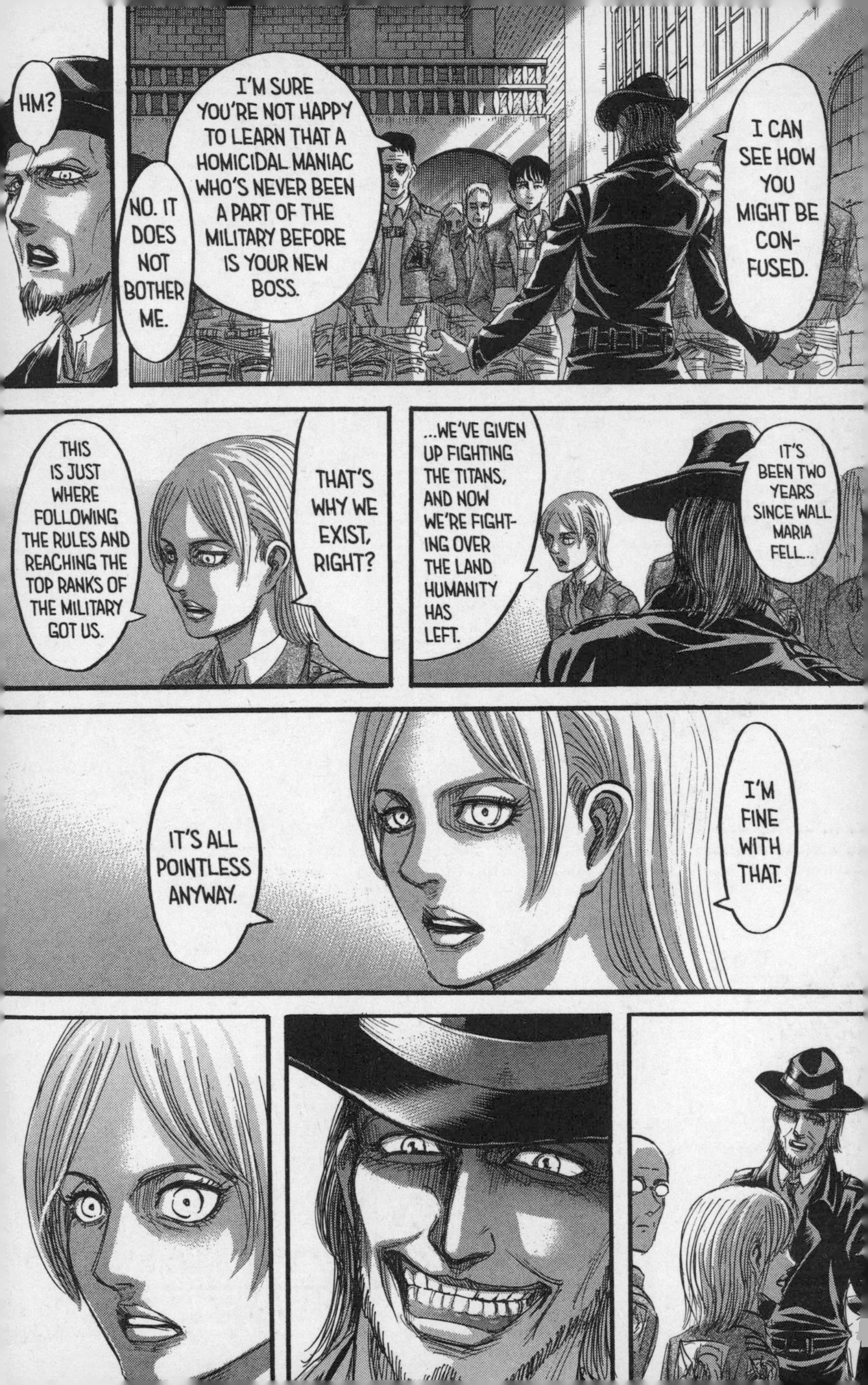
I CAN SEE HOW YOU MIGHT BE CON-FUSED.
I'M SURE YOU'RE NOT HAPPY TO LEARN THAT A HOMICIDAL MANIAC WHO'S NEVER BEEN A PART OF THE MILITARY BEFORE IS YOUR NEW BOSS.
NO. IT DOES NOT BOTHER ME.
HM?
IT'S BEEN TWO YEARS SINCE WALL MARIA FELL...
...WE'VE GIVEN UP FIGHTING THE TITANS, AND NOW WE'RE FIGHT-ING OVER THE LAND HUMANITY HAS LEFT.
THAT'S WHY WE EXIST, RIGHT?
THIS IS JUST WHERE FOLLOWING THE RULES AND REACHING THE TOP RANKS OF THE MILITARY GOT US.
I'M FINE WITH THAT.
IT'S ALL POINTLESS ANYWAY.

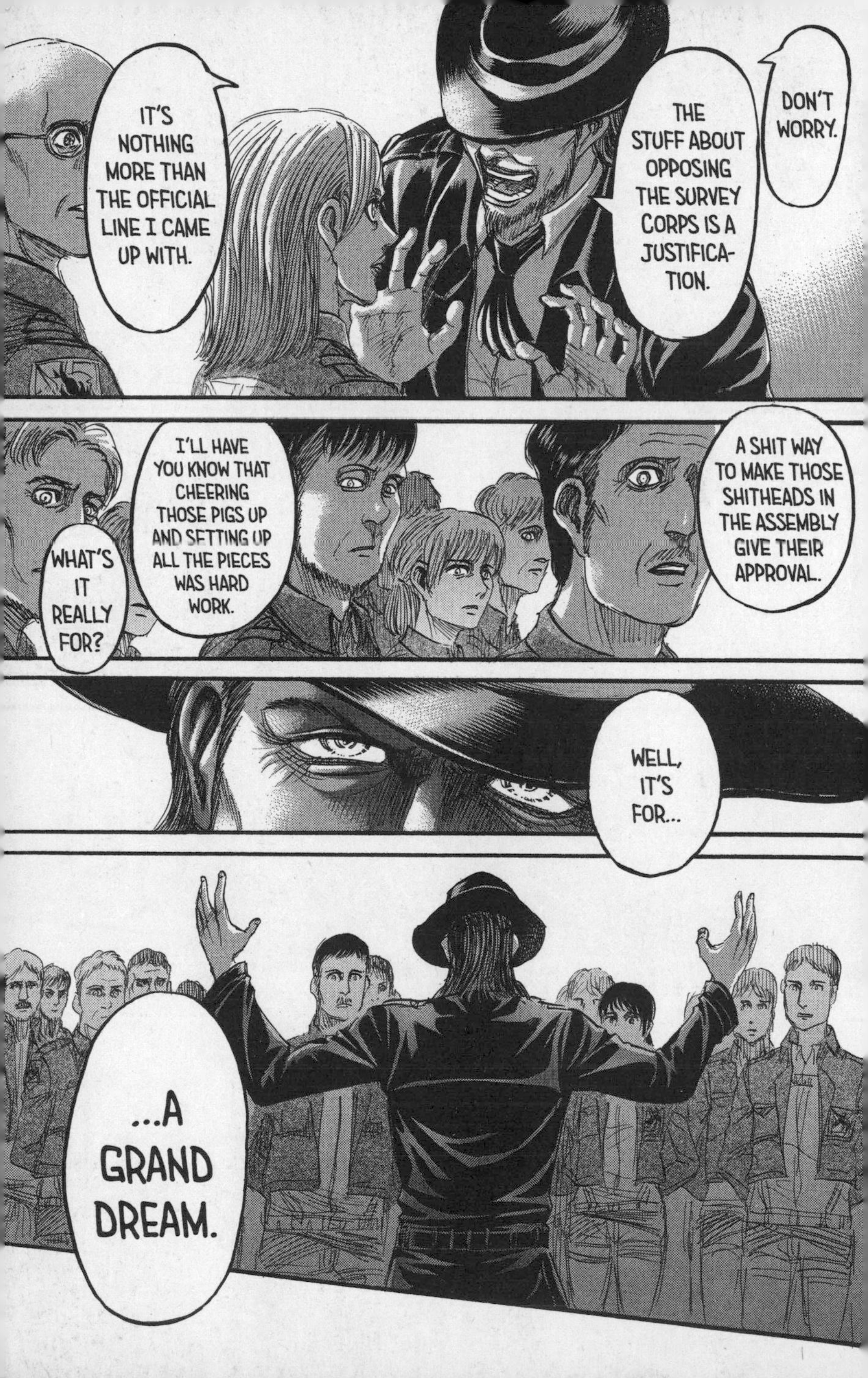
DON'T WORRY.
THE STUFF ABOUT OPPOSING THE SURVEY CORPS IS A JUSTIFICATION.
IT'S NOTHING MORE THAN THE OFFICIAL LINE I CAME UP WITH.
A SHIT WAY TO MAKE THOSE SHITHEADS IN THE ASSEMBLY GIVE THEIR APPROVAL.
I'LL HAVE YOU KNOW THAT CHEERING THOSE PIGS UP AND SETTING UP ALL THE PIECES WAS HARD WORK.
WHAT'S IT REALLY FOR?
WELL, IT'S FOR...
...A GRAND DREAM.

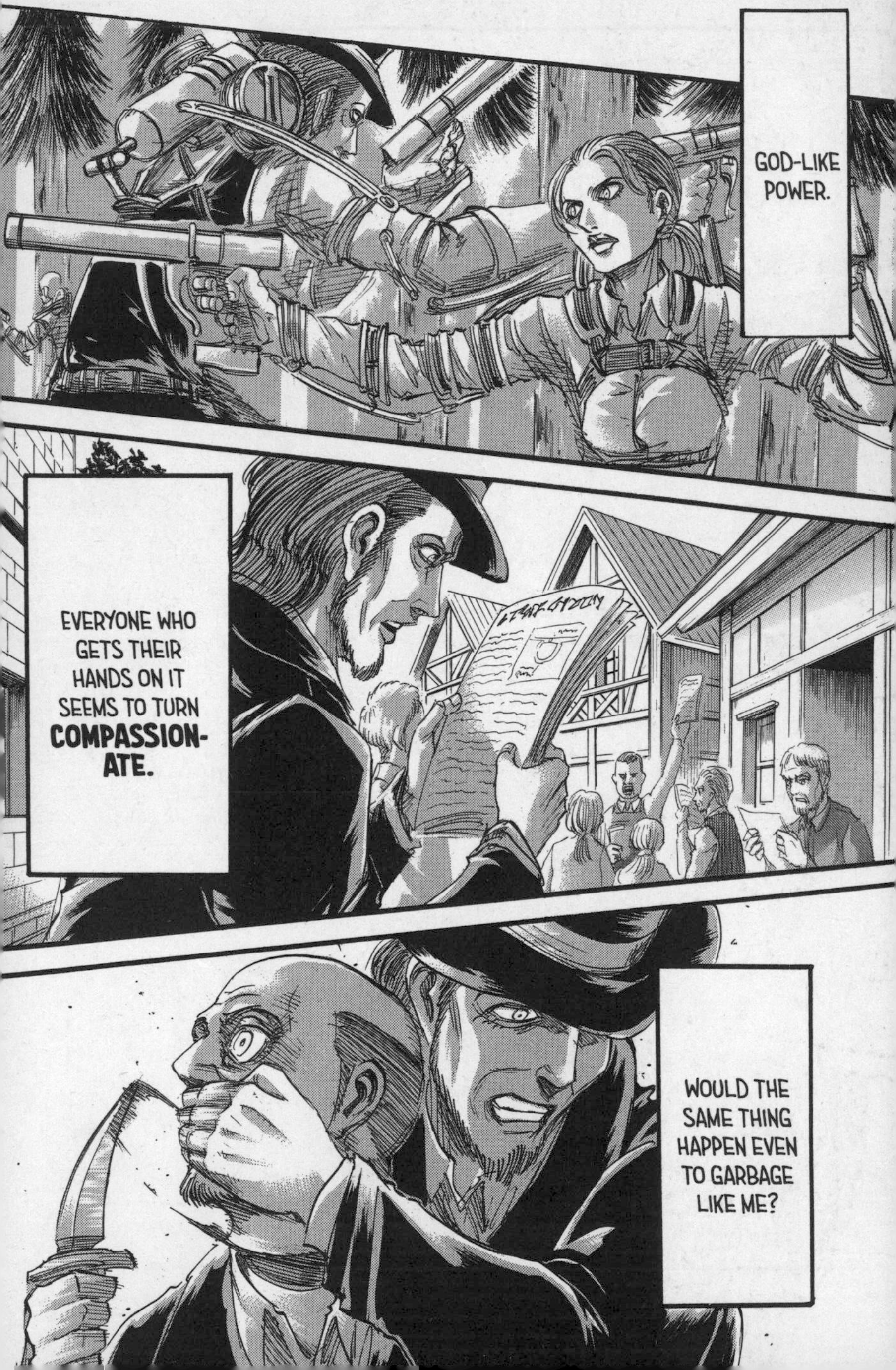
GOD-LIKE POWER.
EVERYONE WHO GETS THEIR HANDS ON IT SEEMS TO TURN **COMPASSION-ATE.**
WOULD THE SAME THING HAPPEN EVEN TO GARBAGE LIKE ME?

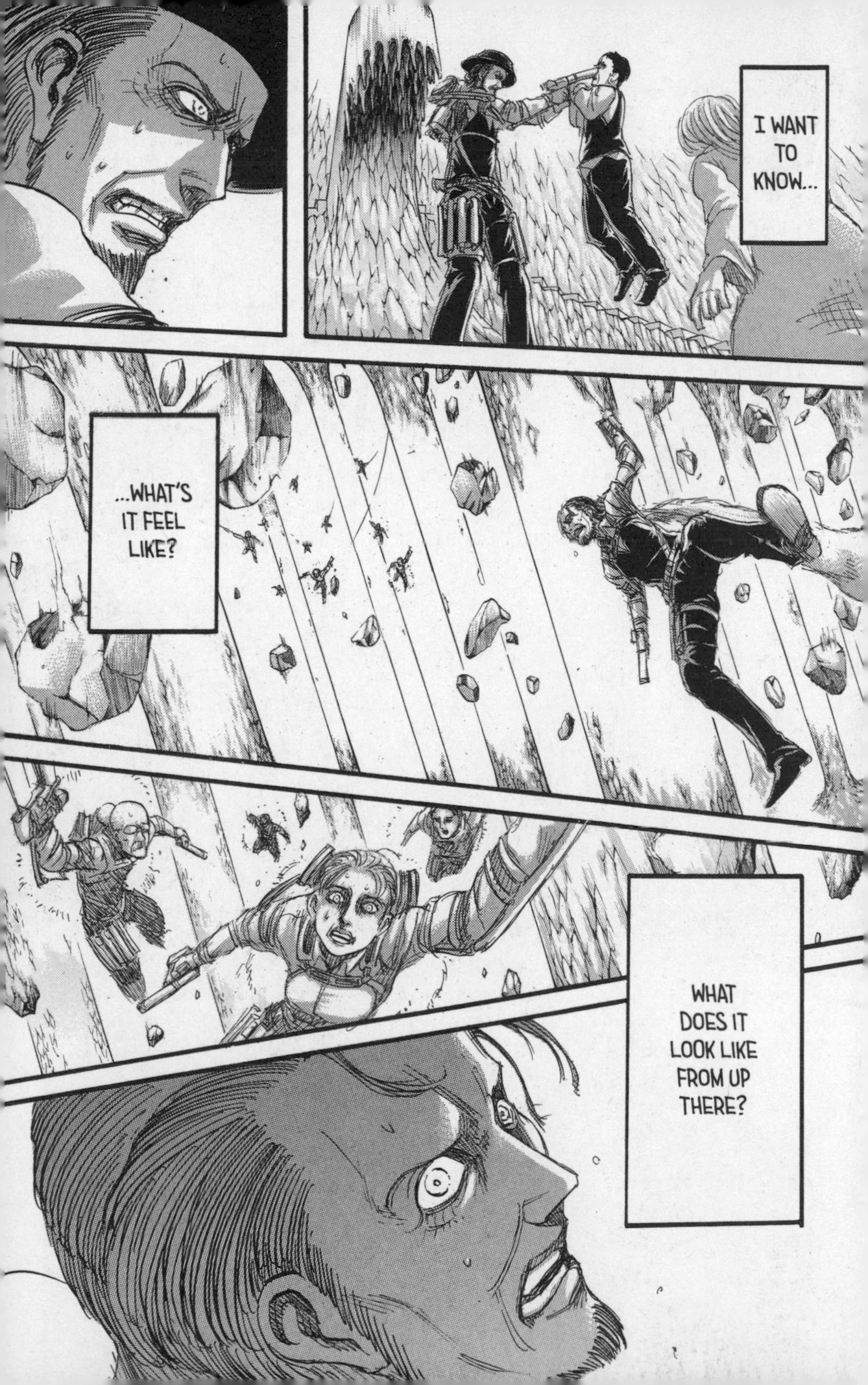
I WANT TO KNOW...
...WHAT'S IT FEEL LIKE?
WHAT DOES IT LOOK LIKE FROM UP THERE?

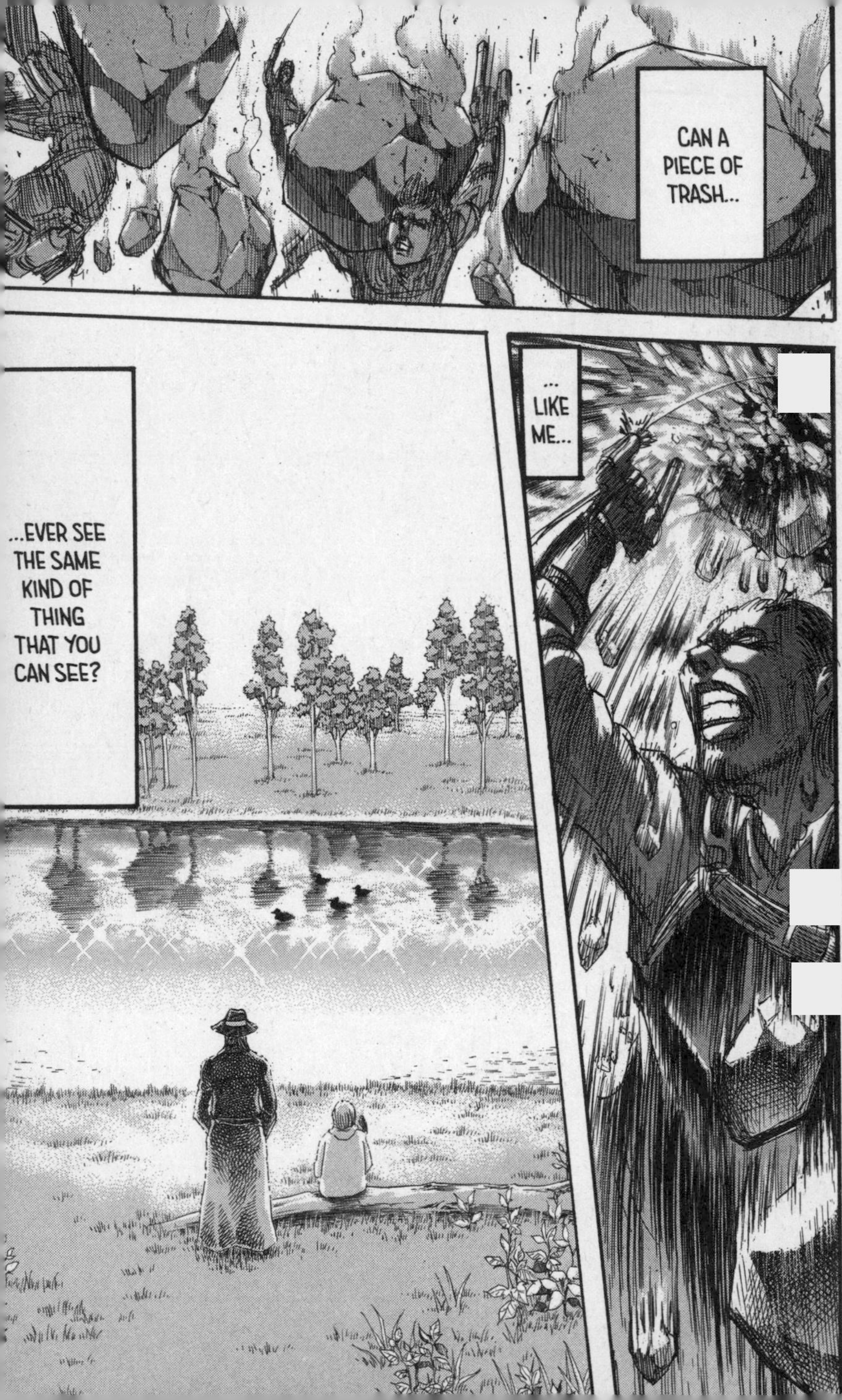
CAN A PIECE OF TRASH...
...LIKE ME...
...EVER SEE THE SAME KIND OF THING THAT YOU CAN SEE?

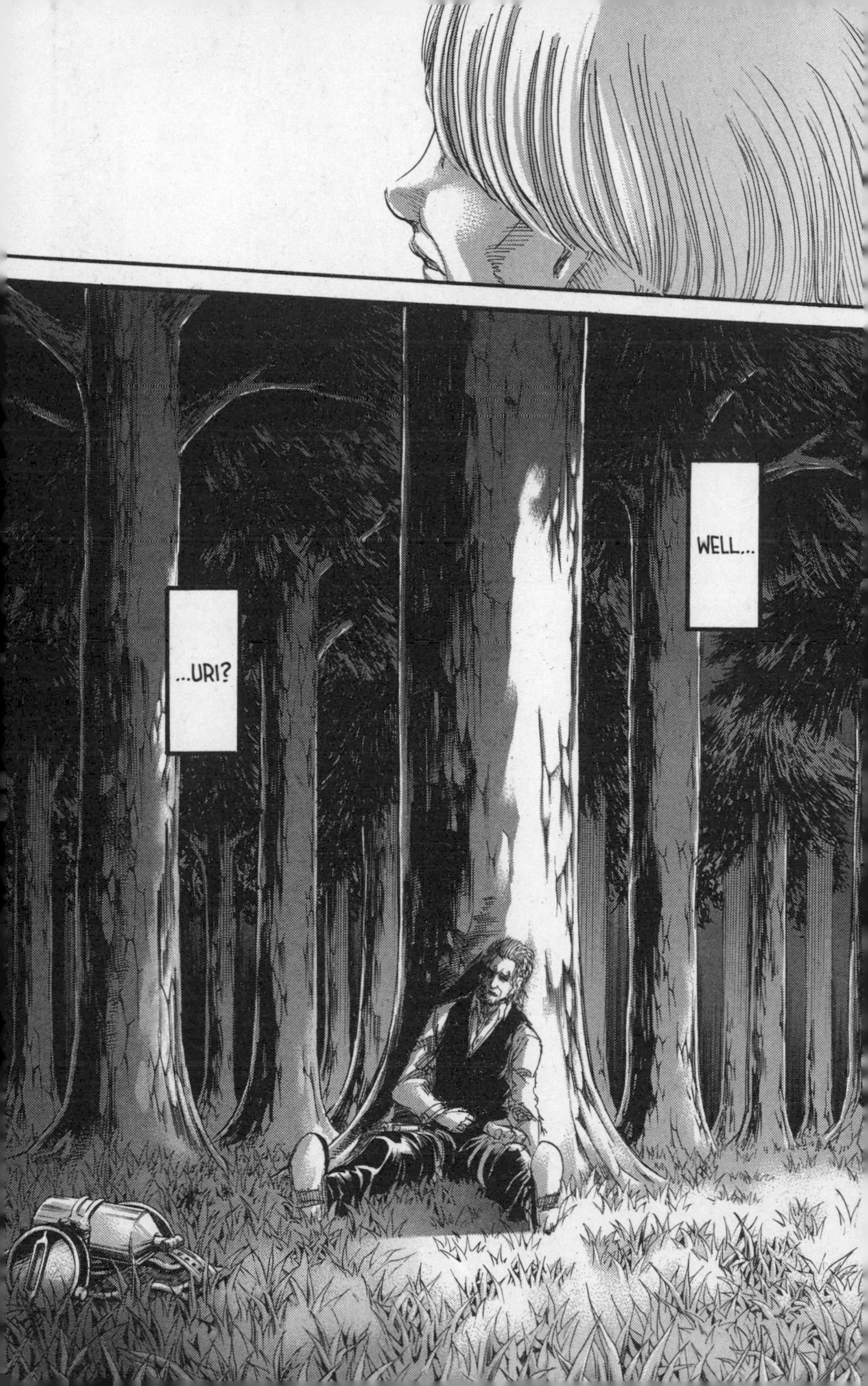
WELL...
...URI?

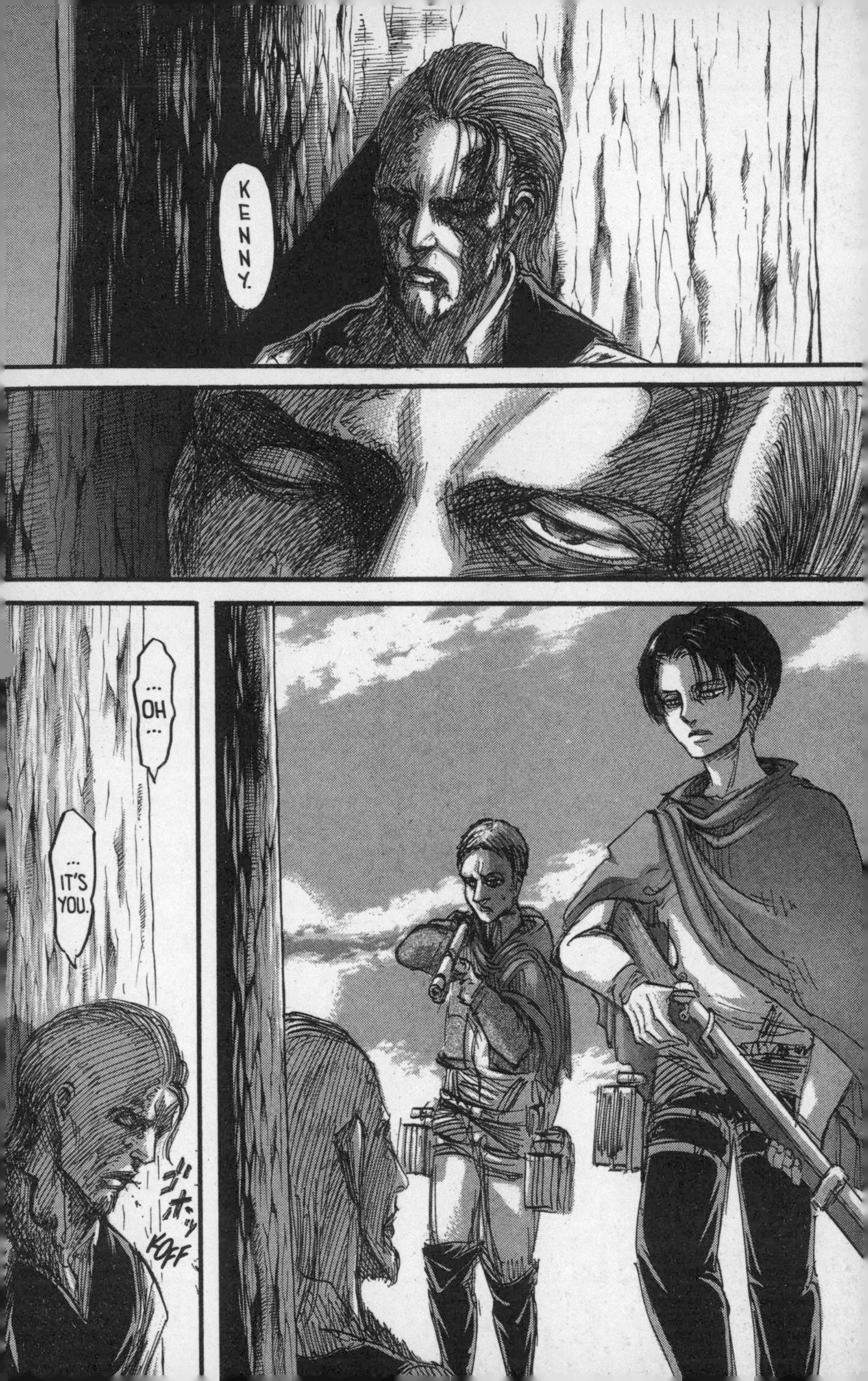
KENNY.
...OH...
...IT'S YOU.
KOFF

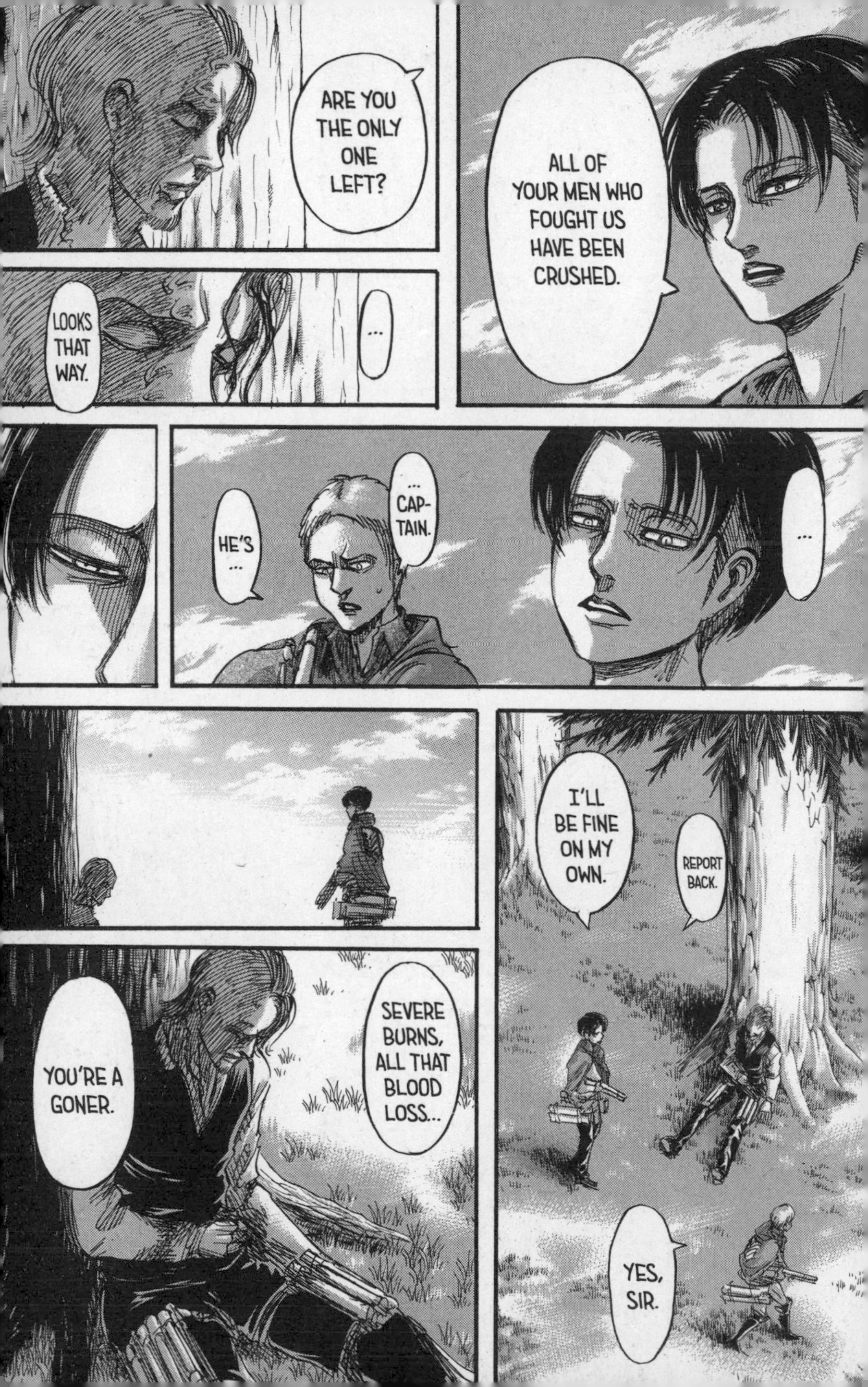
ALL OF YOUR MEN WHO FOUGHT US HAVE BEEN CRUSHED.
ARE YOU THE ONLY ONE LEFT?
...
LOOKS THAT WAY.
...
... CAP-TAIN.
HE'S ...
I'LL BE FINE ON MY OWN.
REPORT BACK.
YES, SIR.
SEVERE BURNS, ALL THAT BLOOD LOSS...
YOU'RE A GONER.

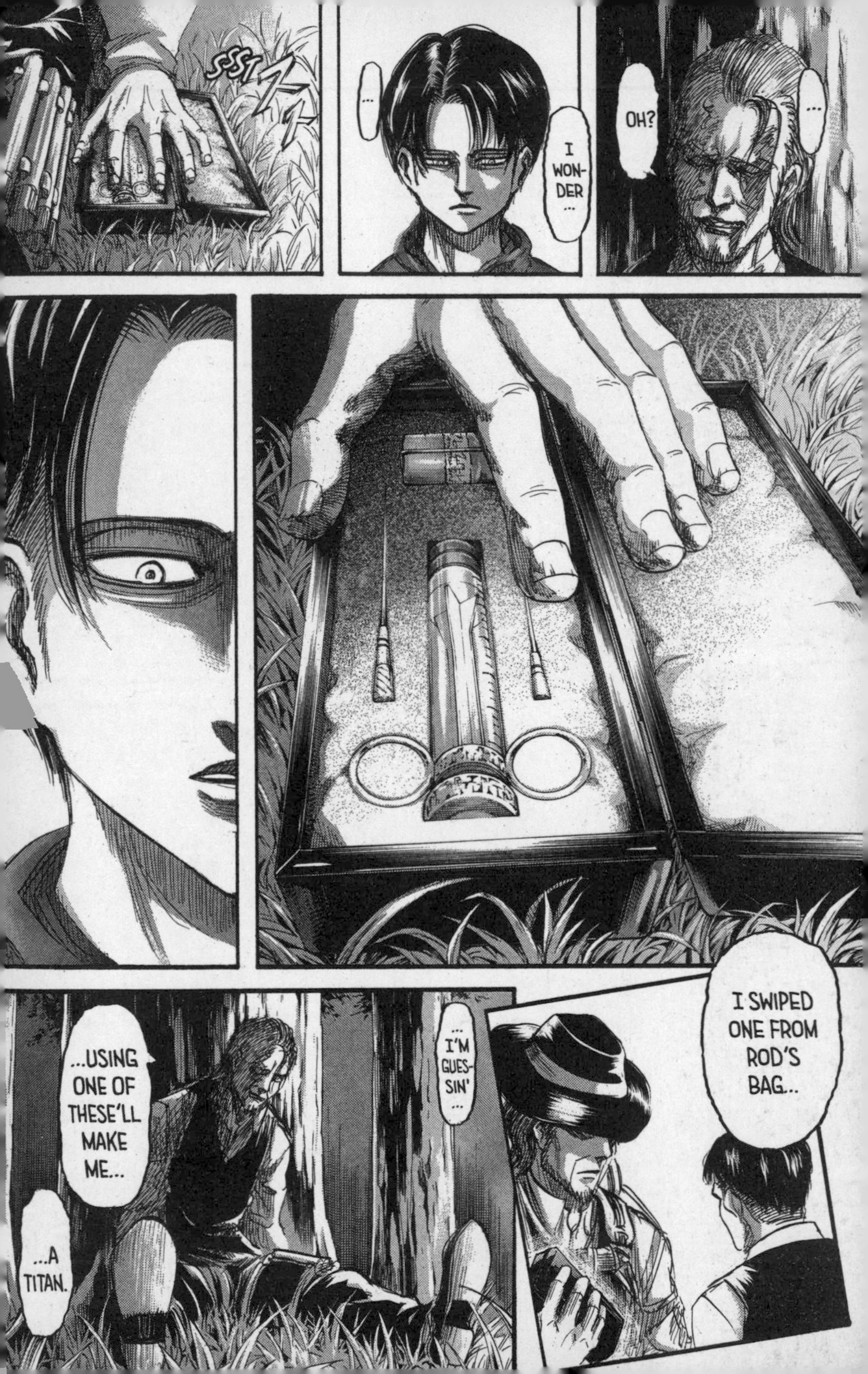

...
OH?
I WONDER...
...
SSST
I SWIPED ONE FROM ROD'S BAG...
...I'M GUESSIN'...
...USING ONE OF THESE'LL MAKE ME...
...A TITAN.

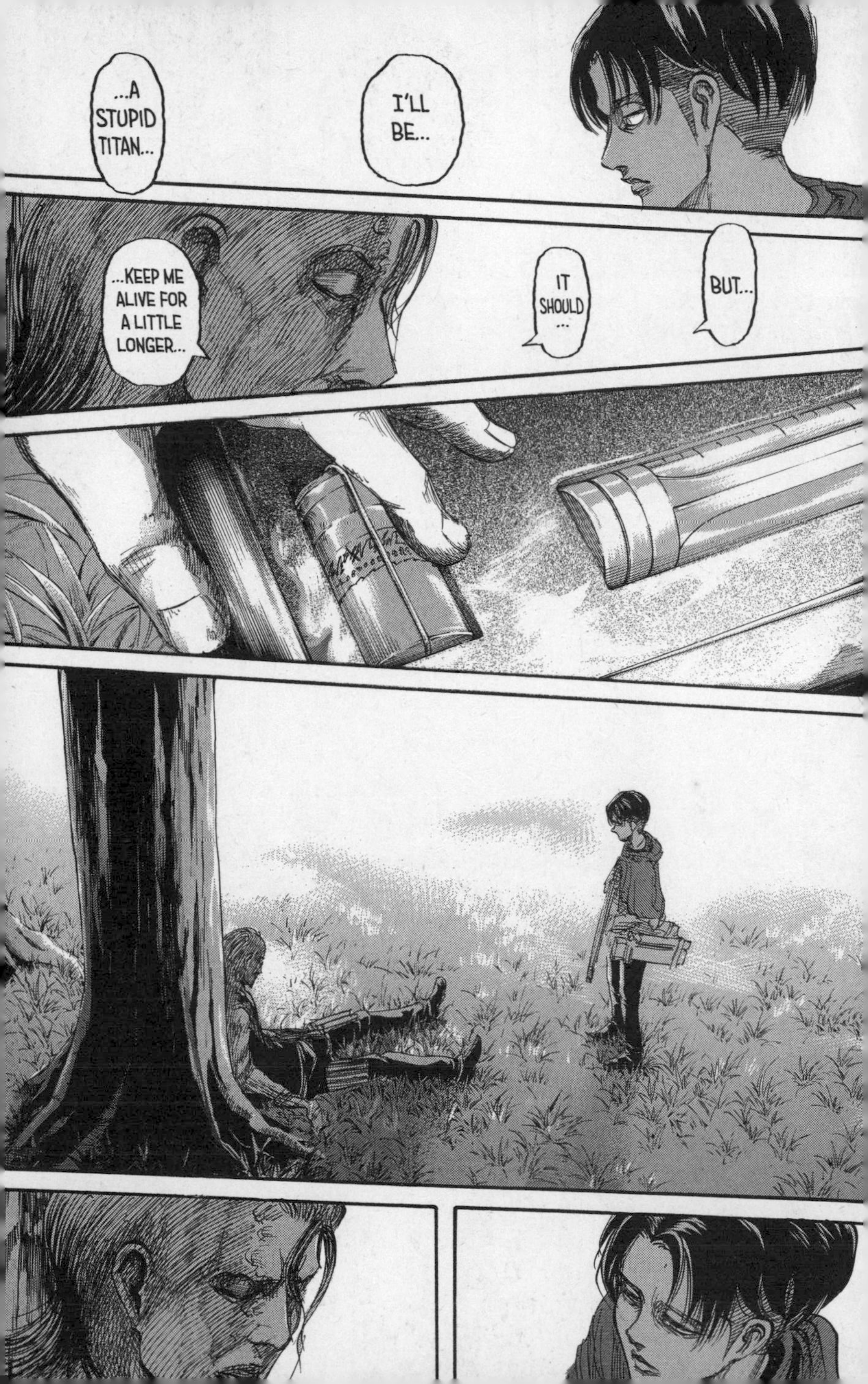
I'LL BE...
...A STUPID TITAN...
BUT...
IT SHOULD ...
...KEEP ME ALIVE FOR A LITTLE LONGER...

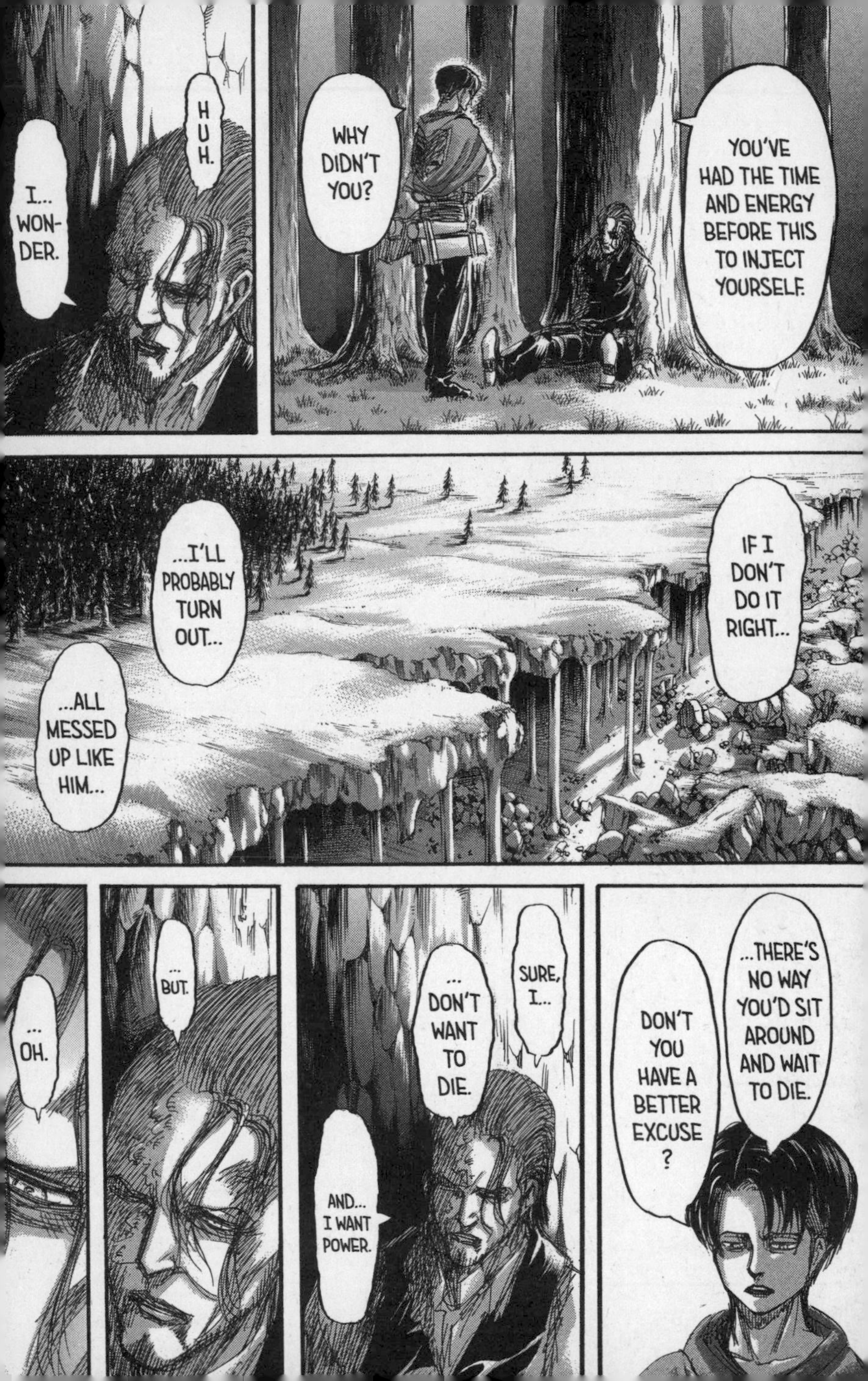
YOU'VE HAD THE TIME AND ENERGY BEFORE THIS TO INJECT YOURSELF.
WHY DIDN'T YOU?
HUH.
I... WONDER.
IF I DON'T DO IT RIGHT...
...I'LL PROBABLY TURN OUT...
...ALL MESSED UP LIKE HIM...
...THERE'S NO WAY YOU'D SIT AROUND AND WAIT TO DIE.
DON'T YOU HAVE A BETTER EXCUSE?
SURE, I...
... DON'T WANT TO DIE.
AND... I WANT POWER.
... BUT.
... OH.

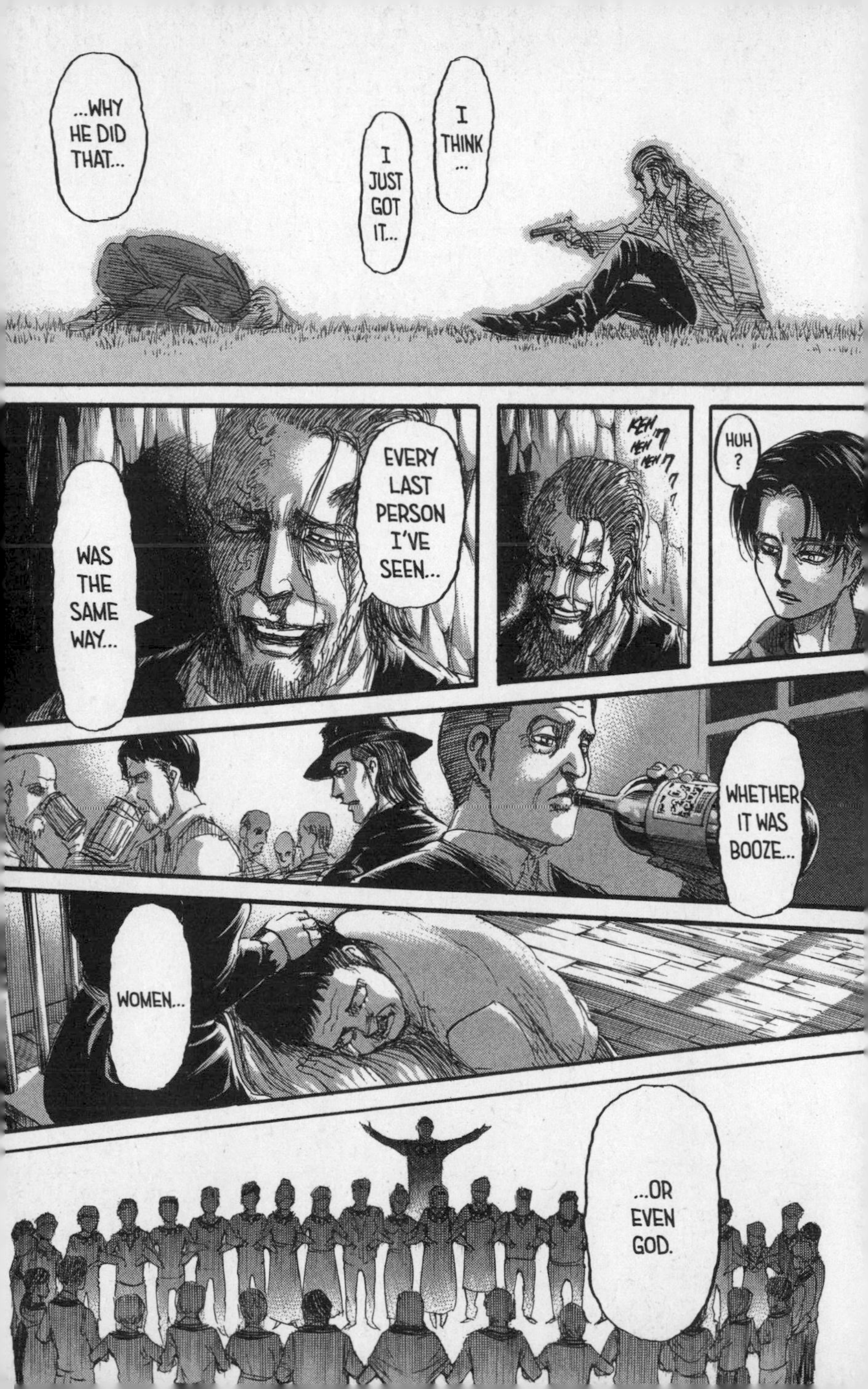
I THINK...
I JUST GOT IT...
...WHY HE DID THAT...
HUH?
KEH KEH KEH
EVERY LAST PERSON I'VE SEEN...
WAS THE SAME WAY...
WHETHER IT WAS BOOZE...
WOMEN...
...OR EVEN GOD.

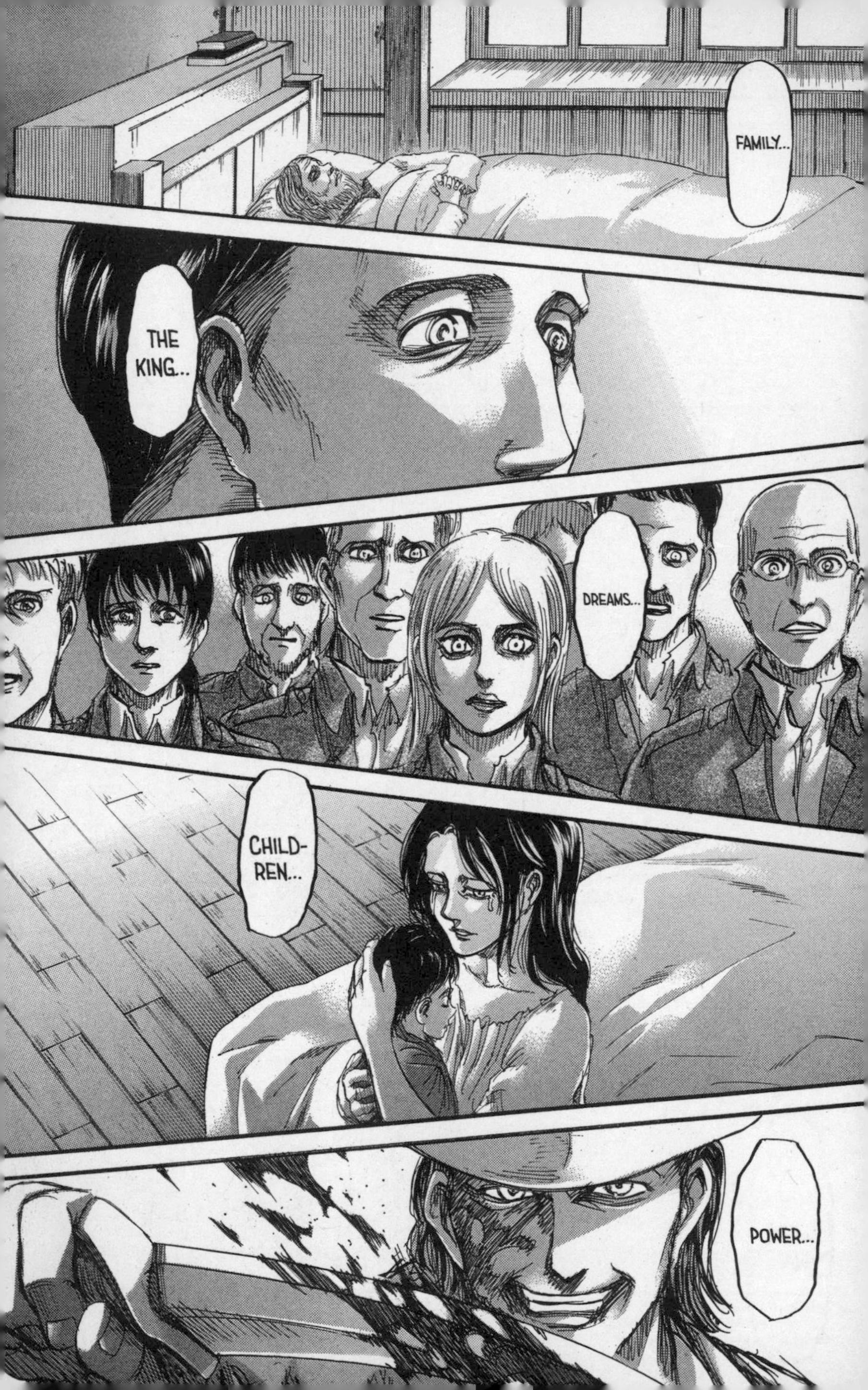
FAMILY...
THE KING...
DREAMS...
CHILD-REN...
POWER...

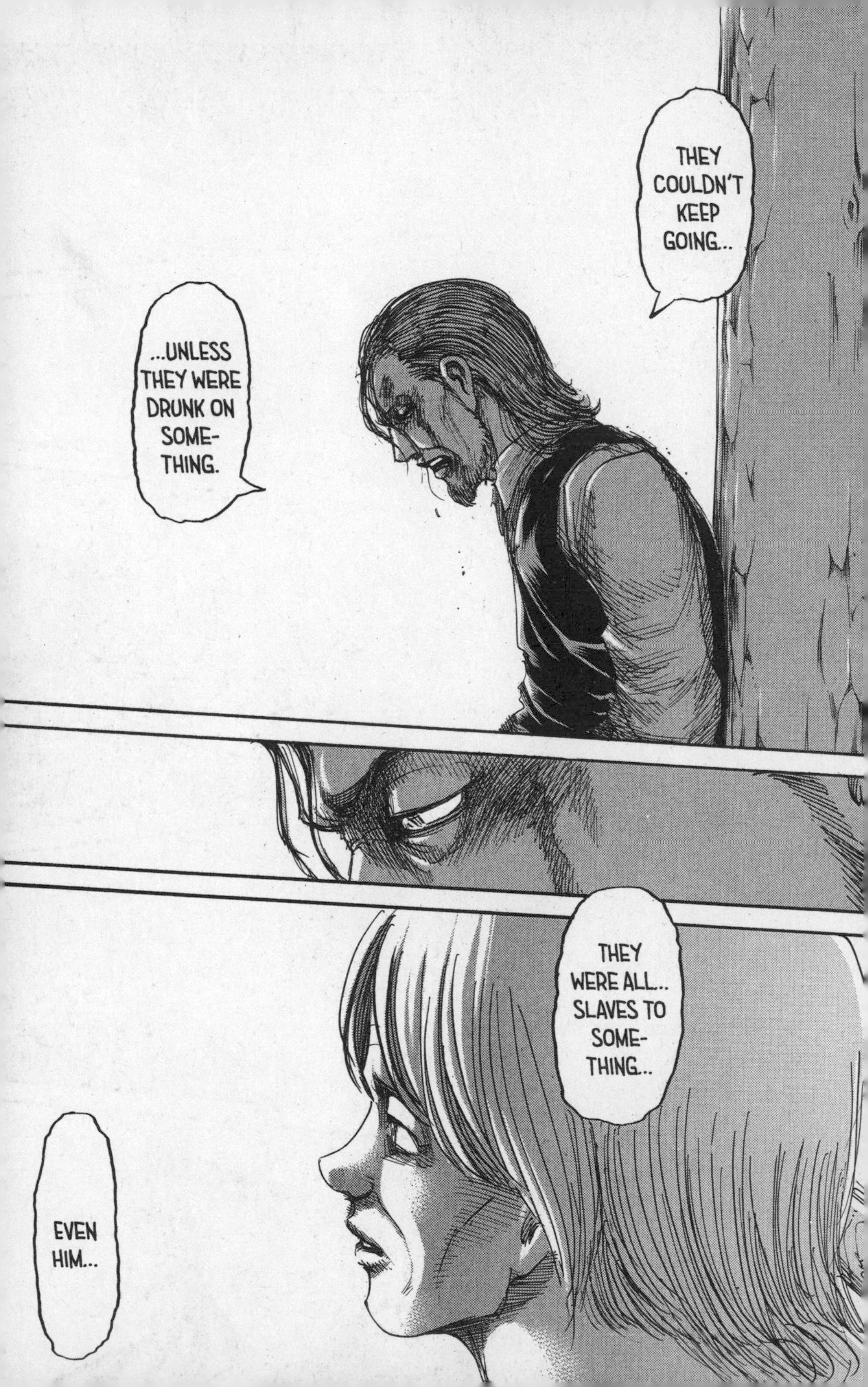
THEY COULDN'T KEEP GOING...
...UNLESS THEY WERE DRUNK ON SOME-THING.
THEY WERE ALL... SLAVES TO SOME-THING...
EVEN HIM...

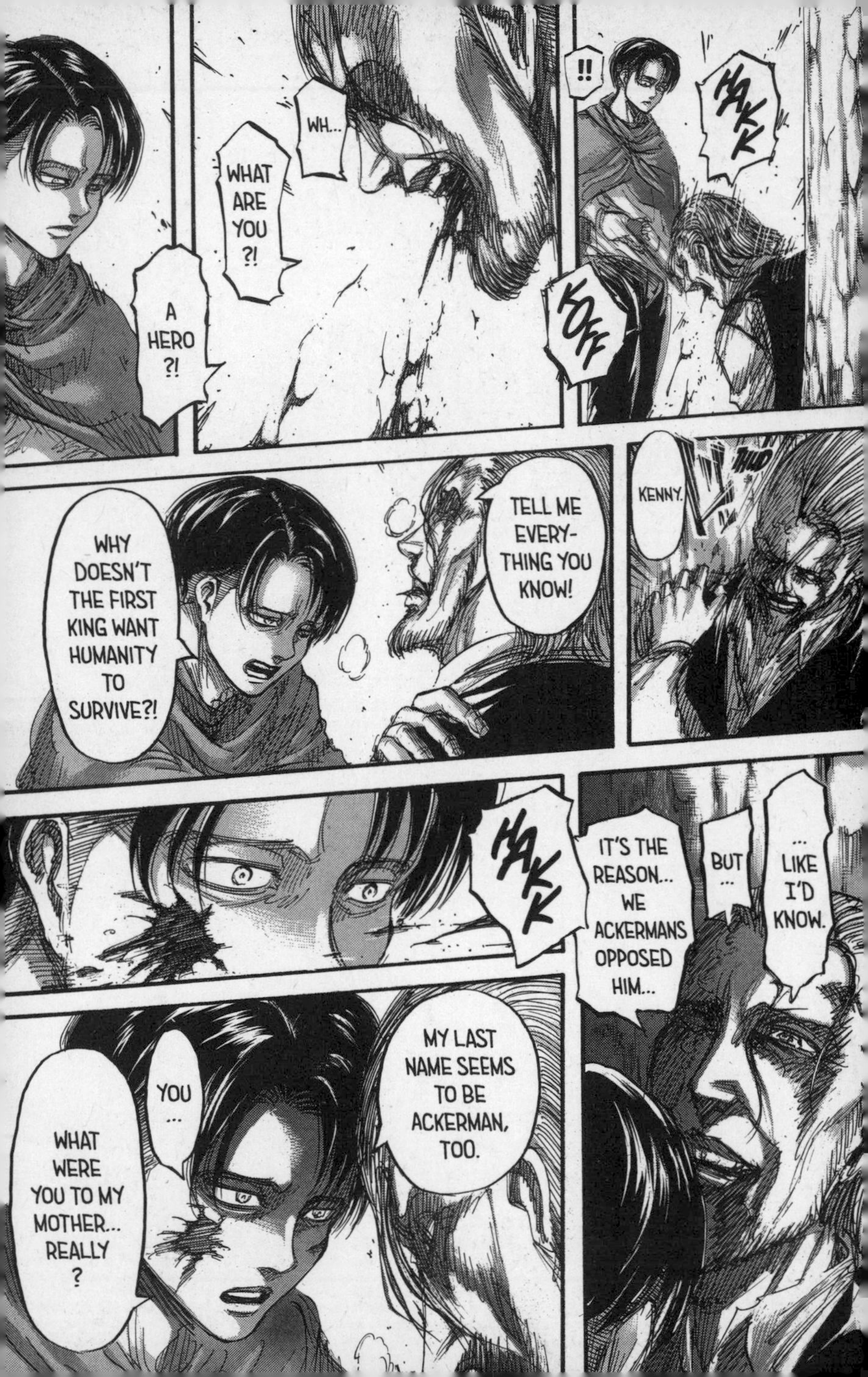
!!
HAKK
KOFF
WH...
WHAT ARE YOU ?!
A HERO ?!
KENNY.
THUD
TELL ME EVERY-THING YOU KNOW!
WHY DOESN'T THE FIRST KING WANT HUMANITY TO SURVIVE?!
... LIKE I'D KNOW.
BUT ...
IT'S THE REASON... WE ACKERMANS OPPOSED HIM...
HAKK
MY LAST NAME SEEMS TO BE ACKERMAN, TOO.
YOU ...
WHAT WERE YOU TO MY MOTHER... REALLY ?

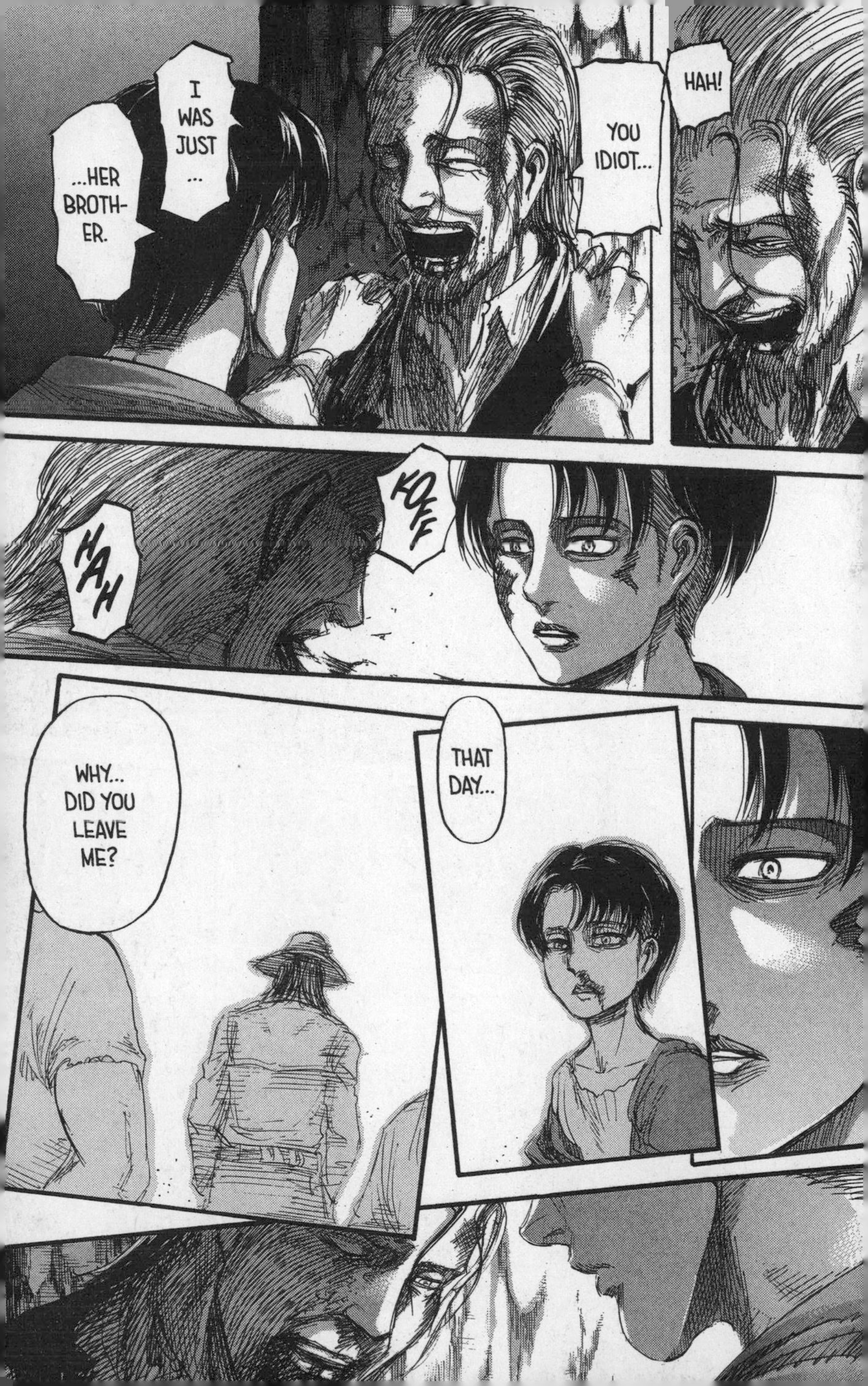
HAH!
YOU IDIOT...
I WAS JUST ...
...HER BROTH-ER.
KOFF
HAH
THAT DAY...
WHY... DID YOU LEAVE ME?

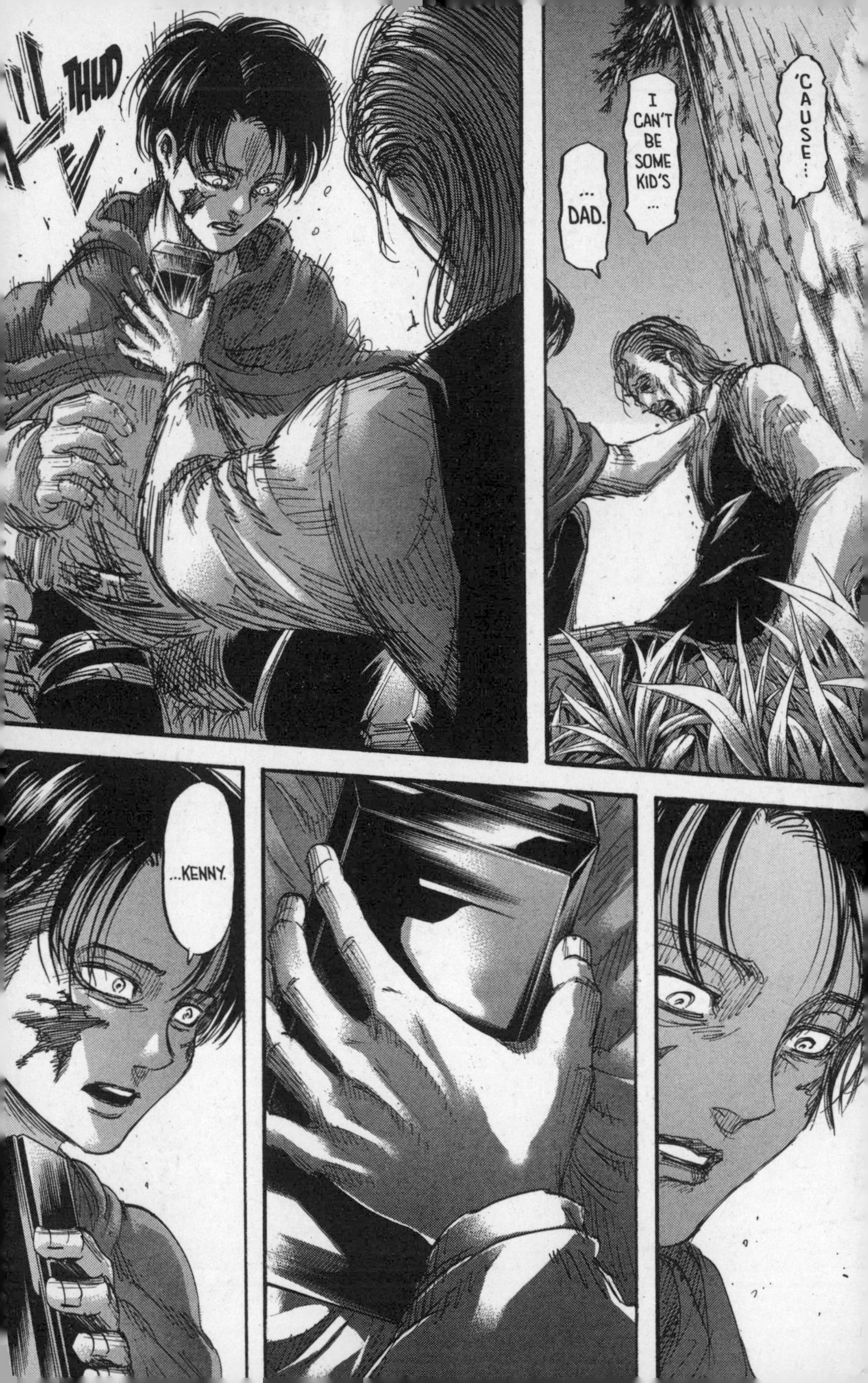
'CAUSE...
I CAN'T BE SOME KID'S ...
... DAD.
THUD
...KENNY.

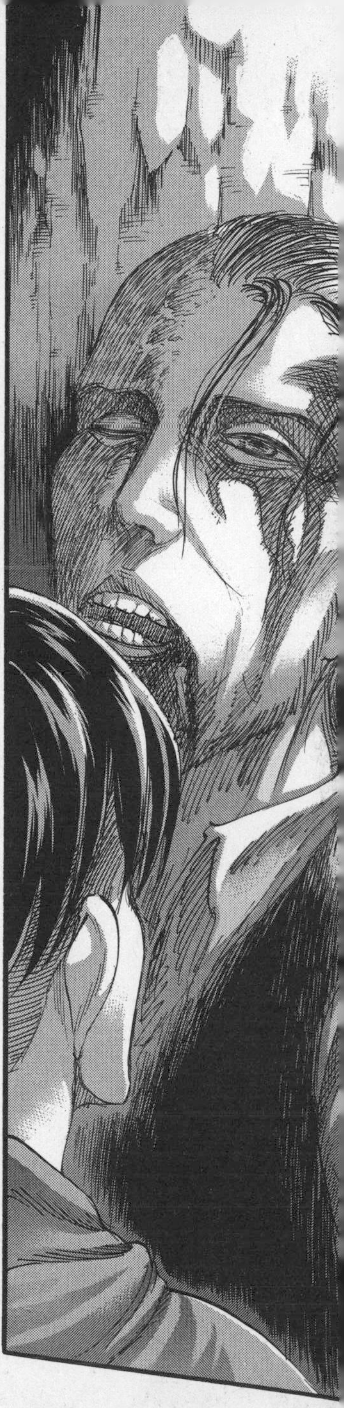
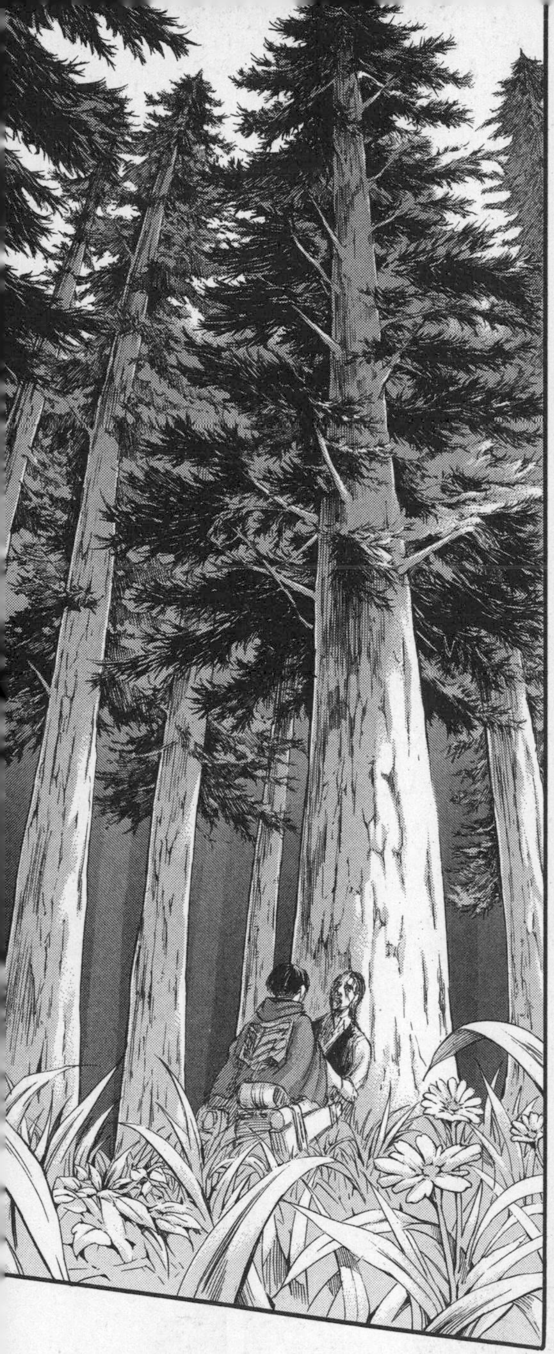

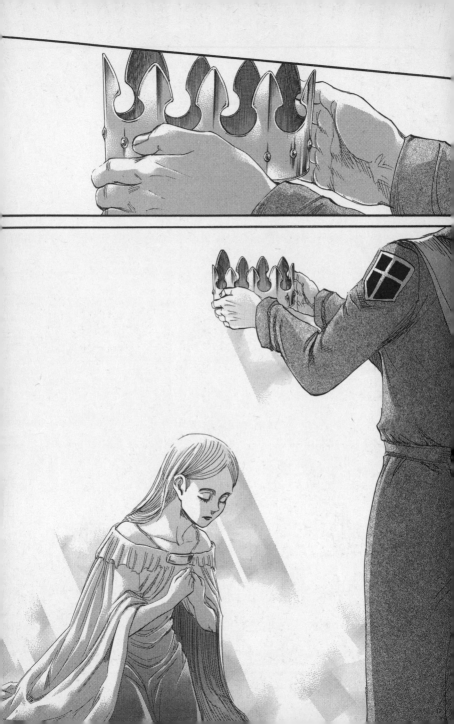

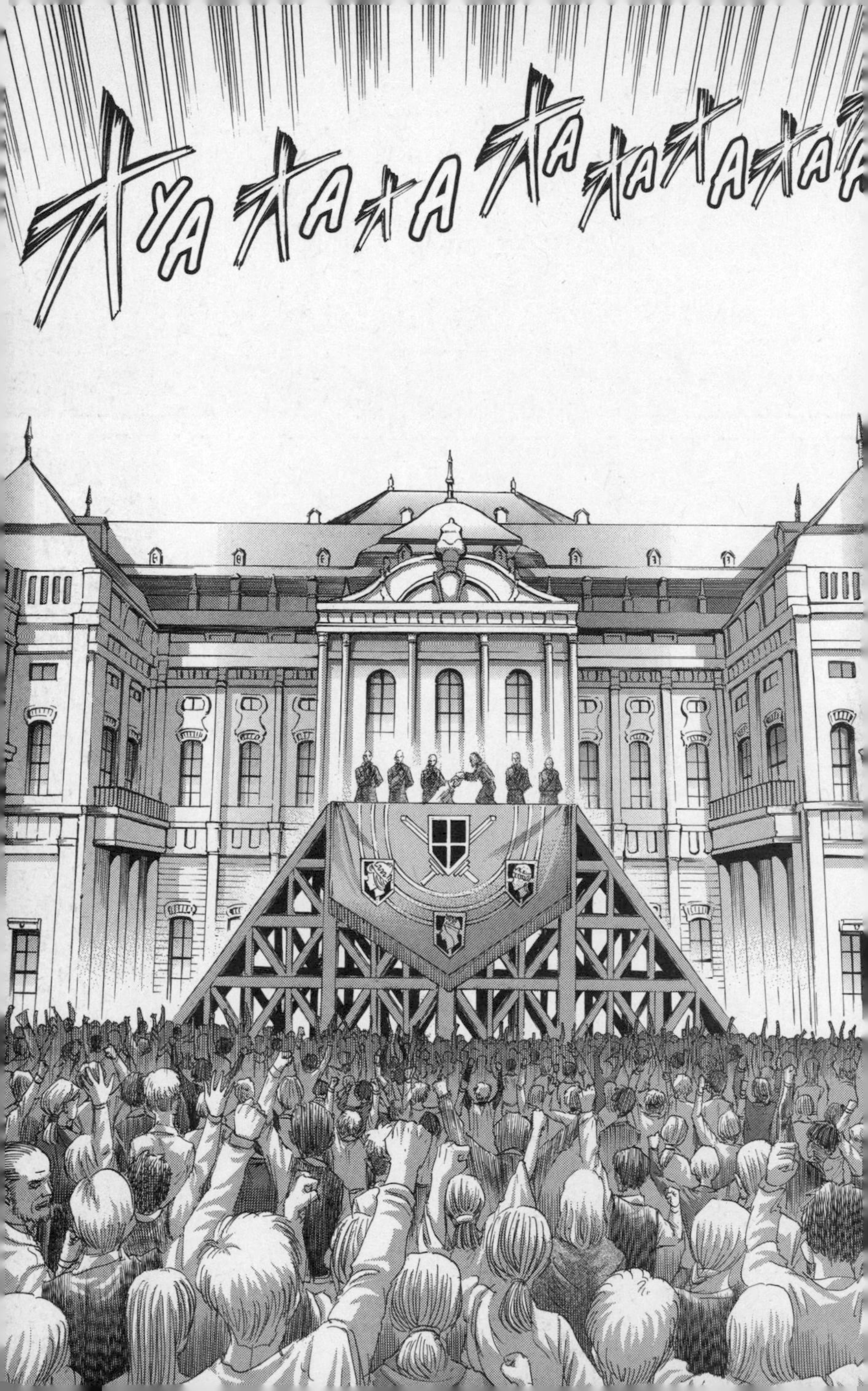

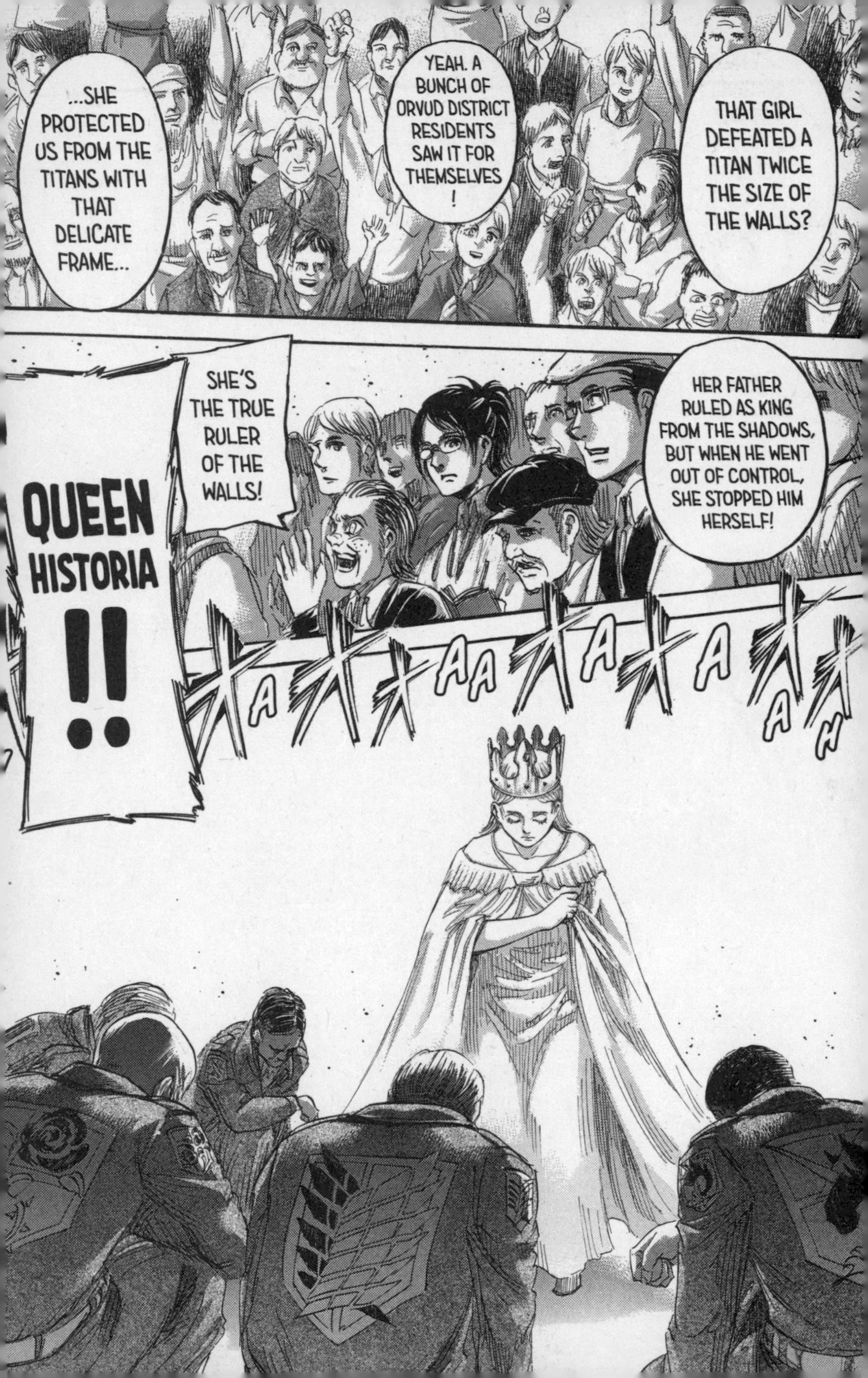
THAT GIRL DEFEATED A TITAN TWICE THE SIZE OF THE WALLS?
YEAH. A BUNCH OF ORVUD DISTRICT RESIDENTS SAW IT FOR THEMSELVES!
...SHE PROTECTED US FROM THE TITANS WITH THAT DELICATE FRAME...
HER FATHER RULED AS KING FROM THE SHADOWS, BUT WHEN HE WENT OUT OF CONTROL, SHE STOPPED HIM HERSELF!
SHE'S THE TRUE RULER OF THE WALLS!
QUEEN HISTORIA!!

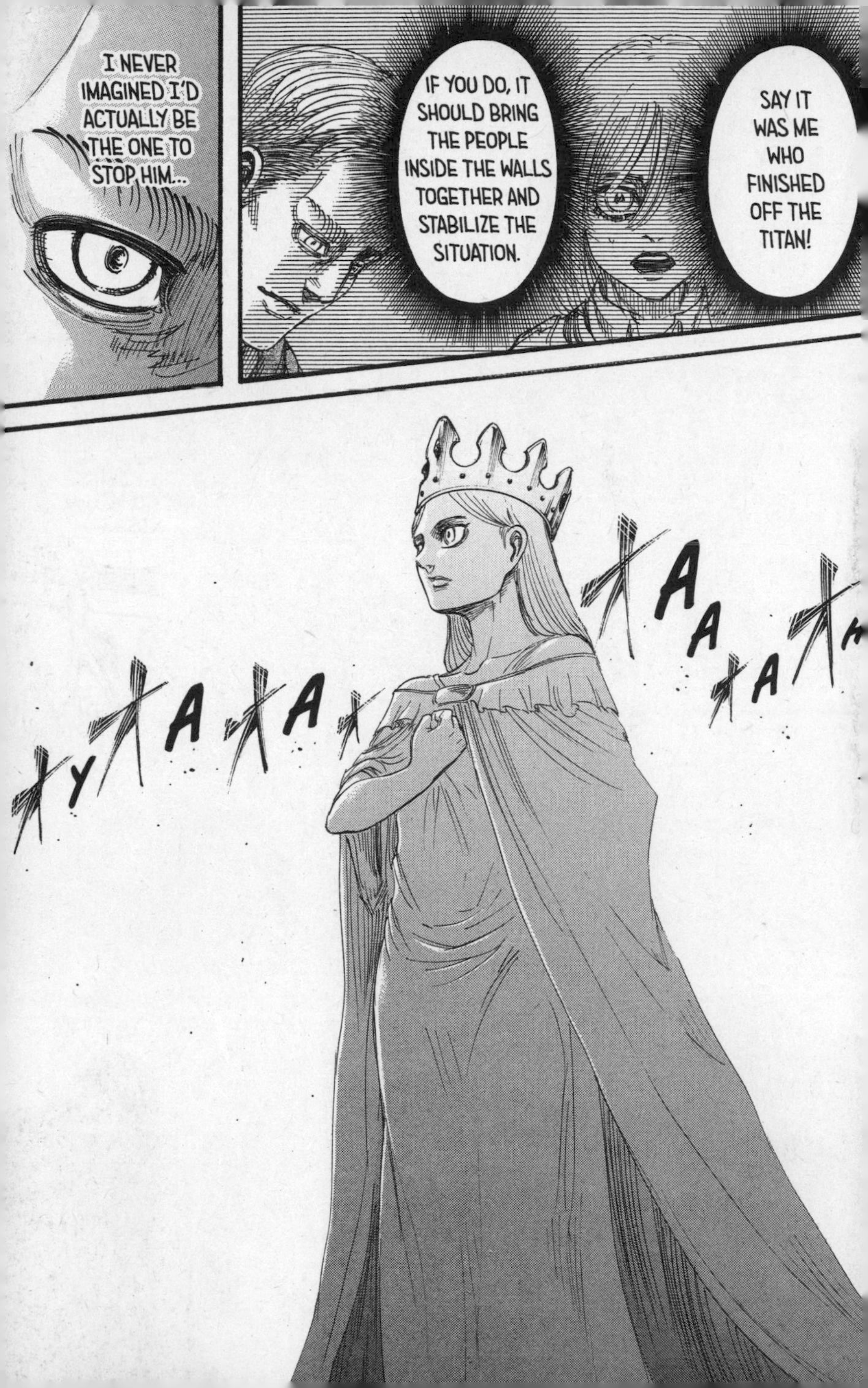
SAY IT WAS ME WHO FINISHED OFF THE TITAN!
IF YOU DO, IT SHOULD BRING THE PEOPLE INSIDE THE WALLS TOGETHER AND STABILIZE THE SITUATION.
I NEVER IMAGINED I'D ACTUALLY BE THE ONE TO STOP HIM...

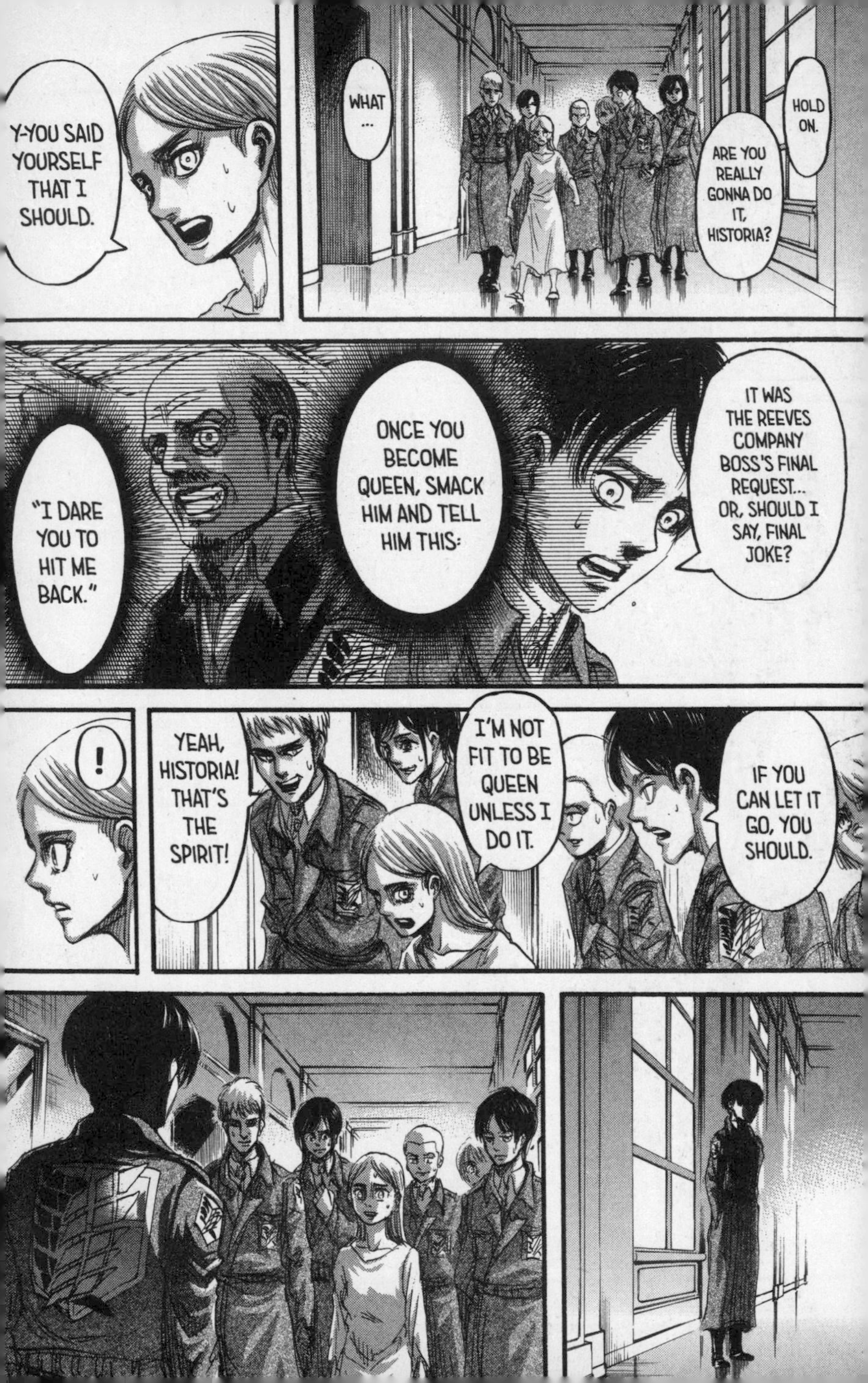
HOLD ON.
ARE YOU REALLY GONNA DO IT, HISTORIA?
WHAT ...
Y-YOU SAID YOURSELF THAT I SHOULD.
IT WAS THE REEVES COMPANY BOSS'S FINAL REQUEST... OR, SHOULD I SAY, FINAL JOKE?
ONCE YOU BECOME QUEEN, SMACK HIM AND TELL HIM THIS:
“I DARE YOU TO HIT ME BACK.”
IF YOU CAN LET IT GO, YOU SHOULD.
I'M NOT FIT TO BE QUEEN UNLESS I DO IT.
YEAH, HISTORIA! THAT'S THE SPIRIT!
!

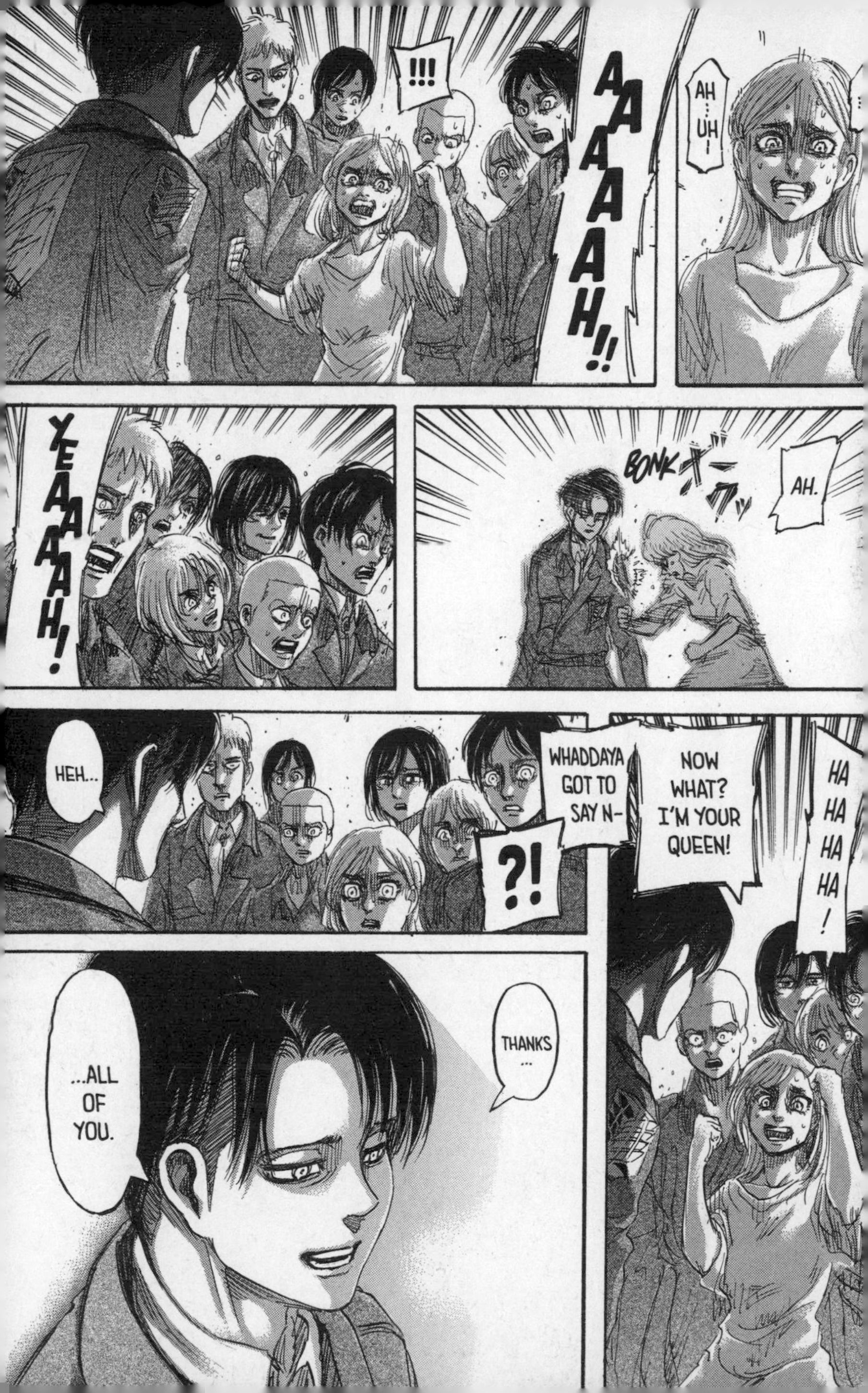
AH... UH!
AAAAAH!!
!!!
BONK
AH.
YEAAAAAH!
HA HA HA HA!
NOW WHAT? I'M YOUR QUEEN!
WHADDAYA GOT TO SAY N-
?!
HEH...
THANKS...
...ALL OF YOU.

ATTACK on TITAN

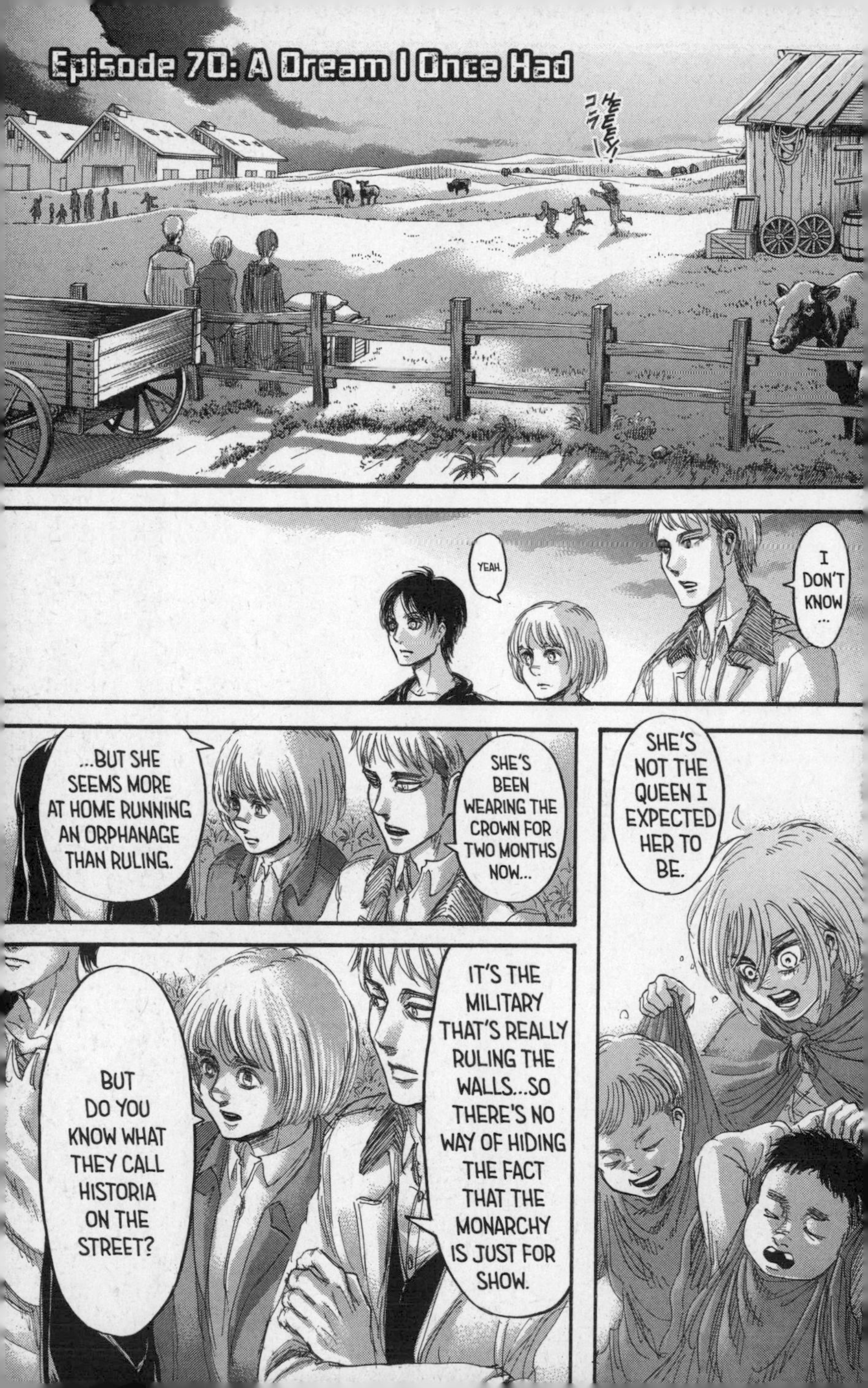
Episode 70: A Dream I Once Had
HEEEY!
コラー
I DON'T KNOW...
YEAH.
SHE'S NOT THE QUEEN I EXPECTED HER TO BE.
SHE'S BEEN WEARING THE CROWN FOR TWO MONTHS NOW...
...BUT SHE SEEMS MORE AT HOME RUNNING AN ORPHANAGE THAN RULING.
IT'S THE MILITARY THAT'S REALLY RULING THE WALLS...SO THERE'S NO WAY OF HIDING THE FACT THAT THE MONARCHY IS JUST FOR SHOW.
BUT DO YOU KNOW WHAT THEY CALL HISTORIA ON THE STREET?

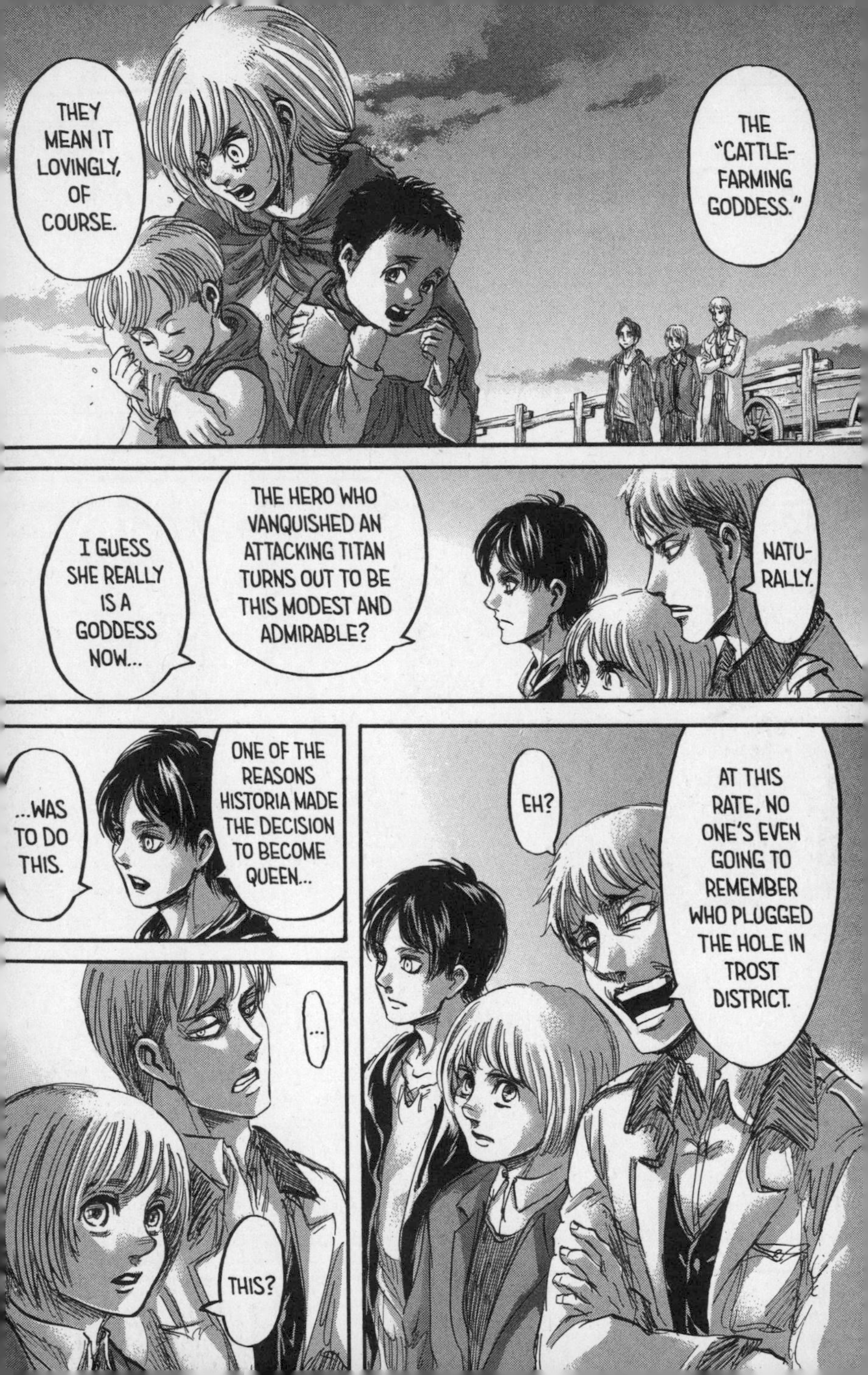
THE "CATTLE-FARMING GODDESS."
THEY MEAN IT LOVINGLY, OF COURSE.
NATU-RALLY.
THE HERO WHO VANQUISHED AN ATTACKING TITAN TURNS OUT TO BE THIS MODEST AND ADMIRABLE?
I GUESS SHE REALLY IS A GODDESS NOW...
AT THIS RATE, NO ONE'S EVEN GOING TO REMEMBER WHO PLUGGED THE HOLE IN TROST DISTRICT.
EH?
ONE OF THE REASONS HISTORIA MADE THE DECISION TO BECOME QUEEN...
...WAS TO DO THIS.
...
THIS?

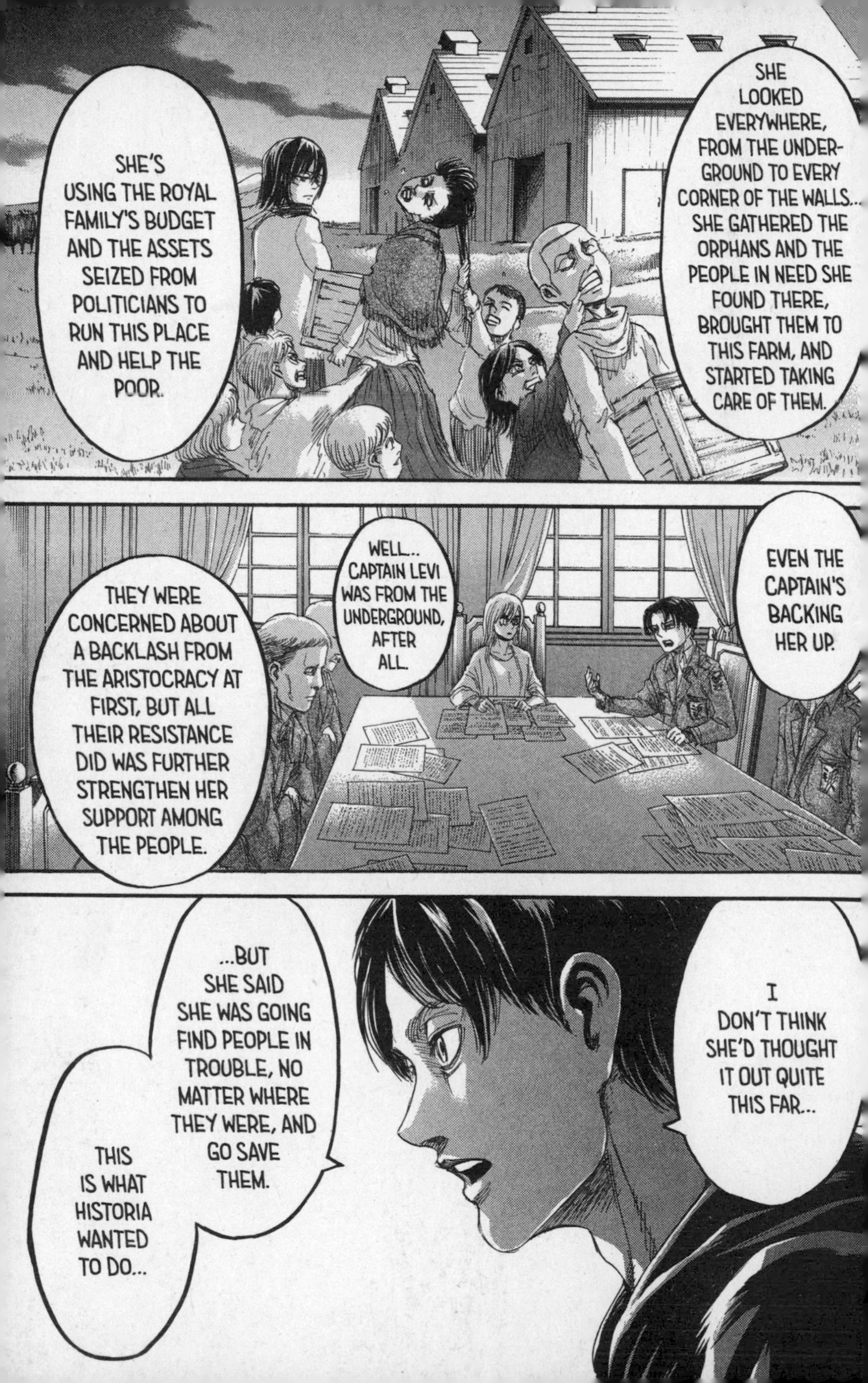
SHE LOOKED EVERYWHERE, FROM THE UNDERGROUND TO EVERY CORNER OF THE WALLS... SHE GATHERED THE ORPHANS AND THE PEOPLE IN NEED SHE FOUND THERE, BROUGHT THEM TO THIS FARM, AND STARTED TAKING CARE OF THEM.
SHE'S USING THE ROYAL FAMILY'S BUDGET AND THE ASSETS SEIZED FROM POLITICIANS TO RUN THIS PLACE AND HELP THE POOR.
EVEN THE CAPTAIN'S BACKING HER UP.
WELL... CAPTAIN LEVI WAS FROM THE UNDERGROUND, AFTER ALL.
THEY WERE CONCERNED ABOUT A BACKLASH FROM THE ARISTOCRACY AT FIRST, BUT ALL THEIR RESISTANCE DID WAS FURTHER STRENGTHEN HER SUPPORT AMONG THE PEOPLE.
I DON'T THINK SHE'D THOUGHT IT OUT QUITE THIS FAR...
...BUT SHE SAID SHE WAS GOING FIND PEOPLE IN TROUBLE, NO MATTER WHERE THEY WERE, AND GO SAVE THEM.
THIS IS WHAT HISTORIA WANTED TO DO...

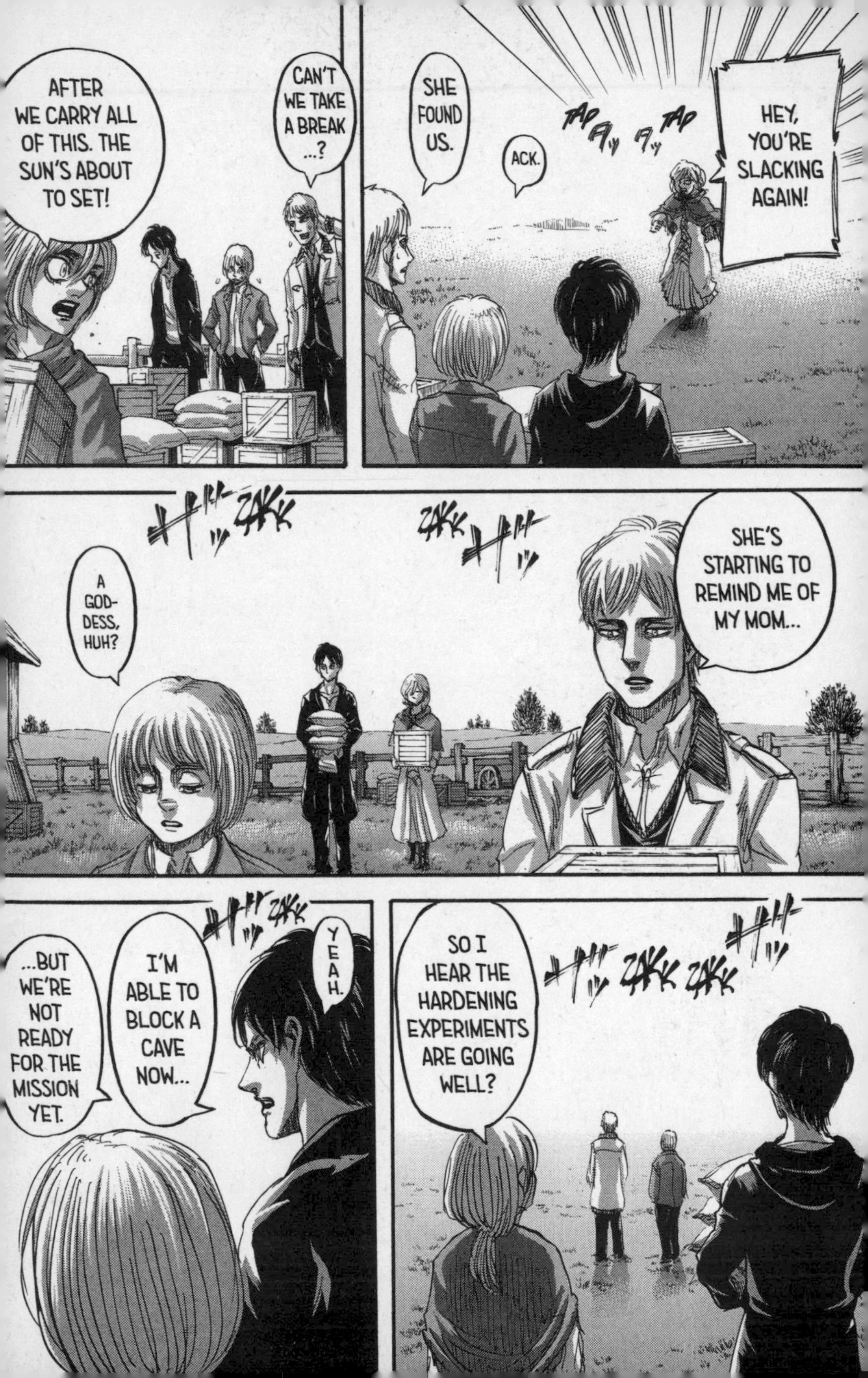
HEY, YOU'RE SLACKING AGAIN!
TAP TAP
ACK.
SHE FOUND US.
CAN'T WE TAKE A BREAK ...?
AFTER WE CARRY ALL OF THIS. THE SUN'S ABOUT TO SET!
ZAK
ZAK
SHE'S STARTING TO REMIND ME OF MY MOM...
A GOD-DESS, HUH?
ZAK ZAK
SO I HEAR THE HARDENING EXPERIMENTS ARE GOING WELL?
ZAK
YEAH.
I'M ABLE TO BLOCK A CAVE NOW...
...BUT WE'RE NOT READY FOR THE MISSION YET.

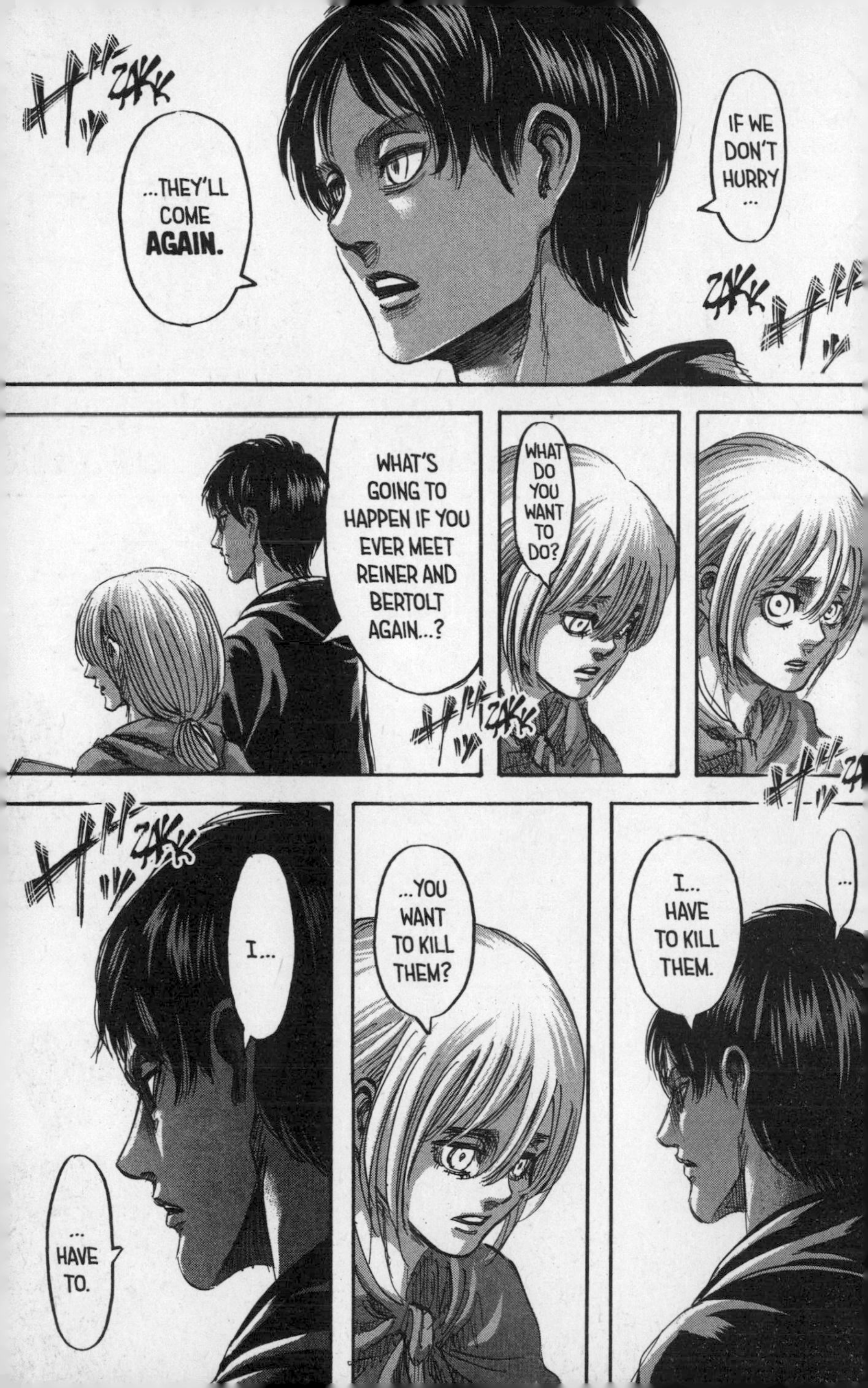
IF WE DON'T HURRY ...
ZAKK
...THEY'LL COME AGAIN.
ZAKK
WHAT DO YOU WANT TO DO?
ZAKK
WHAT'S GOING TO HAPPEN IF YOU EVER MEET REINER AND BERTOLT AGAIN...?
...
I... HAVE TO KILL THEM.
...YOU WANT TO KILL THEM?
ZAKK
I...
... HAVE TO.

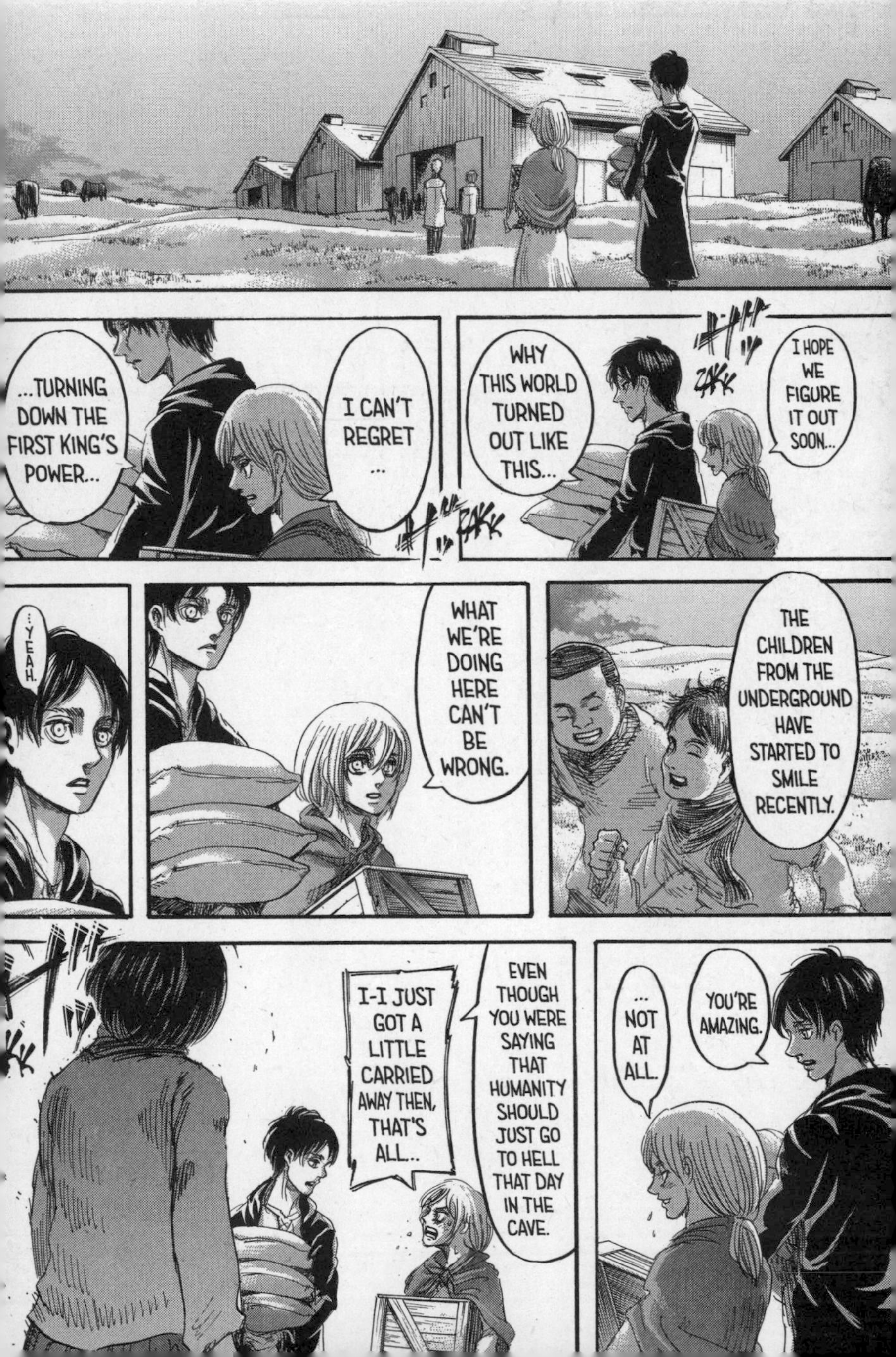
I HOPE WE FIGURE IT OUT SOON...
ZAKK
WHY THIS WORLD TURNED OUT LIKE THIS...
ZAKK
I CAN'T REGRET ...
...TURNING DOWN THE FIRST KING'S POWER...
THE CHILDREN FROM THE UNDERGROUND HAVE STARTED TO SMILE RECENTLY.
WHAT WE'RE DOING HERE CAN'T BE WRONG.
...YEAH.
YOU'RE AMAZING.
... NOT AT ALL.
EVEN THOUGH YOU WERE SAYING THAT HUMANITY SHOULD JUST GO TO HELL THAT DAY IN THE CAVE.
I-I JUST GOT A LITTLE CARRIED AWAY THEN, THAT'S ALL...

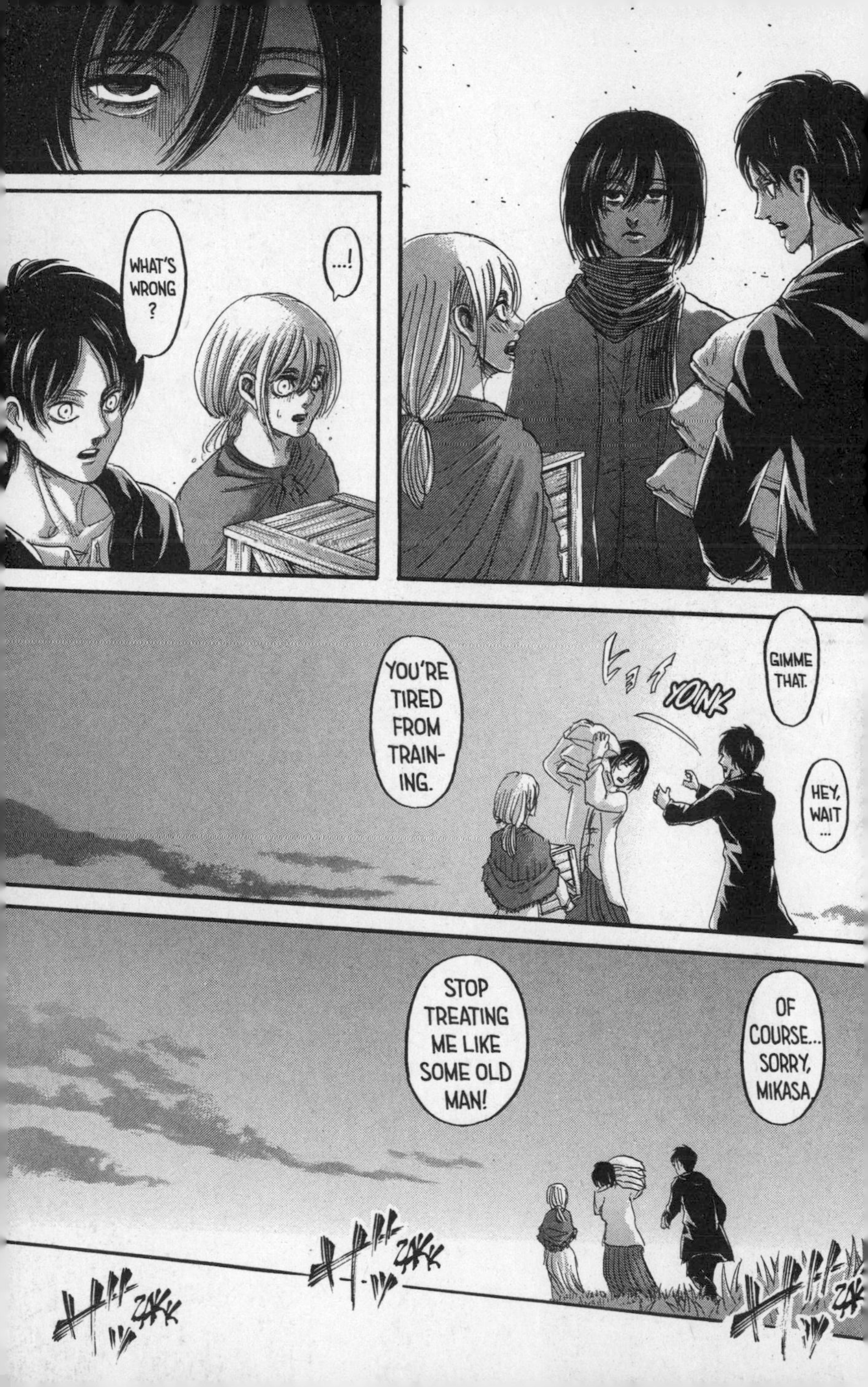
...!
WHAT'S WRONG ?
GIMME THAT.
ヒョイ
YONK
HEY, WAIT ...
YOU'RE TIRED FROM TRAIN-ING.
OF COURSE... SORRY, MIKASA.
STOP TREATING ME LIKE SOME OLD MAN!
ZAKK
ZAKK
ZAKK

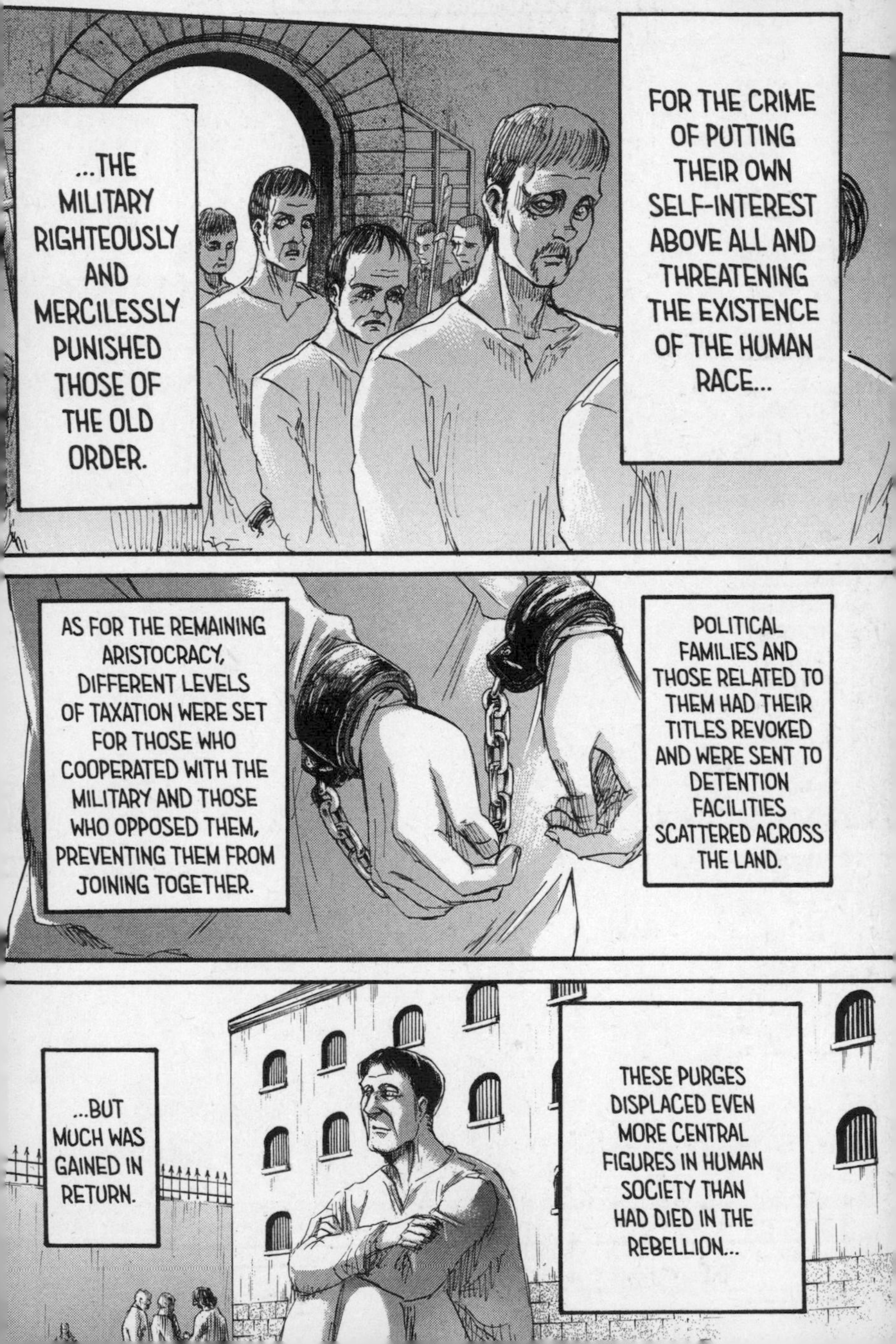
FOR THE CRIME OF PUTTING THEIR OWN SELF-INTEREST ABOVE ALL AND THREATENING THE EXISTENCE OF THE HUMAN RACE...
...THE MILITARY RIGHTEOUSLY AND MERCILESSLY PUNISHED THOSE OF THE OLD ORDER.
POLITICAL FAMILIES AND THOSE RELATED TO THEM HAD THEIR TITLES REVOKED AND WERE SENT TO DETENTION FACILITIES SCATTERED ACROSS THE LAND.
AS FOR THE REMAINING ARISTOCRACY, DIFFERENT LEVELS OF TAXATION WERE SET FOR THOSE WHO COOPERATED WITH THE MILITARY AND THOSE WHO OPPOSED THEM, PREVENTING THEM FROM JOINING TOGETHER.
THESE PURGES DISPLACED EVEN MORE CENTRAL FIGURES IN HUMAN SOCIETY THAN HAD DIED IN THE REBELLION...
...BUT MUCH WAS GAINED IN RETURN.

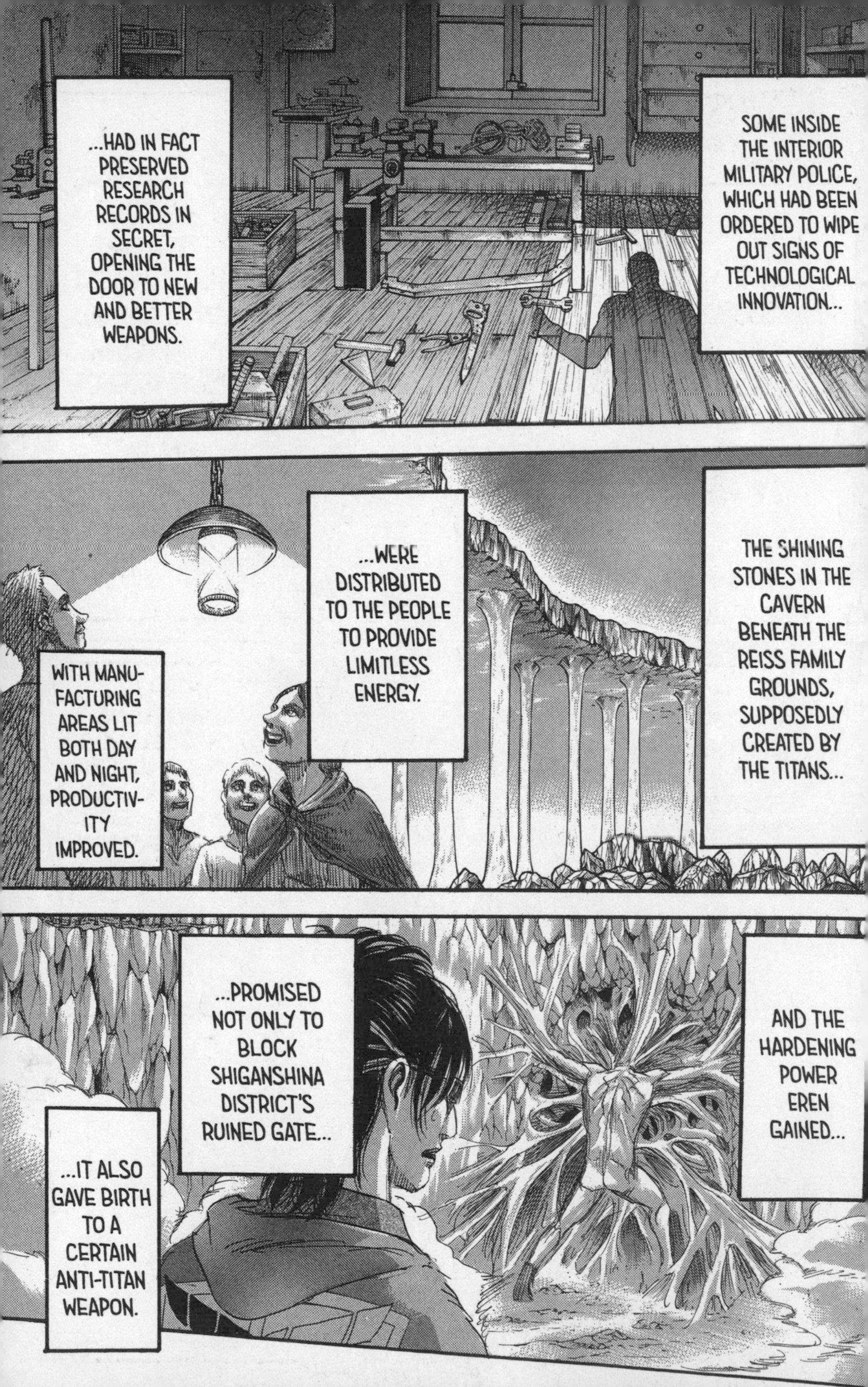
SOME INSIDE THE INTERIOR MILITARY POLICE, WHICH HAD BEEN ORDERED TO WIPE OUT SIGNS OF TECHNOLOGICAL INNOVATION...
...HAD IN FACT PRESERVED RESEARCH RECORDS IN SECRET, OPENING THE DOOR TO NEW AND BETTER WEAPONS.
THE SHINING STONES IN THE CAVERN BENEATH THE REISS FAMILY GROUNDS, SUPPOSEDLY CREATED BY THE TITANS...
...WERE DISTRIBUTED TO THE PEOPLE TO PROVIDE LIMITLESS ENERGY.
WITH MANU-FACTURING AREAS LIT BOTH DAY AND NIGHT, PRODUCTIV-ITY IMPROVED.
AND THE HARDENING POWER EREN GAINED...
...PROMISED NOT ONLY TO BLOCK SHIGANSHINA DISTRICT'S RUINED GATE...
...IT ALSO GAVE BIRTH TO A CERTAIN ANTI-TITAN WEAPON.

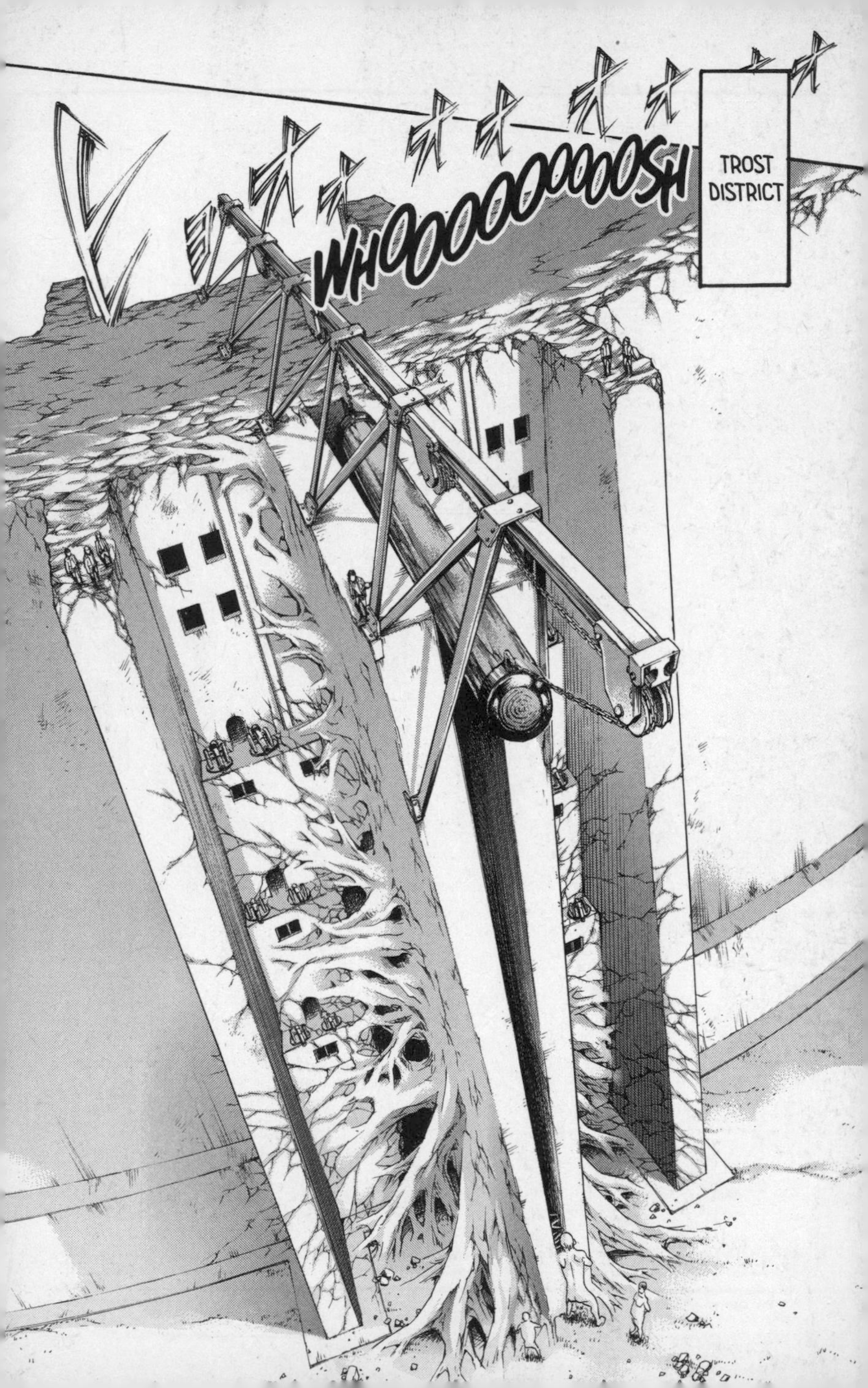
TROST DISTRICT
WHOOOOOOOOOSH

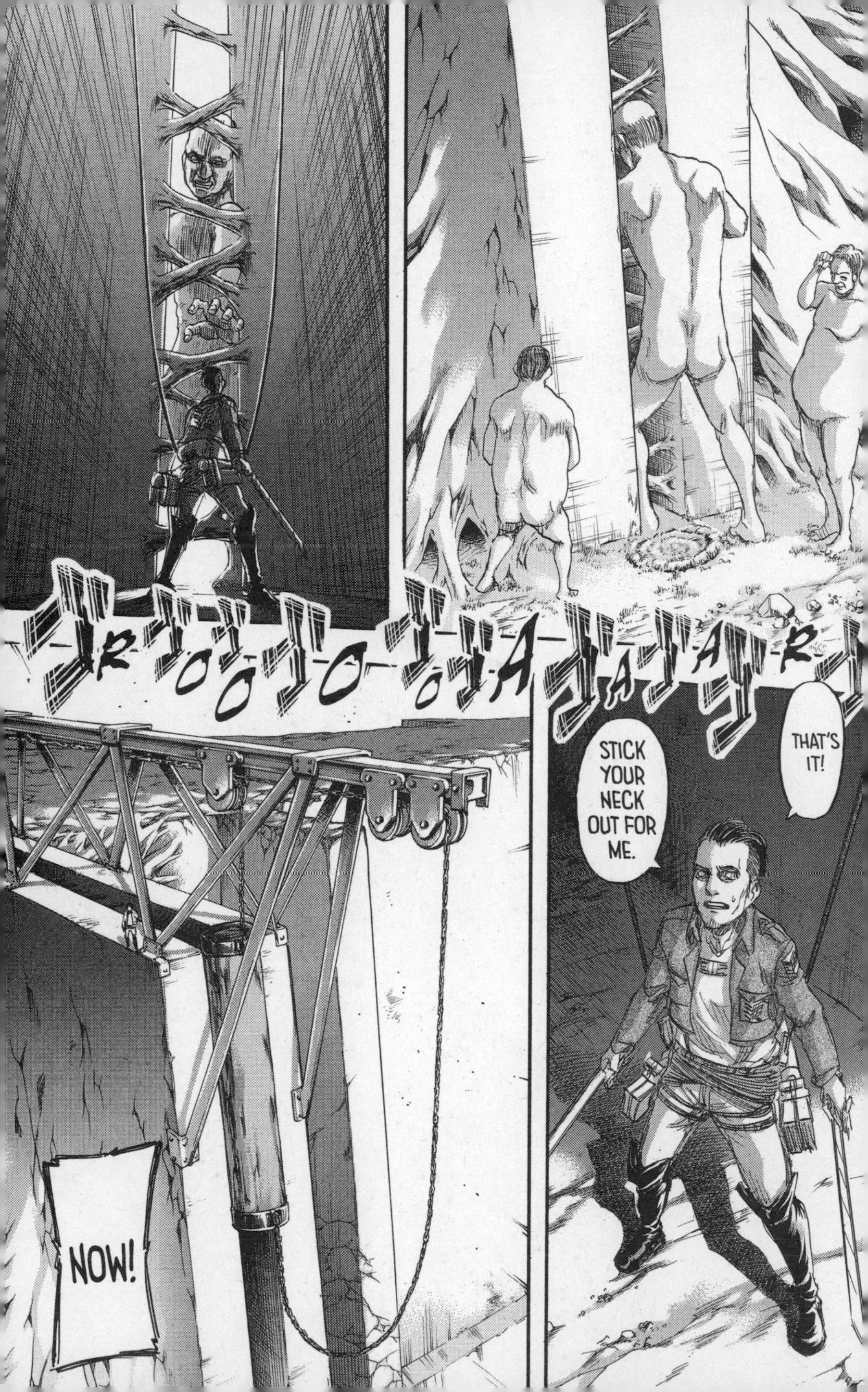
ROOOOAAAR
THAT'S IT!
STICK YOUR NECK OUT FOR ME.
NOW!

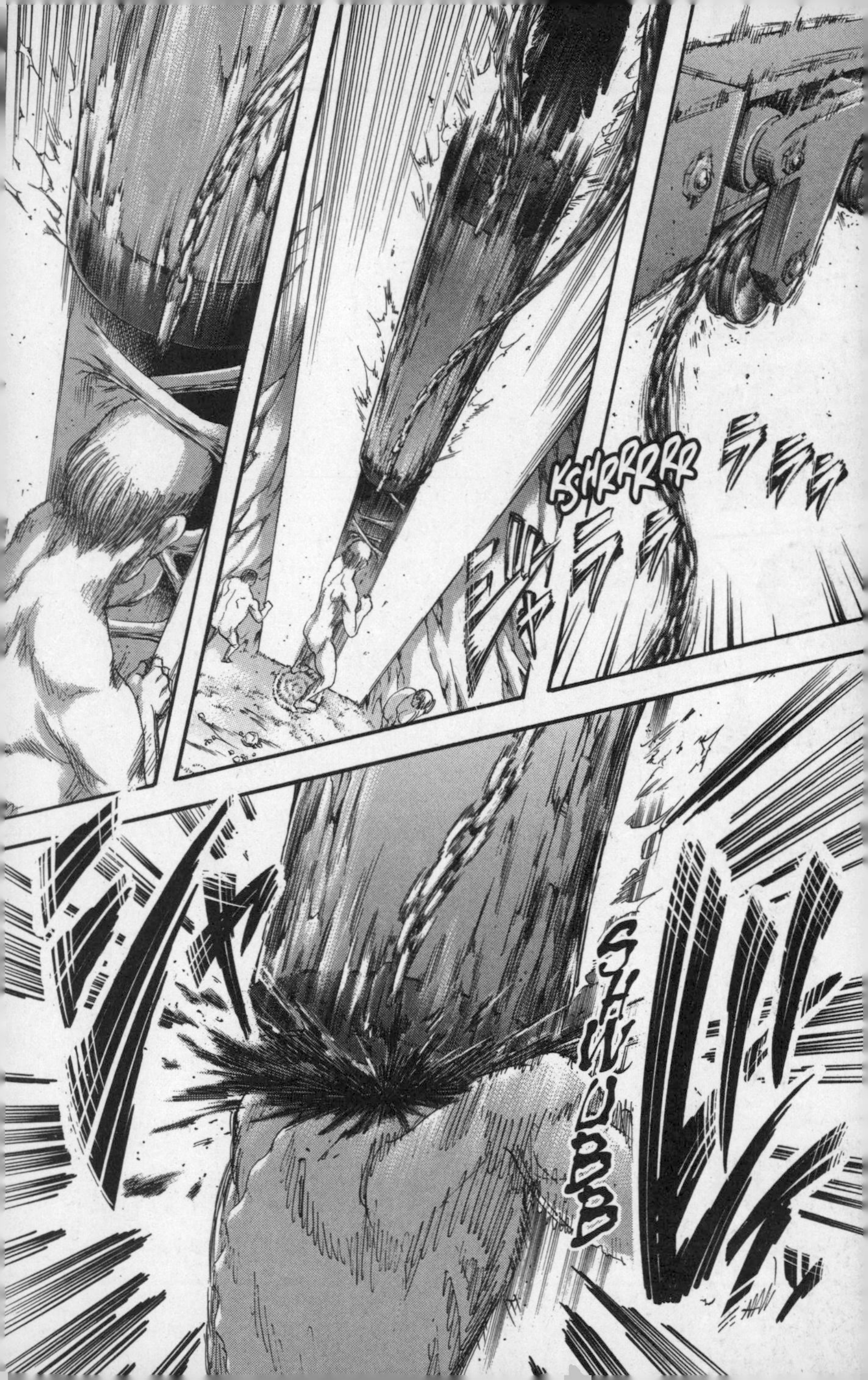
KSHRRRR
SHUUBBB

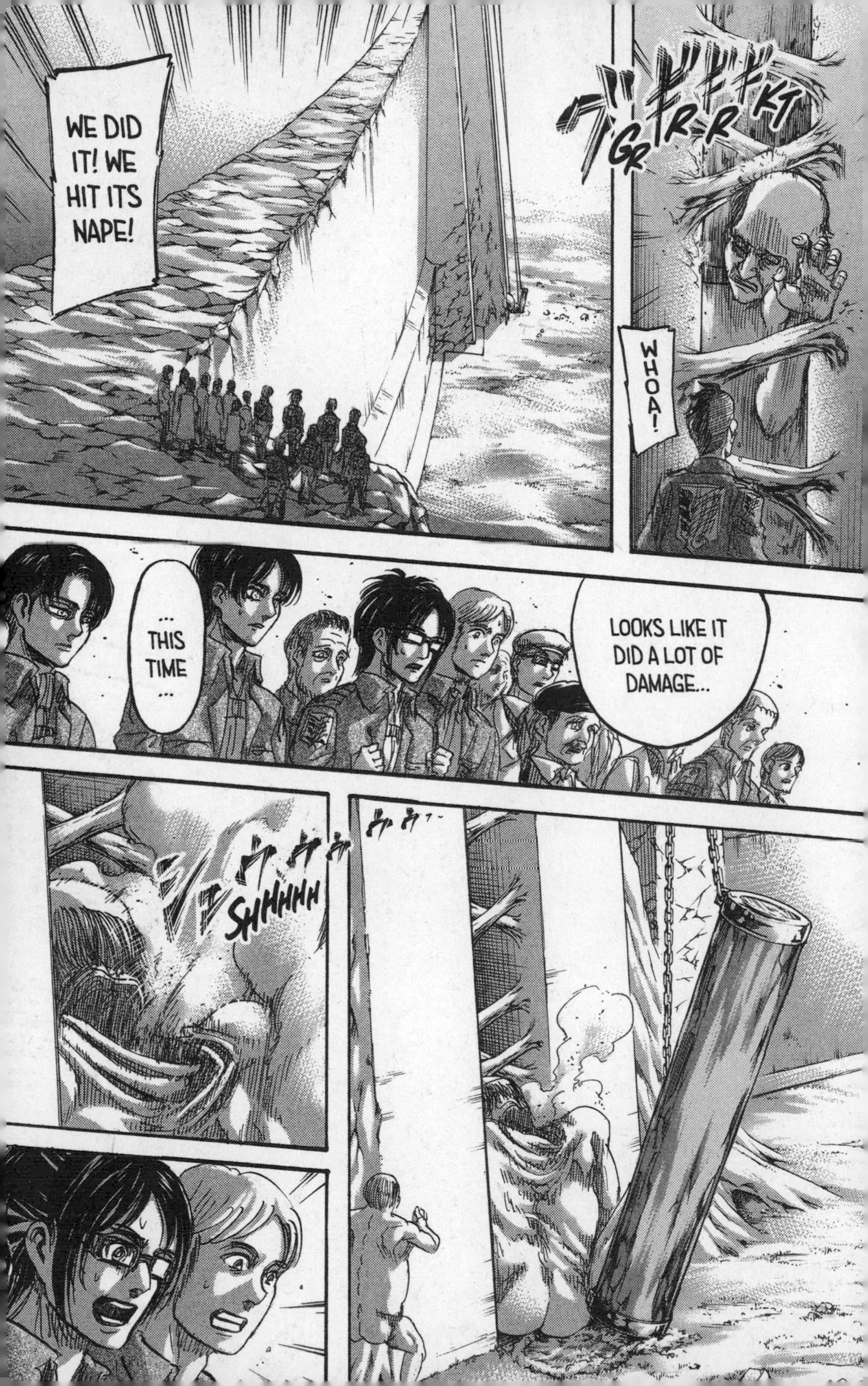
GRR-R-R
WHOA!
WE DID IT! WE HIT ITS NAPE!
LOOKS LIKE IT DID A LOT OF DAMAGE...
...THIS TIME...
SHHHHH

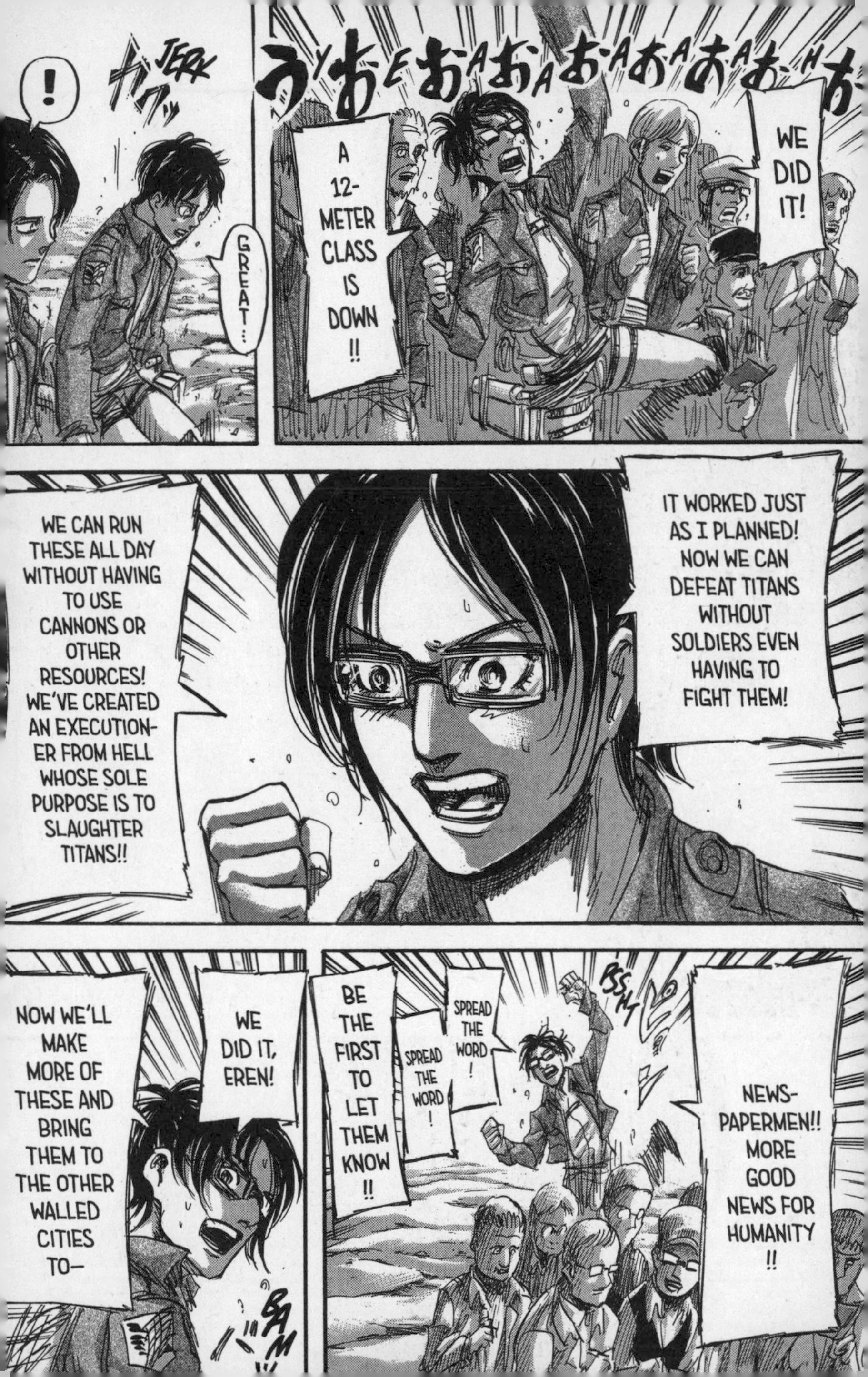
YEAAAAAH
WE DID IT!
A 12-METER CLASS IS DOWN!!
JERK
カクッ
!
GREAT...
IT WORKED JUST AS I PLANNED! NOW WE CAN DEFEAT TITANS WITHOUT SOLDIERS EVEN HAVING TO FIGHT THEM!
WE CAN RUN THESE ALL DAY WITHOUT HAVING TO USE CANNONS OR OTHER RESOURCES! WE'VE CREATED AN EXECUTIONER FROM HELL WHOSE SOLE PURPOSE IS TO SLAUGHTER TITANS!!
PSSH
NEWSPAPERMEN!! MORE GOOD NEWS FOR HUMANITY!!
SPREAD THE WORD!
SPREAD THE WORD!
BE THE FIRST TO LET THEM KNOW!!
WE DID IT, EREN!
NOW WE'LL MAKE MORE OF THESE AND BRING THEM TO THE OTHER WALLED CITIES TO—
BAM
!!

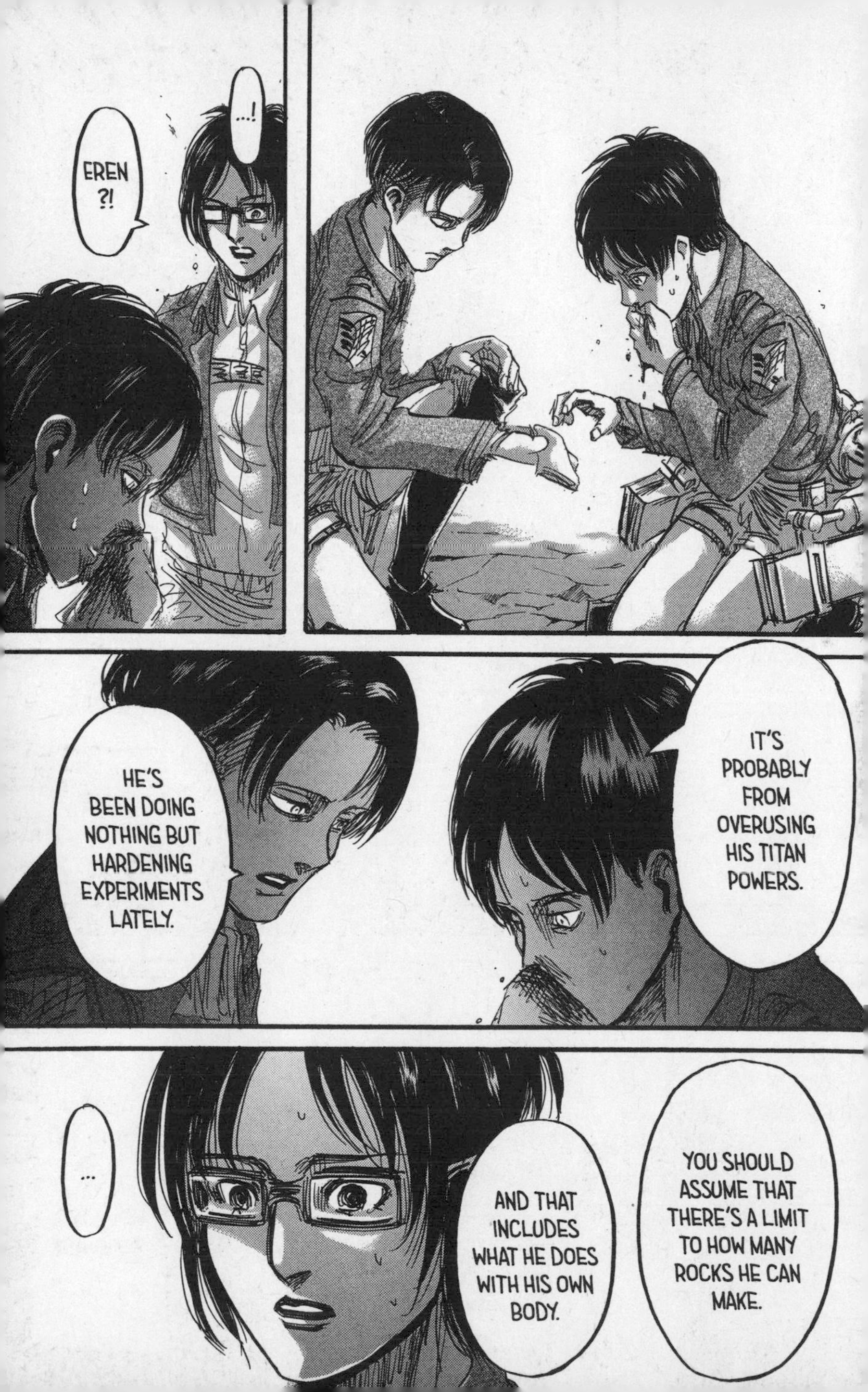
...!
EREN ?!
IT'S PROBABLY FROM OVERUSING HIS TITAN POWERS.
HE'S BEEN DOING NOTHING BUT HARDENING EXPERIMENTS LATELY.
YOU SHOULD ASSUME THAT THERE'S A LIMIT TO HOW MANY ROCKS HE CAN MAKE.
AND THAT INCLUDES WHAT HE DOES WITH HIS OWN BODY.
...

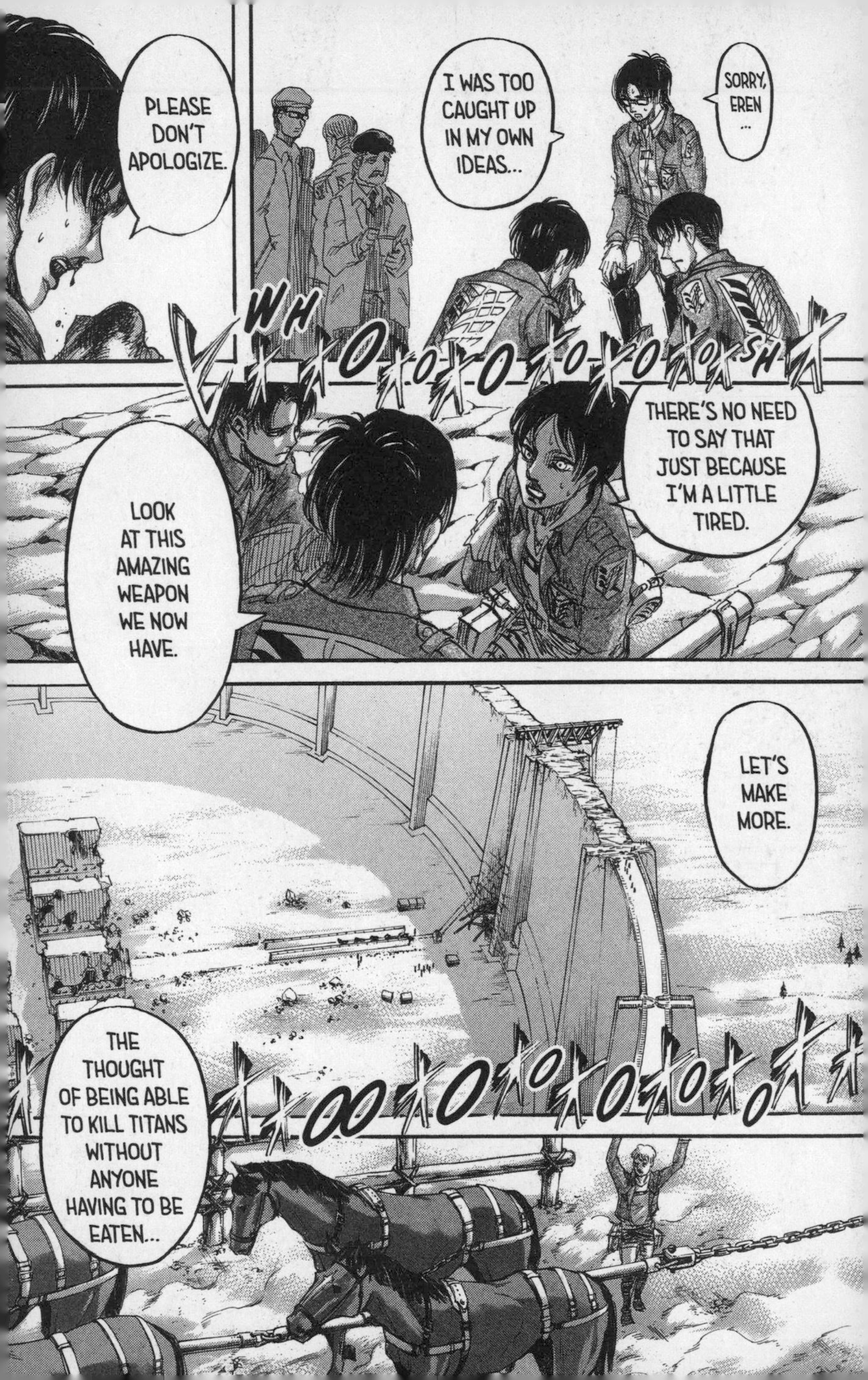
SORRY, EREN ...
I WAS TOO CAUGHT UP IN MY OWN IDEAS...
PLEASE DON'T APOLOGIZE.
THERE'S NO NEED TO SAY THAT JUST BECAUSE I'M A LITTLE TIRED.
LOOK AT THIS AMAZING WEAPON WE NOW HAVE.
LET'S MAKE MORE.
THE THOUGHT OF BEING ABLE TO KILL TITANS WITHOUT ANYONE HAVING TO BE EATEN...

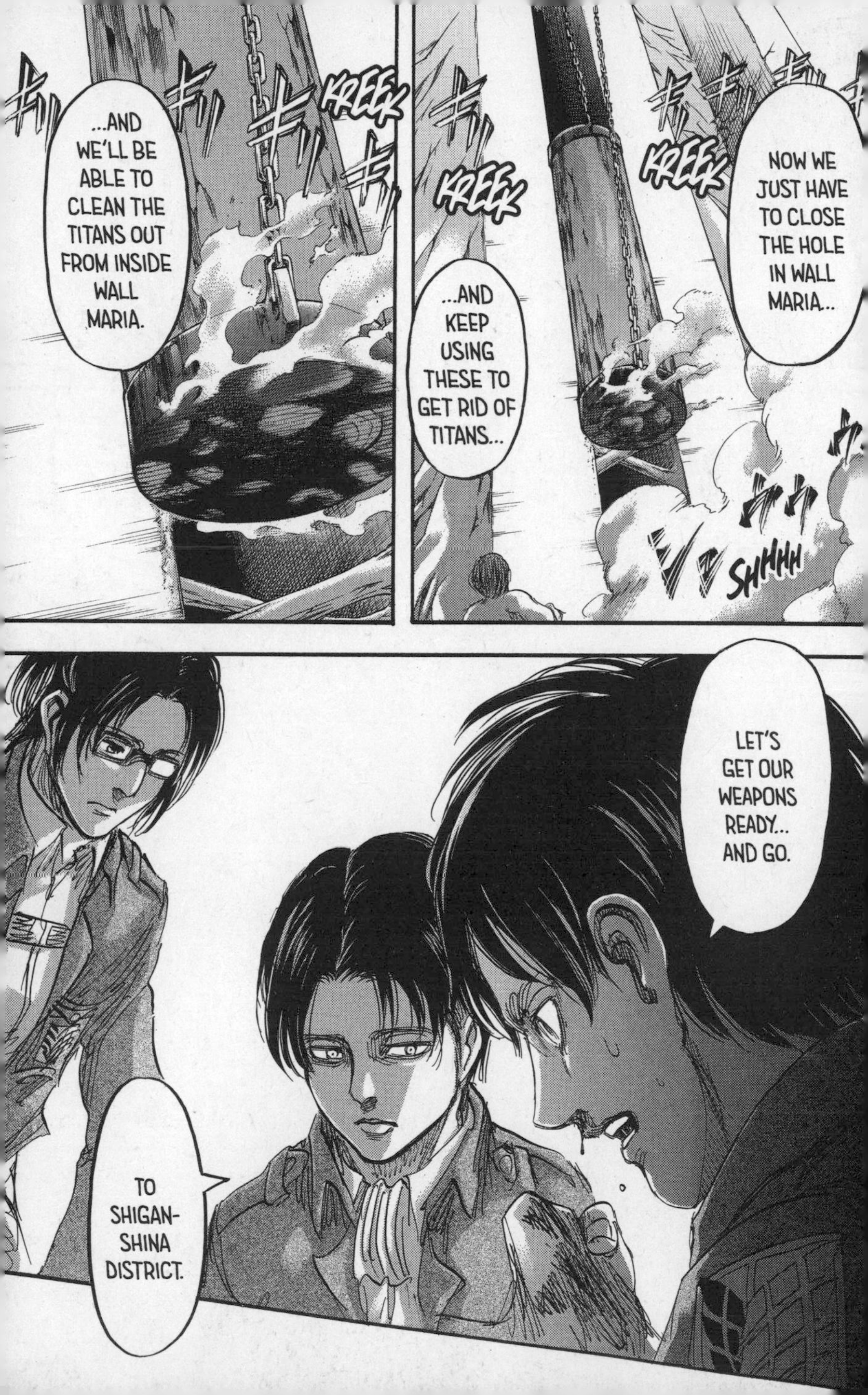
NOW WE JUST HAVE TO CLOSE THE HOLE IN WALL MARIA...
KREEK
KREEK
...AND KEEP USING THESE TO GET RID OF TITANS...
SHHHH
KREEK
...AND WE'LL BE ABLE TO CLEAN THE TITANS OUT FROM INSIDE WALL MARIA.
LET'S GET OUR WEAPONS READY... AND GO.
TO SHIGAN-SHINA DISTRICT.

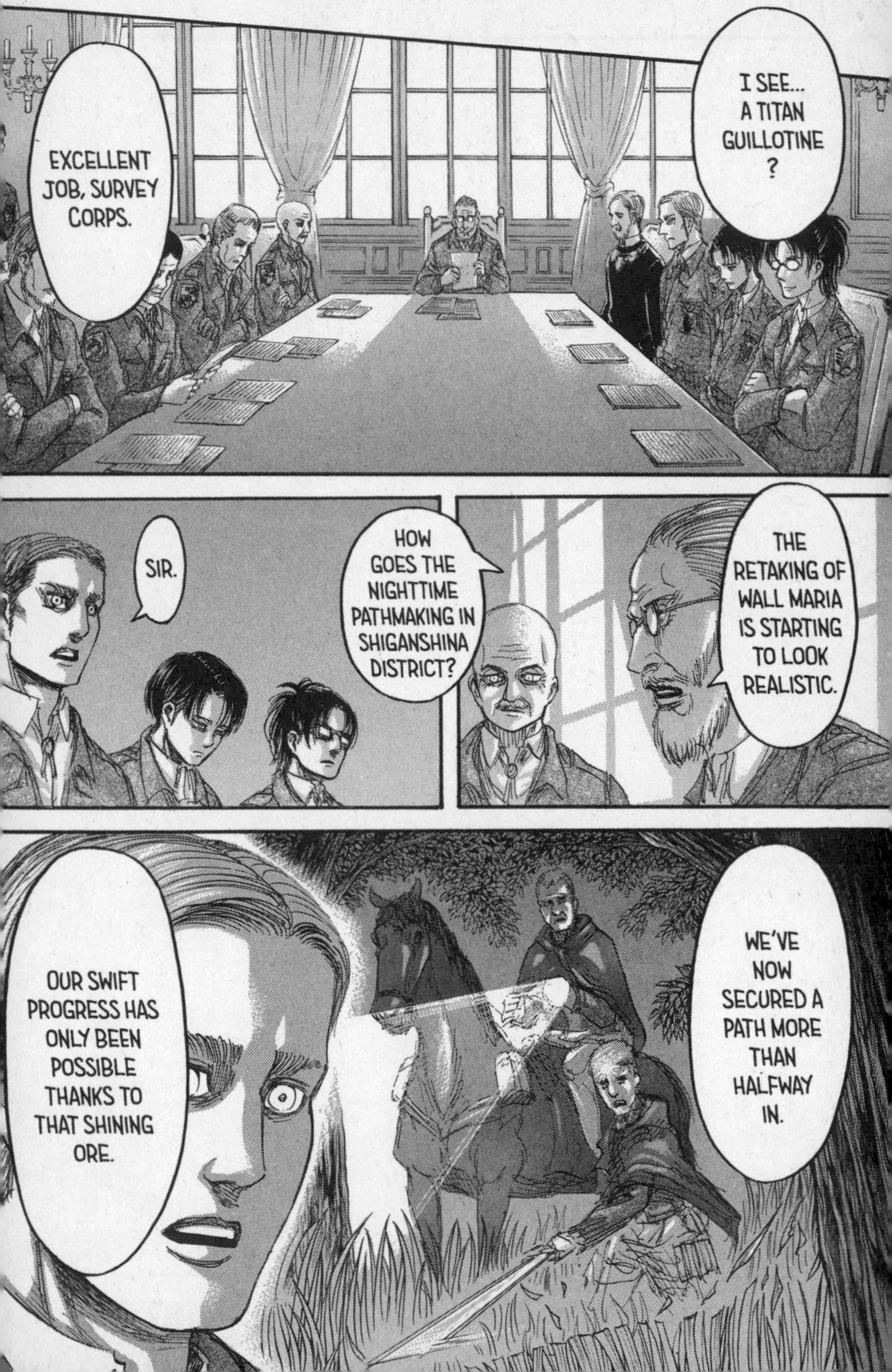
I SEE... A TITAN GUILLOTINE ?
EXCELLENT JOB, SURVEY CORPS.
THE RETAKING OF WALL MARIA IS STARTING TO LOOK REALISTIC.
HOW GOES THE NIGHTTIME PATHMAKING IN SHIGANSHINA DISTRICT?
SIR.
WE'VE NOW SECURED A PATH MORE THAN HALFWAY IN.
OUR SWIFT PROGRESS HAS ONLY BEEN POSSIBLE THANKS TO THAT SHINING ORE.

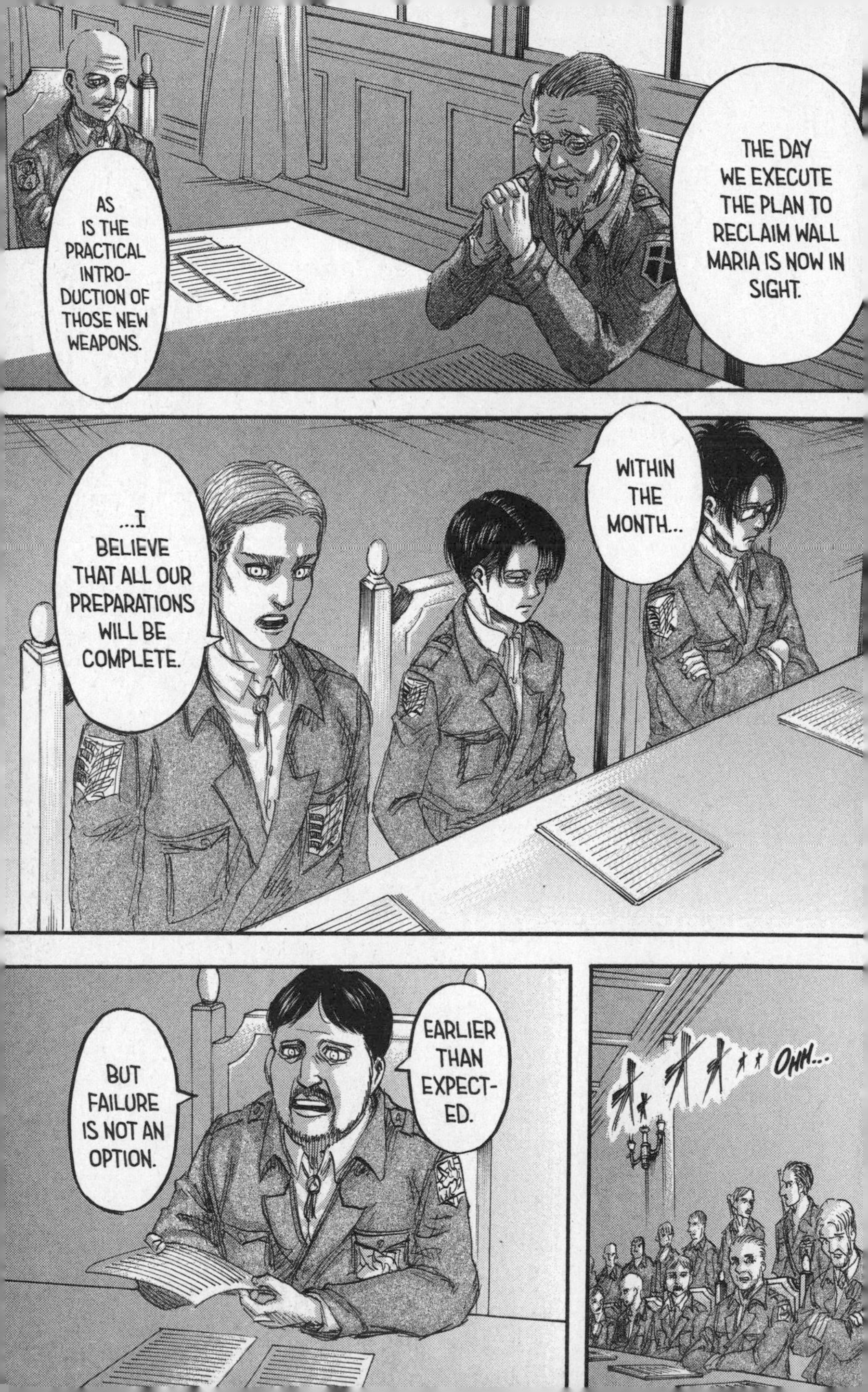
THE DAY WE EXECUTE THE PLAN TO RECLAIM WALL MARIA IS NOW IN SIGHT.
AS IS THE PRACTICAL INTRODUCTION OF THOSE NEW WEAPONS.
WITHIN THE MONTH...
...I BELIEVE THAT ALL OUR PREPARATIONS WILL BE COMPLETE.
OHH...
EARLIER THAN EXPECTED.
BUT FAILURE IS NOT AN OPTION.

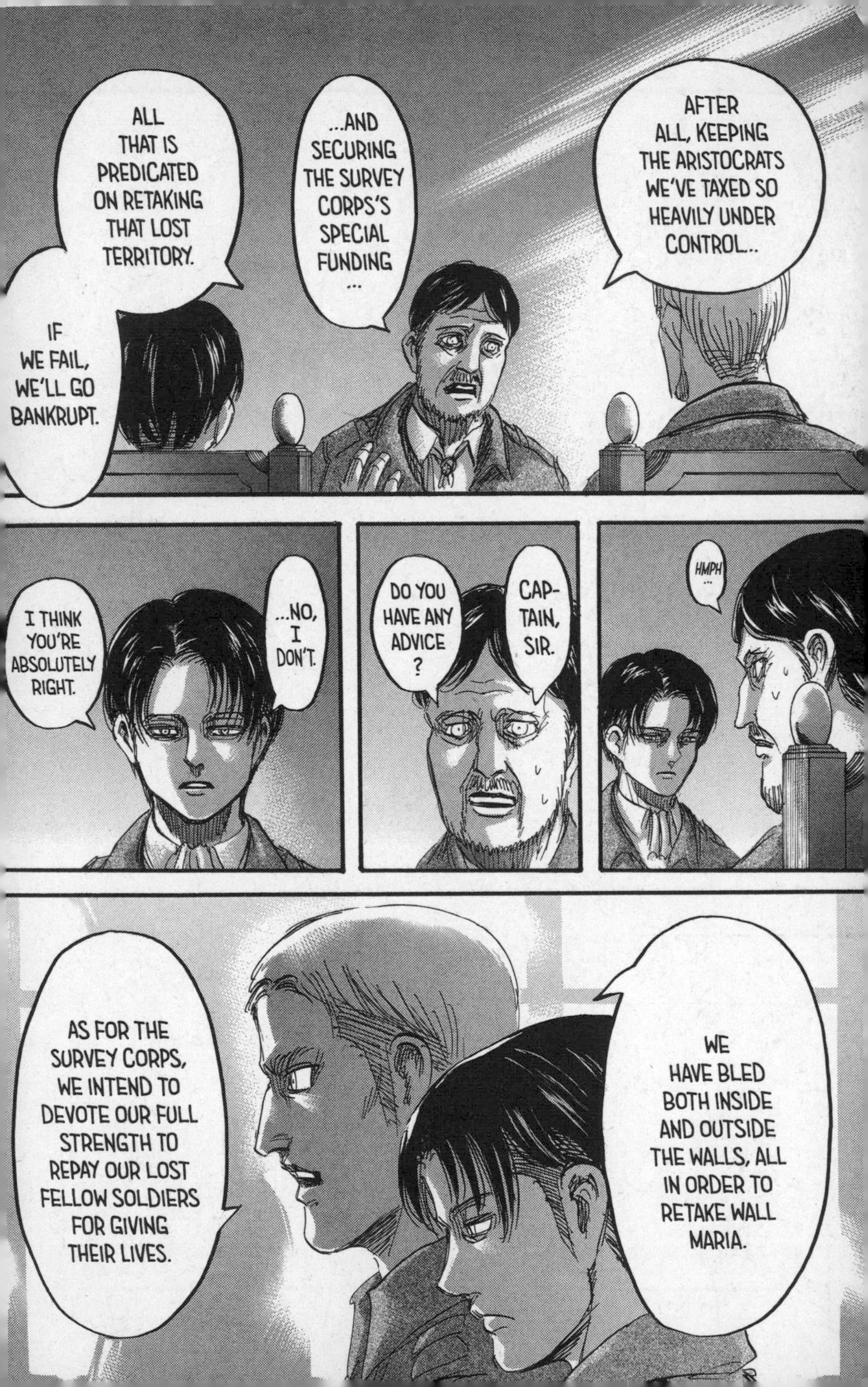
AFTER ALL, KEEPING THE ARISTOCRATS WE'VE TAXED SO HEAVILY UNDER CONTROL...
...AND SECURING THE SURVEY CORPS'S SPECIAL FUNDING ...
ALL THAT IS PREDICATED ON RETAKING THAT LOST TERRITORY.
IF WE FAIL, WE'LL GO BANKRUPT.
HMPH ...
CAP-TAIN, SIR.
DO YOU HAVE ANY ADVICE ?
...NO, I DON'T.
I THINK YOU'RE ABSOLUTELY RIGHT.
WE HAVE BLED BOTH INSIDE AND OUTSIDE THE WALLS, ALL IN ORDER TO RETAKE WALL MARIA.
AS FOR THE SURVEY CORPS, WE INTEND TO DEVOTE OUR FULL STRENGTH TO REPAY OUR LOST FELLOW SOLDIERS FOR GIVING THEIR LIVES.

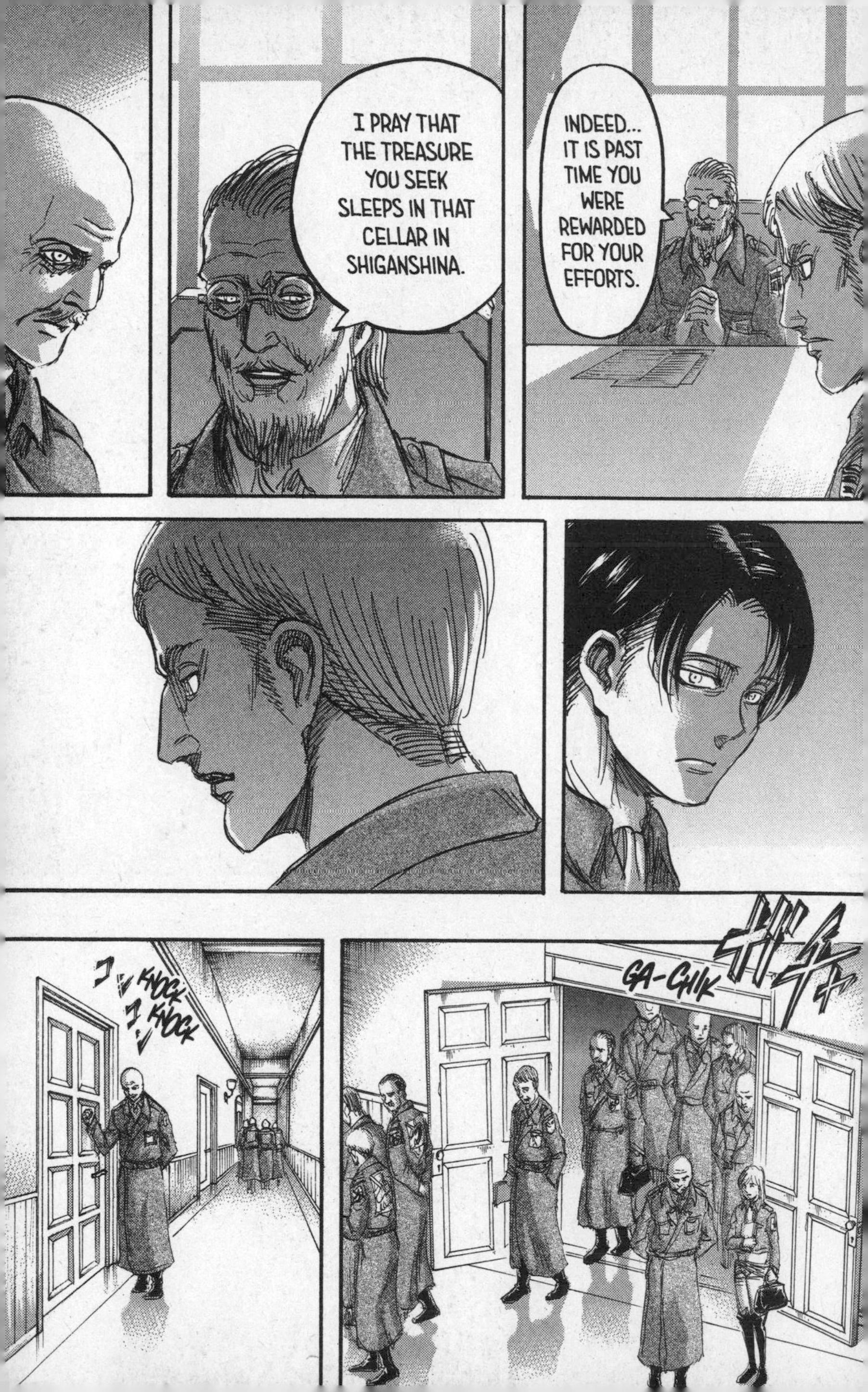
INDEED... IT IS PAST TIME YOU WERE REWARDED FOR YOUR EFFORTS.
I PRAY THAT THE TREASURE YOU SEEK SLEEPS IN THAT CELLAR IN SHIGANSHINA.
GA-CHIK
KNOCK KNOCK

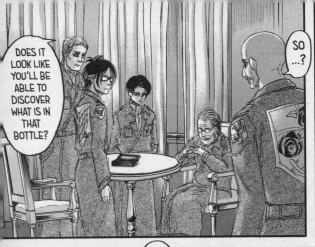

BAM
SO ...?
DOES IT LOOK LIKE YOU'LL BE ABLE TO DISCOVER WHAT IS IN THAT BOTTLE?
WELL, ABOUT THAT...
THIS IS ALL WE CAN FIND OUT WITH THE TECH-NOLOGY WE CURRENTLY POSSESS.
AS WE HEARD FROM EREN AND HISTORIA, IT SEEMS TO CONTAIN INGREDIENTS BASED ON HUMAN SPINAL FLUID. THERE SEEMS TO BE MORE AS WELL, BUT...
AS SOON AS THIS LIQUID TOUCHES AIR, IT EVAPORATES, MAKING ANALYSIS DIFFICULT.

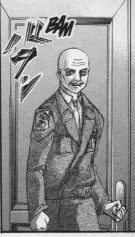

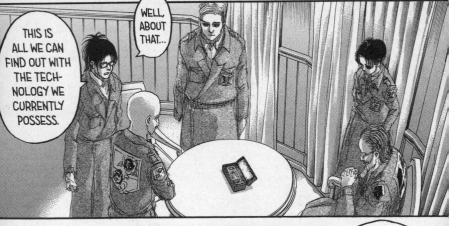

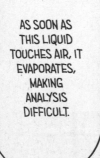

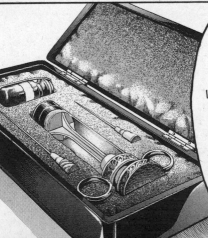

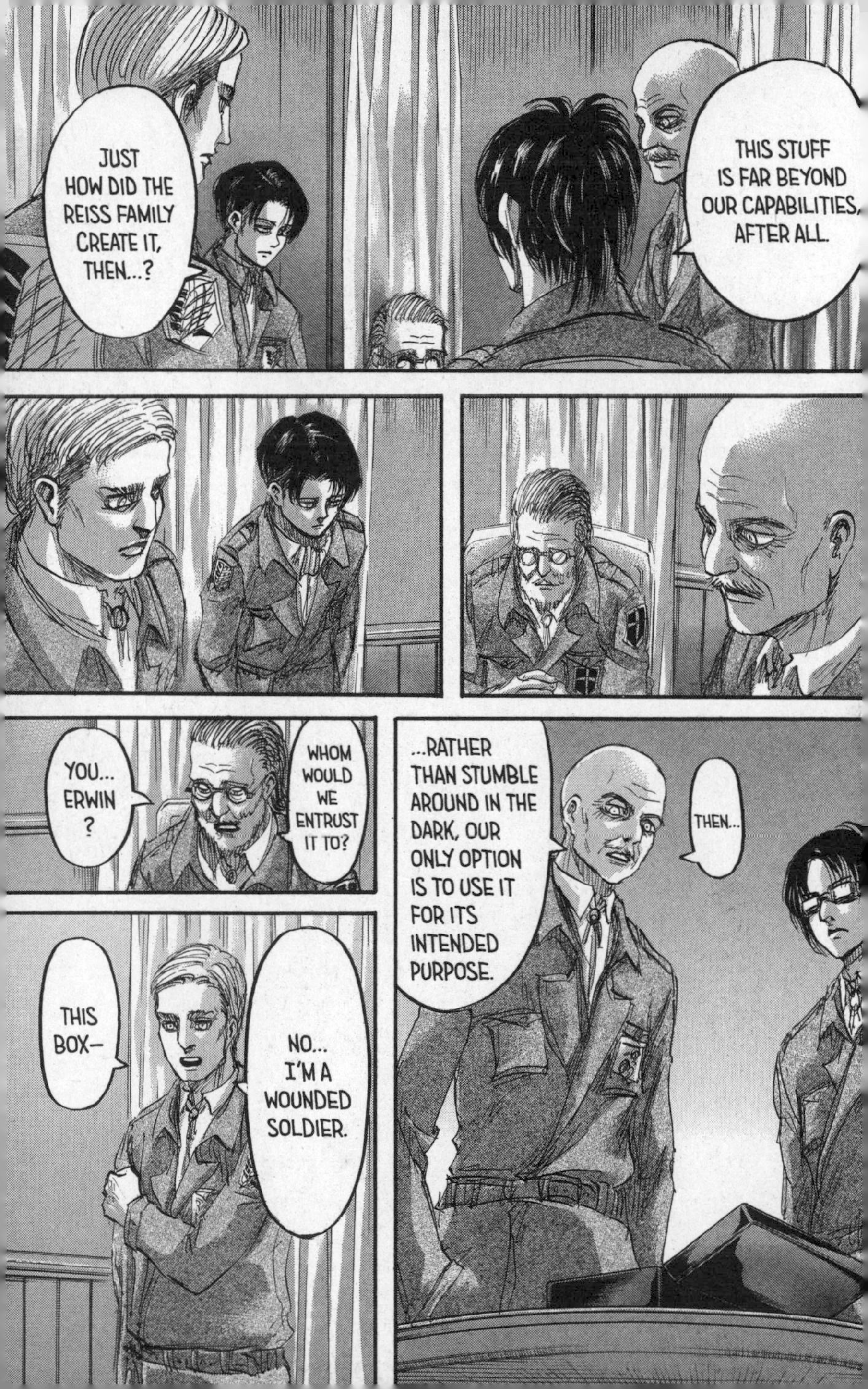
THIS STUFF IS FAR BEYOND OUR CAPABILITIES, AFTER ALL.
JUST HOW DID THE REISS FAMILY CREATE IT, THEN...?
THEN...
...RATHER THAN STUMBLE AROUND IN THE DARK, OUR ONLY OPTION IS TO USE IT FOR ITS INTENDED PURPOSE.
WHOM WOULD WE ENTRUST IT TO?
YOU... ERWIN ?
NO... I'M A WOUNDED SOLDIER.
THIS BOX—

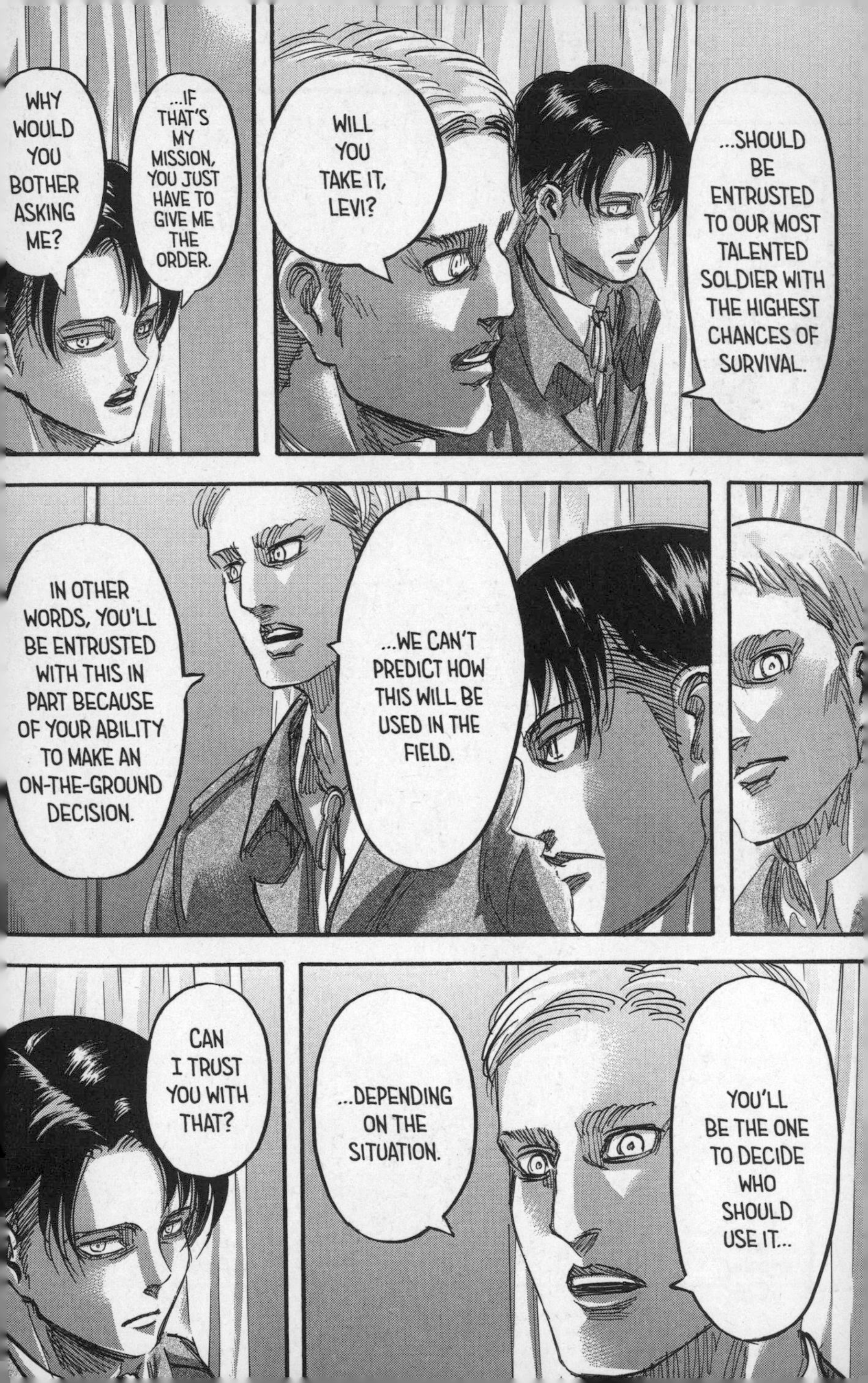
...SHOULD BE ENTRUSTED TO OUR MOST TALENTED SOLDIER WITH THE HIGHEST CHANCES OF SURVIVAL.
WILL YOU TAKE IT, LEVI?
...IF THAT'S MY MISSION, YOU JUST HAVE TO GIVE ME THE ORDER.
WHY WOULD YOU BOTHER ASKING ME?
...WE CAN'T PREDICT HOW THIS WILL BE USED IN THE FIELD.
IN OTHER WORDS, YOU'LL BE ENTRUSTED WITH THIS IN PART BECAUSE OF YOUR ABILITY TO MAKE AN ON-THE-GROUND DECISION.
YOU'LL BE THE ONE TO DECIDE WHO SHOULD USE IT...
...DEPENDING ON THE SITUATION.
CAN I TRUST YOU WITH THAT?

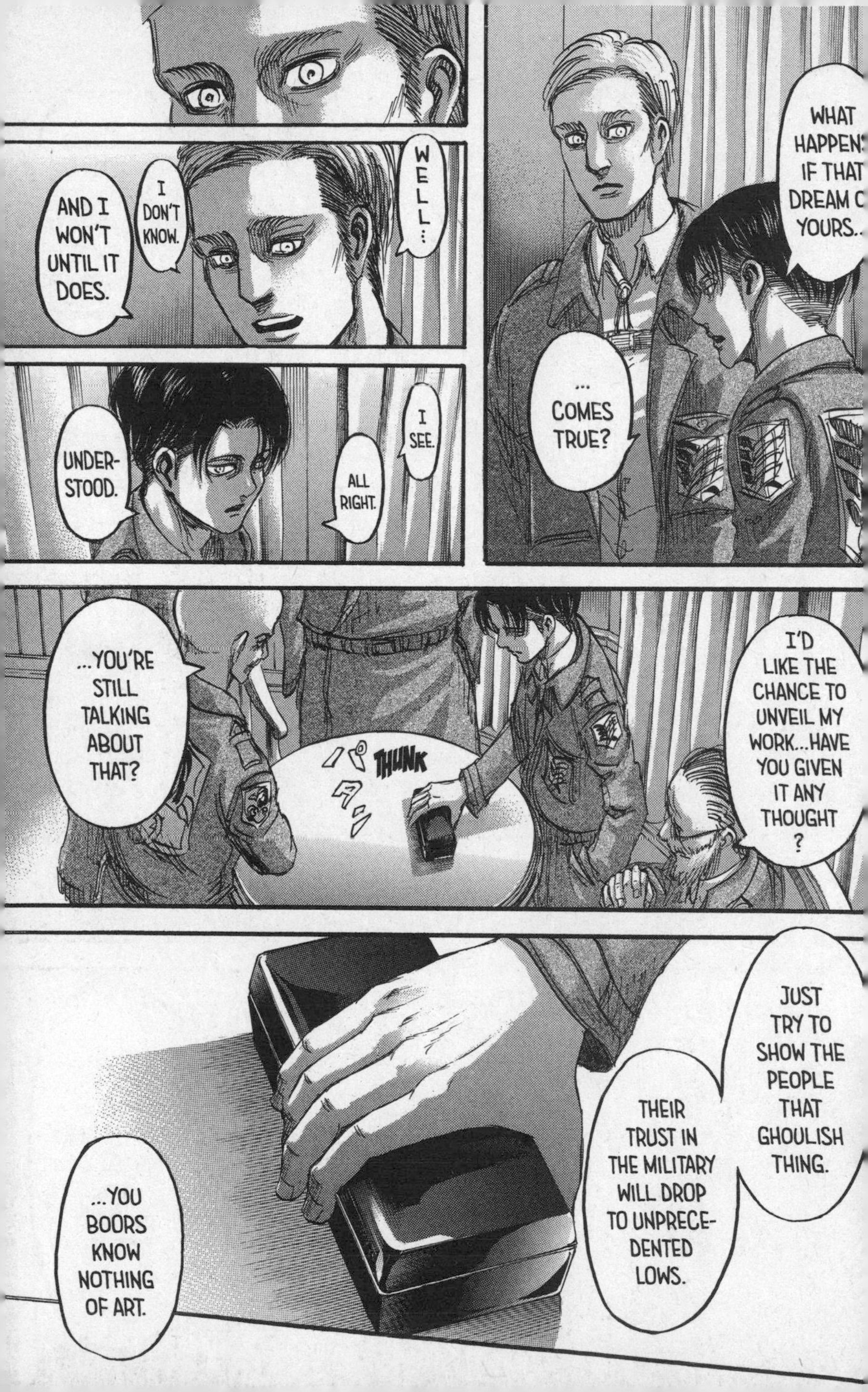

WHAT HAPPEN IF THAT DREAM C YOURS..
...COMES TRUE?
WELL...
I DON'T KNOW.
AND I WON'T UNTIL IT DOES.
I SEE.
ALL RIGHT.
UNDER-STOOD.
I'D LIKE THE CHANCE TO UNVEIL MY WORK...HAVE YOU GIVEN IT ANY THOUGHT?
THUNK
...YOU'RE STILL TALKING ABOUT THAT?
JUST TRY TO SHOW THE PEOPLE THAT GHOULISH THING.
THEIR TRUST IN THE MILITARY WILL DROP TO UNPRECE-DENTED LOWS.
...YOU BOORS KNOW NOTHING OF ART.

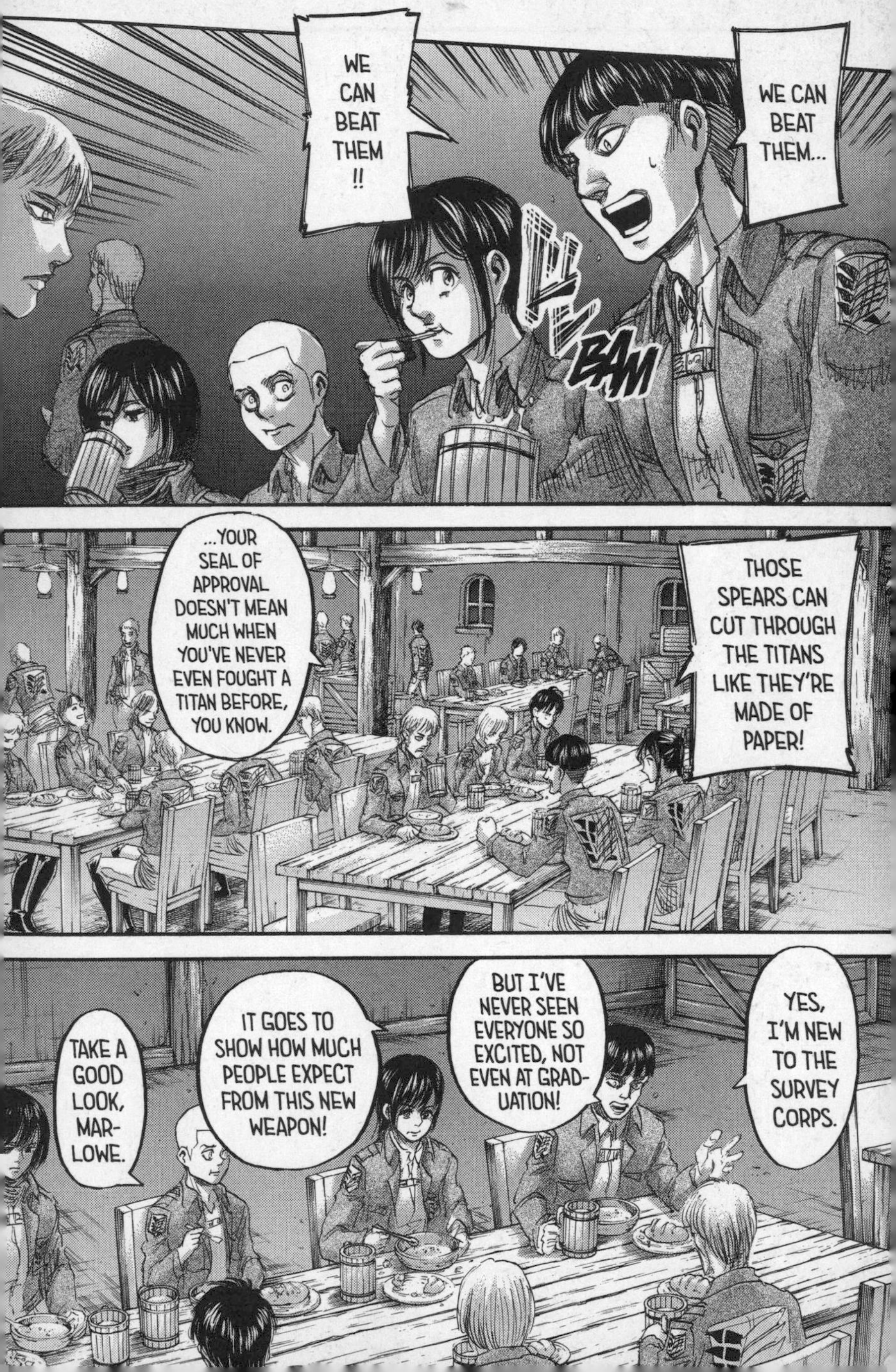
WE CAN BEAT THEM...
WE CAN BEAT THEM !!
BAM
THOSE SPEARS CAN CUT THROUGH THE TITANS LIKE THEY'RE MADE OF PAPER!
...YOUR SEAL OF APPROVAL DOESN'T MEAN MUCH WHEN YOU'VE NEVER EVEN FOUGHT A TITAN BEFORE, YOU KNOW.
YES, I'M NEW TO THE SURVEY CORPS.
BUT I'VE NEVER SEEN EVERYONE SO EXCITED, NOT EVEN AT GRAD-UATION!
IT GOES TO SHOW HOW MUCH PEOPLE EXPECT FROM THIS NEW WEAPON!
TAKE A GOOD LOOK, MAR-LOWE.

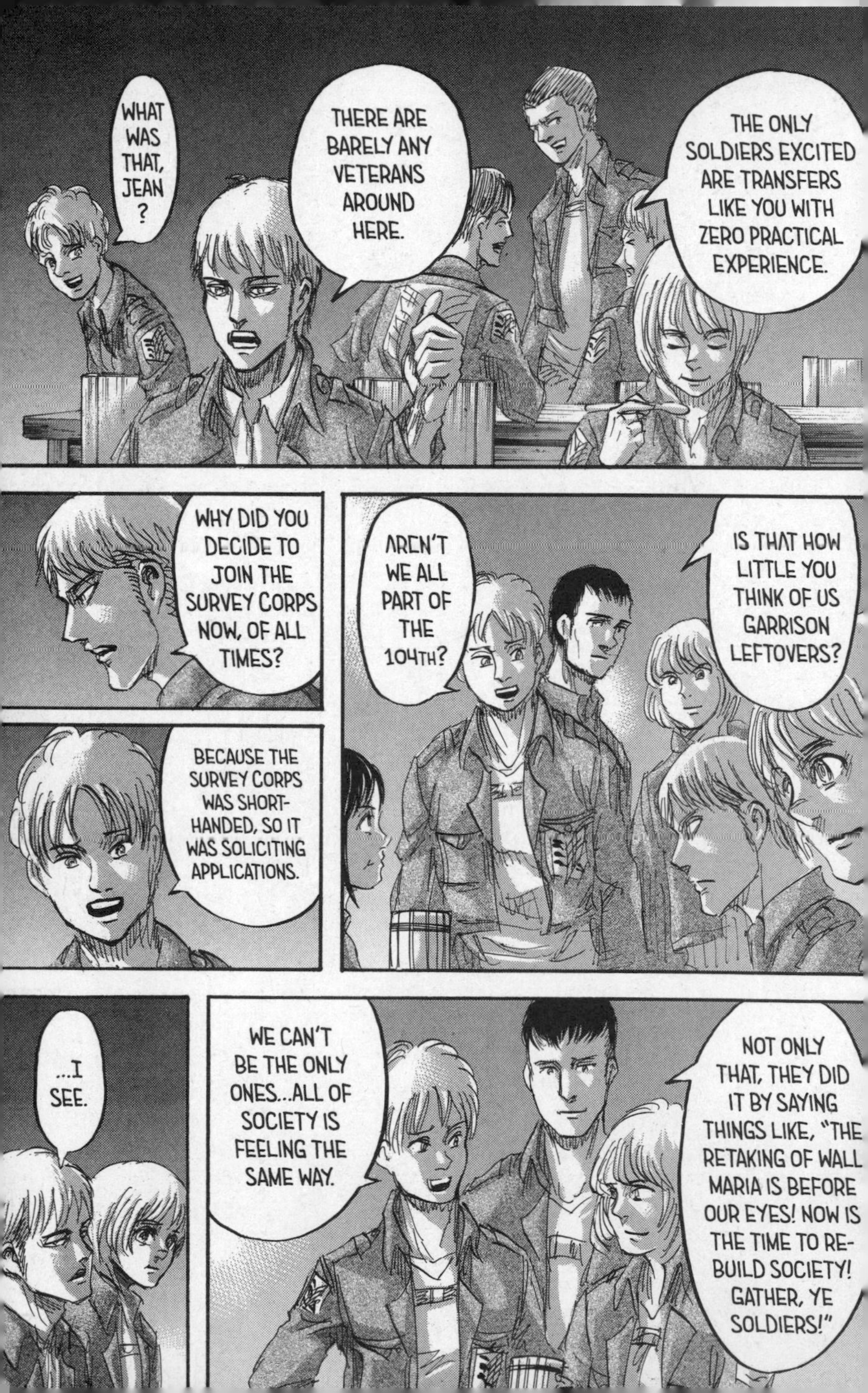
THE ONLY SOLDIERS EXCITED ARE TRANSFERS LIKE YOU WITH ZERO PRACTICAL EXPERIENCE.
THERE ARE BARELY ANY VETERANS AROUND HERE.
WHAT WAS THAT, JEAN?
IS THAT HOW LITTLE YOU THINK OF US GARRISON LEFTOVERS?
AREN'T WE ALL PART OF THE 104TH?
WHY DID YOU DECIDE TO JOIN THE SURVEY CORPS NOW, OF ALL TIMES?
BECAUSE THE SURVEY CORPS WAS SHORT-HANDED, SO IT WAS SOLICITING APPLICATIONS.
NOT ONLY THAT, THEY DID IT BY SAYING THINGS LIKE, "THE RETAKING OF WALL MARIA IS BEFORE OUR EYES! NOW IS THE TIME TO REBUILD SOCIETY! GATHER, YE SOLDIERS!"
WE CAN'T BE THE ONLY ONES...ALL OF SOCIETY IS FEELING THE SAME WAY.
...I SEE.

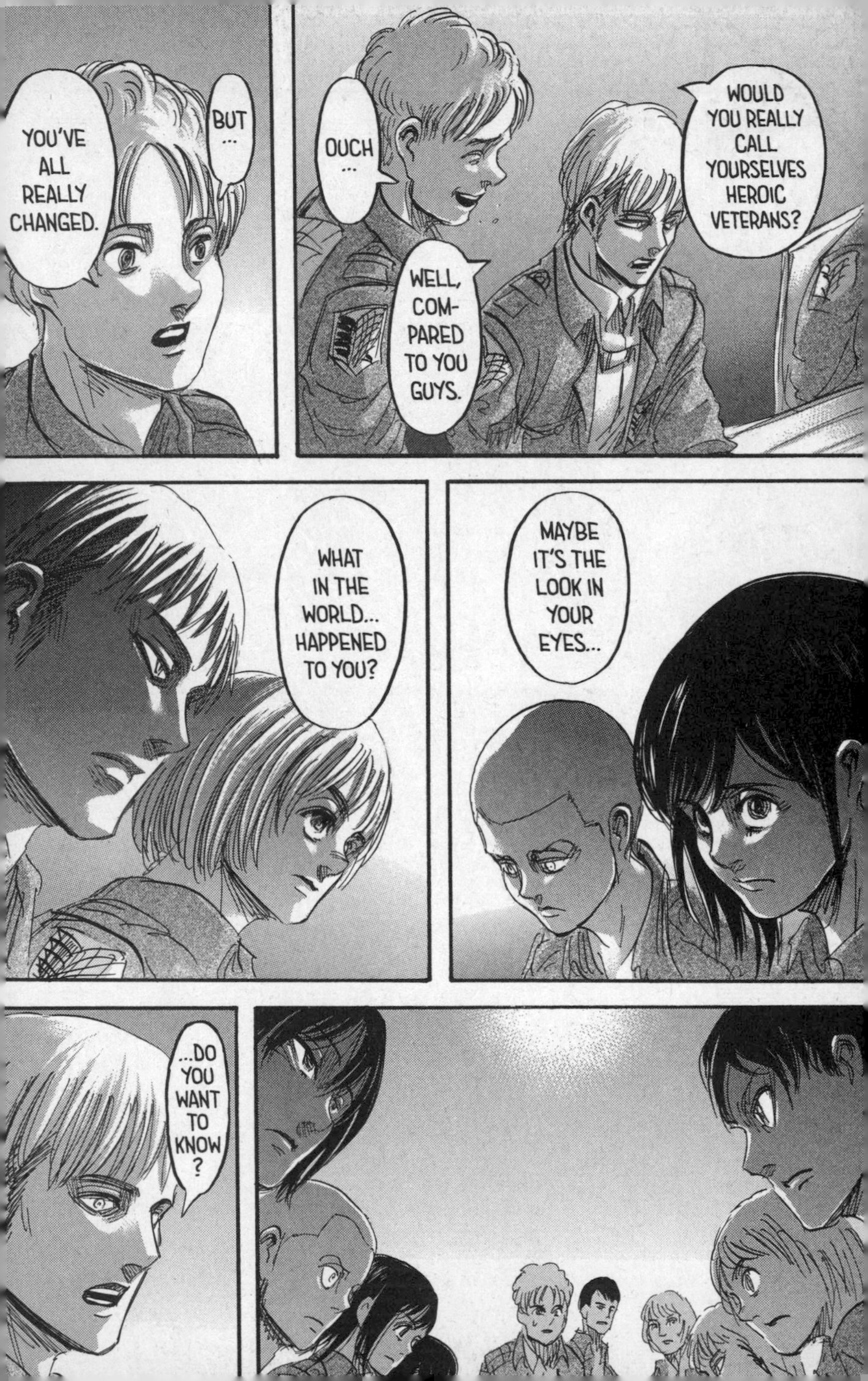
WOULD YOU REALLY CALL YOURSELVES HEROIC VETERANS?
OUCH...
WELL, COM-PARED TO YOU GUYS.
BUT...
YOU'VE ALL REALLY CHANGED.
MAYBE IT'S THE LOOK IN YOUR EYES...
WHAT IN THE WORLD... HAPPENED TO YOU?
...DO YOU WANT TO KNOW?

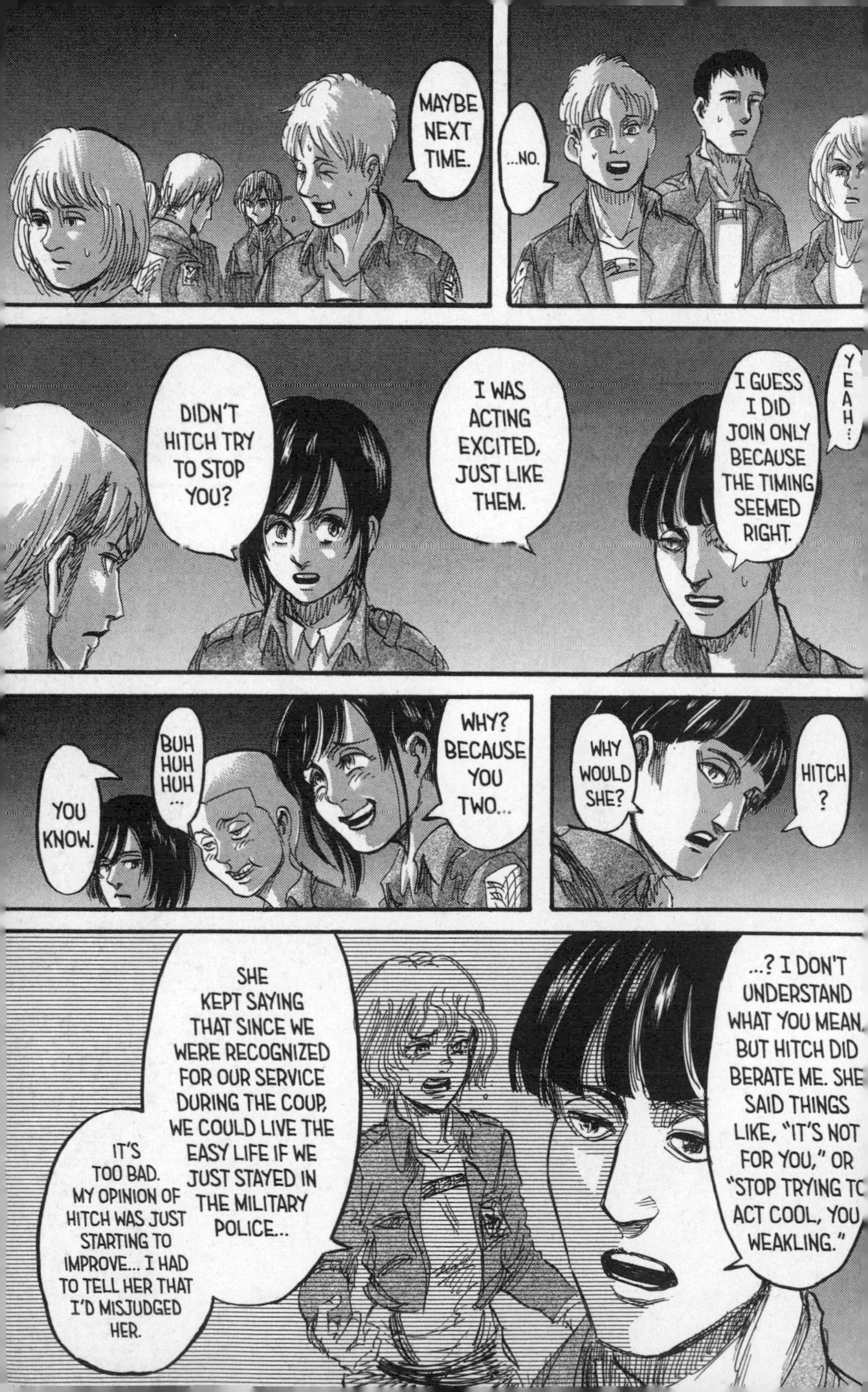
...NO.
MAYBE NEXT TIME.
YEAH...
I GUESS I DID JOIN ONLY BECAUSE THE TIMING SEEMED RIGHT.
I WAS ACTING EXCITED, JUST LIKE THEM.
DIDN'T HITCH TRY TO STOP YOU?
HITCH?
WHY WOULD SHE?
WHY? BECAUSE YOU TWO...
BUH HUH HUH...
YOU KNOW.
...? I DON'T UNDERSTAND WHAT YOU MEAN, BUT HITCH DID BERATE ME. SHE SAID THINGS LIKE, "IT'S NOT FOR YOU," OR "STOP TRYING TO ACT COOL, YOU WEAKLING."
SHE KEPT SAYING THAT SINCE WE WERE RECOGNIZED FOR OUR SERVICE DURING THE COUP, WE COULD LIVE THE EASY LIFE IF WE JUST STAYED IN THE MILITARY POLICE...
IT'S TOO BAD. MY OPINION OF HITCH WAS JUST STARTING TO IMPROVE... I HAD TO TELL HER THAT I'D MISJUDGED HER.

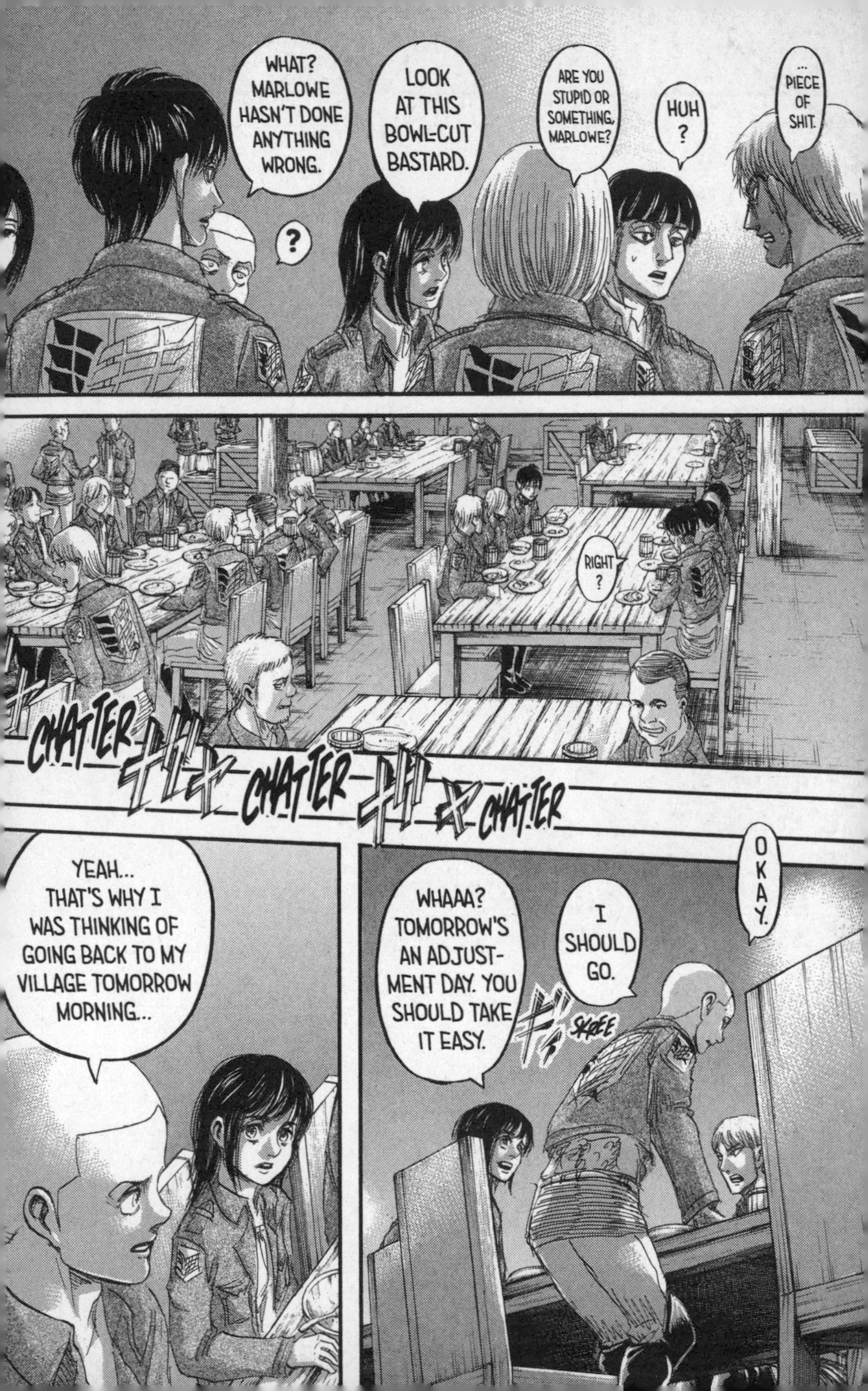
... PIECE OF SHIT.
HUH?
ARE YOU STUPID OR SOMETHING, MARLOWE?
LOOK AT THIS BOWL-CUT BASTARD.
?
WHAT? MARLOWE HASN'T DONE ANYTHING WRONG.
RIGHT?
CHATTER
CHATTER
CHATTER
OKAY.
I SHOULD GO.
SKREE
WHAAA? TOMORROW'S AN ADJUST-MENT DAY. YOU SHOULD TAKE IT EASY.
YEAH... THAT'S WHY I WAS THINKING OF GOING BACK TO MY VILLAGE TOMORROW MORNING...

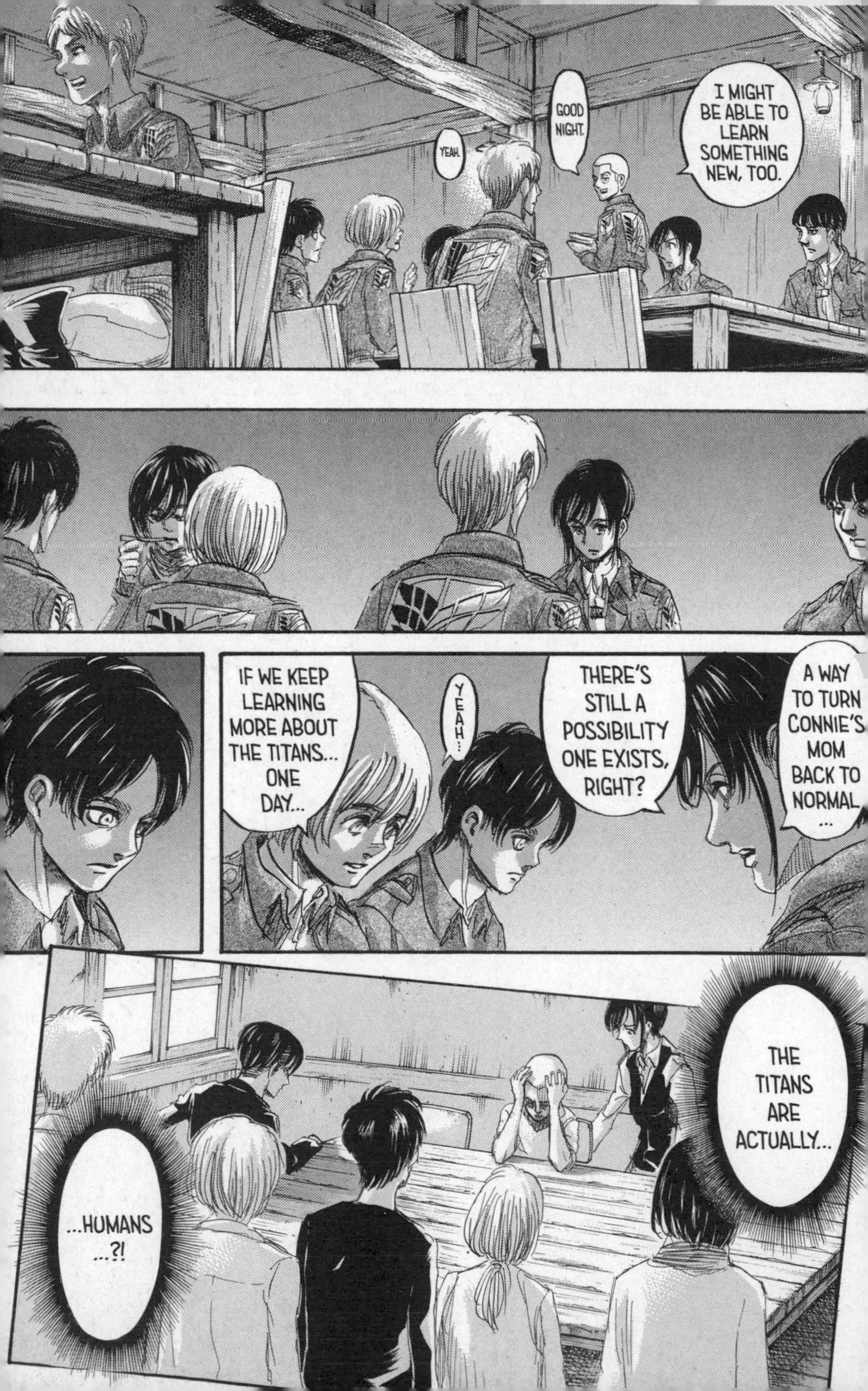
I MIGHT BE ABLE TO LEARN SOMETHING NEW, TOO.
GOOD NIGHT.
YEAH.
A WAY TO TURN CONNIE'S MOM BACK TO NORMAL ...
THERE'S STILL A POSSIBILITY ONE EXISTS, RIGHT?
YEAH...
IF WE KEEP LEARNING MORE ABOUT THE TITANS... ONE DAY...
THE TITANS ARE ACTUALLY...
...HUMANS ...?!

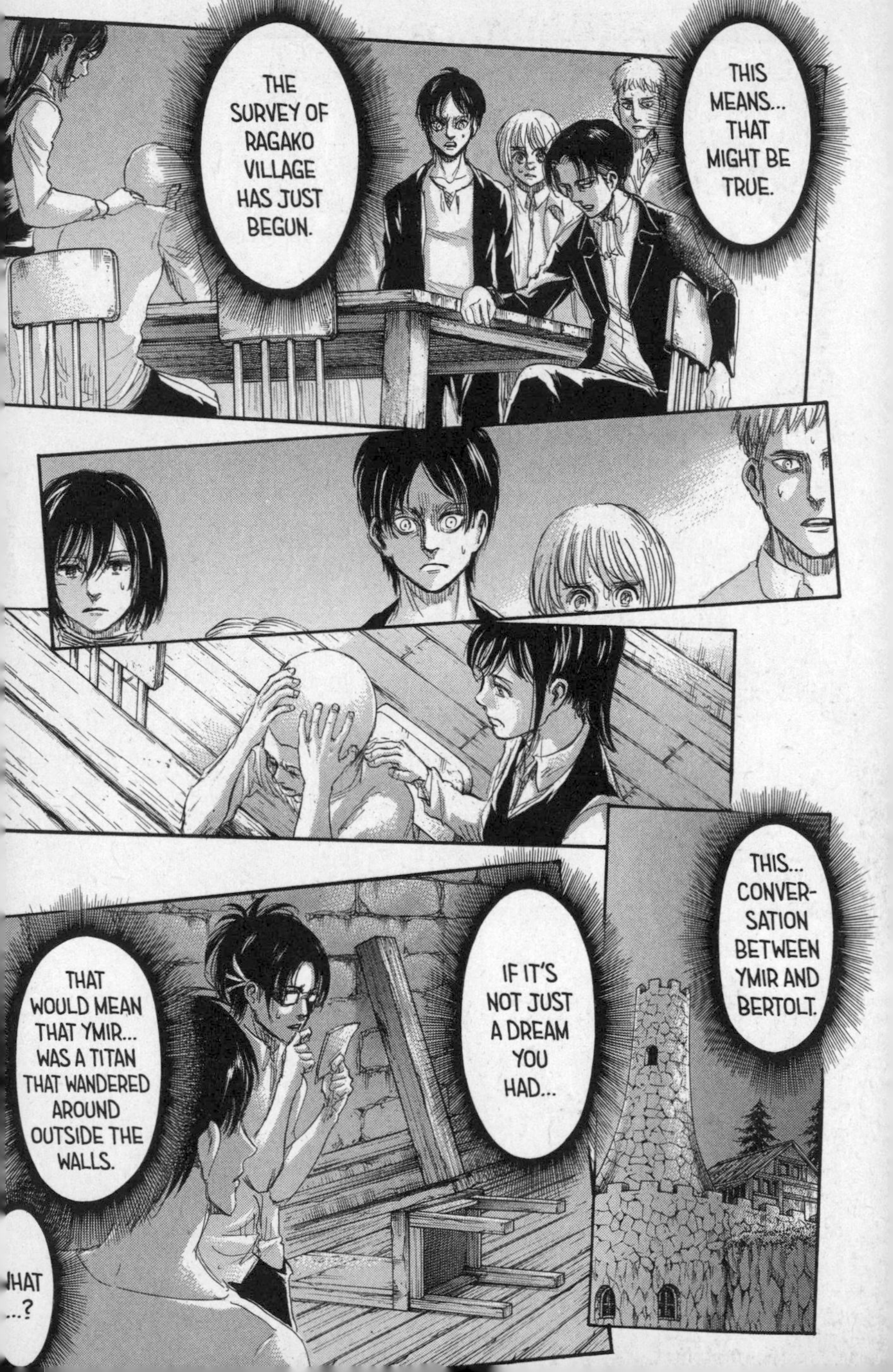
THIS MEANS... THAT MIGHT BE TRUE.
THE SURVEY OF RAGAKO VILLAGE HAS JUST BEGUN.
THIS... CONVER-SATION BETWEEN YMIR AND BERTOLT.
IF IT'S NOT JUST A DREAM YOU HAD...
THAT WOULD MEAN THAT YMIR... WAS A TITAN THAT WANDERED AROUND OUTSIDE THE WALLS.
HAT ...?

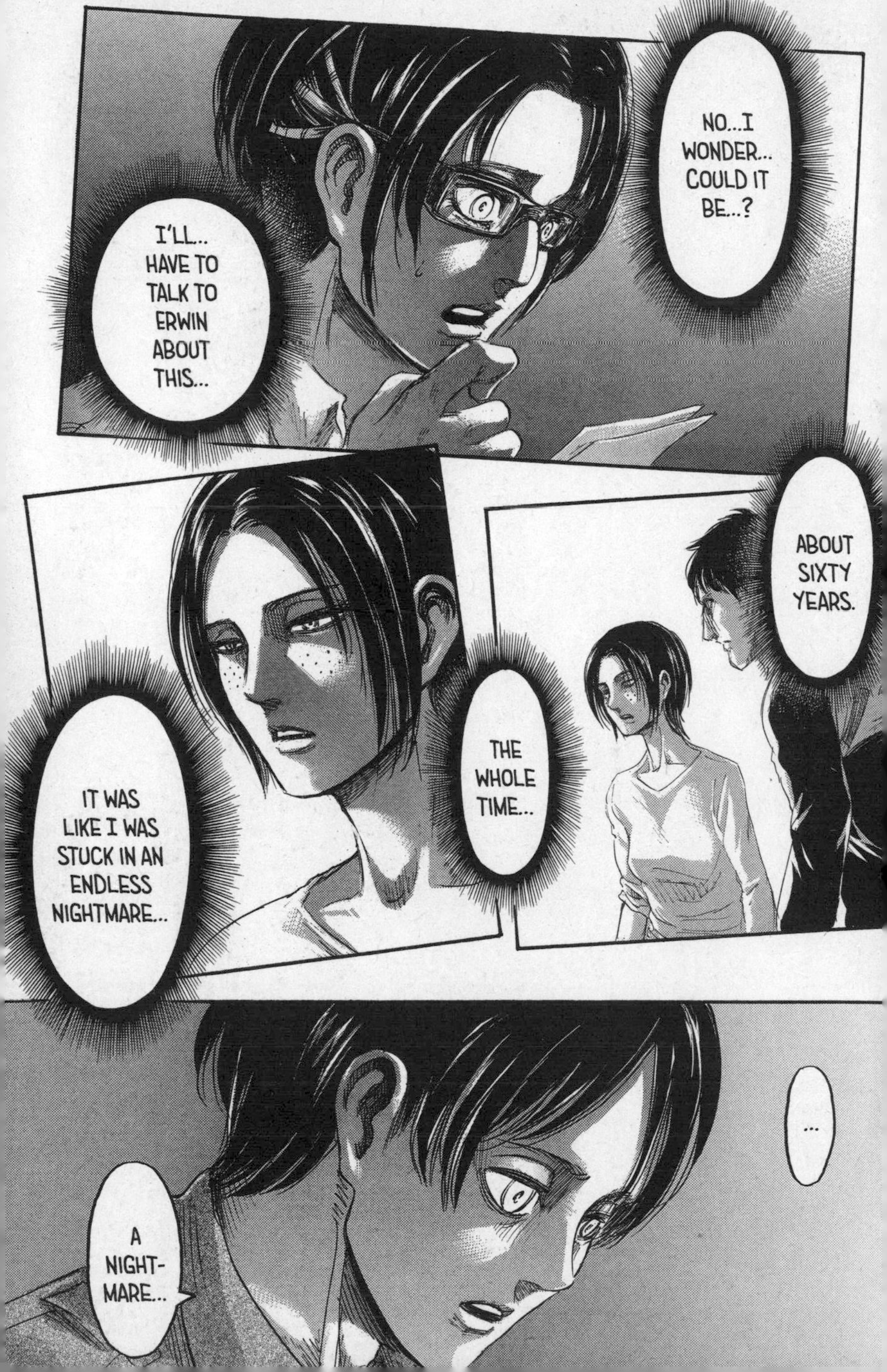
NO...I WONDER... COULD IT BE...?
I'LL... HAVE TO TALK TO ERWIN ABOUT THIS...
ABOUT SIXTY YEARS.
THE WHOLE TIME...
IT WAS LIKE I WAS STUCK IN AN ENDLESS NIGHTMARE...
...
A NIGHT-MARE...

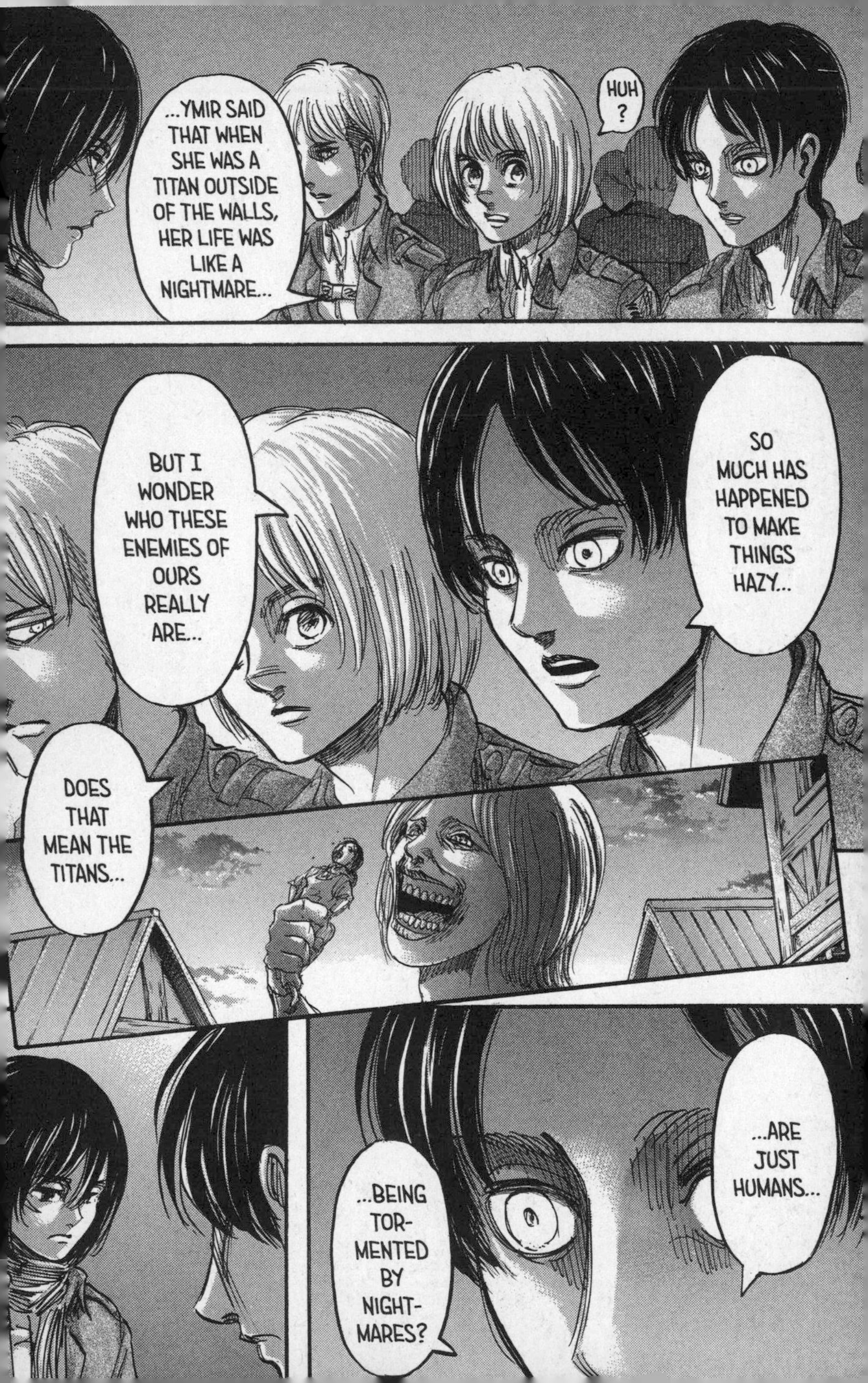
HUH ?
...YMIR SAID THAT WHEN SHE WAS A TITAN OUTSIDE OF THE WALLS, HER LIFE WAS LIKE A NIGHTMARE...
SO MUCH HAS HAPPENED TO MAKE THINGS HAZY...
BUT I WONDER WHO THESE ENEMIES OF OURS REALLY ARE...
DOES THAT MEAN THE TITANS...
...ARE JUST HUMANS...
...BEING TOR-MENTED BY NIGHT-MARES?

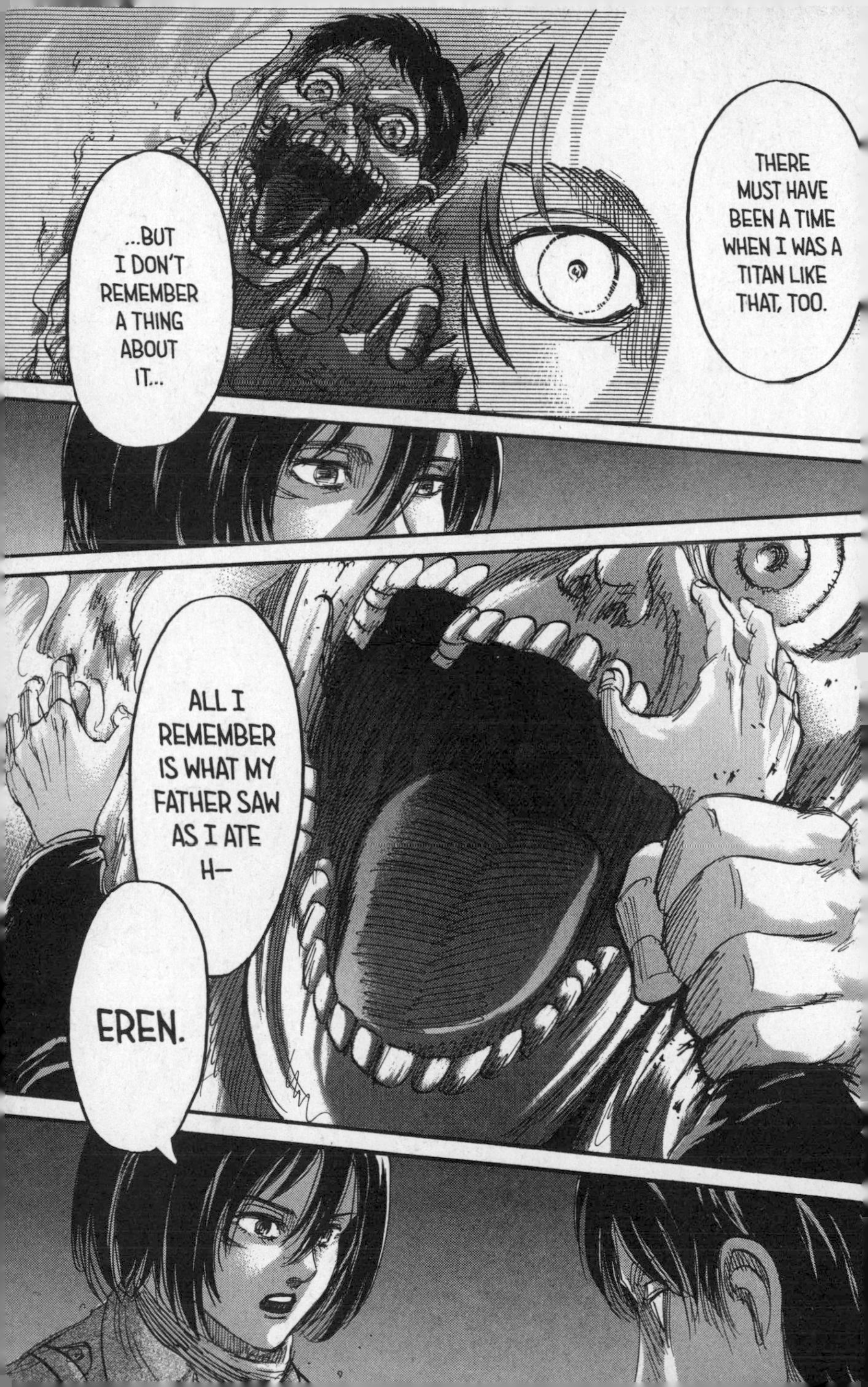
THERE MUST HAVE BEEN A TIME WHEN I WAS A TITAN LIKE THAT, TOO.
...BUT I DON'T REMEMBER A THING ABOUT IT...
ALL I REMEMBER IS WHAT MY FATHER SAW AS I ATE H—
EREN.

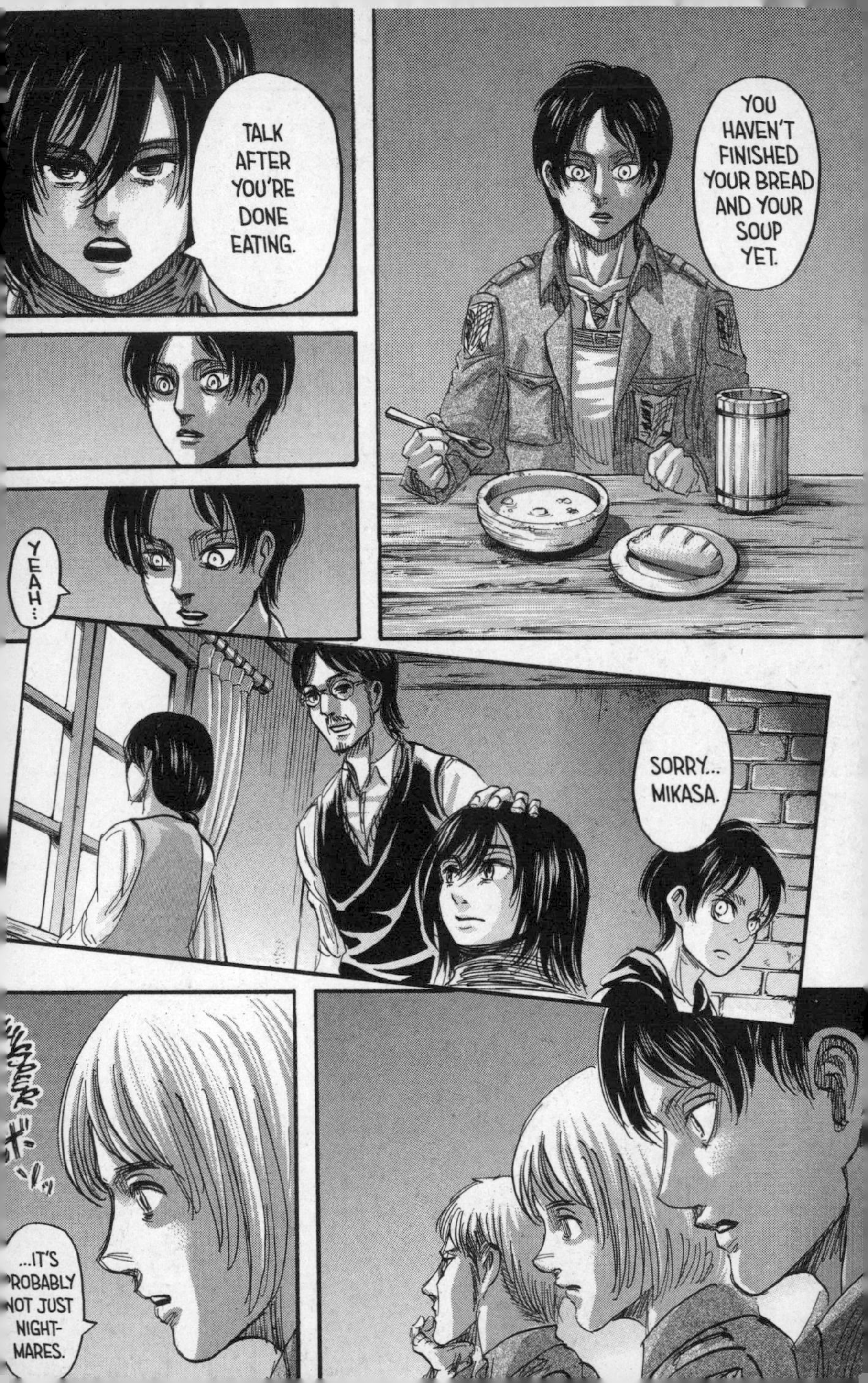
YOU HAVEN'T FINISHED YOUR BREAD AND YOUR SOUP YET.
TALK AFTER YOU'RE DONE EATING.
YEAH...
SORRY... MIKASA.
...IT'S PROBABLY NOT JUST NIGHT-MARES.

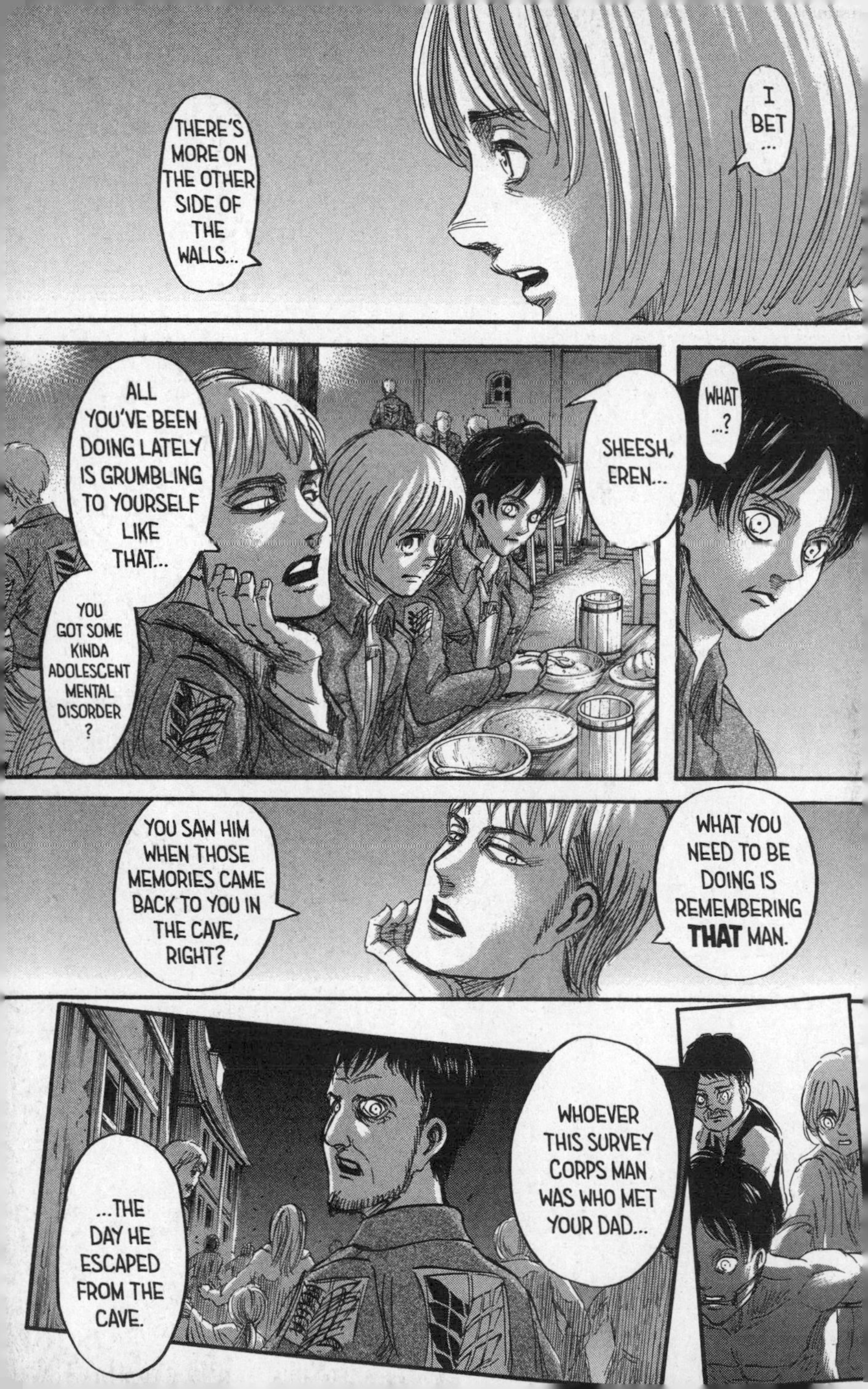
I BET...
THERE'S MORE ON THE OTHER SIDE OF THE WALLS...
WHAT...?
SHEESH, EREN...
ALL YOU'VE BEEN DOING LATELY IS GRUMBLING TO YOURSELF LIKE THAT...
YOU GOT SOME KINDA ADOLESCENT MENTAL DISORDER?
WHAT YOU NEED TO BE DOING IS REMEMBERING **THAT** MAN.
YOU SAW HIM WHEN THOSE MEMORIES CAME BACK TO YOU IN THE CAVE, RIGHT?
WHOEVER THIS SURVEY CORPS MAN WAS WHO MET YOUR DAD...
...THE DAY HE ESCAPED FROM THE CAVE.

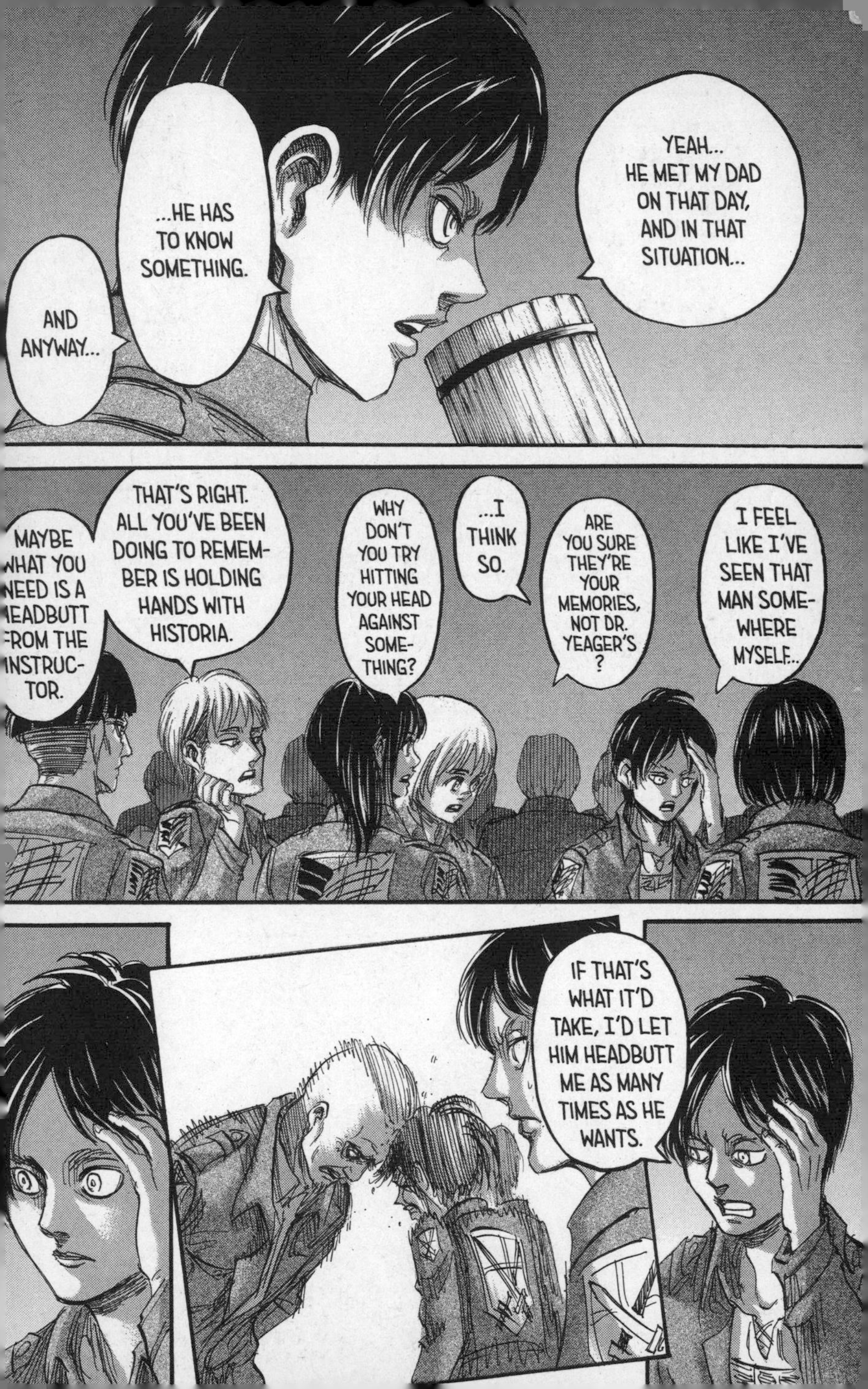
YEAH... HE MET MY DAD ON THAT DAY, AND IN THAT SITUATION...
...HE HAS TO KNOW SOMETHING.
AND ANYWAY...
I FEEL LIKE I'VE SEEN THAT MAN SOME-WHERE MYSELF...
ARE YOU SURE THEY'RE YOUR MEMORIES, NOT DR. YEAGER'S?
...I THINK SO.
WHY DON'T YOU TRY HITTING YOUR HEAD AGAINST SOME-THING?
THAT'S RIGHT. ALL YOU'VE BEEN DOING TO REMEM-BER IS HOLDING HANDS WITH HISTORIA.
MAYBE WHAT YOU NEED IS A HEADBUTT FROM THE INSTRUC-TOR.
IF THAT'S WHAT IT'D TAKE, I'D LET HIM HEADBUTT ME AS MANY TIMES AS HE WANTS.

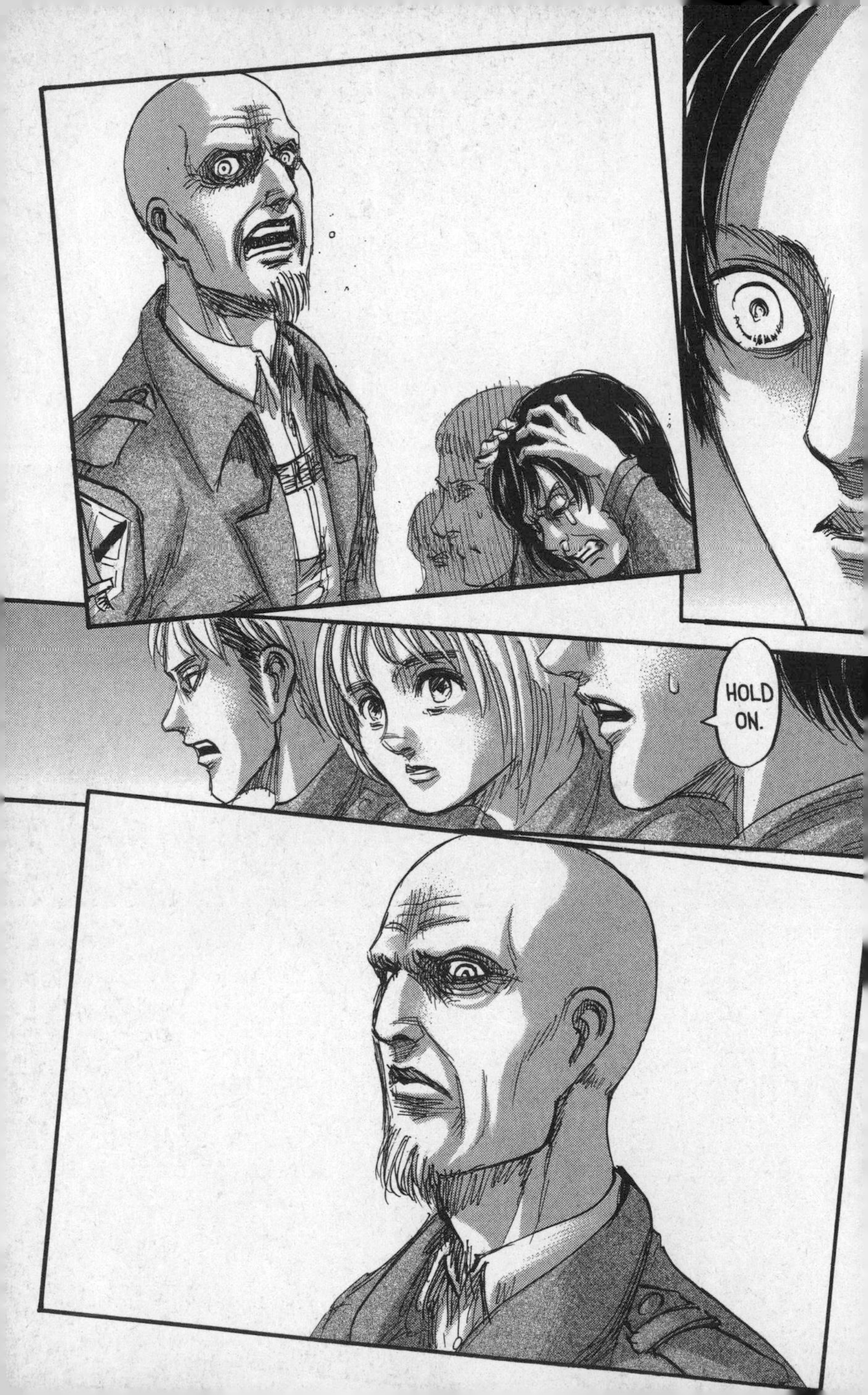
HOLD ON.

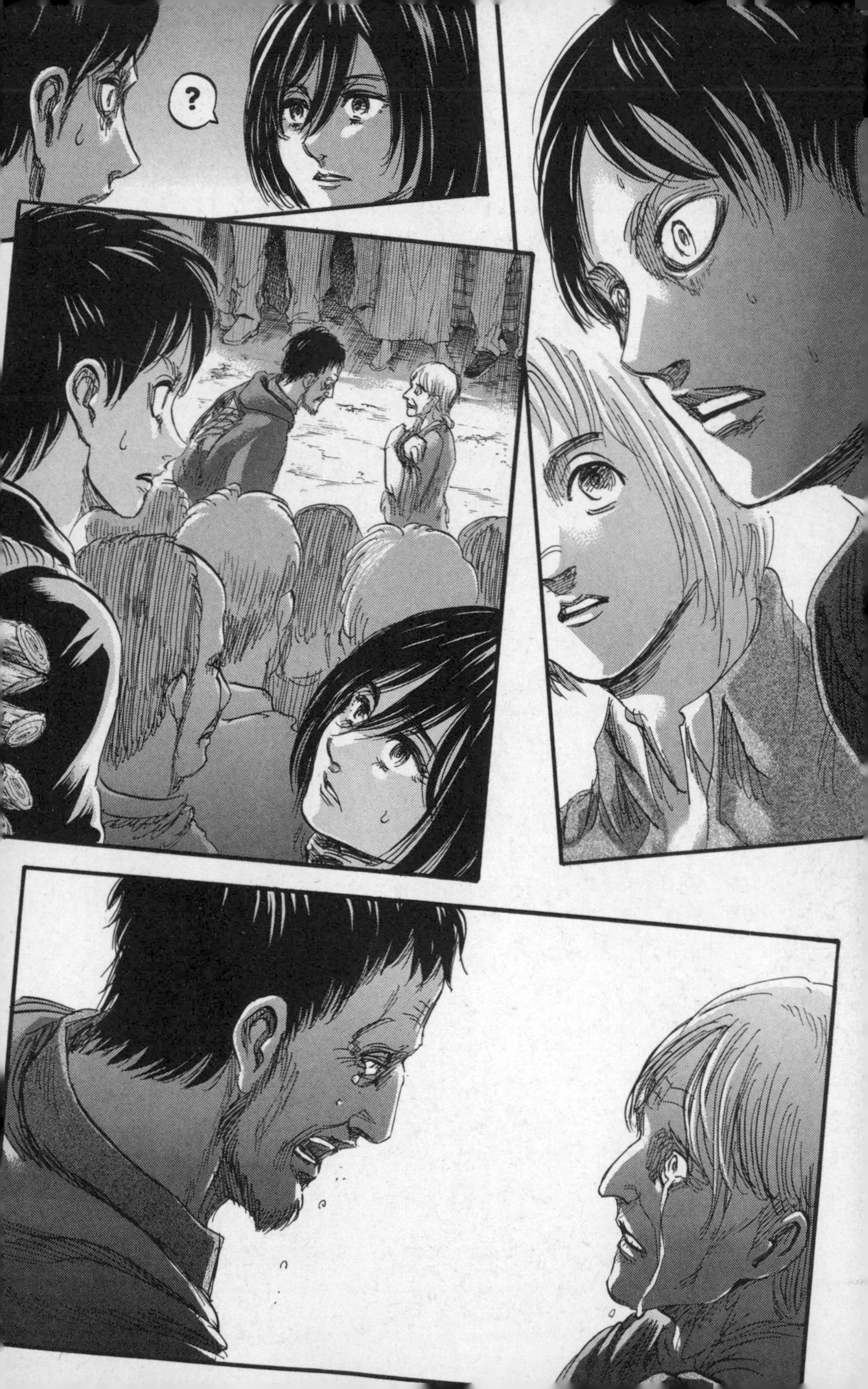
?

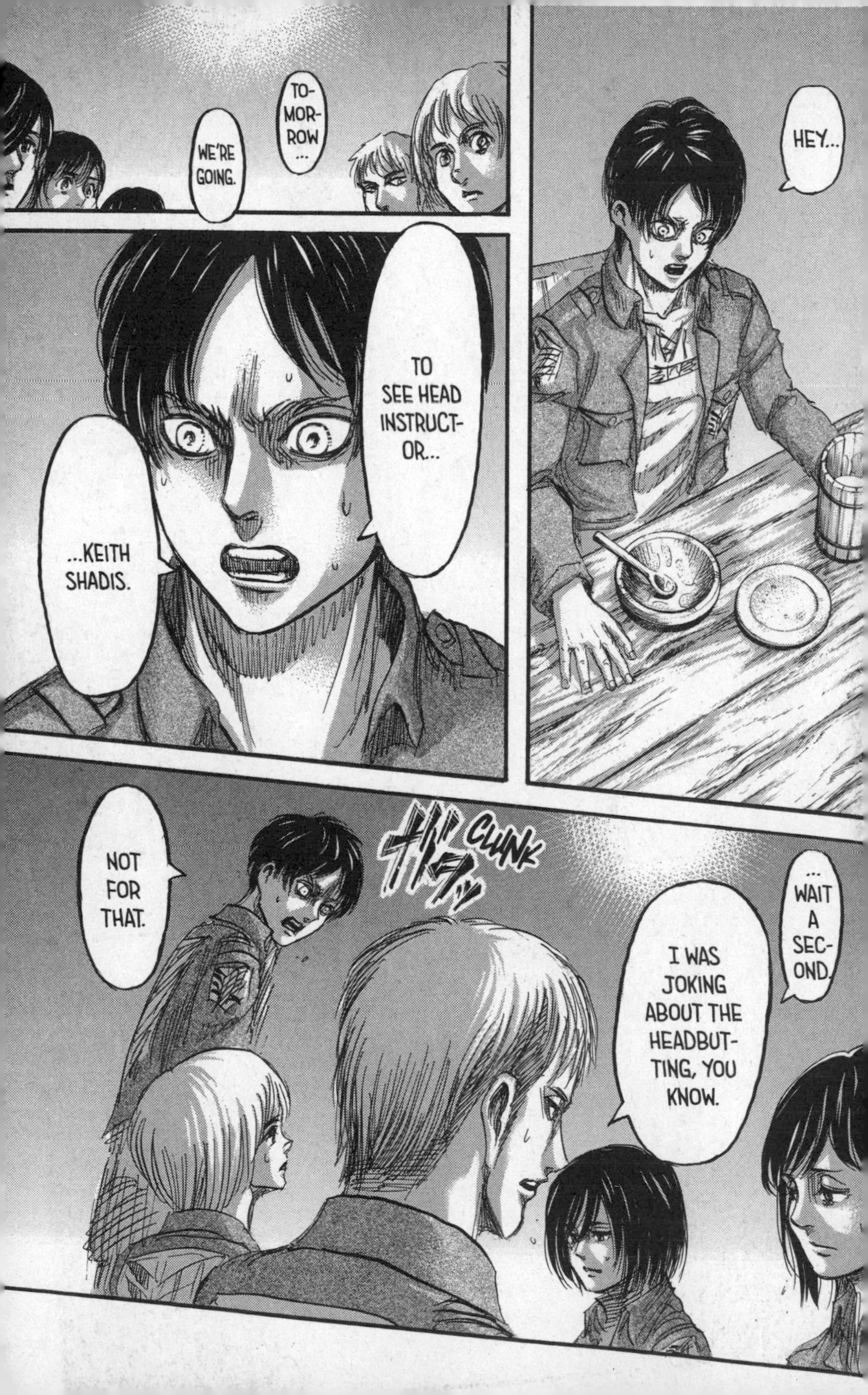
HEY...
TO-MOR-ROW...
WE'RE GOING.
TO SEE HEAD INSTRUCT-OR...
...KEITH SHADIS.
...WAIT A SEC-OND.
I WAS JOKING ABOUT THE HEADBUT-TING, YOU KNOW.
CLUNK
NOT FOR THAT.

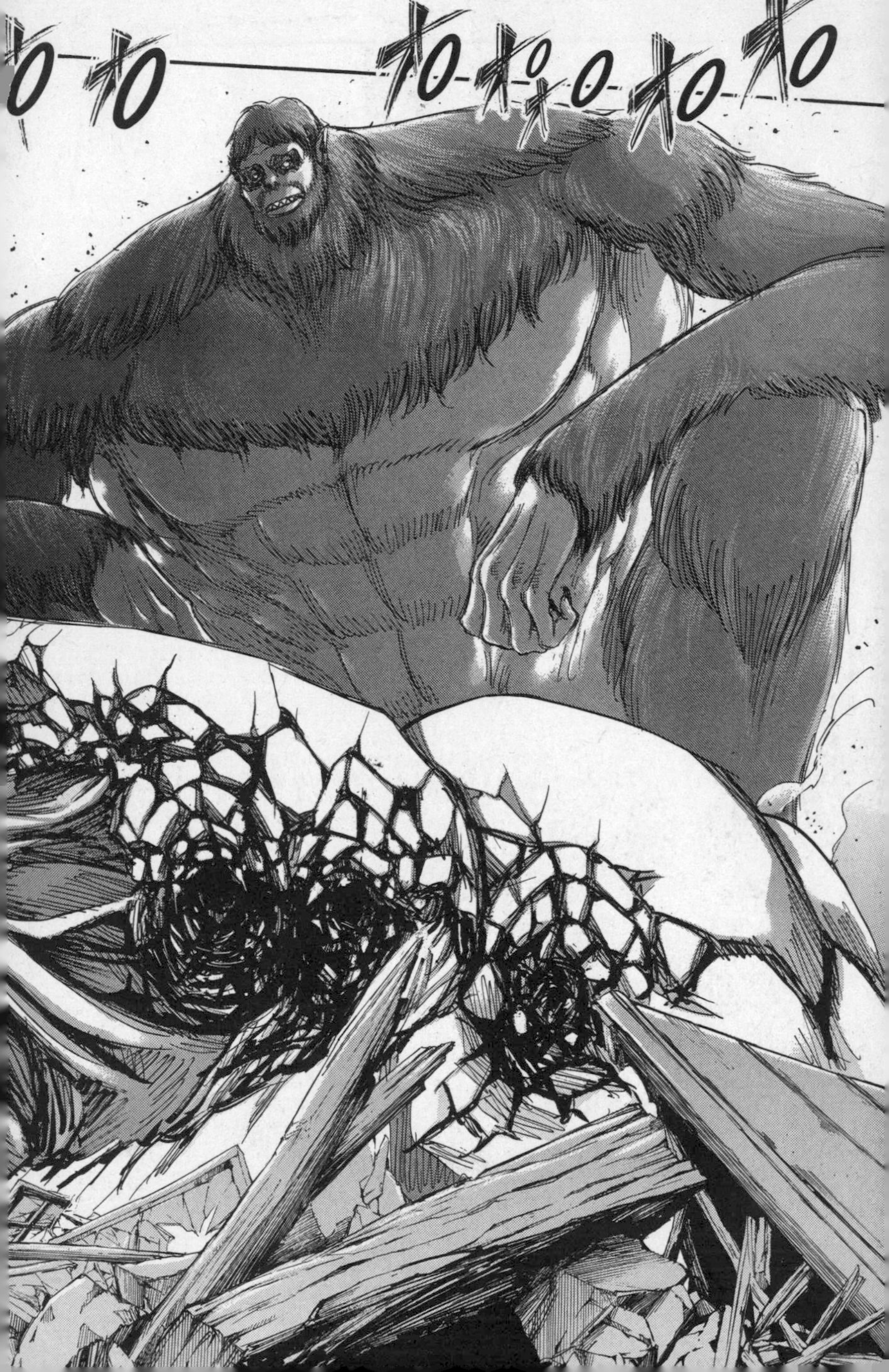

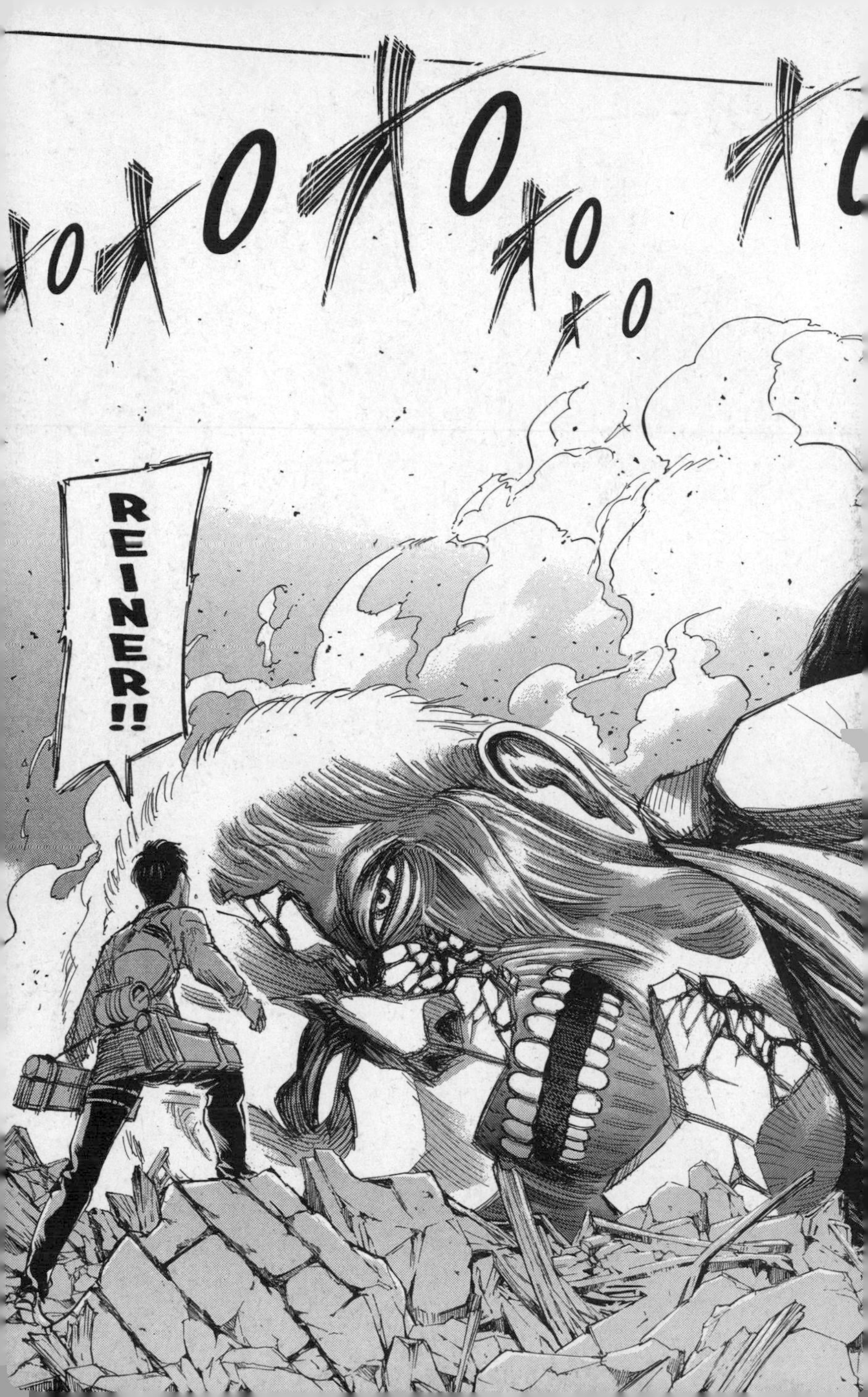
REINER!!

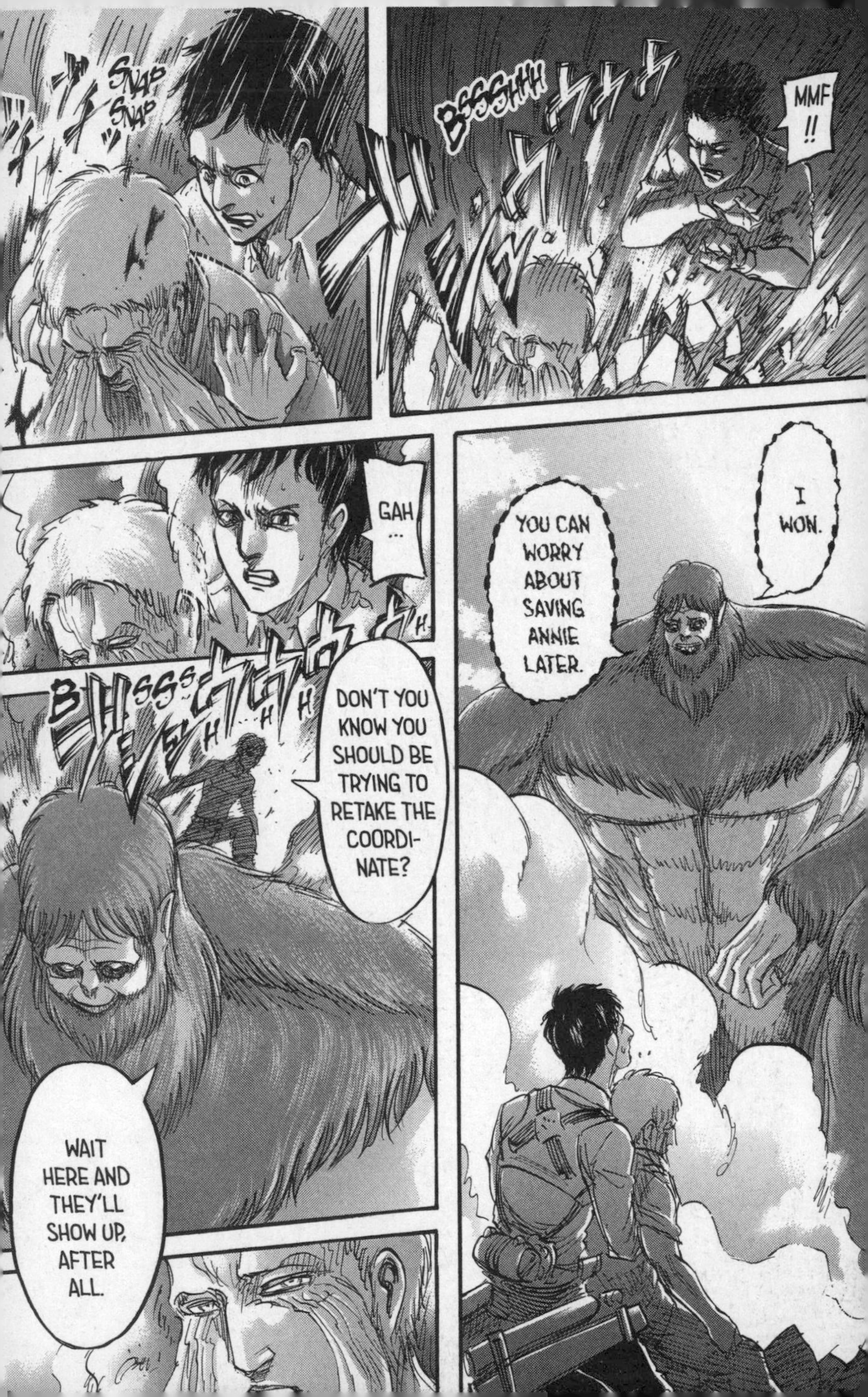
BSSSHHH
MMF !!
SNAP SNAP
I WON.
YOU CAN WORRY ABOUT SAVING ANNIE LATER.
GAH ...
BHSSS
DON'T YOU KNOW YOU SHOULD BE TRYING TO RETAKE THE COORDI-NATE?
WAIT HERE AND THEY'LL SHOW UP, AFTER ALL.

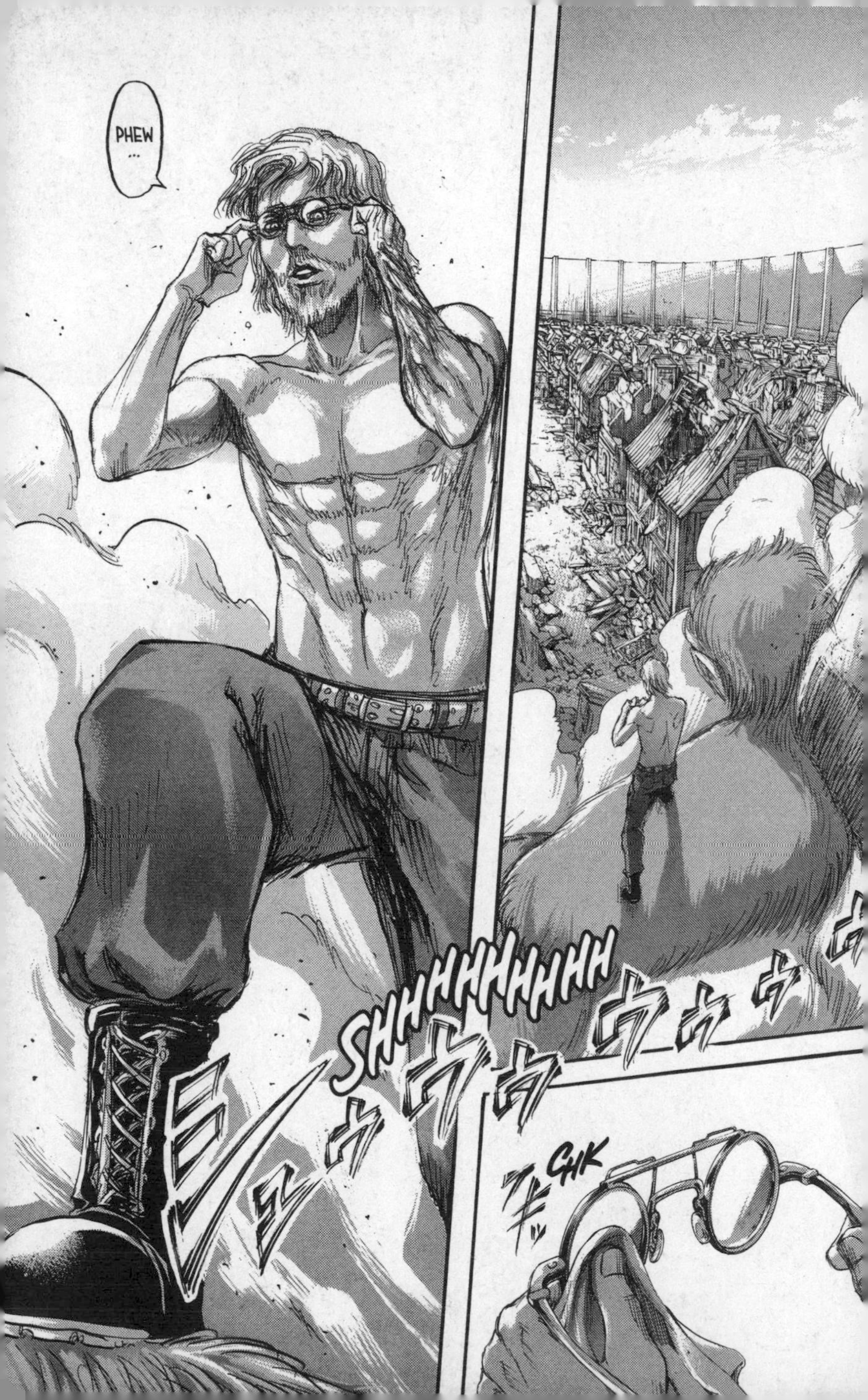
CHK
PHEW
...
SHHHHHHHHHHHH

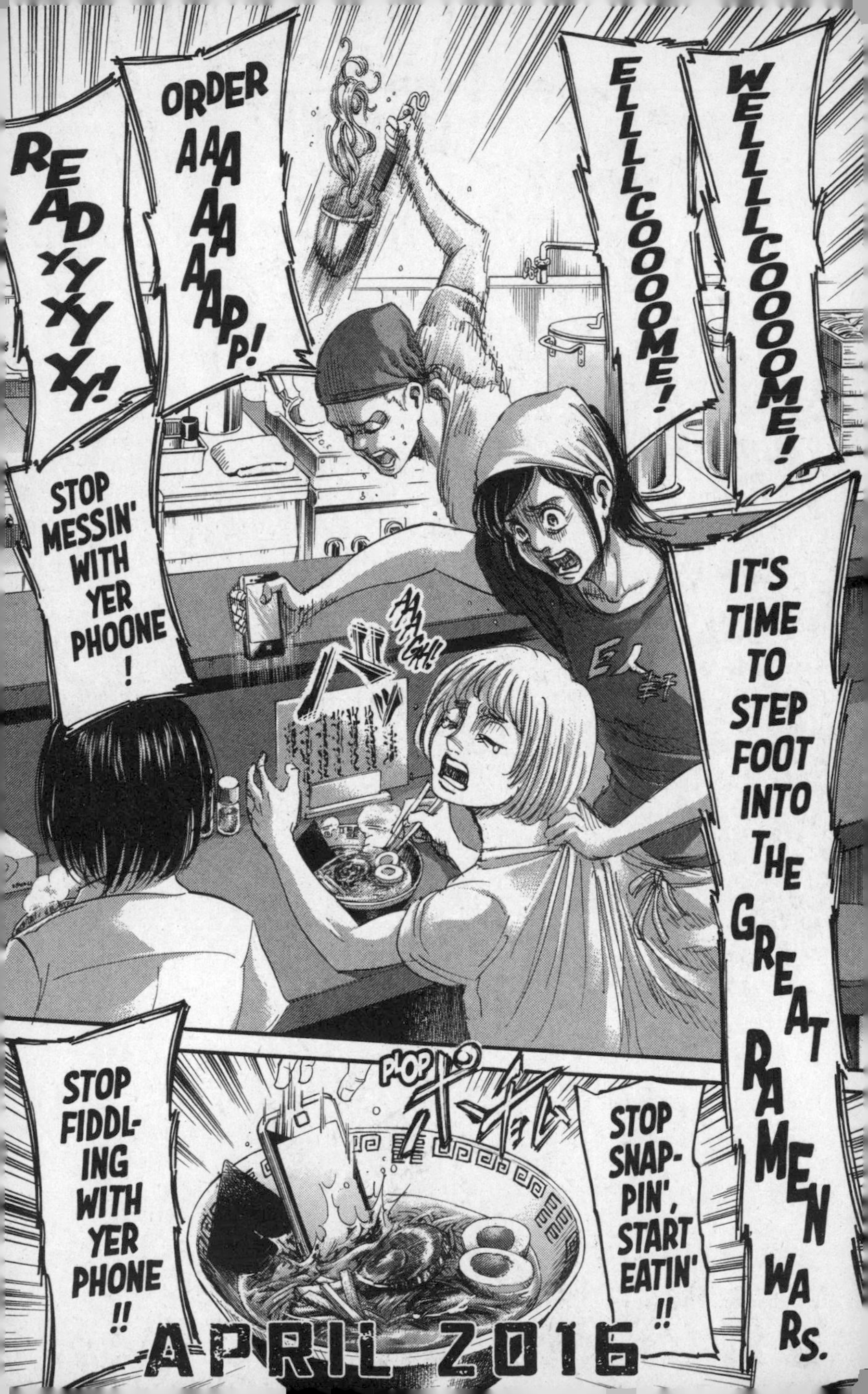
WELLLLCOOOOOME!
ELLLLCOOOOOME!
ORDER AAAAAAAPP!
READYYYYY!
IT'S TIME TO STEP FOOT INTO THE GREAT RAMEN WARS.
STOP MESSIN' WITH YER PHOONE!
AAAGH!!
STOP SNAP-PIN', START EATIN'!!
PLOP
STOP FIDDL-ING WITH YER PHONE!!
APRIL 2016

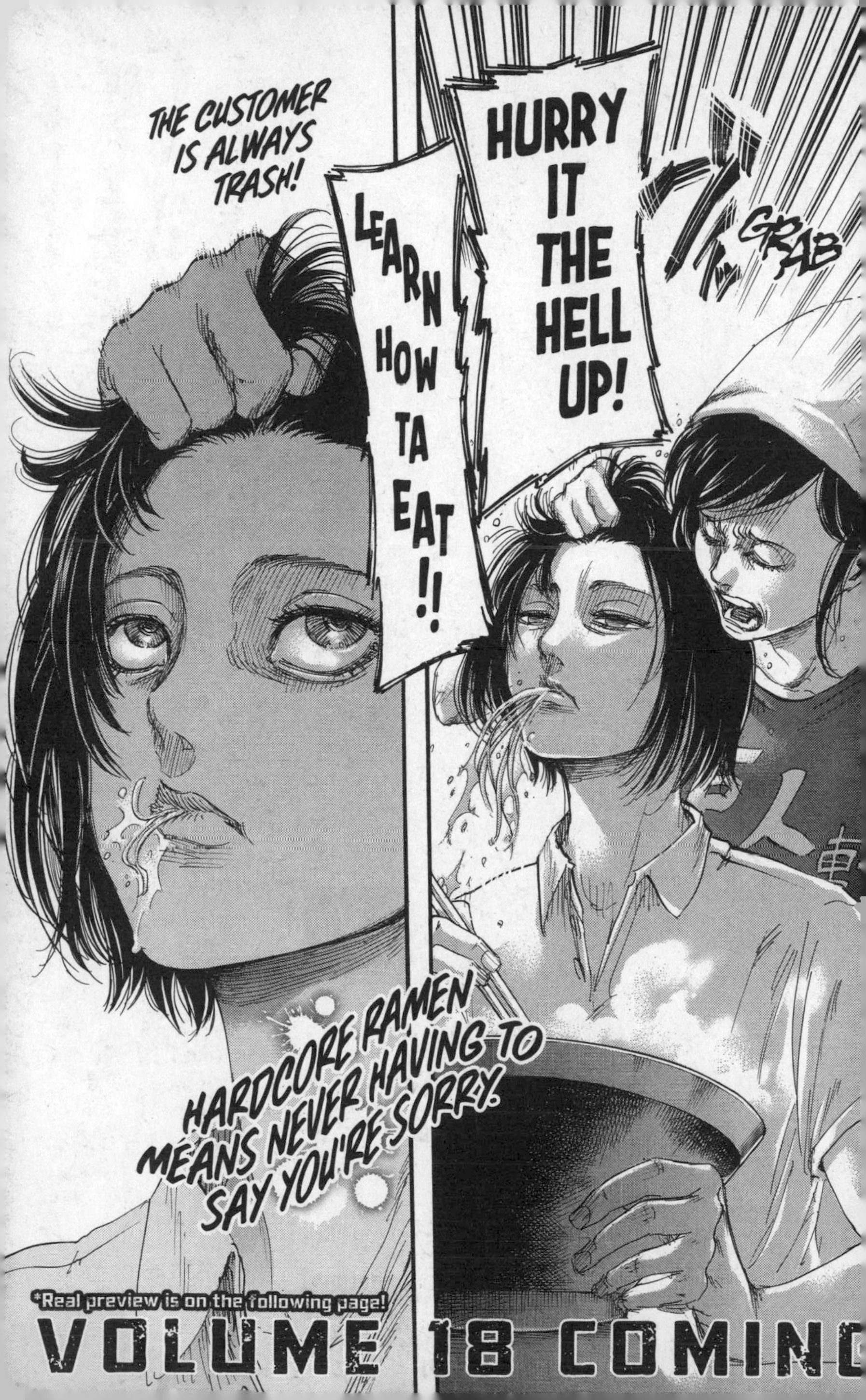
GRAB
HURRY IT THE HELL UP!
LEARN HOW TA EAT!!
THE CUSTOMER IS ALWAYS TRASH!
HARDCORE RAMEN MEANS NEVER HAVING TO SAY YOU'RE SORRY.
*Real preview is on the following page!
VOLUME 18 COMING

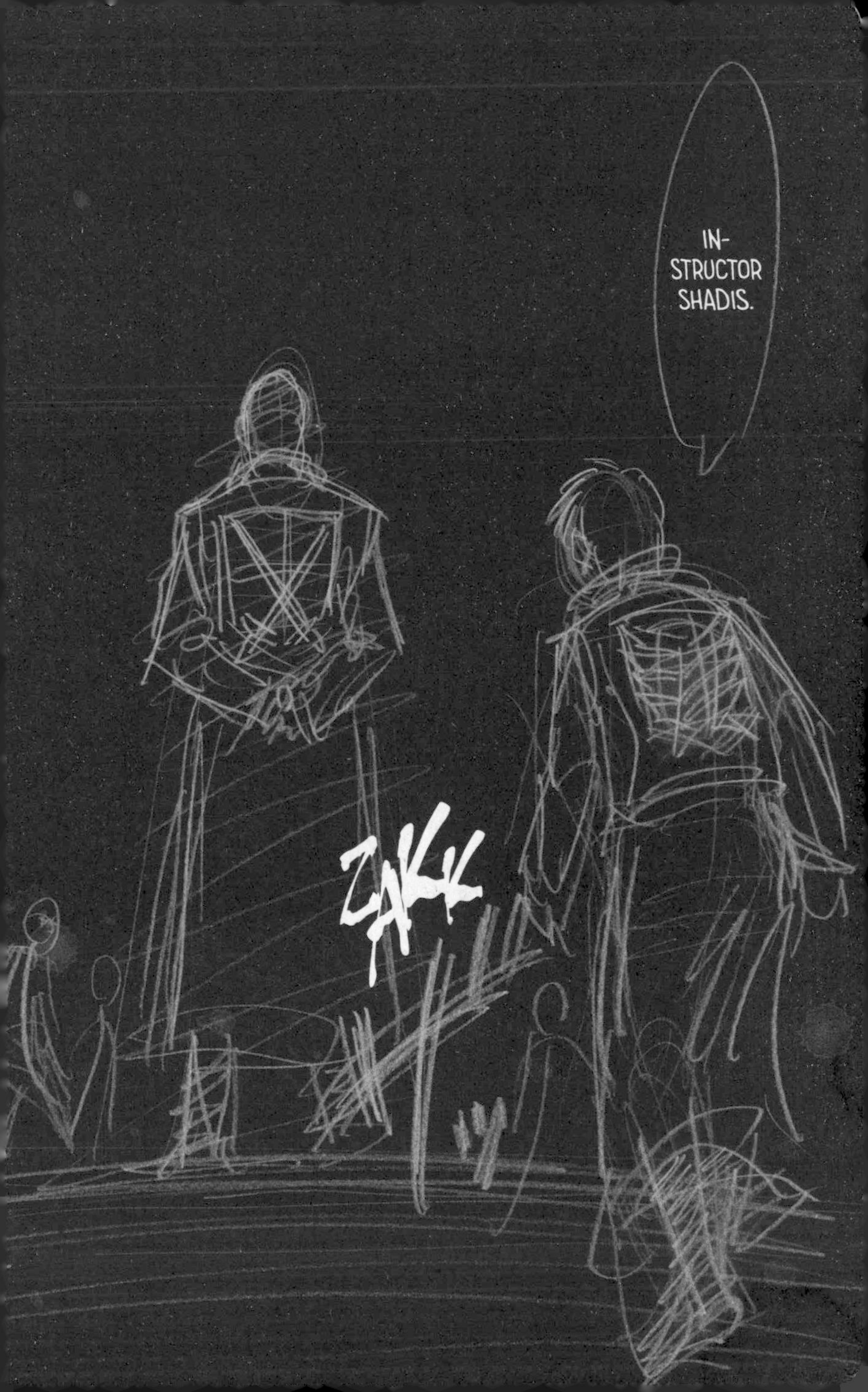
IN-
STRUCTOR
SHADIS.
ZAKK

THE MAN
WHO KNOWS
THE HIDDEN
TRUTH FROM
THAT DAY IN
THE YEAR
845. HOW
DOES HE
FEEL, AND
WHAT WILL
HE SAY...?

Attack on Titan volume 17 is a work of fiction. Names, characters, places, and incidents are the products of the author's imagination or are used fictitiously. Any resemblance to actual events, locales, or persons, living or dead, is entirely coincidental.

A Kodansha Comics Trade Paperback Original

Published in the United States by Kodansha Comics, an imprint of Kodansha USA Publishing, LLC, New York.

Publication rights for this English edition arranged through Kodansha Ltd, Tokyo.

First published in Japan in 2015 by Kodansha Ltd., Tokyo as *Shingeki no Kyojin*, volume 17.

ISBN 978-1-63236-112-7

Original cover design by Takashi Shimoyama (Red Rooster)

Printed in the United States of America.

www.kodanshacomics.com

9 8 7 6 5 4 3 2 1
Translation: Ko Ransom
Lettering: Steve Wands
Editing: Ben Applegate
Kodansha Comics edition cover design by Phil Balsman